An Illustrated Dictionary of South African History

An Illustrated Dictionary of South African History

Christopher C Saunders
Advisory Editor

ISBN 0 620 18080 3

First published in 1994 by
Ibis Books and Editorial Services cc
P O Box 784173
Sandton 2146

Cover illustrations

Black and white, from left to right: Boers on trek (Local History Museum Collection, Durban), Sol Plaatje (South African Library), British prisoners of war – Pretoria, October 1899 (National Cultural History Museum), Jan Smuts (Transvaal Archives), Soweto Riots, 1976 (Mayibuye Centre)

Colour, clockwise from top left: African captives being driven into slavery (Africana Museum), Fleet of Dutch Indiamen at anchor in Table Bay *c* 1760 (Africana Museum), King Mpande by G F Angas (Africana Museum), Peace talks, 14 September 1991 (South African Communication Service), Brakpan mines – coal shaft (The Brenthurst Library), South African War – Spionkop, 24 January 1900 (Africana Museum)

Set in 10 on 12 point Palatino

Cover design and design concept by
Michael Barnett, Johannesburg

Design, phototypesetting and reproduction by
Book Productions, Pretoria

Colour separations by
Lithotechnik, Pretoria

Index by Sharon Rubin, Johannesburg

Printed and bound by
Colorcraft Ltd.,
Hong Kong

Researchers
Alpha Greeff
Lindsey Morton
Jenith Shannon
Terri Strauss (principal researcher)
Kirsten Tatham

Contributors
Mohamed Adhikari, Department of History, University of Cape Town
Thomas Dowson, Department of Archaeology, University of the Witwatersrand
Professor Martin Hall, Department of Archaeology, University of Cape Town
Dr Stuart Jones, Department of Economics, University of South Africa
Dr Timothy Keegan, Senior Lecturer, Department of History, University of the Western Cape
Dr Marcia Leveson, Department of English, University of the Witwatersrand
Tom Lodge, Department of Political Studies, University of the Witwatersrand
Professor Andy Manson, Department of History, University of Bophuthatswana
Professor Paul R Maylam, Department of History, Rhodes University
Dr Uma S Mesthrie, Department of History, University of the Western Cape
Professor W R Nasson, Senior Lecturer, Department of History, University of Cape Town
Professor John Parkington, Department of Archaeology, University of Cape Town
Professor Jeff B Peires, Department of History, University of Transkei
Nigel Penn, Department of History, University of Cape Town
Dr Sara Pienaar, Honorary Research Advisor, South African Institute of International Affairs
Dr Dione Prinsloo, Department of History, University of South Africa
Professor Christopher C Saunders, Associate Professor, Department of History, University of Cape Town
Dr Milton Shain, Department of Hebrew and Jewish Studies, University of Cape Town
Rob F Siebörger, Senior Lecturer, School of Education, University of Cape Town
Professor Andrew B Smith, Associate Professor, Department of Archaeology, University of Cape Town
Nicholas D Southey, Department of History, University of South Africa
Dr Elizabeth B van Heyningen, Department of History, University of Cape Town
Cherryl Walker, Department of Sociology, University of Natal
Dr Nigel A Worden, Senior Lecturer, Department of History, University of Cape Town
Professor John B Wright, Department of Historical Studies, University of Natal

Acknowledgements
Many individuals and organisations have provided invaluable assistance in the sourcing of illustrative material for this book. A special debt of gratitude is owed to the staff of the Mayibuye Centre at the University of the Western Cape, the Africana Museum, the NALN institute, the Transvaal Archives Depot, the Cape Archives Depot, the National Cultural History Museum in Pretoria, the Local History Museum Collection in Durban, the Director of the William Fehr Collection at the Castle in Cape Town, the South African Library, the Brenthurst Library, the Cory Library in Grahamstown, the Pretoria Art Museum, the South Light Photo Library, the South African Museum, the South African National Museum of Military History, the South African Communication Service, the Archaeology Departments of the Universities of Cape Town and the Witwatersrand, and the resources of the following newspapers: *The Argus*, *Beeld*, *Die Burger* and *Rapport*.

Particular thanks are extended to Tom Lodge for the use of photographs from his private collection, to Mrs Dinah Berry for granting permission to reproduce five cartoons from Abe Berry's *Act by Act* (Johannesburg: Lowry Publishers, 1989), and to The Brenthurst Press for permission to reproduce the following material:

p 49 'Landing of the 1820 Settlers in Algoa Bay': oil painting by Thomas Baines, in Jane Carruthers, *Thomas Baines: Eastern Cape Sketches, 1848–1852* (Johannesburg: © The Brenthurst Press, 1990), p 29

pp 50 and 51 'Officer, 8th King's Royal Irish Light Dragoons (1796–1801/2)' and 'Private, 61st (South Gloucestershire) Regiment (1797–1801)': gouache paintings by A B Cree, in Maurice Boucher and Nigel Penn, eds, *Britain at the Cape, 1795–1803* (Johannesburg: © The Brenthurst Press, 1992), p 198

p 54 'Cape Mounted Rifles, officer in full dress, *circa* 1847': lithographed by H Martens, in Basil le Cordeur and Christopher Saunders, eds, *The War of the Axe, 1847* (Johannesburg: © The Brenthurst Press, 1981), p 241

p 60 'The man-of-war *Amsterdam* and other Dutch ships in Table Bay, *circa* 1639': oil painting by Adam Willaerts (© The Brenthurst Press, 1990)

p 89 'General view of the Glencairn Gold Mine, Johannesburg': pencil and ink wash by Melton Prior, in Jane Curruthers, *Melton Prior: War Artist in Southern Africa, 1895–1900* (Johannesburg: © The Brenthurst Press, 1987), p 55

p 105 'Natives going down to work in the New Primrose Mine, Johannesburg': ink wash and crayon by Melton Prior, in Jane Curruthers, *Melton Prior: War Artist in Southern Africa, 1895–1900* (Johannesburg: © The Brenthurst Press, 1987), p 57

p 165 'The warrior Maqoma': wash drawing, unsigned, in Basil le Cordeur and Christopher Saunders, eds, *The War of the Axe, 1847* (Johannesburg: © The Brenthurst Press, 1981), p 266

p 173 'Buffelsdoorn Mine': pencil and ink wash by Melton Prior, in Jane Carruthers, *Melton Prior: War Artist in Southern Africa, 1895–1900* (Johannesburg: © The Brenthurst Press, 1987), p 53

p 261 'Friday June 16 [1848]': water-colour by Thomas Baines, in Jane Carruthers, *Thomas Baines: Eastern Cape Sketches, 1848–1852* (Johannesburg: © The Brenthurst Press, 1990), p 131

p 266 'Xhosa men, one with traditional long-stemmed pipe': pencil sketch by Thomas Baines, in Jane Carruthers, *Thomas Baines: Eastern Cape Sketches, 1848–1852* (Johannesburg: © The Brenthurst Press, 1990), p 110.

FOREWORD

There are many general histories of South Africa, some more popular than others, but no illustrated historical dictionary. In compiling this volume, which is meant for both the general reader and the student, an attempt was made to ensure that all the major topics in the country's history received some coverage. Given the space constraints, however, the volume could not possibly be comprehensive or even nearly so. Some readers will doubtless disagree with the choice of topics, but it is hoped that all will find something of interest in these pages, and that the volume will be found to be a useful reference resource. The illustrations included throw further light on the matters discussed in the text.

Entries will be found on economic, political and social aspects of history, as well as on such topics as architecture and painting, often ignored in histories of the country. The selection of entries was far from easy; many events and individuals were omitted reluctantly. The briefer entries are inevitably descriptive, and only in some of the longer ones were the contributors able to sketch the historiography of their subjects. It is hoped that readers of this Dictionary will be stimulated to go on from its pages to the wealth of more specialised works which explore these topics further. To help in that task, a list of further reading will be found at the end of the volume. Furthermore, the index should help the reader to move from one reference to another, and so acquire greater knowledge about the exciting history of this country.

C C Saunders
(Advisory Editor)

Mossel Bay on the Indian Ocean *c.* 1800 by C Latrobe
(National Cultural History Museum)

A

Dr Abdullah Abdurahman, President of the African People's Organisation
(Mayibuye Centre)

Abdurahman, Abdullah

WELLINGTON, 1872 — CAPE TOWN, 1940

Medical doctor and political leader. Abdurahman was the first Cape Malay doctor in Cape Town and the first coloured person to become a member of both the Cape Town Council and the Cape Provincial Council. In 1905 he was elected President of the African People's Organisation (APO) and he remained its President until his death.

A powerful orator, he was the outstanding coloured leader of his generation, though his conservatism was increasingly rejected by more radical, younger politicians in the 1930s.

Adderley, Sir Charles Bowyer

LEICESTERSHIRE, 1814 — BUCKINGHAMSHIRE, 1905

British industrialist and parliamentarian. A member of the House of Commons (1841–1878) with a keen interest in the colonies, Adderley was a strong supporter of colonial self-government — he helped to draw up the 1853 New Zealand constitution and supported the creation of the Dominion of Canada — but, he opposed the independence given to the Transvaal (1852) and the Orange Free State (1854). Cape Town's main street was named after him because of his opposition to the settlement of convicts in the Cape (1849).

Sir Charles Adderley, after whom the main street in Cape Town was named
(Africana Museum)

Africanism

In the 1940s a small group of men within the African National Congress (ANC) began calling themselves Africanists. Led by Anton Lembede until his death in 1947, the Africanists included men such as Robert Sobukwe, Potlako Leballo and A P Mda, all of whom became increasingly unhappy with ANC policy. They strongly opposed the multiracialism of the Congress Alliance (1953), fearing that the struggle for liberation would be taken over by communists, Indians and whites. They also rejected the Freedom Charter (1956), particularly those sections which guaranteed minority interests, and the charter's declaration that South Africa belonged to all who lived in it, black and white. They believed in the slogan 'Africa for the Africans', and although their definition of Africans included whites, they saw most whites as settlers who had no valid claim to the land they owned.

The Africanists believed that the fostering of a racially assertive nationalism was necessary in order to mobilise the masses, and that the ANC had lost touch with its followers in its concern for the preservation of élitist privileges. They advocated a militant strategy of mass action, using boycotts, strikes, civil disobedience and non-cooperation, and opportunities presented by popular outbursts. They identified their struggle for freedom with that of blacks throughout the African continent; they sought a United States of Africa, and were inspired by the socialist, anti-imperialist leadership of Kwame Nkrumah who led Ghana to independence in 1957, and Tom Mboya of Kenya, who said that whites should 'scram' out of Africa.

In 1958 the Africanists broke away from the ANC and in April the following year they formally established the Pan Africanist Congress (PAC). Sobukwe, the leading theoretician among the Africanists, was elected President of the PAC, which stood for government of the country by Africans for Africans, and the establishment of an Africanist social democracy. One of its first acts was the organising of the anti-pass law campaign of March 1960.

Africanist Robert Sobukwe (second from right) and followers give the PAC salute
(Mayibuye Centre)

African Methodist Episcopal Church (AMEC)

An African independent church movement, affiliated to the African Methodist Church founded by a black congregation in Philadelphia in the United States in 1816. In 1896 James Dwane, a leader of the Ethiopian Church, was appointed general superintendent of the AMEC in South Africa, which then incorporated the Ethiopian Church. Under Dwane's leadership the new church grew rapidly. Subsequently Dwane and others split away in search of religious autonomy. The AMEC remained active in South Africa but it distanced itself from other independent churches and did not engage in overtly political activities.

The South African Native National Congress delegation to London, June 1914. From left to right: Thomas Mapikela, Revd Walter Rubusana, Revd John Dube, Saul Msane and Sol Plaatje
(Mayibuye Centre)

African National Congress (ANC)

Formed in 1912 by members of a tiny professional élite, mostly graduates of Cape mission schools, for the first thirty years of its history the ANC functioned more as a pressure group than as a political party. The curtailment of African political rights in the Act of Union, as well as the looming threat of the Natives' Land Bill, prompted the summoning of a dignified assembly in Bloemfontein of doctors, ministers, teachers, clerks, journalists and landowners to establish the South African Native National Congress as a vehicle for agitation through 'peaceful propaganda'. Various delegations to Cape Town and London between 1914 and 1919 received courteous hearings but failed to affect passage of segregationist laws. Wartime industrial growth and urbanisation contributed to social tensions which found expression in labour strikes and pass law protests in the war's aftermath; for a brief period the Transvaal Congress seemed set on a more militant course. The liberal Joint Council movement, the Government Conferences, the Native Affairs Commission, and the introduction of location advisory boards helped to restore the Congress leaders's confidence in lobbying and consultations.

Right:
In April 1958, the ANC called for a stay-at-home on the occasion of the whites-only general election. During the protest, the police occupied the townships
(Mayibuye Centre)

Through the 1920s and 1930s the ANC (it changed its name in 1923) remained a small organisation with not more than four thousand members grouped in a few dozen branches. Campaigning was sedate: the deputation, the memorandum and the petition were the tactics of choice and on the whole the ANC left mass mobilisation to the Industrial and Commercial Workers Union and the Communist Party. Despite some overlapping membership, the ANC's relationship with the Communist Party was usually uneasy and sometimes tense. Between 1927 and 1930 an uncharacteristically adventurous ANC President, Josiah Gumede, attempted to persuade his executive to support the Party's anti-pass protests; for his pains Gumede was voted out of office and in the western Cape the ANC split, with a communist-influenced 'Independent ANC' building up a militant following among farm workers.

In the 1940s the transformation of the ANC into a mass organisation began. President A B Xuma devised a constitution which laid the foundations for a grass roots structure, allowing branches to retain a portion of subscriptions and paying from his own pocket for full-time officials. A young group of Fort Hare graduates established the Congress Youth League in 1944. The CYL's objectives were to reorient the ANC towards a militant nationalism emphasising African race pride and cultural autonomy, and to persuade their elders to endorse a militant mass-based strategy. Youth Leaguers were inspired by the emergence of African labour organisations as well as the collective force represented by the direct action of the urban poor manifested in bus boycotts and squatter movements. Youth Leaguers won commanding positions in the 1949 ANC executive elections and succeeded in winning the organisation's support for their Programme of Action. The succeeding decade witnessed the implementation of the methods advocated by the League, beginning with a well-supported stay-away strike to protest the prohibition of the Communist Party. Former CYL principals Nelson Mandela, Oliver Tambo and Walter Sisulu, of whom Mandela and Sisulu are now dominant figures within the ANC leadership, revised their earlier advocacy of African exclusiveness as well as their antipathy towards collaboration with communists. The ANC coordinated its activities in an alliance with the Natal and Transvaal Indian Congresses as well as with sister organisations with white and coloured adherents and communists, which helped to predispose the organisation in favour of the multiracial social democracy embodied in the Freedom Charter, adopted by the ANC in 1956. Stay-away strikes and civil disobedience helped to generate a large popular following; ANC membership in the 1950s peaked at about 100 000. But though efforts such as the Defiance Campaign of 1952, in which 8 000 volunteers served prison sentences for civil disobedience, caught the public imagination, the ANC did not represent a serious threat to the authorities. From 1955 the ANC succeeded in disrupting and delaying the implementation of women's pass regulations but this was exceptional; most of its attempts to resist apartheid laws were short-lived.

Organisationally the ANC lacked resources and its members lived and worked on the margins of the industrial economy; they had very little collective leverage. In April 1960, shortly after police had fired into a crowd of anti-pass protesters

Walter Sisulu leads the Human Rights Day march in Alexandra, 10 December 1952
(Mayibuye Centre)

mobilised by the ANC's rival offshoot, the Pan Africanist Congress, the government proscribed both organisations.

After the suppression of a three-day strike in May 1961 to challenge the transition to a Republic and to call for a constitutional convention, Nelson Mandela and other younger ANC leaders, in conjunction with the Communist Party, formed an insurgent wing, Umkhonto we Sizwe. In December 1961, Umkhonto exploded the first home-made bombs in a two-year sabotage campaign. Intended as a last resort 'to bring the government to its senses' the bombs were targeted against property not lives. Meanwhile the ANC's external mission headed by Oliver Tambo began its efforts to secure military training for guerrilla recruits and to win international backing for a South African trade embargo. By 1964 Umkhonto's internal organisation was virtually destroyed and most significant ANC leaders were either in jail or in exile. Umkhonto's commanders, including Mandela, were imprisoned for life.

Until the resumption of guerrilla operations inside South Africa in 1977, the ANC's activities were chiefly conducted in exile. During this period it drew closer to the Communist Party and developed an external bureaucracy in London, Dar es Salaam and Lusaka. In collaboration with the Zimbabwe People's African Union it dispatched two military expeditions across the Rhodesian frontier in 1967 and 1968. ANC soldiers were later to fight in Mozambique and in Angola. The 1969 Morogoro Conference admitted 'non-Africans' to ANC membership and created a Revolutionary Council, both moves which strengthened communist influence within the ANC's senior echelons.

An exodus of refugees after the 1976 Soweto uprising supplied a fresh cohort of recruits for the new training camps established in Angola in the late 1970s. Through the 1980s guerrilla 'armed propaganda' and foreign diplomacy enhanced the ANC's prestige inside South Africa, especially amongst young people. For although the ANC had only a skeletal internal organisation and though it could only field a few hundred armed combatants at any one time, it acquired immense influence especially within the vast federation of voluntary associations formed in 1983, the United Democratic Front. It also enjoyed increasing success in persuading western governments to enforce economic sanctions against South Africa.

Electric pylons sabotaged on 16 December 1961 during Umkhonto we Sizwe's campaign
(Mayibuye Centre)

Above:
Johannesburg, September 1989. Protest march
(Mayibuye Centre)

By the end of the 1980s, economic recession and political stalemate prompted the government to legalise the ANC, release its leaders and initiate negotiations towards racial powersharing. In 1990, the ANC's exile leadership returned home to begin building the largest and most sophisticated political organisation in South Africa and to prepare their radical supporters for the inevitable compromises arising from a bargained constitutional dispensation.

(T Lodge)

Below:
Crowds throng outside the Victor Verster prison to greet Nelson Mandela as he emerges a free man after 27 years of incarceration
(The Argus)

Right:
Translators of the Bible into Afrikaans. From left to right: J D du Toit, E E van Rooyen, J D Kesteil, H C M Fourie and B B Keet
(Africana Museum)

African People's Organisation (APO)

Established in 1902 as the African Political Organisation, it aimed to extend to coloureds in the northern colonies the legal and political rights enjoyed by coloureds in the Cape Colony. Under the presidency of Dr Abdullah Abdurahman (1905–1940) the APO became a powerful and widespread organisation among coloured people throughout South Africa, and remained the most significant body of its kind until the mid-1920s when its influence began to decline. By the 1930s the APO was little more than a mutual benefit, burial and building society, and the new generation of coloured leaders no longer supported it.

African Resistance Movement (ARM)

A group, mostly whites, including a number of university students and lecturers, who in the aftermath of Sharpeville believed that sabotage should be used to shock the white electorate into recognising the need for change in South Africa. Among the members of ARM were a number of radical liberals opposed to the communist-dominated Umkhonto we Sizwe, the military wing of the ANC. ARM used explosives to blow up railway installations and electric pylons. Draconian legislation was introduced in 1962 to combat sabotage, and in 1964 a number of key members of ARM were arrested. Some fled the country, a leading figure turned state's witness, and others were given jail sentences, the longest being fifteen years.

Afrikaans

The language which evolved from the seventeenth century Dutch spoken at the Cape by the first settlers. By the nineteenth century it was spoken by many of the Cape's inhabitants, but it was regarded as the language of the uneducated and considered unsuitable for literary and cultural expression. In the 1870s S J du Toit and others began writing in Afrikaans, producing an Afrikaans journal, grammar and history. After the South African War, the second phase of the Afrikaans language movement commenced, partly in response to Alfred Milner's policies of Anglicisation. Afrikaans periodicals and newspapers began to appear with increasing frequency and in 1925 Afrikaans was recognised as an official language. After 1948 Afrikaans became the language of government and bilingualism was obligatory in the civil service.

Though Afrikaans has been a written language for a relatively short period — the first book published in Afrikaans appeared in 1856 — a significant Afrikaans literature has evolved. It blossomed in the early years of this century in the poems of Eugène Marais and in the poetic triumvirate of Totius (J D du Toit), C Louis Leipoldt and Jan F Celliers. In the 1930s the 'Dertigers' (men of the thirties), a group of talented poets led by W E G Louw and his brother, N P van Wyk Louw, emerged. They were followed in the 1960s by the 'Sestigers' (men of the sixties), Breyten Breytenbach, Ingrid Jonker, Etienne le Roux and André Brink, who led the way with their avant-garde poetry and novels.

Right:
Afrikaans poets Jan F Celliers and Ingrid Jonker
(NALN)

Above:
Etienne le Roux, who led the way with his avant-garde novels
(NALN: Photo by Jakkie Pretorius)

Afrikaner Broederbond

A secret Afrikaner organisation originally established as a cultural organisation named Jong Suid-Afrika (Young South Africa) in 1918. It soon became known as the Afrikaner Broederbond, with the aim of furthering the interests of the Afrikaner people. It sought to promote Afrikaner unity and achieve Afrikaner dominance in the public life of South Africa through a range of political, cultural and economic agencies. The first of these public front organisations, the Federasie van Afrikaanse Kultuurverenigings (Federation of Afrikaner Cultural Organisations) was established in 1929. In the 1930s the Broederbond became increasingly political, siding decisively with Malan and the Purified Nationalists in 1933–1934 and emerging as the vanguard organisation of northern Afrikaner nationalism. The Broederbond was attacked by both Hertzog and Smuts, the latter forbidding teachers and civil servants to belong to it in 1944. Since 1948 every Prime Minister and State President, and most top members of the government and the armed forces have been members of this élite, highly influential organisation.

Afrikaner, Jonker

ROODEZAND, 1790 — OKAHANDJA, 1861

Chief of the Afrikaner tribe from 1823 on the death of his father, Jager Afrikaner. Jonker and his band of followers settled on an island in the Orange River, and armed with rifles they terrorised the surrounding area on horseback for a period of 20 years. Although he established a brief interlude of peace under the influence of missionaries, his insatiable desire for weapons and brandy led him to launch brutal attacks on his Herero neighbours whose cattle he captured to settle his debts. His subsequent raids through Ovamboland left hundreds of villages plundered and burnt.

Afrikaner Rebellion (1914)

A revolt triggered by the government's decision to invade South West Africa during the First World War. Afrikaners who opposed the invasion and hankered for their lost republican independence, under the leadership of former Boer generals, decided to challenge the government by force of arms. The generals used their positions in the Union Defence Force to try to take power in order to restore the Republics. More than 11 400 men in the Orange Free State and the Transvaal went into rebellion in October 1914. Troops under the leadership of Louis Botha put down the rebellion in six weeks. The sentences imposed on the rebels were generally lenient, comprising fines and imprisonment, and before the end of 1916 all were out of jail.

Jopie Fourie was executed by firing squad for his part in the 1914 Rebellion
(Africana Museum)

Jopie Fourie, who was shot by firing squad because he had rebelled without resigning his commission, came to be regarded as a martyr. Botha and Smuts were criticised for their handling of the rebellion and Fourie's execution helped consolidate Nationalist forces behind Hertzog and his newly-formed National Party.

Jonker Afrikaner
(Africana Museum)

Afrikaners

Afrikaners were the descendants of the first Europeans who established themselves in Southern Africa, the free burghers who accepted the Cape as their fatherland in 1657. With the arrival of the Huguenots after 1688 the settlement increased its numbers and the burgeoning population acquired a distinct character. The conclusion that the founding fathers were of Dutch origin however, ought to acknowledge a greater degree of German ancestry. The borders between Germany and German-Dutch Friesland were not clearly demarcated in the seventeenth century. In addition, certain of the Huguenots came to Africa via the Netherlands. According to Pama, an acceptable percentage breakdown of Afrikaner origin is 38 per cent of Dutch ancestry, 35,5 per cent German, 14 per cent French and 3 per cent of Danish-Swedish stock. An 'indeterminable group' of 9,5 per cent display links with Java and with Angolan slaves. By 6 March 1707, Hendrik Bibault's declaration,

Right:
'Boers returning from a hunt', by Samuel Daniell
(African Museum)

Below:
Depiction of the Battle of Blaauwkrantz, 1838, by Thomas Baines. Baines reconstructed the event from eyewitness accounts several years after the battle. The early morning attack by Zulu warriors on a party of Voortrekkers left 500 dead
(Africana Museum)

'*Ik ben een Africaander*', added a new dimension to the idea of an Afrikaner people. Just as immigrants from various European countries became Americans in America, so immigrants to South Africa became native Afrikaners.

With the expansion of the Cape, a natural migration towards the interior followed. By 1800 approximately 25 000 Afrikaners inhabited the region abutting the eastern and northern borders of the country. They had established their own identity and no longer regarded themselves as Netherlanders or Europeans. Although political ties with the Netherlands existed, they saw themselves as a separate people who had become 'indigenous'. They strove strongly towards self-government, but despite their fierce individualism they displayed a certain sense of community: the stock farmers who had trekked into the interior and the wine and wheat farmers spoke the same sort of language and developed certain mutual characteristics.

Before the Great Trek, the Cape Afrikaner was subjected to a gradual Anglicisation process, encouraged by the deliberate efforts of Lord Charles Somerset. The Great Trek initiated a movement of the colonists from the Cape to the unknown interior. Stock farmers probably had some insight into what lay ahead and various exploratory expeditions had been undertaken, but the Trek itself was approached in blind faith; it was a search for a territory where Afrikaners could live independently. Later the establishment of the two Boer Republics in the interior contributed to the Afrikaners' sense of self-reliance and independence

The South African War (1899–1902) was a further attempt to retain independence in the face of a British onslaught. During this war, the suffering in the concentration camps where 26 000 Afrikaner women and children died, and the return of the Boer prisoners of war to burnt and ravaged farms resulted in an embitterment towards the British Empire. The economic recovery of the impoverished Afrikaners was an arduous task, and by the 1930s it had still not been achieved.

The history of Afrikaners in the twentieth century is characterised by urbanisation, a striving towards the maintenance of an own identity and the development of a strong nationalism.

In 1924, J B M Hertzog's National Party came to power with the help of the Labour Party. However, squabbles and differences persisted and political unity remained elusive throughout the 1930s. Coalition and Fusion with General Smuts's South African Party was an attempt at relative reconciliation among Afrikaners and an endeavour to promote cooperation with their English-speaking fellow citizens. But this too failed and a politically divided Afrikanerdom was plunged into the Second World War. In 1948 the Herenigde Nasionale Party, under the leadership of Dr Malan, won the general election, thereby ensuring that a section of Afrikanerdom dominated political life for decades.

In the nineteenth century the Afrikaner concentrated largely on farming — hence the term 'Boer' which was often used interchangeably with 'Afrikaner'. After the South African War (1899–1902), Afrikaners of influence tended to be teachers or ministers and were not well represented in mining, trade and related professions. Economically, Afrikaners played a lesser role than their English-speaking counterparts. A notable exception is the Rembrandt Group of the Rupert and Hertzog families, which in 1993 was recognised as the strongest group financially in South Africa. The emergence of Afrikaners on the

Queuing for rations. Thousands of Boer men, women and children died in concentration camps during the South African War and this left an ineradicable scar on the Afrikaner consciousness (Transvaal Archives TAB 31132)

Hertzog's cabinet, 1929. Front, from left to right: F H P Creswell, D F Malan, J B M Hertzog, N C Havenga, P Grobler. Back, from left to right: O Pirow, J A Kemp, A Fourie, S Jansen, H Sampson, C Malan (Transvaal Archives SAB 2509)

Above:
N P van Wyk Louw, D J Opperman and Elizabeth Eybers, leading Afrikaans writers and poets
(NALN)

economic front was a slow process. Their economic development had a cultural dimension. The Reddingsdaadbond and the Afrikaanse Handelskamer testify to this, as does the establishment of Volkskas Bank and Sanlam. State-funded corporations like Iscor and Sasol depended initially on a sense of Afrikaner loyalty to gain support.

The development of Afrikaans as the language of the Afrikaner was a gradual process. Originally Dutch was the language of common usage and Afrikaans, influenced by French, German, Javanese and Malay, evolved from it. Afrikaans displays a simplified grammatical structure where the gender of nouns and most of the Dutch flexional forms have not been retained. In order to gain recognition for Afrikaans as a written language the Genootskap van Regte Afrikaners was established in 1875. The First and Second Language Movements followed shortly thereafter resulting in Afrikaans acquiring formal status, along with English, as one of the two official languages of the Union of South Africa.

By 1915 the Afrikaans press already played a leading role on the political and cultural fronts. Nasionale Pers with its daily newspapers and its magazines, and the Voortrekkerpers (later Perskor) helped to further the republican ideal and to entrench the Afrikaner's position. Early Afrikaans literature (poetry especially) adopted a strong patriotic tone, and after the South African War it played an important role in the growth of Afrikaner pride and national consciousness. Towards the end of the twentieth century the foremost Afrikaans writers and poets are of world renown — N P van Wyk Louw, D J Opperman, Elizabeth Eybers and Breyten Breytenbach.

The Afrikaner Broederbond, founded in 1918, took the lead in the cultural sphere. Its role in promoting Afrikaner pride and a spirit of cooperation on economic, political, religious and cultural levels should not be underestimated. In 1929 the Federasie vir Afrikaanse Kultuurvereniginge (FAK) was founded and it acted as a central body for the furtherance of Afrikaner cultural interests, particularly in the cities. The church and educational bodies added their weight to the cause and set themselves up as bearers and protectors of cultural aspiration. During these early years the National Party stood at the centre of all endeavours to achieve a spirit of unity and nationalism.

The period from 1929 to 1961 saw the emergence of various cultural organisations such as the Afrikaanse Taal- en Kultuurvereniging (1931), the Voortrekkerbeweging (1931), the Reddingsdaadbond (1940), the Afrikaanse Handelsinstituut (1942), the Afrikaanse Sakekamer (1942), the Rapportryersbeweging (1950), the Afrikaanse Taal- en Kultuurbond (1953) and the Junior Rapportryers (1958). Through their well-organised cultural life — Afrikaner women were involved in community service and charity work (as seen in the activities of the Suid-Afrikaanse Vroue Federasie and the Afrikaanse Christelike

Right:
Afrikaners parade with ox wagons through the streets of Pretoria during the 1938 Voortrekker centenary celebrations
(Transvaal Archives SAB 9420)

Vroue Vereniging) — Afrikaners have ensured that urbanisation has not led to impoverishment and isolation, and even schools and churches have been deliberately enmeshed in cultural activities. But, after 1961 there was talk of the 'New Afrikaner' — a generation of Afrikaners who did not have personal knowledge of the struggle for the recognition of Afrikaans in the unsympathetic cities.

Structures like the Voortrekker monument outside Pretoria, the Vroue monument in Bloemfontein and the Huguenot Memorial in Franschhoek can be described as Afrikaner landmarks. Sculptors such as Anton van Wouw, Coert Steynberg and Hennie Potgieter, amongst others, set high standards. Celebrated artists like J H Pierneef, Hugo Naudé, Maggie Laubser, Pieter Wenning, Gregoire Boonzaaier and Anna Vorster ensure that Afrikaners occupy a leading place in South Africa's artistic heritage.

After the South African War, Afrikaner parents set up numerous Christian National Education schools to prevent a pervasive Anglicisation at school level. The universities of Stellenbosch, Pretoria, Potchefstroom, Bloemfontein and the Rand Afrikaans University in Johannesburg contributed substantially to formal instruction.

Calvinism has played a dominant role in the history of the Afrikaner. The three 'sister' churches — the Nederduits Gereformeerde Kerk, the Gereformeerde Kerk and the Hervormde Kerk — form the backbone of the Afrikaner's religious identity and the church had an enormous influence on the congregant's daily life. In the 1980s the Afrikaanse Protestantse Kerk was established and it took under its wing those Afrikaners with more politically conservative tendencies. Some Afrikaners belonged to the Apostolic mission and the Lutheran and other churches.

(D Prinsloo)

Afrikaner Weerstandsbeweging (AWB)

A white, far-right organisation founded by Eugene Terreblanche in 1973, in reaction to what were seen as modifications to apartheid, in particular the policy of dialogue with black Africa adopted by Prime Minister Vorster. Projecting a neo-Nazi image, with a swastika-like emblem and storm-troopers, the AWB maintained a high profile under Terreblanche's leadership. Registered as a Volkstaat Party, the AWB regarded the Conservative Party as its parliamentary front. It advocated the formation of an independent Afrikaner state in the area of the former Boer Republics, and was militantly opposed to President de Klerk's reform initiative launched in 1990.

Left:
Renowned artist J H Pierneef in his 'grass studio' camp at Pienaars River
(Transvaal Archives TAB 21131)

Below:
Eugene Terreblanche, founder and leader of the AWB
(Rapport Library)

Agriculture

The original base of settler expansion, the southwestern Cape, produced wine and wheat on the estates carved out by the early free burghers, worked by slave labour until 1834. Until the nineteenth century markets were severely restricted and limited to the Dutch East India Company's requirements. In the arid further interior where the trekboers moved with their flocks, a mainly, but never entirely, subsistence economy was practised. Wine production for export boomed for a time in the early nineteenth century as a result of British imperial preference, but it declined in importance with the decline of preference and the abolition of slavery. It was partly as a result of slave compensation

Wool market at Port Elizabeth, 1864, by Thomas Bowler (National Cultural History Museum)

money entering the economy in the late 1830s that the centre of economic gravity moved to the eastern Cape and Midlands districts in the form of merino wool farming to feed the increasingly voracious British textile industry. Cape Town merchant and company capital was largely invested in the promotion of the wool boom which was in full swing by the second half of the 1840s, and which gradually spread out into the more westerly and northerly regions. Many of the pioneer large-scale wool farmers were British settlers who had arrived in the eastern Cape in 1820.

The Boer economy outside the more capitalised regions of the Cape continued to be based in large degree on extensive grazing and hunting, and animal products, hides and skins, ostrich feathers and ivory continued to be major export items. The rise of the British port of Durban and the arrival of British settlers and capital in Natal from the late 1840s intensified the commercial life of the interior, but attempts to turn Natal into a cotton or coffee colony failed, and land became concentrated in the hands of absentee speculators. Natal found its staple export crop in sugar, grown first in the 1850s in the semi-tropical coastal belt. The importation of indentured labourers from India from 1860 provided the industry with its characteristic plantation labour force. During the 1860s and 1870s the planters became increasingly indebted to merchant brokers, and between 1875 and 1898 the industry was consolidated under the control of corporations, which controlled also the factory processing of the sugar. Perhaps the most spectacular export boom in the nineteenth century was in ostrich feathers, a desirable item of fashion in Victorian times. The birds were domesticated by the 1860s, and the farming of ostriches, with its epicentre at Oudtshoorn in the southern Cape, took off in the 1870s, generating huge profits. The eddies reached out far afield wherever alfalfa (lucerne) could be cultivated to feed the birds, and wild land speculations resulted. The feather economy collapsed in 1914, but has revived in more recent years.

Natal sugar mill, Mount Edgecombe, 1918 (Local History Museum Collection, Durban)

The mineral discoveries and consequent rise of internal urban markets had a revolutionary impact on the rural hinterland, and in the longer term were to transform the highveld of the Orange Free State and Transvaal into the region's arable heartland. Maize, wheat and sorghum were soon in great demand to feed the human and animal population of the urban centres; wherever water sources permitted, market gardening was undertaken; dairy cows and beasts of burden were at a premium. Arable production on the highveld was largely in the hands of black peasant producers initially, and a considerable struggle ensued over a long period to equip white farmers with the capital resources and know-how to establish functional control over productive activities on their land. It was initially the Milner regime after the South African War (1899–1902) that set about systematically promoting white capitalist agriculture, and securing and controlling a stabilised black labour force, although its ambitious schemes to introduce large numbers of British land

Far left:
The ostrich, *Struthio camelus*, which was sometimes mistaken at a distance for cavalry
(Africana Museum)

Left:
'Maize cultivation at a South African homestead', by Thomas Baines
(Africana Museum)

settlers were only marginally effective in transforming the countryside.

In the twentieth century, the state intervened massively in the promotion of capitalist farming. The Department of Agriculture was at the forefront in establishing experimental farms and agricultural schools, in importing experts in various branches of production, in providing a variety of agricultural extension services, and in widely circulating instructional publications. Breeding stock were imported and distributed. The colonial land banks, unified in 1912, brought low-interest loans within the reach of white farmers. The railway network was extended through the white farming districts. Export markets were secured for South African fruit and maize, the supply of which outstripped demand early in the century, by means of subsidised freight rates. Cold storage, eradication of disease and quality control all contributed to the export of fruit, eggs and meat. Railway rating policies also facilitated internal distribution of produce. Tariffs protected the Natal sugar industry, the output trebling between 1910 and 1927, leading to an export drive. Wool yields climbed dramatically, exports quadrupling in value between 1910 and 1927.

The government sponsored and subsidised the creation of co-operative societies, designed to bypass the grip of middlemen by supplying farmers' needs and marketing their produce. A wine farmers' co-operative (KWV) was formed in the southwestern Cape in 1917, and a Fruit Growers' Co-operative Exchange was set up in 1922. In the 1920s grain elevators were erected at railway stations under co-operative control, permitting bulk handling. The level of state support continually increased in order to maintain the viability of white agriculture, in the face of recurring climatic and market crises. The Great Depression — when export prices slumped dramatically — combined with the terrible drought of the early 1930s, caused a mass efflux of failed white farmers. State controls over farming methods and marketing were greatly elaborated in consequence. By the time the Marketing Act was passed in 1937 in order to coordinate their regulations and activities, control boards had been established for meat, maize, dairy produce, wheat, wine and tobacco. Several others followed. These boards fixed prices and

Left:
Imported breeding stock improved local flocks greatly. This advertisement placed in the Graaff-Reinet Herald of 10 March 1860 proclaims the merits of 'eleven splendid French merino rams'
(Africana Museum)

Oranges being delivered to a centralised fruit packer in Rustenburg (Transvaal Archives TAB 753)

controlled marketing to the benefit of the producers, restricted competition from imports, where necessary issued quotas and subsidised exports (sometimes effectively dumping produce), and maintained stringent quality controls.

In the 1990s, commercial agriculture is almost exclusively under the control of white farmers. The areas of intensive agricultural production are to be found in the central highveld plateau where maize, sorghum, cereal crops, cattle, sheep and dairying predominate; along the south-western and southern Cape coastal belt where are to be found fruit, vines, wheat, sheep and dairying, tobacco, ostriches and lucerne; and the Natal coastal strip where sugar plantations dominate. Maize (accounting for about a half of the cultivated acreage in South Africa) is the major agricultural export product, followed by wool, sugar, fruit and jam. Newer crops that have been adopted successfully in various parts of the country include groundnuts, sunflowers, tea, coffee, sisal and cotton. However, the debt of South Africa's white farmers by the 1990s was approaching twenty billion rands; and as drought and economic decline again threatened agriculture, it was clear that the state was no longer willing, or able, to subsidise white farmers as it had previously.

(T Keegan)

Airlinks

The first commercial air service in South Africa was introduced in 1919: it conveyed passengers across South Africa and Rhodesia. By 1939 there was an extensive network of air routes linking all the major centres of the country, with regional flights to Rhodesia, Mozambique, South West Africa, Uganda and Angola. International flights were begun when a British airline started flying between Cape Town and London in 1931. Three years later the state-owned South African Airways (SAA) came into existence.

As a result of South Africa's apartheid policies, African states imposed a ban on landing and overflying rights on all South African aircraft in 1963. In 1986 the US Congress banned direct air travel, begun in 1969, between South Africa and the United States. With the repeal of apartheid legislation in 1991, SAA was once again permitted to fly over Africa, flights to New York were resumed, and many new airlines began flying into and out of South Africa.

Alexandra

A black township north of Johannesburg between the old Pretoria Main Road and the eastern bypass, Alexandra is one of the few black townships completely surrounded by white suburbs. Notorious for overpopulation and squalid conditions — it was originally intended to house 5 000 people, but by the early 1990s its population was estimated at 200 000 people — it adjoins affluent Sandton. After major unrest in the township in the 1980s, the government decided to try to upgrade it, but with little success, and it remains a stronghold of resistance to the apartheid state.

Right:
Alexandra township. A street scene in the 1940s (Africana Museum)

All African Convention (AAC)

A federal body set up in 1935 to co-ordinate resistance to the proposed land legislation, which was intended to compensate Cape Africans for the loss of common-roll voters' rights. Its president, D D T Jabavu (1936–1948), led a delegation to meet Prime Minister Hertzog to discuss its opposition to the abolition of the African vote, but without success. In 1943, the AAC became affiliated to the Non-European Unity Movement (NEUM).

Amabutho

Zulu word for age sets, into which young men, on reaching puberty, were formed. In *amabutho* men fought, worked, hunted and raided for their king, and had to wait until granted permission to marry. In this way the king had control over their labour, he could check population growth, and at the same time he provided himself with a highly efficient device for the maintenance of public order. *Amabutho* developed amongst most northern Nguni chiefdoms in the late eighteenth century, but it was particularly in the Zulu kingdom that they became the source and confirmation of the king's power.

Andrews, William Henry

SUFFOLK, 1870 — RONDEBOSCH, 1950

Labour leader and communist. Andrews was brought up in an atmosphere of religious dissent and political radicalism. A life-long champion of the working class, he introduced the shop stewards' movement to South Africa, and was involved in numerous labour disputes, including the miners' strike in 1907 and the Rand gold mining strikes of 1913 and 1914. He was Chairman of both the South African Labour Party (1909) and the International Socialist League. He was a founder member of the Communist Party (the result of an amalgamation of several organisations) and became its general secretary in 1921. He was also the first secretary of the South African Trade Union Congress, a position held from 1925 until his retirement in 1932.

William Henry Andrews
(Africana Museum)

Anglican Church

The Church of England was introduced into South Africa after the second British occupation of the Cape (1806) to minister to the spiritual needs of the English in the new colony. After Robert Gray became first Anglican bishop of Cape Town in 1848, the activities of the church were greatly expanded. The church was, however, riven with disputes, which led Gray to create an autonomous Church of the Province of South Africa (1870), which retained close ties with Canterbury and the church in Britain. A small separate Church of England survived in South Africa, but was not important. The main Anglican church, after a long period in which it did little to challenge the racism of the governments of the day, began to take a leading role in opposition to apartheid in the 1950s, and in the 1980s Archbishop Desmond Tutu became a national and international leader in that struggle.

Anglo American Corporation

The largest company in South Africa. A predominantly mining and finance conglomerate, Anglo American was formed in 1917 by Sir Ernest Oppenheimer (1880–1957) with considerable backing

'St George's Cathedral from Wale Street, Cape Town', by Thomas Bowler.
The activities of the Anglican Church were greatly expanded after 1848
(Africana Museum)

from American financier J P Morgan, to exploit the east Witwatersrand goldfields. Oppenheimer was a key figure in the diamond industry and from 1929 chairman of De Beers Consolidated Mines, which became part of the Anglo empire. Anglo American extended its operations into Northern Rhodesia (now Zambia) from 1929, where it exploited copper, and also Southern Rhodesia (now Zimbabwe). In the 1950s and 1960s it began to diversify into industry, finance and property. Today it has extensive investments throughout the world through Minorco, its offshore investment company. Since its inception Anglo American has been closely identified with subsequent generations of the Oppenheimer family: Sir Ernest's son Harry succeeded him as chairman, and Harry's son is today one of the leading figures in the organisation.

Anglo-Boer War (First), *see* Anglo-Transvaal War

Anglo-Boer War (Second), *see* South African War

Anglo-Transvaal War (1880–1881)

Sometimes known as the Transvaal War of Independence or the First Anglo-Boer War, it was a struggle in which the Transvaal Afrikaners attempted to regain their independence, lost when Britain annexed the Transvaal in 1877. After three years of peaceful protest and petition had failed to have the annexation revoked, the Transvaal Afrikaners rebelled. Their strategy was to besiege British garrisons stationed in towns in the Transvaal, and to prevent British reinforcements from entering the Transvaal from Natal. The Transvalers scored a number of victories, culminating in the overwhelming victory at Majuba (February 1881), which shook Britain and captured the attention of the world. Negotiations for peace, begun by Kruger in January, were concluded forthwith. The Pretoria Convention (1881) revoked Britain's annexation of the Transvaal, and granted the Boers self-government. The Transvaal was regarded as a British suzerainty, its foreign relations remained under British control and it was forbidden to alter its boundaries without British consent.

Anglo-Zulu War (1879)

In 1878, determined to break Zulu power, the British High Commissioner, Sir Bartle Frere, served a stiff ultimatum on Cetshwayo, the Zulu king. When Cetshwayo rejected his unreasonable demands, British troops invaded Zululand, suffering a spectacular defeat at Isandlwana (January 1879). A Zulu advance on nearby Rorke's Drift was fended off, and in July 1879 British troops took Ulundi, the Zulu capital. Cetshwayo was captured and the Zulu army ceased to be effective. Zululand was divided into thirteen separate chiefdoms and, after a ruinous civil war, was annexed by Britain (1887) and then incorporated into Natal (1897).

Antisemitism

Prior to the 1930s antisemitism was limited to negative literary and cultural stereotyping: Jewish knavery; financial

The Anglo-Transvaal War: the Boer method of fighting, as depicted in one of the illustrated newspapers of the time (Africana Museum)

Painting of the Battle of Rorke's Drift by M E Newman, an episode in the Anglo-Zulu War. Troops arrive to relieve the beleaguered garrison (Local History Museum Collection, Durban)

machinations (exemplified in Hoggenheimer, a notorious cartoon caricature); military 'shirking'; 'Bolshevik' subversion and 'unassimilability'. Calls to curtail the influx of eastern European Jews, made from the turn of the century, culminated in a Quota Act of 1930. The 1930s and early 1940s witnessed a popular surge of antisemitism, ensuring a prominent position for the 'Jewish Question' on the public agenda. Antisemitism formed an important and influential component of the Afrikaner nationalist world-view. It was particularly evident in the rhetoric and actions of the Greyshirts, the Ossewabrandwag and the New Order. The groundswell of anti-Jewish feeling prompted the United Party to introduce stiffer educational and financial requirements in an Aliens Act of 1937 which prevented large-scale German-Jewish immigration.

The 'Jewish Question' receded rapidly from the public agenda after the war. Anti-Jewish outbursts were restricted to fringe elements on the ultra-right, including Holocaust 'revisionists'. Close ties between South Africa and Israel from the 1970s tarnished the image of the Jew in the mind of the black majority. There are indications of substantial social distance between blacks and Jews, including negative attitudes towards Jews among black élites.

(M Shain)

Apartheid

Apartheid means, literally, 'apartness'. It is the term generally applied to the rigid race policy devised and implemented by the National Party government after its election to power in 1948. Apartheid did not represent a radical departure from the segregation era that preceded it. Rather, it took segregation to its logical conclusion. Apartheid amounted to a more systematic, more monolithic set of policies, and was more rigidly and ruthlessly enforced than segregation.

The word 'apartheid' first came to be used by Afrikaner intellectuals in the 1930s. But it was not until the 1940s that National Party thinkers began to formulate ideas that would come to be embodied in the apartheid system. Even by the 1940s these ideas were lacking any real coherence or finality. Indeed some have argued that apartheid ideology never developed any such coherence or finality. This view counters the widely held assumption that apartheid was the product of a grand plan or blueprint masterminded by Dr Verwoerd.

A key figure in the elaboration of apartheid theory in the 1940s was Geoffrey Cronjé, professor of sociology at Pretoria University. He saw apartheid as the only way to safeguard cherished ideals, such as racial purity and the diversity of nations. But it was left to the Sauer Committee to formulate more specific policy directions. This committee had been set up by the National Party with the task of drafting policy before the 1948 election. The Sauer Report firmly rejected racial integration and assimilation, for Indians and coloureds as well as for Africans. It saw the reserves as providing the basis for a more complete system of political separation for Africans. It also recommended state control over African education, and severe restrictions on African urbanisation.

In the two decades after 1948 the main elements of apartheid were gradually put in place. The crux of apartheid was the homeland or Bantustan system. It was the development and elaboration of this system that differentiated apartheid from segregation. The system was developed with some vigour, especially after Dr Verwoerd became Minister of Native Affairs in 1950. In 1951 he piloted through Parliament the Bantu Authorities Act, a key measure in the creation of Bantustans. It provided for a three-tier system of African self-government in the reserves: the bottom tier would be a Tribal Authority, consisting of local chiefs and headmen; in the middle was the Regional Authority, which overlay two or more Tribal Authorities and drew upon the membership of the latter; at the top, the Territorial Authority would be responsible for the whole area of a reserve. The Act was to be implemented gradually with different 'tribal groups' moving to the various levels of government at different stages. The structure was implemented first in the Transkei where a Territorial Authority was in place by 1957.

The 1959 Promotion of Bantu Self-Government Act further developed the system by proclaiming the existence of eight African 'national units', based on assumed linguistic and cultural diversity, but not on territoriality. Provision was made for the gradual transfer of some power of self-government to these units. Again the Transkei, in 1963, was the first Bantustan to be granted such status. Other homelands gradually, one by one, followed the same path. Eventually ten such homelands were created; four of these (Bophuthatswana, Ciskei, Transkei and Venda) were granted 'independence' by the South African government, but they failed to gain recognition of this independence from the rest of the world.

Insofar as various other apartheid policies and measures depended on it, the Bantustan system was the corner-stone of apartheid. The whole process of political differentiation between black and white rested on the homelands. Apartheid's apologists argued that blacks would exercise their political rights in their own homelands, and in so doing would automatically renounce any claim to political rights under the South African constitution. Indeed, one of the ultimate objectives of apartheid planners was that there would eventually be no black South Africans. This was the purpose of the 1970 Bantu Homelands Citizenship Act, which stipulated that all blacks would become citizens of one of the homelands; this was to apply even to persons who had never set foot in a homeland.

There was also a close connection between the homeland system and urban apartheid. One of the objectives of urban apartheid was to limit the movement of

The Bantustans came to take on the function of dumping grounds, accommodating those who were surplus to the labour requirements of white South Africa. Pictured here, Illinge Camp in Natal (Mayibuye Centre: photo by John Seymour)

blacks into urban areas. The apartheid ideal was that black urban presence would be limited according to the labour needs of urban areas. As far as was possible, blacks would be required to live in a Bantustan. Various measures and mechanisms were devised in an effort to achieve this ultimately unattainable objective. First, an elaborate system of influx control and pass laws was constructed, and increasingly tightened over time, in order to limit the movement of blacks into urban areas. The machinery of influx control had been put in place during the segregation era, but from the 1950s it became much more rigid. A key measure was the 1952 Native Laws Amendment Act. This designated all towns and cities as prescribed areas in which influx control would be automatically applicable; and no African could remain in these areas for more than seventy-two hours unless he or she met certain qualifications — the notorious 'section 10 rights'. The state developed a massive apparatus to enforce influx control. Millions of blacks were arrested under the pass laws, especially during the 1960s and 1970s; and hundreds of thousands were endorsed out of urban areas, where they were not entitled to be under the law, and removed to one or other of the Bantustans.

Other mechanisms were devised in an effort to limit the size of the urban black population in 'white' South Africa. Some cities and towns were situated quite close to homeland borders. In many of these cases whole townships, originally built close to the urban centre, were destroyed and rebuilt inside the homeland, further away from the workplace but still within commuting distance. Another mechanism was simply to redraw the boundaries of homelands, already heavily fragmented, to include existing black townships. Thus, for instance, Umlazi and KwaMashu, outside Durban, were in 1977 incorporated into KwaZulu.

In many cases urban areas were too far removed from a Bantustan to make this option viable. Apartheid planners considered circumventing this problem by establishing high-speed commuter rail links between Bantustans and cities to convey black workers to the urban workplace. The other approach, which was implemented, was to take industry close to the Bantustans. Thus incentives were offered to industrialists to set up factories in areas where cross-border labour could be tapped. These were the so-called border industries.

Millions of blacks were arrested under the pass laws. Here, demonstrators give the thumbs-up salute during the ANC pass burning campaign of 1960
(Mayibuye Centre)

The apartheid system both built upon and entrenched territorial segregation, as set down in the 1913 and 1936 Land Acts. The reserves provided the territorial basis for the homelands, but not the basis for a viable rural economy. In the mid-1950s the government appointed the Tomlinson Commission to recommend ways of developing African rural areas. It proposed extensive investment towards such development, but the government failed to act on this recommendation. Instead the rural areas of the Bantustans, during the apartheid era, slid deeper and deeper into poverty. Increasingly they came to take on the function of dumping-grounds, taking in people who were surplus to the labour requirements of white South Africa. Thus the homelands came to be integral to the whole process of forced removals, a process which will almost certainly go down in history as the most horrendous feature of apartheid.

The ultimate objective of forced removals was to 'cleanse' white South Africa of its black population without endangering the labour supply. Forced removals took various forms. There were those

Below:
Countless Africans suffered as a result of the process of forced removals. Here, a white farmer profits from the situation by charging to transport the goods of those forcibly removed from his farm
(Mayibuye Centre)

people, already referred to, who were endorsed out of urban areas. There were blacks forcibly removed from so-called 'black spots', black-owned freehold land which fell outside the homelands. Black cash tenants, sharecroppers and labour tenants occupying white-owned land increasingly came to be victims of forced relocation, ending up in the Bantustans. As capitalist agriculture mechanised more intensively from the 1950s, so many farm labourers lost their jobs. They too were forced into the homelands. It is now reckoned that about 3 500 000 people were relocated under these and other categories of removals. One of the dire consequences of this process was to aggravate the overpopulation of the Bantustans and so also to accelerate their impoverishment.

It has been suggested that apartheid was a more intensified, rigidified form of segregation. This was certainly so in many other spheres of South African life. The differential treatment of black and white in the industrial workplace can be traced back to the early years of diamond mining. Job reservation came to be extended by the 1956 Industrial Conciliation Act, which intensified race discrimination and segregation in industry.

Segregation in the educational field was taken onto a new plane in the apartheid era. The key measure was the Bantu Education Act of 1953. This placed black education under the control of the Department of Native Affairs, and in the process destroyed the independent mission schools. The syllabus for black schools was also changed, in such a way as to prepare pupils for a subordinate role in society. A few years later apartheid was extended to tertiary education. The 1959 Extension of University Education Act imposed segregation on universities by providing for the creation of four new ethnic colleges and forcing all existing universities, except Fort Hare, to become white institutions.

Under the Bantu Education Act, African pupils received inadequate and inferior schooling designed to prepare them for a subordinate role in society (Mayibuye Centre)

The Native (Urban Areas) Act of 1923 had allowed for, but not compelled, residential segregation. Urban areas, in varying degrees, came to adopt the practice of residential segregation, especially for Africans, over the next two or three decades. It was the Group Areas Act of 1950 that imposed a rigid, nationwide system of urban segregation. The Act empowered the government to proclaim residential and business areas for particular race groups. It was designed to create racially homogeneous residential areas. Those most severely affected by the measure were thousands of coloureds and Indians who had for long been living alongside whites in many communities.

Another distinguishing feature of the apartheid era was the imposition of racial segregation across a broad spectrum of social and cultural spheres. Soon after the National Party's accession to power in 1948, legislation was passed prohibiting marriage or any sexual liaison between whites and other race groups. Further legislation in 1953 required a whole range of public amenities to be segregated, including beaches, sporting facilities, restaurants, cinemas, theatres, post offices, buses, trains, public toilets and park benches. This form of segregation came to be known as petty apartheid.

The distinction has often been drawn between 'petty apartheid' and 'grand apartheid' — the latter referring to the broader system of political and economic discrimination and differentiation, based on the homelands. However, both petty apartheid and grand apartheid depended on one key measure — the Population Registration Act of 1950. This made provision for every person to be classified into a racial group. Without this measure it would have been impossible to enforce other discriminatory laws with the desired degree of rigidity.

While apartheid depended on a rigid system of racial classification, it also required an enormous repressive apparatus. Apartheid policy-makers may have hoped that they could obtain the consent of blacks for a policy that brought their own subordination and exploitation. But this was a

Left:
A distinguishing feature of apartheid was the imposition of racial segregation across a broad spectrum of social and cultural spheres. Signs such as these were commonplace
(Mayibuye Centre)

naïve hope, and over the years black opposition to apartheid became stronger and more militant. Thus the government passed ever more repressive laws, restricting political organisation and action. At the same time the state's security apparatus was both enlarged and given wider powers, so that the police came to act more and more ruthlessly against the opponents of apartheid. Ultimately an extraordinary degree of repression was required in order for the apartheid system to be maintained.

Scholars, commentators and observers have for long considered and debated the essential character and function of apartheid. Certain questions have arisen: was apartheid a massive piece of social engineering based on a carefully drawn blueprint, or was it a pragmatic response to changing circumstances? Was it a monolithic or a flexible system? Was its function primarily political or economic?

Both apartheid's apologists and liberal analysts have, from their different perspectives, viewed apartheid as primarily a political phenomenon, designed to preserve racial identities and secure white supremacy. Marxist analysts, on the other hand, have explained apartheid in materialist terms, seeing it as a system designed primarily to secure the exploitation of cheap black labour. Such analysts have observed that the high point of the apartheid era — the 1960s, when the system came closest to functioning as intended — coincided with a period of considerable economic growth. It thus seemed that apartheid was highly functional to the capitalist economy — a view long disputed by liberal writers who argued that apartheid was economically irrational and inefficient insofar as it went against free market principles.

For a long time the conventional wisdom also held that apartheid was the product of a blueprint carefully worked out by Afrikaner nationalist ideologues, with Dr Verwoerd playing the leading role. Recent research has disputed this view. It is argued that there was no systematic model from which apartheid was derived; and at crucial stages Afrikaner nationalists were divided among themselves over future policy directions. Rather, apartheid was a pragmatic policy that evolved in response to particular circumstances.

Apartheid was also flexible and adaptable. In the four decades after 1948 it changed its character. It began as a fairly crude form of white supremacy, known as *baasskap*. In the 1960s the emphasis shifted more towards 'separate development' in an effort to mask white supremacism. From the late 1970s the government began to tamper with apartheid, abandoning some of its more rigid features and trying to make it look more acceptable to the outside world. Ultimately, though, apartheid broke down, unable either to fulfil its own contradictory objectives or to withstand growing, fierce opposition inside the country and from the international community. This reality forced the government of F W de Klerk to abandon the ideology and policy of apartheid. But as the country moved haltingly and violently towards a new order in the early 1990s, a number of the old structures and institutions of apartheid still remained intact.

(P Maylam)

Below:
Troops in Crossroads squatter camp, 1987. To maintain the apartheid system effectively, the state's security apparatus was enlarged and given even greater powers
(Mayibuye Centre)

Apprenticeship

In the eighteenth century Khoisan children and adults captured by Boer commandos during raids were distributed as apprentices among the farmers. Though apprenticeship was supposed to be for a limited number of years, and in theory to involve training of some kind, in reality apprentices were held in virtual slavery. A British proclamation in 1812 attempted to regulate this practice by enforcing apprenticeship from eight years to eighteen years of age only, with the employer responsible for food, clothing and education. When slavery was abolished in 1834, slaves were obliged to serve as apprentices to their former masters for a further four years.

Architecture

South Africa's many different architectural styles are reflected in the beehive and cylindrical-shaped dwellings of Bantu-speaking people, Cape Dutch, Georgian and Victorian buildings, the houses of the Malays in Cape Town, and the architecture of Indians in Natal.

Early Dutch, Flemish, German and French settlers built in the European style, but adapted buildings to local climatic conditions and availability of local materials. Gradually a unique, Cape Dutch vernacular architecture evolved, in the form of stark white-plastered walls, smooth grey thatch, elaborately fashioned mouldings, and a great central gable rising over the main doorway, the hallmark of the style. Cape Dutch architecture reached its highest expression towards the end of the eighteenth century, and lingered on throughout the Georgian era. During the early years of the nineteenth century, fashions in architecture changed completely with the introduction by the British of Georgian and Regency styles, adapted to local conditions by features such as shutters and verandas. The 1820 settlers created the peculiarly eastern Cape version of these styles, while the Voortrekkers carried the basic Cape style into the interior.

The Victorian vernacular which followed used corrugated-iron roofs and incorporated front verandas (stoeps). The mineral discoveries and the advent of the railways gave a tremendous impetus to building. Typical of this era were buildings using mass-produced, pre-fabricated components, often ordered by catalogue from abroad. It was during the late nineteenth century era of prosperity that Sir Herbert Baker came to the Cape from England. Probably the most significant figure in South African architecture, Baker designed and built some of the country's finest buildings, such as the Union Buildings in Pretoria and Groote Schuur in Cape Town, and his work long influenced the character

The beehive-shaped dwellings typical of the Bantu-speaking people are depicted in this painting of a Zulu kraal near Umlazi, Natal, by George French Angas (Local History Museum Collection, Durban)

Sir Herbert Baker designed some of the country's finest buildings, among them the Union Buildings in Pretoria
(Institute of South African Architects)

of South African architecture. The twentieth century brought the Art Nouveau, Bauhaus, Art Deco and Modern Movements, imported from Europe. Though the central business districts of all the major cities were marred by much hideous building, previous tastes and styles lingered on, as in the Arts and Crafts style adapted to South African needs by Baker. Reacting against post-modernism, Revel Fox, one of the most prominent architects of the 1980s and early 1990s, returned to neo-classicism in Bank City, Johannesburg.

Arms Embargo

In reaction to the Sharpeville massacre (1960) and its aftermath, the United Nations (UN) Security Council imposed a non-mandatory arms embargo on South Africa in 1963. South Africa's response was the establishment in 1966 of a public armanent manufacturing corporation, Armscor, to promote self-sufficiency. In 1977, following Steve Biko's death in detention, the UN Security Council imposed a mandatory arms embargo on South Africa, making it illegal for any member state of the UN to sell arms to South Africa. By then Armscor had established a flourishing arms industry, and some arms continued to flow in from Eastern Europe and Third World countries, with Israel and Taiwan acting as intermediaries.

In the mid-1980s the United States threatened to cut off military aid to allies suspected of breaking the international arms embargo against South Africa. Despite the lifting of most sanctions against South Africa in 1991, the international arms embargo remained in place in the early 1990s.

Autshumao (Harry)
d. 1663

A leader of the Goringhaicona, otherwise known as the Peninsular Khoikhoi (Strandlopers), who had lost their stock and been forced to resort to scavenging. Autshumao was taken by the British to the East (Bantam) in 1631, and there taught English and trained as an intermediary. He became the postal agent for the British and lived for a number of years on Robben Island. He then acted as an agent between Van Riebeeck's officials, who were intent on stock bartering, and the Khoikhoi further inland. He prospered from his position to such an extent that, in the late 1650s, he became a significant stockowner of over 200 cattle and sheep respectively. The Dutch expedition inland in 1655 to the Malmesbury-Saldanha area exposed Autshumao's role in preventing Khoikhoi in the outlying districts from bartering directly with officials at the Fort. Autshumao accompanied another Dutch expedition in 1655 which proved unprofitable, and the Dutch, on the recommendation of rival leaders of the Peninsular Khoikhoi (Gogosoa and Doman) banished

Autshumao to Robben Island. Doman subsequently assumed Autshumao's position as intermediary.

Azania

A word derived from the Greek *azainein* meaning 'dry'. Some 2 000 years ago, the area south of Ethiopia stretching down the coast of East Africa from Somalia to Kenya was called 'Ajan' or 'Azania'. In 1965 the Pan Africanist Congress (PAC) adopted the name Azania for South Africa, and the name was taken over by the Black Consciousness movement and the Azanian People's Organisation.

Azanian People's Organisation (AZAPO)

A Black Consciousness group formed in 1978 to fill the gap after the banning of most Black Consciousness organisations in 1977. AZAPO laid down a rigidly Africanist line, rejecting dependence on whites. It stood for non-collaboration with the oppressor, anti-racism, independent trade union organisation, free and compulsory education, popular control of the means of production and a unitary state. It drew its support chiefly from black intellectuals and the urban middle classes.

B

Baasskap

Afrikaans word for 'mastery', it was used to mean white domination or supremacy. Prime Minister Strijdom in the 1950s admitted that the National Party policy of apartheid was one of *baasskap*. His successor Verwoerd realised that *baasskap* was morally indefensible and hoped to deflect international criticism by reformulating the policy as separate development.

Baden-Powell, Robert Stephenson Smyth

LONDON, 1857 — KENYA, 1941

British soldier, writer, founder of the Boy Scouts. Baden-Powell participated in the Anglo-Zulu campaign of 1888, was secretary to the British and Transvaal Commission in Swaziland, and then chief staff officer in Matabeleland in 1896. After commanding the Fifth Dragoons in India, he was sent back to South Africa in 1899 to raise two regiments for the protection of the Rhodesian and British Bechuanaland borders, and the railway lines. When the South African War broke out later that year, one of these regiments remained with him at Mafeking and it was here that he became famous for his leadership during the seven-month siege of the town. The genius for organisation and improvisation which he displayed during his defence of Mafeking, earned him great credit in Britain. After the siege was lifted he trained a South African constabulary and prepared these men for the task of policing the country.

After resigning from the army in 1910, he devoted himself to the founding of the Boy Scouts and later the Girl Guides movement in Britain. In his capacity as Chief Scout he twice revisited South Africa, in 1925 and 1936.

Lieutenant-Colonel Baden-Powell
(Transvaal Archives TAB 4357)

Bailey, Sir Abe

CRADOCK, 1864 — MUIZENBERG, 1940

Rand mining magnate and politician. Bailey, who joined the gold rush to the Transvaal in 1886, acquired an immense fortune from gold, diamonds, coal, platinum and tin, as well as land in both South Africa and Rhodesia. His wealth enabled him to devote himself to politics and he became a member of the Cape and later the Transvaal Parliaments. He was a staunch supporter of British interests in South Africa.

A cartoon of Sir Abe Bailey
(Cape Archives E 5182)

Baines, Thomas

KING'S LYNN, 1820 — DURBAN, 1875

Artist and explorer. Baines came out to South Africa in 1842 and established himself as a marine and portrait painter in Cape Town. He made various journeys of exploration throughout southern Africa — to the war-torn eastern Cape, with Living-

Thomas Baines, self-portrait at the age of 38, *c.* 1858
(William Fehr Collection)

stone to the Zambezi and on two occasions to Matabeleland in what is now Zimbabwe.

He was an acute observer of the peoples and places he visited and these impressions are accurately reflected in the many paintings and sketches he made, as well as in his journals and diaries.

Baker, Sir Herbert

KENT, 1862 — KENT, 1946

Architect. After training as an architect in London, Baker came out to South Africa in 1892 and stayed for twenty years. He used natural, indigenous materials in his buildings, which ranged from artisans' houses to Groote Schuur, the house he designed for C J Rhodes, from great administrative buildings such as the Union Buildings in Pretoria to churches and Cape Dutch houses which he restored. He initiated a new style of imperial architecture, which he carried from South Africa to India.

Right:
Sir Herbert Baker. His work changed the face of South African architecture
(Institute of South African Architects)

Ballinger, Margaret

GLASGOW, 1894 — CAPE TOWN, 1980

Politician and university lecturer. A brilliant scholar, Ballinger lectured in the History departments of first Rhodes and then the Witwatersrand Universities (1919–1934). At both institutions she was prevented from occupying the Chair of the department because she was a woman. In 1937 she entered Parliament as one of four members elected by black voters, and she retained her seat until 1960. A founder member of the Liberal Party (1953), she was elected its first leader but resigned two years later. Her constant support for African interests gained her international recognition. In retirement she wrote a history entitled *From Union to Apartheid.*

Bambatha Rebellion (1906)

The last act of resistance to colonialism in South Africa to have been organised by a traditional leader. Bambatha

Far right:
Margaret Ballinger, a founder member of the Liberal Party
(Africana Museum)

(c. 1865–1906), a minor Zulu chief in the Greytown area of Natal, had repeatedly clashed with the colonial authorities. When he refused to pay a new poll tax, he fled across the Tugela River to join with Sigananda in the Nkandla Forest to avoid capture by colonial forces. The rebels were ambushed in the Mome Gorge and suffered heavy losses; Bambatha and 500 others were killed and Sigananda was captured. After this, rebellion flared up among Zulu people elsewhere in Natal, but was soon suppressed. The brutality shown by the Natal forces, however, and the panic that had ensued, cast doubt in many white minds about the capacity of the Natal government to keep order in its territory, and in that way the Bambatha Rebellion promoted the move towards unification of the various states in South Africa.

Indaba held at Greytown to explain details of the hut tax collection to Bambatha and other African chiefs. The imposition of this tax led to the Bambatha Rebellion of 1906 (Local History Museum Collection, Durban)

Banking

Commercial banking in South Africa dates back to 1793 when the Bank van Leening (Lombard-Loan Bank) was established by the Dutch East India Company to remedy the grave shortage of currency. The expansion, albeit uneven, of the Cape's economy in the early nineteenth century required the organisation of finance, and in 1837 the first commercial bank, that of the Cape of Good Hope, was founded in Cape Town. Thereafter numerous small district banks emerged in nearly every village in the colony. In 1861, the establishment of the London and South African Bank marked the advent of the Imperial banks, the first South African banks funded by capital raised abroad. They not only had access to the London capital and money markets, but operated a system of branch banking. With the depression of the 1860s about half of the twenty-nine existing banks in the Cape Colony were either absorbed by one of the larger Imperial banks or were liquidated.

The mineral discoveries and the subsequent development of the mining sector led to the small local banks of the nineteenth century evolving into the highly concentrated commercial banks of the twentieth century. The two largest banks by the twentieth century were Standard and Barclays (which changed its name to First National in the 1980s when Barclays disinvested). A central reserve bank was established — the South African Reserve Bank (1920) — and other financial institutions were set up to meet specific needs, such as the Land Bank, the discount and accepting houses, hire-purchase institutions and numerous building societies.

This thatched mud hut housed the first Standard Bank in Johannesburg (Cape Archives J1695)

Banning

Various forms of banning were imposed by law, especially in the era of apartheid. These included the banning of people, organisations, meetings and publications. A banned person was subject to a number of restrictions, was required to report to the police regularly and was confined to his or her home, usually from 6 p.m. to 6 a.m. every day. Banning orders generally lasted for five years and were often renewed. By the end of 1978 a total of 1 378 people had been banned, and many others driven into exile. By 1988 fifty-six organisations were outlawed, most notably the Communist Party (1950), the African National Congress (1960) and the Pan Africanist Congress (1960). Open-air public meetings could only be held with special permission, and marches were rarely allowed. Some 30 000 publications were banned, a large proportion for political reasons.

Bantu Education

A separate educational system introduced by the Bantu Education Act (1953) whereby schooling for Africans was removed from the hands of the Christian missions and placed under the control of the Department of Native (Bantu) Affairs. The Act laid down a differential syllabus designed to prepare Africans for their special, inferior place in apartheid society. Bantu Education meant the provision of many more schools, and the number of pupils at schools greatly increased, but black indignation at being given a separate and inferior education was a major cause of the Soweto uprising of 1976. Protests continued throughout the 1980s, and the rejection of Bantu Education often meant that no education was received at all.

Cramped classrooms were a feature of the Bantu Education system (Mayibuye Centre)

Bantu-speaking People

What linguists call the Bantu language group, classified as part of the Niger-Congo language family, includes hundreds of related languages, spoken throughout a large part of the African continent. Archaeologists and linguists think it likely that Bantu languages were spread southwards by the movement of people, and that people speaking a Bantu language crossed the Limpopo River about 2 000 years ago, after which the language family dispersed southwards through much of what is now South Africa. It is also assumed that those who spoke Bantu languages practised mixed farming and used iron, and were the direct ancestors of the Bantu-speaking people first encountered by Europeans in the sixteenth century in the Transkeian region, and later in the interior.

Bantu-speaking people in South Africa are divided linguistically into four groupings; Nguni and Sotho the two major ones, and Venda and Tsonga. Though these language groupings roughly correspond to certain cultural differences, it is wrong to link language and culture and assume that each language group had a separate history. Broadly, however, one can say that the Nguni people, living in the coastal region between the escarpment and the Indian Ocean, were cultivators, hunters and above all herders, with cattle playing an important role in most aspects of their life. They lived in scattered homesteads and were organised into relatively small chiefdoms, though by the late eighteenth century a process of political consolidation, especially among the northern Nguni, was well underway, and culminated in the emergence of powerful states in the nineteenth century. The Sotho, inhabiting the interior plateau, preferred to live in large villages situated in the midst of communal pasturage, although divergent settlement patterns existed. Besides herding, cultivating and hunting, they were skilled craftsmen, mining and smelting various metals in which they carried on an extensive trade.

Bantustans

The Bantustans, or black homelands, embodied the grand design of apartheid, to create a South Africa ruled by a

Left:
Inanda kraal, Natal, by G F Angas. Cattle played an important role in the lives of the Nguni people who inhabited the region between the escarpment and the Indian Ocean
(Local History Museum Collection, Durban)

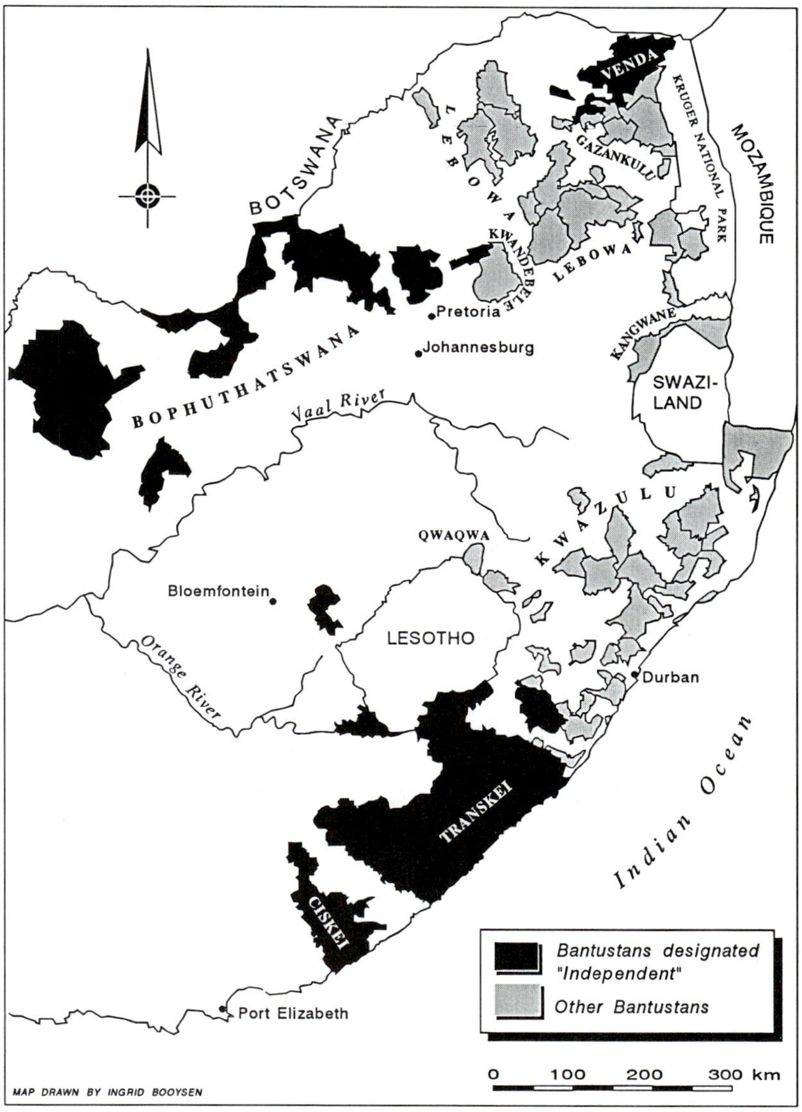

Below:
The Bantustans as they were in 1993

white majority, enveloping ten independent tribal states where blacks could fulfil their political aspirations. Separate 'locations' for blacks existed under British colonial government, but after the Act of Union in 1910 the idea developed of transferring political functions to blacks in their own homelands, as a way of preventing a black majority from eventually swamping the white minority. The Natives Land Act (1913) and the Native Trust and Land Act (1936) laid foundations for the Bantustan areas. The Tomlinson Commission (1954) set out a basis for the policy of separate development that was subsequently adopted by the Nationalist government under Dr H F Verwoerd. The Promotion of Bantu Self-Government Act (1959) indicated future ethno-political boundaries for the Bantustans, which were gradually consolidated by the purchase and incorporation of millions of hectares of land.

By 1974, self-governing status had been conferred on the Transkei, Lebowa, the Ciskei, Bophuthatswana, QwaQwa, Gazankulu, Venda and KwaZulu; it was conferred on KwaNdebele in 1981. Independence was subsequently accepted by the Transkei (1976), Bophuthatswana (1977), Venda (1979) and the Ciskei (1981).

The Bantustans were not recognised by the United Nations on the grounds that they were creations of apartheid, and their sixteen million residents have never freely determined their political status. The

Above:
Lady Anne Barnard. Her series of letters to Henry Dundas is an important source of information on social and political life at the Cape during the first British Occupation
(Transvaal Archives TAB 12898)

Above:
A cartoon of Barney Barnato which appeared in 1895
(Africana Museum)

Right:
Sir Henry Barkly, Governor of the Cape from 1870 to 1877
(Transvaal Archives TAB 13211)

policy of clearing 'black spots' from white-designated areas by forced removals, corruption, and the failure of the Bantustans to become economically viable, have reinforced opposition to their existence. The possible reincorporation of the Bantustans, nominally independent, remains a controversial issue; in the view of some experts, bilateral treaties would have to be concluded and approved by the South African Parliament.

Barbier, Etienne

FRANCE, *c.* 1699 — CAPE TOWN, 1739

Rebel. Barbier came to the Cape as a soldier in the service of the Dutch East India Company. Deserting from the Castle in 1738, he championed a group of discontented farmers charged with robbing cattle, and incited them to revolt against the Dutch East India government. A seditious document which he wrote and pasted up on the Paarl church door was responsible for his arrest and eventual execution.

Barends, Barend

c. 1770 — BOETSAP, CAPE, 1839

Griqua leader. A grandson of Adam Kok I, Barends was forced to flee east along the Orange River after a clash with the Khoikhoi leader Jager Afrikaner. There he invited missionaries of the London Missionary Society (LMS) to join him in 1801. This was the start of a stable, settled Griqua community in what was to be called Griqualand West. He spent the next thirty years trying unsuccessfully to remain independent of missionary control and to maintain his position as leader.

Barkly, Sir Henry

LONDON, 1815 — LONDON, 1898

Governor of the Cape (1870–1877). During his term of office, Barkly had the difficult task of paving the way for responsible government, after which the self-governing colony would be permitted to annex the disputed diamond-fields and Basutoland. He encountered considerable opposition to these ideas in the Cape Colony, and the eventual annexation of Griqualand West led to the Diggers' Revolt of 1875.

Barnard, Lady Anne

SCOTLAND, 1750 — LONDON, 1825

Writer and hostess. The wife of Andrew Barnard, the Colonial Secretary to Governor Macartney, Lady Anne was, in the absence of the governor's wife, first lady of the colony and a renowned hostess to British officers and bureaucrats, Xhosa chiefs and the Dutch élite. She was a remarkable woman of great energy and during her stay from 1797 to 1802, she travelled widely in the Cape, recording her observations in her shrewd, insightful style. Her journals, letters and many sketches provide valued information on life at the Cape and the affairs of the colony in the early years of British occupation.

Barnato, Barney

LONDON, 1852 — AT SEA, OFF MADEIRA, 1897

Financier and diamond magnate. In 1873 Barnato followed his brother to Kimberley to seek his fortune in the diamond rush. In 1880 he formed the Barnato Diamond Mining Company and thereafter challenged C J Rhodes's De Beers Company. In this struggle, Rhodes was victorious and Barnato's company was merged in De Beers, of which Barnato was made life governor. He was a member of the Cape Legislative Assembly from 1889 until his mysterious death some eight years later.

Barry Commission (1881)

Commission on Native Laws and Customs appointed by Sir Bartle Frere, Governor of the Cape and High Commissioner. It was to devise a system of law and administration for a post-conquest society in the territories annexed to the

Left:
Members of the Cape Colony Natives Law and Customs Commission. Back, right to left: Thomas Ayliff, Sir Theophilus Shepstone, 3 unidentified black witnesses, E S Rolland. Front, right to left: W E Stanford, W Bisset, Judge Sir Jacob Dirk Barry (chairman), Thomas Upington, Revd James Stewart, Richard Solomon
(Cape Archives AG 14293)

Cape Colony. The Commission sat under the chairmanship of Sir J D Barry (1832–1905), a supreme court judge in the Eastern Cape Division. The report of his Commission, which was published in 1883, directed Cape policy towards differential administration for the large black population of the Transkei. The report remained a basic source for an understanding both of Cape policy towards Africans in the early years of conquest and of African law.

Left:
Joseph Barry
(South African Library)

Barry, James
SCOTLAND, *c.* 1795 — LONDON, 1865

Distinguished military surgeon. Barry qualified as a surgeon in London in 1813 and was posted to the Cape in 1816. He was appointed personal physician to Lord Charles Somerset, Governor of the Cape, and was later promoted to Medical Inspector for the Cape Colony and Principal Medical Officer of the army. Cantankerous and quarrelsome, his career was marked by controversy; his sustained campaigns for improved conditions in prisons and hospitals proved to be unpopular with the authorities. It was not until his death that his true sex was revealed — in order to pursue his career, Barry had spent a lifetime disguised as a man.

Above:
Dr James Barry, the distinguished military surgeon who spent a lifetime disguised as a man in order to pursue a medical career
(Africana Museum)

Barry, Joseph
HERTFORD, ENGLAND, 1796 — CAPE TOWN, 1865

Entrepreneur. A successful merchant, Barry exercised an important influence in the Overberg region for fifty years. When the Overberg grain crop failed in 1822, he assisted local inhabitants by transporting a consignment of grain to Port Beaufort. This was the beginning of a regular shipping service for agricultural goods down the Breede River and opened a new route to the Cape markets, signalling a period of prosperity and economic revival in the Overberg. The commercial enterprise which he founded in 1834, Barry and Nephews, dealt in a wide variety of goods and extended its activities over the whole Overberg region. Barry introduced agricultural improvements in sheep and wine farming, and tried to persuade farmers to increase productivity. Apart from his business interests, he also acted as an attorney and was deputy-sheriff of the district. In 1854 he was elected to represent the Overberg in the Cape Parliament.

Bastards (Basters, Bastaards)

The term used for frontiers-people of mixed race. Bastard frontier communities in the northern Cape were in fact hybrid societies, including runaway slaves, adventurous whites, Khoi and those who wished to escape the jurisdiction of the Cape government. The Bastards owned guns, professed an adherence to Christianity and spoke a dialect of Dutch. The missionaries of the London Missionary Society persuaded a group of them to change their name to Griqua, a name chosen in recognition of the Grigriqua (Khoi) element in their make-up.

Basutoland

State created by Moshweshwe (*c.* 1786–1870), who brought together different Sotho people threatened by various enemies and saw his country annexed in 1868 by the British, at a time when it was under threat from the Boers of the Orange Free State. In 1871, after his death, it was incorporated into the Cape Colony, but as a separate entity, not subject to the usual laws of the colony. The Sotho went into rebellion against Cape rule in 1880, specifically to an order that they hand in their weapons, and in 1884 the Cape, having failed to suppress the revolt, decided to hand the territory back to Britian. Basutoland was then a High Commission territory, eventually led to independence in 1965 as the Kingdom of Lesotho, though totally surrounded by South Africa. In the 1980s South Africa used force against Lesotho to ensure that it stopped aiding guerrillas of Umkhonto we Sizwe and eventually through a blockade succeeded in removing the government of Chief Leabua Jonathan. A major highlands water scheme nevertheless went ahead, intended to provide water from northern Lesotho to the Witwatersrand and other parts of the Transvaal.

Alfred Beit, mining magnate and financier (Africana Museum)

Beaumont Commission (1913–1916)

Appointed under the Natives Land Act (1913) to investigate the allocation of additional land to blacks. The Commission sat under the chairmanship of Sir William Beaumont (1851–1930), a supreme court judge in Natal. It reported in 1916 and recommended enlarging the land available to Africans in each province. Though its recommendations were accepted by the Smuts government, additional land was not provided for until 1936, and then the land released was much less than that allocated by the Commission.

Bechuanaland

Land of the Tswana people. Name for the large territory north and south of the Molopo River. In 1885, believing that this territory had an important role to play as a springboard for the colonisation of central Africa, the British government annexed it. The area north of the Molopo River was administered as a British protectorate until it was given independence in 1966 as Botswana. The territory south of the Molopo River — British Bechuanaland — became part of the Cape in 1895.

Beit, Alfred

GERMANY, 1853 — ENGLAND, 1906

Mining magnate, financier and co-founder with Rhodes of Southern Rhodesia. In 1875 Beit was sent to Kimberley by Lipperts, a prominent firm of Hamburg-based gem importers, to act as their diamond-buying agent. But after three years he established himself as an independent buyer and later joined forces with Rhodes in an intricate financial struggle to amalgamate the diamond mines. This culminated in 1888 in the foundation of De Beers Consolidated, with Beit becoming one of its four 'life governors'. From 1889 he began to devote equal attention to gold mining, sinking a series of deep level shafts around Johannesburg, thus becoming a pioneering leader of the

Witwatersrand gold industry. In 1904 he became vice-president of the British South Africa Company, which he had helped to finance in 1889.

Although he had displayed little interest in political affairs, Beit found himself implicated in the crisis of the Jameson Raid (1895) and he and Rhodes were forced to resign from the board of the British South Africa Company. Despite this, Beit's wealth continued to grow and the scope of his benefactions widened to include education and the provision of public amenities and social services.

Berlin Missionary Society

The first group of five missionaries, sent out to South Africa in 1834, established the Society's first mission station, Bethanien, on the Riet River in the Orange Free State. By 1894 some sixty-four missionaries were active in South Africa, working among the Korana, Zulu, Sotho, Xhosa, Pedi and Tswana people, as well as among migrant labourers on the mines. The Berlin Society missionaries made a major contribution in writing the languages of the people among whom they worked.

Bethelsdorp

Famous mission station established by the London Missionary Society among the Khoi near Algoa Bay in the Cape in 1803. Under its first missionaries, Dr van der Kemp and James Read, Bethelsdorp was much criticised by British and Batavian authorities and by colonists, and the missionaries in turn were strong critics of government policy and of the way the farmers treated the Khoi. Bethelsdorp went through ups and downs in succeeding decades, but remained an important centre for missionary work, much visited by a wide range of people. Today its site is within Port Elizabeth.

Beyers, Christiaan Frederik

STELLENBOSCH, 1869 — VAAL RIVER, 1914

General, politician and attorney. Beyers was practising as an attorney in the Transvaal Republic when war broke out in 1899. He then joined the Boer forces, and became Assistant-General commanding the forces in the northern Transvaal. After the war he became a founder member of Het Volk (1904), speaker of the Transvaal Legislative Assembly (1907), and first Commandant-General of the Union Defence Force (1912). When South Africa entered the First World War on the British side, he resigned in protest and resorted to armed resistance against the government. He drowned while trying to escape from government forces.

Above:
A group of German missionaries sent to South Africa by the Berlin Missionary Society
(Cape Archives AG 10391)

Above:
Bethelsdorp mission station, an important centre for missionary work in the eastern Cape
(Cape Archives E 2184)

Left:
Portrait of General C F Beyers by Hugo Naudé
(National Cultural History Museum)

Above:
Although Steve Biko's death in police custody provoked world-wide outrage, no one was found to be responsible for his murder
(Mayibuye Centre)

Biko, Steve

KING WILLIAM'S TOWN, 1946 — PRETORIA, 1977

Founder of the Black Consciousness movement in South Africa, and martyr. A man of great intelligence and remarkable qualities of leadership, he was, while attending Natal Medical School, co-founder and first president of the all-black South African Students' Organisation (SASO), the aim of which was to raise black consciousness and self-esteem. He also became honorary president of the Black Peoples' Convention (BPC), an umbrella organisation which attracted mainly young professionals and intellectuals.

From 1973 onwards Biko suffered banning, detention and other harassment at the hands of the state. His death in police custody, which provoked world-wide outrage, was followed by the banning of the Black Consciousness organisations and helped lead to the imposition of a mandatory arms embargo against the country by the United Nations Security Council. An inquest revealed something of the appalling treatment to which he had been subjected before his death, but no-one was held responsible for his murder.

Bisho Massacre

On 7 September 1992 thousands of African National Congress (ANC) supporters marched from King William's Town to Bisho, capital of the Ciskei. Some of the leaders hoped that the march would lead to the removal from power of the Ciskei military leader, Brigadier Oupa Gqozo. The march was part of an ANC campaign to unseat Bantustan leaders who had been allies of the government at Codesa. When some of the demonstrators left the agreed path of the march, Ciskei soldiers opened fire on the unarmed marchers, killing twenty-eight and injuring 200. The slaughter contributed to the atmosphere of mistrust following the breakdown of Codesa II, the massacre at Boiphotong, and the increase in violence generally.

Below:
Ciskei soldiers opened fire on ANC supporters at Bisho on 7 September 1992
(Beeld)

Blaauwberg, Battle of (1806)

The Batavians occupied the Cape in 1803 under Governor Lieutenant-General Jan Willem Janssens. In 1805 the British decided to re-occupy the Cape in order to secure it as a supply point on the passage to India. In January 1806 a British force under Major-General Sir David Baird marched towards Cape Town. About twenty-five kilometres north of the town, the British defeated a force under Janssens. The Batavians then surrendered at Papendorp (Woodstock).

Black Circuit (1812)

In 1812 circuit courts were established at the Cape. The first sat at Uitenhage and investigated accusations of maltreatment of Khoi by colonists on the basis of testimony collected by Revd James Read and Dr van der Kemp of the London Missionary Society at Bethelsdorp. Eight of the colonists brought before the court for assault or murder were convicted, but the court found that other charges were unjustified. The colonists were incensed at the very idea of the trials, threw scorn on the missionaries, and spoke of the Black Circuit as a travesty of justice, but the trials probably had an educative effect and lessened the abuses to which the Khoi were subject.

Black Consciousness Movement

Black Consciousness aimed to raise black self-esteem and to overcome the psychological oppression of blacks by whites. The movement emerged in the late 1960s under the leadership of Steve Biko, with the birth of the South African Students' Organisation (SASO). Black students led by Biko broke away from NUSAS to form their own organisation. Thereafter a number of Black Consciousness organisations were established, including the Black Peoples' Convention (1972) which operated on the political front, and Black

Community Programmes, an association which promoted health and welfare work in black communities. From the early 1970s the movement and its leaders were subject to repression. A year after the Soweto uprising (1976), in which Black Consciousness played a significant part, Biko was detained and in September 1977 he died in police custody. The following month all the Black Consciousness organisations were banned. The Black Consciousness philosophy was however continued in the Azanian People's Organisation (AZAPO).

Left:
Revd James Read (Snr) of the London Missionary Society. His protests to London of ill-treatment of Khoi servants by white farmers led to the establishment of the Black Circuit Court
(South African Library)

Left:
Steve Biko addressing the second general students' council of the South African Students' Organisation (SASO), at the University of Natal, July 1971
(Mayibuye Centre)

Black Politics

Since the advent of the Black Consciousness movement in 1968, any discussion of black politics has to refer to developments affecting members of the Indian and coloured communities as well as the African majority. Often, though, different institutions and separate developments have affected the representation, organisation and mobilisation of the three groups.

Representation. Africans, Indians and coloureds in the Cape had direct representation in Parliament through the colour blind 1853 constitution, though they all lost the right to be elected to Parliament in 1910. In Natal, Africans were denied the vote in 1865 and Indians in 1896; in the Afrikaner Republics from their inception the vote was limited to whites. Despite progressively restrictive property qualifications, the size of the African, and coloured and Indian electorates in the Cape was sufficiently substantial for their excision from the common voters' roll to be a major preoccupation among white political leaders during the Union. In 1936 the 10 000 Cape African voters were taken off the common roll and were given instead the right to elect three 'Native Representatives' to the House of Assembly. The 'Native Representation' established by the 1936 legislation also included four senators chosen by African electoral colleges in each of the provinces and an advisory Native Representative Council chaired by the Secretary for Native Affairs with twelve elected African members. Cape blacks could also elect two special representatives to the Provincial Council. Coloureds and Indians in the Cape were dismissed from the common roll in 1956, again receiving instead the right to elect special white representatives, four to Parliament and two to the Cape Provincial Council.

Even this truncated representation in central government disappeared with the full implementation of apartheid. Africans and coloureds lost their parliamentary representatives in 1959 and 1970 respectively. Henceforth Africans were supposed to exercise their political rights within whatever representative institutions developed in the homelands, and a Coloured Representative Council with forty elected members was substituted for coloured parliamentary representation. The CRC had no executive authority; all its decisions had to be approved by the Minister of Coloured Affairs. A rather similar body existed for Indians, the South African Indian Council, from 1974, with fifteen members elected by members of Indian local authorities. Indians before then were never given any form of communal parliamentary representation, largely because until 1961 the government persisted in considering Indians as aliens who would one day be repatriated. Indians in the Cape, though, had the same common roll voters' rights as coloureds until these ended in 1970.

Apart from the very limited representation which black South Africans were allowed historically in central government, Africans, Indians and coloureds had varying degrees of access to municipal and local government and for Africans Bantustan institutions provided another officially sanctioned arena for political activity. In Natal, subject to property qualifications, Indians could stand for office and vote in municipal elections until 1924; coloureds continued to vote in local council elections in Natal until 1956. Non-racial municipal rolls existed in the Cape until 1971: during the 1950s 15 000 coloureds and Indians qualified as registered local voters and in 1962 twelve coloured councillors held office, six in Cape Town. Partly elected segregated management committees were instituted for coloured and Indian townships during the 1970s. In African townships Advisory Boards were set up in 1923. In 1961, these began to be replaced by Urban Bantu Councils. Like the Boards, the UBC's were partly elected and largely consultative though they did have the authority to allocate trading licences and determine similar issues. In 1982, the Black Local Authorities Act granted full local government status to Councils in the townships; elections for twenty-four of these new municipalities were held in October 1983.

The Black Local Authorities Act was one of a series of political reforms enacted in the early 1980s intended to incorporate or co-opt African political leadership. The 1983 constitution reorganised the parliamentary system established in 1910. From 1984, Parliament comprised three chambers, a white House of Assembly, a coloured House of Representatives and an Indian House of Delegates, varying in size according to an entrenched formula of 4: 2: 1. Each of these chambers was invested with the power to legislate for its community's 'own affairs' (social welfare, education, health, housing and local government). Joint standing committees drawn from the three houses were to busy themselves with 'general affairs' (finance, foreign policy, defence, justice). What constituted an own or general affair was at the ultimate discretion of the State President, chosen by a multiracial college nominated by the majority parties in each house.

The tricameral constitution made no provision for Africans, who officially were still required to develop their political institutions around Bantustan administrations. The Transkei possessed a measure of elected government from 1895 with the establishment of district councils, of which some members were elected by tax payers. District councils were represented in a General Council or Bunga chaired by the Chief Magistrate. In the other reserves local councils also existed but they did not have elected members; even in the Transkei elected representatives played a largely advisory function; real power remained in the hands of white functionaries. The council system was legally superseded by Bantu Authorities in 1951 which emphasised chiefly prerogatives and exalted ethnic distinctions. Through the 1950s and 1960s, Tribal, Regional and Territorial Authorities were installed in ten ethnically designated Bantustans. Territorial Authorities later became legislative assemblies, with appointed chiefly majorities and elected members chosen through universal adult suffrage. Though in certain cases, elected members later formed majorities in their legislatures, in practice, chiefs remained very influential.

The tricameral constitution of 1984 made no provision for Africans (Cartoon by Abe Berry)

Organisation. Black access to central government was never permitted to endanger white monopolies over power and resources. Even so, token representation of one form or another helped to stimulate or provoke black political organisation. The genesis of black political organisation can be traced at least as far back as the formation of Elijah Makiwane's Native Education Association in 1879. The Transkei and the eastern Cape were the spawning grounds for a succession of associations led by the graduates of the mission schools and colleges. These were not mass movements but rather small élite bodies which directed their energies at increasing black voter registration and lining up voters behind white liberal personalities active in Cape parliamentary politics. With the capacity to influence the outcome of elections in at least five constituencies, this first generation of black political leadership was treated with a degree of consideration by white politicians. Political divisions existed within this black élite, sometimes mirroring those across the racial divide.

After the South African War, the extension of British colonial authority and the negotiations towards Union prompted a proliferation of African organisations in the Transvaal, Free State and Natal, as well as in the Cape. A South African Native Convention assembled in March 1909 in reaction to the segregationist provisions of the South Africa Bill. The Convention decided to become a permanent body and laid much of the groundwork for the formation of the African National Congress in 1912, the first truly national body representing black opinion. From 1909, black politicians placed much less emphasis on attempting to influence white parliamentary spokesmen; the Act of Union reduced their relative influence as voters to insignificance. Instead they first attempted to solicit the help of the imperial power through sending or participating in deputations to Britain and secondly by making direct appeals to the South African authorities. Until the Second World War, the tactics generally favoured by the educated professional blacks who tended to predominate in politics remained politely circumspect: lobbying, petitioning and submitting memorandums. For a brief period after the First World War, the ANC lent its support to a groundswell of popular protest in Johannesburg. Police treatment meted out to strikers and pass protesters as well as the palliatives contained in legislation enacted in the early 1920s helped to restore the decorum of its leaders. Instead the initiative in channelling the political energies of the popular classes passed to the Industrial and Commercial Workers Union, a labour organisation started amongst Cape dockworkers by a Nyasaland migrant, Clements Kadalie. Kadalie's ICU spread with amazing speed through the 1920s, building an enormous following among farmworkers and squatters threatened with displacement from white-owned land. Ostensibly a trade union, it functioned as a surrogate political party fired by nationalist rhetoric and millenarian hope. Its success helped to convince the leadership of the Communist Party (founded in 1921) that organising black workers should be the prime objective of socialist revolutionaries.

From 1924 onwards the communists, hitherto mainly white, began building black industrial trade unions. In the late 1920s communists recruited a remarkable generation of black activists, many of them teachers. This group included such figures as Moses Kotane and John Marks, men who played a formative role in black politics until their deaths in the 1970s. Communists favoured dramatic methods: mass meetings, demonstrations and civil disobedience characterised their efforts to oppose the pass laws in the late 1920s. They tended to ignore representative institutions, contesting elections only when they wished to mobilise protest, not to win office. Communists also joined the ICU, contributing to ideological tensions within that organisation which helped it to fracture into competing segments. For its

Above:
The South African Native National Congress deputation to England. They attempted to solicit the help of the imperial power against oppression and segregation
(Mayibuye Centre)

Moses Kotane (top) and John Marks, communists who played a formative role in black politics
(Mayibuye Centre)

members, though, the ICU promised more than it could deliver; like a great wave it rolled across the countryside, arousing the enthusiasm of entire communities but leaving little in the way of durable organisation in its wake.

The 1936 laws which deprived Africans in the Cape of their common roll franchise and which extended the provisions of the Land Act, heralded a second more systematic phase of organisation building. An All African Convention failed to develop effective opposition to Native Representation; instead the efforts by communists and white liberals to win seats in Parliament and the NRC through securing the support of advisory boards and electoral colleges helped to promote the development of local branch-based political organisation amongst blacks. Communists and ANC members started contesting Advisory board elections at the beginning of the Second World War. Communists also began to establish a following amongst coloured common roll voters in the Cape; a course which was to win them municipal, provincial and parliamentary seats during the 1940s and early 1950s.

Amongst coloureds, though, there were alternative political attractions to the communists. Coloured electoral politics between 1905 and 1940 was dominated by Dr Abdullah Abdurahman's African People's Organisation. Abdurahman, himself Cape Town's first coloured councillor, acquired considerable political leverage and public credibility through his efforts to resist and delay the imposition of residential segregation through encouraging coloured voters to favour sympathetic white parliamentarians. By the late 1930s, though, as for blacks two decades before, white liberal clientalism was offering considerably diminished returns and the APO was beginning to be eclipsed by left-wing rivals, first the communist inclined National Liberation League, and then a series of Trotskyite-influenced groupings which advocated electoral boycotts and 'non collaboration'. These latter groups coalesced into the Non-European Unity Movement, intellectually prevalent in middle class coloured politics during the 1950s. Communist coloured support tended to be largely proletarian. The NEUM was nonracial in ethos and it acquired a number of affiliates with African members including the rump of the All African Convention whose remaining members were opposed to participation in native representative elections. The AAC believed peasant opposition to the Land Act represented the nucleus of a revolutionary nationalist movement. A group of AAC adherents, mainly Transkeian African school teachers, began trying to sustain peasant opposition to official land rehabilitation measures.

By the end of the 1940s, though, the ANC was emerging as the major force in black politics, a position which it maintained thereafter. Organisational overhaul and ideological reinvigoration in the 1940s helped it to meet the challenge of supplying leadership to an increasingly restive urban working class. The prohibition of the Communist Party in 1950 helped to radicalise the ANC further as it absorbed the activist networks developed by communists in townships and factories in the preceding decade. The Communist Party reconstituted itself on a clandestine basis in 1953. For party theoreticians the national movement was to represent the vehicle for the achievement of a non-capitalist peoples' democracy, a vital stage in the transition to socialism. To non-communists within the ANC as well as outsiders, communist efforts to strengthen the ANC through contributing to its leadership as well as developing a base in organised labour looked suspiciously like a take-over. Strengthening such fears was the emergence after the 1952 Defiance Campaign of an alliance between the ANC and the Indian Congresses as well as smaller bodies formed by left-wing whites and coloureds, many of them previously and some still active within the banned Communist Party.

Of the ANC's new allies, the Natal Indian Congress was the most substantial. The NIC was the oldest political organisation in the country. It was founded amid efforts led by Indian merchants to oppose the 1894 Franchise Amendment Bill. A key figure in the agitation against the Bill was Mohandas Gandhi, a London-trained lawyer who had arrived in Durban one

Right:
Protestors arrested during the 1952 Defiance Campaign
(Mayibuye Centre)

year earlier. Gandhi aroused the antipathy of the local authorities by touring India to mobilise public sentiment in 1896. South African Indians had a powerful ally in the Indian colonial government which on several occasions embarrassed the British Colonial Secretary into attempting to alleviate discriminatory legislation against South African Indians. In 1903 Gandhi formed the British India association to resist trader segregation in the Transvaal. Three years later, the Transvaal government introduced pass laws for Indians and in 1907 Gandhi and his colleagues launched a passive resistance campaign in which 2 000 protesters were jailed for refusing registration. Internal disagreements brought the campaign to a ragged close in 1909 and Gandhi, by now an isolated figure within the affluent merchant community, turned his attention to the plight of Natal indentured labourers. Natal Indian Congress officials helped to coordinate and support a series of strikes by plantation and colliery workers against a tax imposed on ex-indentures. After a bitter struggle, the tax was abolished and on the eve of the First World War Gandhi left South Africa for India.

In the interwar period the NIC and its Transvaal sister organisation lost much of their assertiveness as their wealthy leaders once again resorted to letter-writing, petitioning, and appealing to the Indian government's representative in Durban. Both organisations were revived on the eve of the Second World War by young radicals, some of them communists active in a burgeoning trade union movement, and spurred by the threat of legislation to curtail 'Asiatic' land occupation. The war held up the legislation but its introduction in 1946 prompted another passive resistance campaign led by Yusuf Dadoo and Monty Naicker and encouraged from across the Indian Ocean by Gandhi and the Indian government. In 1947, Naicker and Dadoo signed a pact with Dr A B Xuma, the ANC President, undertaking future joint campaigning for a full franchise and other basic rights.

Cooperation with the Indian Congress and other groups in the 1950s brought many benefits, including financial resources as well as strategic and organisational know-how, but within the ANC it was not universally approved of. Despite the ANC's acquisition of a large popular following, some of the young nationalist intellectuals who had helped to rejuvenate the movement at the beginning of the decade believed that Congress's advocacy of multiracialism weakened its mass appeal and diverted it from militant courses. In 1959 a Transvaal-based group broke away to form a new organisation, the Pan Africanist Congress. At the end of the year, the PAC announced that it would conduct an anti-pass campaign, the first of several endeavours which its leaders hoped would culminate in a struggle for independence by 1963. The PAC never had time to build a large national organisation but it had strong pockets of support in Johannesburg, Pretoria, Vereeniging and Cape Town. On the first day of its pass resistance, clusters of supporters appeared outside police stations in these centres and crowds gathered around them. Police fired

Left:
Yusuf Dadoo, one of the leaders of the 1946 Passive Resistance Campaign
(Mayibuye Centre)

Above:
Dr G M Naicker, President of the Natal Indian Congress, held aloft after addressing a Passive Resistance rally on 26 June 1946
(Mayibuye Centre)

Above left:
The horrifying result of police opening fire on anti-pass resistors in Sharpeville. Sixty-nine protestors were killed and many more were injured
(Mayibuye Centre)

Above right:
Robert Sobukwe (front, left), President of the Pan Africanist Congress, leads a march
(Mayibuye Centre)

Below:
SACP meeting in London, 1987. The ANC's alliance with the Communist Party was a decisive factor in its survival
(Mayibuye Centre)

into such a crowd in Sharpeville, Vereeniging, killing sixty-nine people. In the nation-wide tumult which followed, the ANC and the PAC were banned.

Between 1961 and 1964 both the ANC and the PAC and a number of smaller groups including former adherents of the non-racial Liberal Party attempted to mount armed insurgencies. These were suppressed and several thousand political activists were jailed and many others went into exile. In the three decades that followed, both the ANC and the PAC established exile bureaucracies and small guerrilla armies. The ANC's alliance with a disciplined and resourceful Communist Party was a decisive factor in its survival; by contrast, the PAC's exile history was a sorry one, with poverty, demoralisation, internal squabbles and mutinies rendering it ineffective for most of the time.

Inside South Africa the expansion of black education, industrial growth and the proliferation of homeland bureaucracies helped to generate new political forces during the 1970s. Students at the segregated universities formed the first organisations in what came to be known as the Black Consciousness movement. Black Consciousness emphasised cultural regeneration as the essential prelude to any political assertion. After 1973, a new generation of trade unions grew out of a spasm of strikes in Durban clothing factories; in contrast to previous decades black workers possessed skills and industrial presence and these gave them considerable collective power. Finally Bantustan leaders attempting to legitimise their administrations began to create mass organisations to animate voters in (largely ritualistic) elections and to distribute patronage. The most effective of these, Chief Mangosuthu Buthelezi's Inkatha, constructed a formidable army of supporters. Unlike most Bantustan political parties, Inkatha was associated with an ethnic state tradition which retained considerable public legitimacy especially among older rural people.

In 1976 an uprising led by children in Soweto schools in protest against a recently implemented Afrikaans language requirement opened a new era of mass resistance. Now the generational solidarity of black youth and organisational sophistication of factory labour gave to black political movements an unprecedented potency. The collapse of neighbouring colonial administrations allowed the ANC exiles to re-establish an internal presence within South Africa and facilitated recruitment for guerrilla training. During the opening stages of a theatrical urban guerrilla campaign, activists from the Black Consciousness groups suppressed in the aftermath of the Soweto uprising turned their attention to local civic organisation in Indian, coloured and black townships. A vast matrix of community associations underpinned organised efforts to oppose the constitutional

and local government reforms of 1983–1984. This resistance had an explosive character as popular anger was fuelled by inflation, unemployment and administrative corruption. A United Democratic Front was established in 1983 with many ANC sypathisers in its senior echelons. The UDF attempted to coordinate political opposition to the tricameral constitution but increasingly it became a movement driven by the enthusiasms and passions of its different supporters. UDF campaigning became an insurrectionary revolt as crowds marched on the homes of city councillors and local organisations announced the installation of 'People's Power'. The revolt spread to the countryside too as UDF affiliates sprang up in remote homeland villages in the northern Transvaal. Compared to earlier popular uprisings in South Africa, this rebellion was distinctly violent. In 1986, 1 298 people were killed, 412 by police. That year, the army began a systematic occupation of the townships. By mid-1987 the uprising had been checked but the political and economic costs of regimented quiescence were unsustainable.

In August 1989 the authorities permitted a civil disobedience movement against segregated public facilities led by a coalition of UDF, trade union and church leaders to assemble huge crowds in virtually every significant town. In September, the new De Klerk administration began discreet negotiations with the ANC's diplomats in Lusaka. With the unbanning of all prohibited organisations in February 1990, the opening phases of a new epoch started to unfold. In the 1990s, the complex alliances and political bargains arising from a negotiated transition to power sharing rendered the traditional distinctions between white and black politics obsolete.

Mobilisation. For much of their history, the modern political organisations which functioned within black South African communities were not mass movements. The persistence of token forms of élite representation helped to dissuade black leaders from mobilising popular support. But in any case, before the Second World War, the development of large, powerful organisations would have been inconceivable. Black South Africans did not have the resources to organise. Except in the mining industry, black workers performed the most menial and least skilled tasks, the literate middle class was tiny, and vast distances, poverty and illiteracy isolated different communities. Even in the 1950s, when the ANC was able to develop a functioning branch structure and boast a 100 000 membership, it remained a movement of the poor; vulnerable and ill-equipped. Living on the edges of the urban economy, the collective sanctions which the ANC's followers could employ were fairly weak. In the 1980s the situation was very different. By then black workers were performing virtually all of the vital tasks

Above left:
Chief Mangosuthu Buthelezi surrounded by Inkatha youth, 1980. The Inkatha Freedom Party constructed a formidable army of supporters
(Mayibuye Centre)

Above right:
The 1976 uprising led by Soweto pupils. Their protest against the use of Afrikaans in schools opened a new era of mass resistance
(Mayibuye Centre)

Below:
Daduza township, 1985. In popular uprisings in the mid-1980s, many thousands lost their lives
(Mayibuye Centre)

Nelson Mandela addressing a rally in Soweto after his release. With the unbanning of all prohibited organisations in February 1990, a new political epoch began to unfold
(Mayibuye Centre)

within industrial production. Mass literacy ensured an extraordinarily rapid spread of political ideas. The industrial growth of earlier decades had nurtured a clerical and professional class with the skills to maintain effective political bureaucracies, and communications technology supplied an international audience for local political activists. The white minority's monopoly of power was over.

(T Lodge)

Members of the Black Sash protest against the introduction of the Senate Bill in 1955
(Mayibuye Centre)

Black Sash

An organisation of white women which began as the Women's Defence of the Constitution League in 1955, when the government introduced the Senate Bill to change the constitution in order to remove coloured voters from the common voters' roll. With the passing of the Senate Act, the Black Sash turned its attention to other unjust legislation. Nation-wide protests and marches were held at which white women wore black sashes as a sign of mourning for the deprivation of rights. While that kind of protest continued, from the 1960s the Black Sash's most important work was done in its Advice Offices, helping victims of the pass laws and other apartheid legislation.

Bleek, Wilhelm Heinrich Immanuel

BERLIN, 1827 — CAPE TOWN, 1875

Scholar and librarian. Bleek was a pioneer in the field of Bantu philology and was one of the first researchers to produce extensive studies on indigenous South African languages, particularly that of the San people. While under the tutelage of K R Lepsius at the University of Berlin, he became familiar with this eminent philologist's phonetic script which was used widely at the time for the transcription of African languages. In 1853 he met Bishop Colenso in Britain, and at the bishop's request he left for South Africa to compile a Zulu grammar.

At the Cape Bleek was appointed interpreter to the Governor, Sir George Grey, and during this time he catalogued most of the books in the Grey collection. When Sir George presented his collection to the South African Public Library, Bleek was appointed librarian.

Shortly after his arrival in South Africa, Bleek developed an interest in the San and from 1870 he devoted almost all his attention to the study of their languages. Although unable to complete his work before his death, his daughter Dorothea based *A Bushman Dictionary* on his research.

Bloemfontein

Capital of the Orange Free State and judicial capital of the Republic of South Africa. It was founded by Major Douglas Warden in 1846 as a fort and residency. It became the seat of the British-administered Orange River Sovereignty

A depiction of Bloemfontein in 1851, by Thomas Baines
(William Fehr Collection)

(1848–1854) and of the Orange Free State (an independent Boer Republic in 1854). Negotiations between President Kruger and Sir Alfred Milner were held in Bloemfontein in May to June 1899; the failure of those negotiations led directly to the outbreak of the South African War in October that year. At the National Convention of 1908–1909, it was agreed that when South Africa was united, Bloemfontein should be the site of the Appellate Division of the Supreme Court.

Bloemfontein Convention (1854)

This document gave the Boers living between the Orange and Vaal rivers their independence. It therefore made possible the establishment of the Republic of the Orange Free State. The British government, which had renounced sovereignty over the territory in 1853, undertook not to make any treaties prejudicial to the interests of the Orange River Government. Furthermore, the Boers agreed to honour a treaty with the Griqua chief Adam Kok, there was to be no slavery in the new state, and access to munitions supplies was guaranteed.

Blood River, Battle of (1838)

From February 1838 Dingane, the Zulu king, tried to force the Voortrekkers out of his country. This attempt was finally defeated at the battle of Blood River (16 December), which was fought between some 10 000 Zulu and a Voortrekker commando of 470 men under the leadership of Andries Pretorius. The tributary of the Buffalo River, on the banks of which the battle was fought, became known as Blood River after the slaughter of some 3 000 Zulu. Thanks to their firepower, the Boers suffered only three minor casualties, and after the battle the white presence in Natal was never again seriously threatened. As Afrikaner nationalism grew, so the victory was given ever more heroic stature and was seen as a sign of divine favour. In the mid-twentieth century the Day of the Vow or Covenant was celebrated as the holiest day in the calendar of Afrikaner festivities. Murals depicting the battle of Blood River occupy a central place in the Voortrekker monument outside Pretoria.

The Battle of Blood River during which some 3 000 Zulu lost their lives
(Africana Museum)

Boers

An Afrikaans word meaning 'farmers'. In the eighteenth century it meant white farmers, many of whom became trekboers; semi-nomadic pastoral farmers who dispersed into the Cape's interior. Be-

Boers on trek. This etching appeared in *The Graphic* in 1879
(Local History Museum Collection, Durban)

tween 1834 and 1840 some 15 000 whites left the Cape Colony for the highveld and Natal in a mass migration which came to be called the Great Trek. These early settlers of the Orange Free State and the Transvaal, people determined to maintain 'proper relations between master and servant', were called Boers. By the nineteenth century the term had come to mean Afrikaners in general, and the states founded in the interior by the Voortrekkers were called the Boer Republics. Those who fought against the British in the South African War, often referred to as the Anglo-Boer War, were also called Boers. For some blacks, 'Boer' has come to mean any white associated with a racist order.

Boer War, *see* South African War

Boomplaats, Battle of (1848)

Battle which firmly established British rule north of the Orange River. When Sir Harry Smith, Governor of the Cape Colony and High Commissioner for South Africa, annexed the lands north of the Orange River in 1848, those Boers who did not want to live under British rule appealed to the Voortrekker leader Andries Pretorius to take up arms and help restore their independence. A Boer commando under Pretorius marched to the Orange River to confront Smith, then retreated northwards in the face of Smith's advance with 1 200 men, but at Boomplaats was defeated by Smith, who was aided by a force of Adam Kok's Griqua. Pretorius and his men had then to retreat north of the Vaal River.

Bophuthatswana

Bantustan of the Tswana. Given nominal independence in 1977, it consisted of seven separate territorial units in the central and western Transvaal and the north-western Cape, as well as Thaba 'Nchu in the Orange Free State. Some of its citizens lived in what was in effect a dormitory suburb of Pretoria. Under the chief ministership of Lucas Mangope, Bophuthatswana became self-governing in 1972. When given its nominal independence, its population was 2,5 million Tswana, 1,4 million of whom worked and lived in South Africa, many on the Witwatersrand. Bophuthatswana's considerable mineral wealth includes platinum, of which it is one of the world's major producers, asbestos, chromium, gold, iron ore and manganese. It has nevertheless remained financially dependent on South Africa. A new capital was established at Mmabatho, adjacent to the town of Mafikeng, which became part of Bophuthatswana in 1980. Casinos — of which the largest is Sun City

Right:
Mmabatho, 10 February 1988. Four people were killed in the failed coup by members of the Bophuthatswana army.
(Mayibuye Centre)

Below:
Defeat of the Dutch rebels at Boomplaats, 29 August 1848, by J Corden
(© The Brenthurst Library)

— became a source of income after nominal independence. Mangope's insistence that Bophuthatswana citizens renounce South African citizenship rights was much resented, especially by non-Tswanas, who also tried to resist the imposition of the Tswana language on them. Though Bophuthatswana's constitution contained a Declaration of Rights and allowed for a multiparty system, the territory inherited South African laws, including those relating to terrorism and the job colour bar. In 1988 an attempted coup against the Mangope government, led by dissident elements in the Bophuthatswana Defence Force who accused the administration of corruption, was crushed by South African troops. The People's Progressive Party was banned, and political parties other than the ruling party were barred from holding meetings without official permission. In the Codesa deliberations (1991–1992), Bophuthatswana rejected proposed re-incorporation, reserving its position as a sovereign and independent state.

Bosman, Herman Charles

KUILS RIVER, 1905 — JOHANNESBURG, 1951

Author. Bosman worked as a journalist in Europe from 1930 to 1939, but it was his days as a school master in the Marico district of the western Transvaal that he immortalised in his volumes of short stories.

Among the stories and novels for which he became famous are *A Cask of Jerepigo* (1957), *Unto Dust* (1963) and *A Bekkersdal Marathon* (1971). His character, Oom Schalk Lourens, in *Mafeking Road* (1947) became the mouthpiece of rural Boer humour. Convicted in 1926 of the murder of his step-brother, Bosman chronicled his experience of prison life in the volume *Cold Stone Jug*.

Botha, Louis

NEAR GREYTOWN, NATAL, 1862 — PRETORIA, 1919

General and statesman. An outstanding military commander, Botha rose to become a general during the South African War. After the war he returned to politics and became chairman of Het Volk (1904), Prime Minister of the Transvaal (1907), and then first Prime Minister of the Union of South Africa (1910), a post which he held until his death.

After the war he was a staunch advocate of reconciliation between Boers and English-speakers and a believer in the maintenance of the imperial connection.

Left:
An outstanding military commander, Louis Botha rose to become a general during the South African War
(Die Burger)

Botha, Pieter Willem

PAUL ROUX, 1916 —

Politician. At the age of twenty he became a full-time organiser for the National Party, and later became its Cape leader. He was elected to Parliament in 1948 and held a number of cabinet portfolios, amongst them defence. In 1978 he became Prime Minister and six years later was elected the country's first State President under a new constitution which

Below:
P W Botha, South Africa's first State President under a new constitution
(South African Communication Service)

gave the holder of that office vast powers. Though he told his people to 'adapt or die' and was responsible for some reforms, including the abolition of the pass laws, Botha failed to realise the need for fundamental internal change. An imperious man, he dominated his cabinet and was deaf to advice. In 1988 he accepted the settlement which provided for Namibian independence. When he suffered a stroke early the following year, he stepped down as leader of the National Party but not as State President, which led to conflict between him and his cabinet. In August 1989 he resigned as State President, accusing his cabinet colleagues of betrayal.

Bowler, Thomas William

HERTFORDSHIRE, 1812 — LONDON, 1869

Artist. He accompanied Thomas Maclear, Astronomer Royal, to the Cape as his manservant in 1834, and subsequently set himself up as an artist and art teacher in Cape Town. His chief importance lies in his role as a pictorial historian in an age before photographs were commonplace. He travelled extensively throughout the Cape Colony, and recorded important local events over a thirty-five year period. His prolific output included watercolours, pencil sketches, oils and lithographic prints.

Right:
Portrait of artist Thomas William Bowler, aged 21
(William Fehr Collection)

Boycotts

Especially from the 1940s to the late 1980s, boycotts of various kinds were a much-used form of protest by Africans against white domination, at a time when few other legal forms of protest were possible. Between 1940 and 1945 a rise in bus fares led to a series of bus boycotts on the Witwatersrand, forcing the government to investigate living conditions and wages of workers. Consumer boycotts became a notable feature of the 1950s, but there were also major bus boycotts in the townships of Evaton (1950) and Alexandra (1957). The Alexandra bus boycott, which lasted over three months and involved over 60 000 people, led the government to pass a bill requiring employers to subsidise the transport costs of their African workers. In 1957 the ANC announced a boycott of goods produced by Afrikaner Nationalists and of Nationalist-controlled finance houses, and in 1959 it organised a successful three-month consumer boycott of potatoes, in protest against the oppressive treatment of farm labourers.

In the field of labour relations, the consumer boycott emerged as an effective form of pressure in support of striking workers and a weapon in the struggle for union recognition. In response to the implementation of Bantu Education in 1955, schools were boycotted, and since then school boycotts have been a notable feature of African education. Numerous rent and service boycotts mounted by township inhabitants were so successful that by 1990 R1,15 million was owed to local authorities. Bond boycotts led some developers and lending institutions to withdraw from the African housing market.

Far right:
Residents of Alexandra township begin the long journey to work on foot during the 1957 bus boycott
(Mayibuye Centre)

Brand, Dollar (Abdullah Ibrahim)

CAPE TOWN, 1934 —

Jazz musician. In the 1950s Dollar Brand played the piano with the 'Jazz Epistles' on Sunday evenings at the Odin Cinema in Sophiatown. Among the group were Moeketsi (alto), Gwangwa (trombone), Gertse (guitars), Mabuza (drums) and Masekela (trumpet). Their music had a strong flavour of black American music, and the distinctive penny whistle and later the saxophone contributed to what became known as 'kwela-jazz'.

With the extension of the Group Areas Amendment Act to the field of entertainment, many clubs and venues excluded black performers, and black artists were forced to pursue their careers in Europe or America. Dollar Brand went to America in 1962, and only in the early 1990s did he and other former exiles including Masekela, Makeba and Mbulu perform again in South Africa. His most popular record was 'Manenberg' with Moeketsi.

Brand, Sir Johannes Henricus

CAPE TOWN, 1823 — BLOEMFONTEIN, 1888

Lawyer, politician and long-time President of the Orange Free State. Brand gave up a flourishing law practice in Cape Town and a seat in the Cape Parliament to become President of the Orange Free State in 1864. He was re-elected to that office four times and occupied it until his death. His prudent administration resulted in prosperity for the Orange Free State which became known as 'the model Republic'. He dealt harshly with the Sotho, but sought to promote harmony between the Boer Republics and the British colonies in South Africa.

Left:
Sir J H Brand, President of the Orange Free State in 1864
(National Cultural History Museum)

Breytenbach, Breyten

BONNIEVALE, WESTERN CAPE, 1939 —

Afrikaans writer and poet. Breytenbach went into exile in 1961 and has since lived in Paris. His perspective from exile on life in South Africa informs much of his writing. In 1973 he and his Vietnamese wife were granted a temporary visitor's permit to accept a literary prize in South Africa, and he chronicled the experience of that visit in *A Season in Paradise*. In 1975 he returned in disguise and travelled around the country in an attempt to gain supporters for a largely white, anti-communist section of the ANC named Okhela. Arrested and charged with terrorism, he was sentenced to nine years imprisonment. After seven years confinement, he was released in 1982. After his release he published *Mouroir, The True Confessions of an Albino Terrorist* and *End Papers*.

Brink, André Philippus

VREDE, ORANGE FREE STATE 1935 —

Writer and lecturer. Brink was educated at Lydenburg High School, Potchefstroom University and the Sorbonne. After a long career as Professor of Afrikaans at Rhodes University, he was appointed Professor of English at the University of Cape Town in 1991. He introduced an innovative style of Afrikaans prose in such novels as *Lobola vir die Lewe* (1962) and *Die Ambassadeur* (1963). Later novels were concerned with the implications of apartheid, most notably *Rumours of Rain* (1978), *A Dry White Season* (1979) and *A Chain of Voices* (1982), all of which were translated into many languages. He published a collection of essays, speeches and articles in 1983.

Britain in South Africa

British ships occasionally stopped to rest crews at the Cape of Good Hope in the late sixteenth and early seventeenth centuries, and two fleet commanders, Humphrey Fitzherbert and Andrew Shilling, even considered establishing a permanent British presence at Table Bay in 1620. British contact with South Africa was

Celebrated jazz musician Dollar Brand
(South African Library)

Afrikaans poet, Breyten Breytenbach
(NALN)

André Brink introduced an innovative style to Afrikaans prose
(NALN: photo by Jakkie Pretorius)

Capture of the Dutch East India Company fleet in Saldanha Bay. Painting by Thomas Luny
(Africana Museum)

'Expulsion of the Xhosa', by Ludwig Alberti. During the brutal Fourth Frontier War of 1811–1812, British and Cape forces drove the Xhosa back over the Great Fish River
(Africana Museum)

thereafter confined to its ships, which stopped regularly in Cape Town while engaged in lucrative trade with India and the East. The growth of French military power in Europe after 1789, partly at the expense of the Dutch, threatened the continued security of Britain's trading routes, and gave the impetus to the military conquest of the Cape by the British in September 1795.

Initially, Britain wished only to preserve the sea route and prevent the French from capturing the Cape. The British had no desire to antagonise the Cape's Dutch population, and they guaranteed language rights, the legal system and religious freedom. They also won local approval for loosening the trading monopoly of the Dutch East India Company. In terms of the Treaty of Amiens between Britain and France, the Cape was handed back to the Dutch (the Batavian regime in the Netherlands) in 1803. Peace between the two European rivals did not last, however, and the British, deeply conscious of the Cape's strategic value, reoccupied the Cape in January 1806. Again, Britain regarded its presence there as temporary, although it became increasingly aware of the economic potential of the Cape. Little was done to disturb the status quo or basic social structures. Only after the London Convention in August 1814, when the Dutch formally

Landing of the 1820 settlers in Algoa Bay, by Thomas Baines. Baines visited the eastern Cape some 30 years after the settlers had arrived and by that time the influence and permanence of the English settlement had become apparent
(© The Brenthurst Press)

ceded the Cape to Britain, did British control become permanent. From this time, the British began to move swiftly towards the establishment of a far stronger and more efficient colonial state. Britain was poised to become the dominant power in southern Africa for the remainder of the century.

The strategic significance of the Cape was an important consideration to the British, who did not want this disturbed by instability in the interior. Military action was thus taken to ensure that the balance of power in the Zuurveld region, where Xhosa and whites had been in conflict since the 1770s, swung decisively in favour of the frontiersmen. This was achieved after the short but brutal Fourth Frontier War of 1811–1812 and by colonial success at the Battle of Grahamstown in 1819. British settlers were located in the region in 1820, with the intention of strengthening colonial control. This was the first indication of the formidable role British troops would play in securing Britain's authority in southern Africa during the remainder of the century.

Important economic reforms — though their implementation was slow and uneven — were also introduced during the first decades of British control. Britain, keen to draw the Cape into a commercial system of free trade and private enterprise in their Empire to enable the Cape to generate its own profits, encouraged exports by loosening stringent monopolies and trade restrictions. As a result, wheat cultivation had increased by fifty per cent by 1820, while wine exports, which trebled between 1812 and 1822, generated more income than all other exports put together. From the 1830s, eastern Cape wool became the most important colonial export, greatly strengthening the commercial significance of the Cape. Economic development occured in various sectors. The volume of shipping in Cape ports quadrupled between the 1820s and 1840s; roads and communications within the colony were greatly improved; the land tenure system was reformed; sterling was introduced as the currency of the Cape; and banking and insurance companies were founded.

Another crucial change initiated by the British during this period of transformation was an emphasis on free labour. The economy and social order were based on slavery, which had no place in the free

Slave trading. Although the British banned slave importation in 1807, and slaves were officially granted freedom in 1834, the majority of former slaves found that their positions barely changed
(Local History Museum Collection, Durban)

Extent of the Cape Colony in the year 1800, showing the boundaries proclaimed by Earl Macartney in 1798
(The Brenthurst Library)

Right:
A missionary settlement at Groenkloof, by C Latrobe
(Africana Museum)

Above:
Private of the 61st (South Gloucestershire) Regiment, by A B Cree. This regiment fought in the campaign of May to September 1799, and served on the frontier between Graaff-Reinet and Algoa Bay in 1800
(© The Brenthurst Press)

market economy. Slave importation was banned in 1807, and slaves were officially granted freedom in 1834, though they were obliged to be apprenticed to their former masters until 1838. A further move towards free labour was the passing of Ordinance 50 in 1828, which repealed pass laws and granted Khoisan and free blacks the right to own land and equality before the law. Although economic motives underpinned these developments, British humanitarians and missionaries at the Cape used moral and religious arguments against bonded labour. The majority of former slaves found, however, that their positions barely changed. Many colonists objected to the difficulties they encountered in securing regular and reliable labour supplies during this period, and raiding occurred in the interior of southern Africa to replenish labour resources at the Cape.

Government and administration were streamlined and altered. Legal reforms in 1828 were far-reaching, and made provision for an independent judiciary, courts were modelled on British lines and the entire central and local systems for the administration of justice were overhauled. An efficient civil service bureaucracy was established. Journalists meanwhile won the right to publish political comment and report on government affairs. And, after three decades of pressure from both within and outside the Cape, a new constitution which conferred representative government was granted in 1854. Although the two-chamber Parliament was to be elected by all males who qualified for the franchise — by earning £50 per annum or occupying property worth £25 — political power was effectively transferred by the British to the Cape's white inhabitants.

British military, economic and administrative intervention at the Cape thus determined the shape of colonial society during the first half of the nineteenth century and beyond, but Britain's involvement in southern Africa was not confined solely to the areas of white settlement at the Cape. The eastern frontier remained volatile until the 1880s, and a considerable number of troops and supplies were deployed in the area for decades. The disastrous cattle-killing of 1856–1857 seriously weakened the Xhosa economy and eased colonial conquest; but before it could confidently control the region, Britain found it necessary to annex additional territory and to inflict further military defeats on the Xhosa.

Meanwhile, British traders, hunters, missionaries and speculators had penetrated remote interior areas from the beginning of the century, but particularly from the 1830s. In Natal, conflict between Voortrekkers, English traders and Africans between 1838 and 1842 provoked Britain to intervene. Britain feared the involvement of a rival European state, was anxious lest conflict exacerbate tensions on the Cape eastern frontier, and responded to commercial and missionary pressures by annexing Natal in 1843. Natal thereafter became a second focus of British political authority in southern Africa. A constitution was granted in 1856, whereby the white minority could elect the legislature but the British continued to control executive appointments.

Considerable tension also existed on the northern frontiers of the Cape during the 1830s and 1840s, which increasingly occupied British attention. Conflicting Boer, Griqua, Tswana and Sotho claims to hegemony were complicated by internal cleavages within these communities and by missionary rivalries. In 1848, the British government annexed the area between the Orange and Vaal Rivers, called the Orange River Sovereignty, in the hope of settling various territorial disputes. Military defeat of British forces by the Sotho paramount, Moshweshwe, at Viervoet in 1851, however, persuaded Britain to withdraw from the region. The independence of the Voortrekkers north of the Vaal was recognised in 1852, and of the Orange River Sovereignty (thereafter known as the Orange Free State), where issues were more complex because of the permanent settlement of both trekkers and English-speakers, in 1854. Britain concluded that the costs of administration and military obligations in the interior were not warranted.

A decade later, Britain again became involved in the affairs of the interior for strategic reasons. The British were worried that continuing disputes between the Orange Free State and Moshweshwe's Sotho would jeopardise the stability of the Cape frontiers, and they threatened to curtail the supply of arms to the Free State. Basutoland was annexed as a separate British colony in March 1868.

Britain's chief motives for involvement in the interior were to ensure that its main economic interests further south were secure. It was committed to the control of the Cape sea route and to the complete domination of the external trade of southern Africa. Mineral discoveries at the end of the 1860s, however, gave the imperial power a new and significant political and economic interest in the interior of the subcontinent.

The discovery of a diamond near Hopetown in 1867, followed by further findings in the area which became known as Kimberley and Griqualand West, sparked a rush of local and foreign diggers and prospectors to the region, and also attracted the attention of competing political claimants. In 1871, Britain annexed Griqualand West after a British arbitrator

Officer of the 8th King's Royal Irish Light Dragoons who came to the Cape in 1796 and served in the Frontier War of 1800. Painting by A B Cree (© The Brenthurst Press)

Early diggings at Kimberley. Securing a reliable labour supply to the diamond fields became a priority of the British during the 1870s (South African Library)

Griqua chief Nicholas Waterboer had the strongest claim to the diamond diggings in Griqualand West
(Cape Archives AG 14152)

ruled that the Griqua chiefdom of Nicholas Waterboer had the strongest claim to the diggings, and Waterboer was persuaded to seek British protection. Local diggers' committees and major industrialists effectively controlled the area with the support of British officials. Griqualand West was incorporated into the Cape in 1880.

The securing of a reliable and regular labour supply to the diamond fields became a priority of the British during the 1870s. The main source of labour were the Tswana living in the vicinity of the mines and the Pedi in the eastern Transvaal, but the latter were hindered by the Boer authorities in the Transvaal from gaining easy access to Griqualand West. Natal sugar farmers, a powerful lobby, also demanded a stable source of labour from the eastern Transvaal and Mozambique, and resented the powerful Zulu kingdom which itself refused to satisfy labour demands and had the potential to block trade going north and labour coming south.

Powerful interests argued that the political fragmentation of southern Africa into British colonies, independent Boer Republics and autonomous African societies was economically disadvantageous to Britain. The British Colonial Secretary after 1874, Lord Carnarvon, believed that a confederation of southern African states under the British crown would provide the solution. Despite various discussions and even the passage of legislation through the British Parliament, confederation schemes failed because of opposition from various southern African parties. Britain then pursued a more vigorous option: the Transvaal was annexed in 1877 (but regained its independence in 1881 after a brief war) and war was provoked with the Zulu in 1879, after which their kingdom was divided, greatly weakening it. The British also defeated the Pedi in 1879. Yet again, Britain achieved what the white colonists could not: it secured a decisive change in the balance of power in southern Africa in favour of whites.

Increasing competition among European powers and growing threats to Britain's status as the premier world power during the 1880s meant that Britain maintained a keen political and economic interest in southern Africa. Bechuanaland was annexed in 1885 to prevent the Germans, who had established a military presence in South West Africa the previous year, from forming a common boundary with the Transvaal. Cecil Rhodes, a wealthy mining magnate and the pro-British Cape Prime Minister, brought Rhodesia under the British flag in 1890. But it was the discovery of rich gold deposits on the Witwatersrand in 1886 which was to deepen still further Britain's commitment and investment in the region and also to lead to its most costly involvement in southern Africa.

Within a decade of the discovery of gold, over 44 000 Uitlanders (fortune-seeking foreigners, many of whom were British) had settled on the Witwatersrand, posing a numerical, cultural and political threat to the rural-based Calvinist Afrikaners in the Transvaal. By the mid-1890s, the competing mining magnates and industrialists in Johannesburg had also come to regard

Right:
The Anglo-Zulu War: before going to battle at Ulundi on 4 July 1879
(Cape Archives AG 782)

the republican government of President Paul Kruger as a hindrance both to the regional economy and their personal wealth. The Transvaal was keen to escape British commercial domination, and conducted much of its foreign trade through Delagoa Bay rather than Cape and Natal ports, which further alienated Rhodes. The appointment of an arch-imperialist, Joseph Chamberlain, as British Secretary of State for the colonies in 1895 ushered in a period of more aggressive British involvement in southern African affairs.

The Jameson Raid at the beginning of 1896 — an attempt to invade Johannesburg and proclaim a provisional government, led by an associate of Rhodes, Leander Starr Jameson — ended in failure and polarised relations between English-speakers and Afrikaners throughout southern Africa. Kruger consolidated his position, while Chamberlain became convinced that more direct action was necessary to secure British interests. In 1897, the jingoistic and autocratic Sir Alfred Milner was appointed British High Commissioner in South Africa, and despite the efforts of many to avert conflict, tensions between Britain and the Transvaal continued to increase until the latter's declaration of war in October 1899.

Essentially, Britain went to war to ensure that its economic and political hegemony over the region was strengthened rather than diminished. Pressures on Britain's international position were mounting and it was becoming increasingly vital to control the material resources of southern Africa. Britain expected an easy conflict, but stubborn Boer resistance, skilled commandos and effective guerrilla warfare tactics meant that the war lasted for almost three years. Over 71 000 soldiers and civilians — 34 000 Boers, 22 000 British and 15 000 blacks — lost their lives. Britain was forced to deploy almost 450 000 soldiers and spend over £200 million, making it the most costly war it fought between 1815 and 1914.

Britain was forced to deploy almost 450 000 soldiers, making the South African War the most costly it fought between 1815 and 1914 (National Cultural History Museum)

Milner wished to cement British supremacy in South Africa thereafter. He intended to rule the defeated Transvaal and Orange Free State autocratically until he had imported a sufficient number of British settlers to outnumber the Afrikaners; only then would he grant representative government, which he believed would be loyal to British interests. He failed in his bid to Anglicise the Afrikaners, despite some British immigration and an increase in investment by British merchants and companies. By 1905, sentiment was swinging strongly against Milner in both South Africa and Britain, and the election of a Liberal government in Britain in 1906 inaugurated a new approach to the subcontinent.

British troops repelled by Boer forces at the Tugela (Africana Museum)

The Liberals wished to preserve British interests in South Africa, but believed that this would best be achieved by cooperating with, rather than alienating, Afrikaners. They thus granted self-government in 1906 and 1907 to the Transvaal and the Orange Free State. The drive towards a more united South Africa — since the 1870s a goal of various British imperialists who hoped to strengthen British involvement — was now taken forward by South Africans who hoped to weaken that influence.

The constitution negotiated in Durban in 1908 and 1909 by representatives of the four southern African parliaments was passed by the British parliament as the South Africa Act in 1909. Britain's interests were taken care of, as it was now in a position to withdraw troops and lessen direct political and financial involvement in South Africa, while so long as South Africa remained within the empire there would be no threat to her economic or strategic interests. The Union of South Africa thus came into being on 31 May 1910 as a self-governing dominion within the British Empire with full British approval.

Britain was far less directly absorbed in South African affairs after 1910 but strong links between the two countries were retained. South Africa fought on Britain's side in the two world wars and firm ties persisted between English-speaking South Africans and Britain, laying them open to repeated charges of disloyalty from Afrikaner nationalists. Britain remained South Africa's chief trading partner and largest source of foreign investment, even after South Africa declared itself a Republic and left the Commonwealth in 1961.

(N D Southey)

British Kaffraria

In 1847, as the War of the Axe came to an end, Sir Harry Smith, Governor of the Cape Colony and High Commissioner, annexed the territory between the Keiskamma and Kei Rivers and called it British Kaffraria. Initially it was ruled directly by the High Commissioner. In 1860 it was proclaimed a Crown Colony, and in 1866 it was incorporated into the Cape Colony. After the cattle-killing (1857), considerable parts were opened to white settlement. The main town was King William's Town, and the area was also known as the Ciskei.

British Occupation of the Cape

In 1795, during the Napoleonic Wars, Britain wrested the Cape from the Dutch East India Company in order to secure her sea routes to India. The Cape was a valuable strategic base and Britain's primary aim was to prevent the Cape from falling into the hands of her arch imperial rival, France. The British assumed that the occupation would be temporary and set out to maintain the status quo, making few changes in the law or constitution. They abolished restrictions on internal trade, and maintained a large garrison at the Cape, which helped bring about an economic revival in the southwestern part of the colony. However, in their main task of restoring peace on the colony's eastern frontier, they were no more successful than their Dutch predecessors had been.

In 1803 the Cape was handed over to the new Batavian Republic in terms of the Treaty of Amiens between Britain and

Far right:
Cape Mounted Rifles, officer in full dress *c.* 1847
(© The Brenthurst Press)

Below:
The hill, fort and mess house in King William's Town, British Kaffraria
(National Cultural History Museum)

France. Then war resumed, and in 1806 Britain once again ousted the Dutch. The new British administration was autocratic and conservative. Dutch remained the official language, Roman-Dutch law was retained and local administration remained in the hands of *landdrosts* and *heemraden*. Free trade replaced the Dutch trading monopolies, and wine farmers profited from their access to British markets where their wine sold well thanks to a substantial tariff preference. Some changes were introduced; the slave trade was abolished (1808), a code was promulgated for the treatment of Khoi servants (1809), and a circuit court system brought justice nearer to the frontier (1811). The government for the first time tried to impose a frontier settlement by force, the British army expelling 20 000 Xhosa from the Zuurveld, which then became available for white settlement. But only some time after the Cape was officially ceded to Britain under the general peace settlement of 1814 were attempts made to restructure the colonial economy and society, and to make British influence predominate.

British South Africa Company (BSAC)

A mercantile company founded in 1889 by Cecil Rhodes after he had obtained a mining concession from Lobengula, ruler of the Ndebele north of the Limpopo River. The company was granted a royal charter giving it rights to govern and administer, mine, make treaties and distribute the vast territory north of the Limpopo. The charter was initially granted for twenty-five years and was extended for a ten-year period in 1915. The BSAC was obliged to report annually to the Secretary of State, maintain order, check slavery and promote free trade. Based in London, it was under British control, and so obtained territory for Britain without any financial contribution by the imperial government. At the same time, it thwarted any expansionist plans to the north which the South African Republic may have nurtured.

In 1890 Rhodes sent a Pioneer Column, accompanied by whites from all over southern Africa in search of farms, through Ndebele raiding grounds into Mashonaland. In 1893 company forces defeated the Ndebele under Lobengula and took over control of Matabeleland, opening it up to mining and farming. Dr Jameson, whom Rhodes had appointed administrator of Mashonaland in 1891, incorporated Matabeleland to create the embryo colony of Rhodesia. Further Ndebele and Shona uprisings were put down, and by 1897 the BSAC controlled all the territory up to the Zambezi River, and had acquired substantial land and mineral rights. Company rule in Southern Rhodesia ended in 1923 when voters chose self-government over incorporation in the Union of South Africa, and the territory was annexed by Britain as a colony. The following year the company transferred control of Northern Rhodesia to Britain, but continued with the development of the territory. The BSAC retained commercial assets in these territories, including mineral rights and railways, until they were acquired by the governments of Southern Rhodesia and Zambia. In 1965, through a merger, the company's history effectively ended.

Broederbond, *see* Afrikaner Broederbond

Broom, Robert

SCOTLAND, 1866 — PRETORIA, 1951

Medical doctor and palaeontologist. Broom founded the departments of zoology and geology at Victoria College, University of Stellenbosch and in his later years was appointed palaeontologist at the Transvaal Museum. He was a world authority on mammal-like reptiles, having unearthed rich fossil deposits in the Karoo. His studies threw much light on the origins of mammals from reptilian ancestors and his discovery in 1947 of the first adult skull of an *Australopithecus* (dubbed 'Mrs Ples') at Sterkfontein, confirmed and extended Raymond Dart's earlier findings. His tireless, life-long devotion to palaeontology contributed significantly to scientific knowledge of mammal and human evolution.

Bulhoek Massacre (1921)

A tragic incident which began in 1920 when Enoch Mgijima, leader of a religious sect known as the Israelites, squatted with his followers on the commonage near Queenstown in the eastern Cape and defied attempts at removal by the Smuts government. Eventually the police were sent to force the issue, the Israelites continued to believe in Mgijima's prophecies and refused to move, and in the en-

Cecil John Rhodes, Managing Director of the British South Africa Company
(Transvaal Archives TAB 15078)

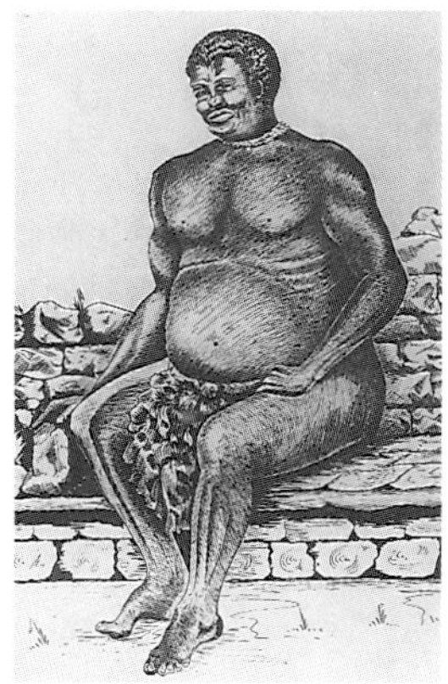

Rhodes was able to found the BSAC after he had obtained a mining concession from Lobengula, ruler of the Ndebele
(Transvaal Archives TAB 4838)

Dr Robert Broom's life-long devotion to palaeontology contributed significantly to scientific knowledge of mammal and human evolution
(South African Library)

Prophet Enoch Mgijima whose followers met a tragic end at Bulhoek when they defied attempts at removal by the Smuts government
(Africana Museum)

Right:
General Sir Redvers Buller, Commander-in-Chief of the British forces in South Africa in 1899
(Africana Museum)

Above:
Thomas François Burgers was elected President of the Transvaal Republic in 1872
(Transvaal Archives TAB 1923)

suing massacre 163 Israelites were killed and 129 wounded. Those arrested were found guilty of sedition and Mgijima and two others received six years' imprisonment with hard labour.

Buller, Sir Redvers Henry
DEVON, 1839 — DEVON, 1908

British soldier. After a successful army career, including serving in the Zululand campaign of 1879, Buller was appointed Commander-in-Chief in South Africa in 1899. He suffered heavy losses in three attempts to relieve Ladysmith, and was criticised for his indecisiveness, lack of nerve and inability to follow through attacks. He was replaced as Commander-in-Chief by Field Marshall Lord Roberts. Buller subsequently captured Dundee, Volksrust and Lydenburg, but his reputation never reached its previous standing, and, after he tried to clear his name, he was relieved of his command at half pay.

Burchell, William John
LONDON, 1781 — LONDON, 1863

Naturalist, traveller, artist and author. With headquarters at Klaarwater, Griquatown, Burchell made botanical collections in 1811 and 1812, later travelling for four years around the Cape in a wagon built specially to suit his requirements. He covered a vast and varied stretch of country amassing a total of 63 000 specimens, including about 50 000 plant specimens, skins, skeletons, insects, live seeds, bulbs and preserved fish. He annotated his collections copiously, compiled a *Catalogus geographicus* of his route and collecting area, and described previously unknown genera and species. He is commemorated in the genus *Burchellia*.

In 1819 Burchell was called before a select committee in the British House of Commons to advise on the suitability of South Africa for the settlement of British emigrants. His recommendation of the Albany district for this purpose influenced Parliament to make funds available for emigration. He wrote his authoritative *Travels in the Interior of Southern Africa* between 1822 and 1824.

Bureau of State Security (BOSS)

Created by Prime Minister Vorster in 1969, BOSS coordinated and evaluated intelligence, and engaged in clandestine operations both within South Africa and abroad, infiltrating agents into a number of anti-apartheid organisations and engaging in bribery and 'dirty tricks' campaigns. Under Vorster, BOSS was the élite security apparatus of the state, and it gained a major influence on all aspects of security policy. Its head, General Hendrik van den Bergh, worked closely with Vorster, and like the Prime Minister was implicated in the Information Scandal of 1978. A year later a discredited BOSS was restructured and renamed the Department of National Security.

Burgers, Thomas François
LANGFONTEIN, 1834 — RICHMOND, CAPE, 1881

Theologian and President of the Transvaal. After graduating as a Doctor of Theology in Holland, he returned to the Cape in 1859 and became a minister of the Dutch Reformed Church in Hanover. In 1872 he was elected President of the Transvaal Republic. His relatively sophisticated ideas on government, education and religion antagonised the Boers, and he found governing an almost bankrupt state increasingly difficult. In April 1877 Shepstone annexed the Transvaal for the British Crown. Burgers died a few years later in obscurity and poverty.

Far left:
Empty buses head back to town as commuters stream to work on foot during the bus boycotts
(Mayibuye Centre)

Left:
Chief Minister Mangosuthu Buthelezi addressing an Inkatha rally in Soweto, 1986
(Mayibuye Centre)

Bus Boycotts

Rising transport costs led to a series of bus boycotts by blacks on the Witwatersrand and in Pretoria between 1940 and 1945. The best-known involved commuters from Alexandra, to the north of Johannesburg, who over many years refused to accept higher fares and instead walked many kilometres to work. These boycotts helped to politicise black opinion on bread-and-butter issues and forced the government to investigate the living conditions and wages of workers, though conditions did not improve. In trying to keep fares down, a Public Utility Transport Corporation (PUTCO), subsidised by the government, was established in 1945.

Bushmen, *see* Hunter-gatherers; San

Buthelezi, Mangosuthu Gatsha

MAHLABATINI, ZULULAND, 1928 —

Chief Minister of KwaZulu and President of Inkatha. Buthelezi is a direct descendant of Cetshwayo, Zulu ruler at the time of the Anglo-Zulu war. He was educated at Fort Hare (where he joined the African National Congress Youth League) and Natal Universities. In the early 1970s he founded Inkatha yeNkululeko yeSizwe as a black liberation movement. After becoming Chief Minister of KwaZulu (1977), he rejected independence for his fragmented and impoverished territory and emerged as the most outspoken of the Bantustan leaders. In 1979 he attended a meeting with the ANC in London, but rejected their overtures and in the 1980s Inkatha increasingly took an anti-ANC position on a number of issues, though he continued to demand the release of Nelson Mandela. He campaigned strongly against sanctions and called for a free enterprise economy. When it was revealed that Inkatha had been receiving state funding, he denied knowledge of it. Though he condemned violence, he was unable to prevent his followers from clashing with the ANC in Natal and KwaZulu, and he refused to support the banning of the carrying of so-called cultural weapons.

Buthelezi, Wellington (Dr Butler Hansford Wellington)

MELMOUTH, NATAL, *c.* 1895 — *c.* 1940

Religious leader. A charismatic figure, who sold medicines and lied blatantly about his origins and qualifications, he preached a version of Garveyism. In the late 1920s he boasted a following of 25 000 in the Herschel district of the eastern Cape, especially among members of the Amafela, a popular religious movement of rural women who tried to resist land registration and taxation. His supporters were active in independent schools and churches. Harassed by missionaries and magistrates, Buthelezi was imprisoned and fined on several occasions. In 1927, as a result of his resistance to taxes and cattle dipping, he was prohibited from entering the Transkei. His following decreased steadily from the mid-1930s. Attempts to deport him to the United States were thwarted when his South African origins were confirmed.

Bywoner

A white tenant farmer or share-cropper who gave a part of his crop or herd to his landlord as rent for the land he used. By the 1870s a shortage of farming land on the highveld had resulted in widespread share-cropping, squatting and labour tenancy. As land values rose and agriculture became more capitalised, many *bywoners* were driven off the land. These impoverished people, most of whom were Afrikaners, were commonly known as poor whites.

C

Calvinism

Historians once claimed that white race attitudes and racial segregation in South Africa were the result of the Calvinist ideas of the Dutch settlers of the late seventeenth and eighteenth centuries, and especially of the trekboers on the frontier. These people, believing in predestination, viewed themselves on the one hand as the elect or 'chosen' people, the children of Israel seeking the promised land, and the blacks on the other as 'damned'. But historians now question the extent of the hold of Calvinism over the settlers at the Cape at this time and look elsewhere for the origins of racism.

When the Voortrekkers left the Cape Colony around 1835, the Dutch Reformed synod refused to support them, but they kept their Calvinist faith alive and its tenets emerged in some of their laws, such as the Rustenberg Grondwet of 1859, which provided that members of the Volksraad of the South African Republic were to be members of the Hervormde Kerk. At the Cape, the Afrikaner Bond adopted a severe form of neo-Calvinism which reflected the ideas of Dr Abraham Kuyper of Holland.

Two strands of Calvinism fed into Afrikaner nationalism. Volkskerk Calvinism (People's Church) was nurtured within the Dutch Reformed church. Central to its tenets was the concept that church and state were separate entities, but that the former should reinforce the latter. The Kuyper type of neo-Calvinism, dominant within the Broederbond, held sway in Potchefstroom in the 1930s. According to its precepts the church, the family and the state were absolute and answerable only to God, and they also functioned as interlocking theocracies within society as a whole.

Thomas Bowler's depiction of Adderley Street in Cape Town, with a view of the Dutch Reformed Church (Africana Museum)

Cape

The Cape Colony was initially established by Jan van Riebeeck in 1652 as a refreshment station for Dutch ships en route to Java and the Indonesian spice islands. The Dutch East India Company had no thought of establishing a colony of settlement. Indeed, they seriously considered digging a canal from Table Bay to False Bay to permanently separate the Cape Peninsula from the rest of Africa.

Because Van Riebeeck was unable to establish satisfactory trading relationships with the indigenous Khoikhoi people, he allocated farms along the Liesbeeck River to nine 'free burghers' in 1657. These were the first of South Africa's white settlers. Since the colonists were unable or unwilling to labour for themselves, and since they were forbidden to enslave the Khoikhoi, slaves were imported from the Dutch East Indies and Madagascar. From 1710 onwards, the slave population of the Cape consistently outnumbered the burgher population, establishing the pattern of white landownership and black servitude that has marked South Africa ever since.

By 1703, the colonists had settled the arable wheat and winelands of the south-western Cape, and crossed the Hottentots-Holland mountains into the South African interior. A new type of cattle-farmer emerged, the trekboer, who demanded extensive tracts of land. The Dutch East India Company policy of 'loanplace' tenure, whereby the farmers fixed their own boundaries, facilitated the rapid territorial expansion of the colony. The Khoikhoi offered little resistance after the trekboers seized control of their water resources, and they were mostly reduced to the condition of informal servitude on the white farms. Near the Fish River, however, the advancing trekboers encountered the Xhosa kingdom. The Xhosa effectively obstructed the eastward expansion of the Cape over a period of one hundred years and in nine frontier wars (1779–1878).

The British occupied the Cape in 1795, and consolidated their control thereafter, despite a brief interlude of Batavian rule (1803–1806). The settlement of 5 000 British immigrants in the eastern Cape during 1820 accelerated demands for a reform of the corrupt administrative structures inherited from the Dutch. The 'revolution in government', instituted by Acting Governor Bourke in 1828, cleaned up the system of justice, installed an impartial civil service, deregulated the Cape economy, and declared all British subjects of whatever colour equal before the law (Ordinance 50 of 1828). These changes seriously threatened the social and economic status quo, and triggered the Afrikaner Great Trek.

This 'revolution in government' was not accompanied by greater democratisation.

The man-of-war *Amsterdam* and other Dutch ships in Table Bay, *c.* 1636, by Adam Willaerts (© The Brenthurst Press)

The landing of Van Riebeeck, by Charles Bell, 1850. Van Riebeeck was unable to establish satisfactory trading relationships with the indigenous Khoikhoi people
(South African Library)

'Fighting in the Fish River Bush, September 1851', by Thomas Baines. The British tried to drive the Xhosa out of the area but during the attack over 30 soldiers of the Queen's Regiment were killed in an ambush where dogs were reputedly used to pull down the men
(Africana Museum)

Robert Godlonton, editor and owner of the influential *Graham's Town Journal*
(South African Library)

There were five 'unofficial' members of the Cape Legislative Council, but they were all nominated by the Governor. Demands for popular representation erupted in 1849, when the British government sent a shipload of convicts to the Cape. The government was backed by the extreme settler faction of Robert Godlonton, while the popular party was headed by the veteran liberal, Andries Stockenström, who enjoyed the support of the Cape's coloured population. The Kat River Rebellion of 1851 further reminded the government of the need to incorporate a broad spectrum of social classes into the political dispensation. The Cape's first representative Parliament (1853) was therefore elected on a non-racial franchise with relatively low qualifications (£25 worth of property, or £50 annual income). Much of the early

Settlers encamped on the Great Fish River, by F T I'Ons, 1837. The arrival of 5 000 British immigrants in the eastern Cape in 1820, accelerated demands for administrative reform
(William Fehr Collection)

politicking revolved around the ultimately sterile issue of eastern Province separatism, but the Cape's commitment to a non-racial franchise and colour-blind legislation laid the foundations of the so-called Cape liberal tradition.

Meanwhile, the expansion of the Cape's boundaries continued unabated. Sir Harry Smith added 50 000 square miles with a single stroke of his pen in 1847, by unilaterally extending its northern border to the Orange River. Thereafter, the Cape expanded by swallowing up the Crown Colonies established on its immediate frontiers: British Kaffraria (1866), Griqualand West (1880) and British Bechuanaland (1895). Transkei was annexed piecemeal between 1879 and 1894. Only Basutoland stood its ground. It was annexed to the Cape in 1871 against the will of its inhabitants but freed itself through the Gun War (1880–1884), which resulted in its coming directly under the British government.

In 1872, the Cape attained Responsible Government. John Molteno of Beaufort West was the first Prime Minister. At first, there was no such thing as party politics. Members were elected for their personal qualities, and ministries coalesced around cliques of local politicians. Cape liberalism flourished in this environment, as the black vote held the balance of power in seventeen parliamentary constituencies. The situation began to change in 1880, with the formation of South Africa's first political party, the Afrikaner Bond. The Bond aimed to mobilise Cape Afrikaners in defence of their political and economic interests. But its leader, Jan Hofmeyr, was sufficiently attuned to Cape political traditions not to seek office for himself, and to support the principles of 'best man' government and the non-racial franchise.

It is significant to note that the non-racial franchise was adopted at a time (1853) when only two Cape districts had substantial numbers of African voters. The continuing accretion of Xhosa- and Tswana-speaking territories gave rise, however, to the possibility that black voters might one day outnumber white ones. This led to the Registration Act of 1887 and the Franchise and Ballot Act of 1892, which effectively reduced the number of black voters. Most radical of all was the Glen Grey Act of 1894, dubbed a 'Bill for Africa' by its author, Prime Minister Cecil Rhodes. This proposed to divide the African population between a peasant class of prosperous smallholders and a landless proletariat available for mine labour. But even the black peasants were to be politically marginalised: landholders on Glen Grey titles were eligible to vote only for local councils and not for the Cape Parliament.

The split between the Afrikaner Bond and the pro-British Progressive Party, which crystallised after the 1896 Jameson Raid, was parallelled by an ethnically-based split between the black leaders J T Jabavu (a Mfengu) and W B Rubusana (a Xhosa). The fact that both white political parties commanded some black support buttressed the non-racial franchise until the National Convention of 1908 which negotiated the Union of South Africa. The Cape delegation did not insist on a non-racial franchise for all of South Africa, but

Map of the Cape Colony in 1851, engraved by John Rapkin
(The Brenthurst Library)

contented itself with the agreement that each province could maintain its own franchise laws after Union.

Britain refrained from interference in the franchise question, expressing the hope that the Cape would extend its liberal influence over the northern provinces once the question of unification was settled. This pious hope was never realised. It was the northern provinces which prevailed over the Cape tradition, and not the other way around.

(J B Peires)

Cape Town

The geographical setting of Table Bay, watered by springs from Table Mountain, favoured early settlement by hunter-gatherers. Khoikhoi pastoralists occupied the peninsula at the time of European contact.

Europeans discovered its existence when the Portuguese explorer, Bartolomeu Dias, rounded the Cape in 1488. The seamen who followed as the European commercial empires expanded in the East were grateful for the protection of the bay from the summer south-easterly gales, while the streams and trade with the Khoi furnished refreshment.

White settlement resulted from the expansion of the Dutch colonial empire. In 1652 the Dutch East India Company (VOC) sent a small expedition, commanded by Jan van Riebeeck, to establish a refreshment station in Table Bay. Initially known as the Kaapsche Vlek, the settlement was characterised by its military and restorative functions.

The Castle, which took its modern form from 1665, symbolised the military aspect. Until the mid-nineteenth century it was the centre of government and élite social life, while the common soldiers helped to shape Cape Town's unique urban proletariat.

Although the VOC had intended only to provide fresh food, the town soon took on a modest commercial function. It provided accommodation and recreation for visitors, hence the title 'Tavern of the Seas'. Until the late nineteenth century it was also the largest trade centre in southern Africa.

In its spatial structure, Cape Town was a typical colonial city, modified by local conditions. Built on a grid, the houses, about 550 in 1770, were low, white and flat roofed, while the streets were bounded by open canals. The introduction of slaves, combined with the multinational character of the VOC, ensured that it was cosmopolitan. The adoption of Islam by the

Jan Hofmeyr, leader of the Afrikaner Bond, South Africa's first political party
(Transvaal Archives TAB 12906)

Khoikhoi pastoralists occupied the Cape peninsula at the time of European contact
(© The Brenthurst Library)

Entrance to the Castle, by T W Bowler. Until the mid-nineteenth century the Castle was the centre of government and élite social life
(Africana Museum)

Table Bay in 1683, by Aernout Smit
(William Fehr Collection)

slaves added to its diversity. In 1786 a burgher council was constituted of three Company officials and three appointed free burghers to govern the town.

In 1795, during the Napoleonic wars, the British first occupied the Cape, and annexation was confirmed by the Treaty of Vienna in 1814. From a backwater ruled by a declining trading company, Cape Town became the metropolis of an expanding African empire, integrated into a global industrial economy. The Commercial Exchange built in 1819 symbolised the new spirit of free enterprise and liberal ideology. The first stones of the harbour breakwater were laid in 1860, the beginning of the docks.

Growing prosperity transformed the city. The building of the suburban railway line to Wynberg in 1864 accelerated the tendency of wealthier inhabitants to migrate to the suburbs. The insanitary canals were covered. The Dutch buildings of the Heerengracht, renamed Adderley Street after Sir Charles Adderley, a British politician who had supported the local stand against the introduction of convict labour in 1849, gave way to ornate Victorian banks, insurance companies and department stores. At the same time the urban poor, expanded by freed slaves after 1838, clustered in decaying urban mansions and in the new estate developments of Bo-kaap and District Six.

The ornate Victorian structure of the Standard Bank, corner of Adderley and Darling Streets, Cape Town
(Cape Archives AG 1567)

Population growth, from 17 570 in 1817 to 51 251 in 1891, necessitated more effective local government. The Burgher Senate was dissolved in 1827, to be replaced in 1840 by a municipal council. With a franchise based on property rather than race, the Cape Town municipality tended to reflect the interests of commerce and business. The overriding issue, which shaped municipal politics until 1913 when Cape Town united with the suburban municipalities, was water supply. A programme of dam building culminated in the opening of the Hely Hutchinson Dam on Table Mountain in 1904.

The mineral revolution, which brought greater wealth to Cape Town, made possible other public works. An increase in shipping resulted in the enlargement of the docks, which became the greatest local employer of labour. These workers were mainly Mfengu and Xhosa. Other immi-

'The Public Library and Museum from the Botanic Gardens, 1864', by Thomas Bowler
(Africana Museum)

grants poured in, especially from Britain and Eastern Europe, and the city became very cosmopolitan. The end of the nineteenth century was the height of British influence in Cape Town.

The South African War (1899–1902) marked a turning point in Cape Town's fortunes. After a brief wartime prosperity, a long depression followed which was linked to Cape Town's increased dependence on the economy of the interior. With Union in 1910 Cape Town became politically dependent too, although it was the new legislative capital of South Africa.

In the twentieth century Cape Town became an industrial city, with an increased pace of urbanisation. The textile industry was the most prominent enterprise. An influx of Afrikaners led to the expansion of northern suburbs like Parow and Bellville, which became independent municipalities. Although culturally lively, inner city slums like District Six became more overcrowded and some coloured people reluctantly spilled into new townships on the Cape Flats like Athlone and Kew Town. Africans had already been segregated in a location at Ndabeni in 1901 during a plague epidemic, and in 1927 they were moved to Langa. After 1945, with increased urbanisation, the locations of Nyanga and Gugulethu were erected. Cape Town became a highly segregated city.

Nevertheless, apartheid after 1948 was traumatic for Capetonians. In 1966 District

Although culturally lively, inner city slums like District Six became increasingly overcrowded
(Mayibuye Centre)

Six was proclaimed white under the Group Areas Act and thousands of people were driven from homes which they had occupied for generations. In 1972 coloured representation on the municipality was abolished. Africans suffered from influx control legislation combined with the coloured labour preference policy but their desire for work and homes led, from the 1970s, to the growth of illegal squatter settlements like Crossroads, which became a focus of local conflict and international criticism.

Political resistance became part of the pattern of life. White Capetonians tended

The 1970s saw the growth of illegal squatter settlements like Crossroads (Mayibuye Centre)

to support the moderate opposition. Amongst coloureds the African People's Organisation, formed in 1902, gave way to more militant parties like the South African Communist Party and the National Liberation League in 1935 with such leaders as the municipal councillor, Cissie Gool. Clements Kadalie led dock workers in strikes after 1919. Langa became a Pan Africanist Congress base, its residents participated in the pass law demonstrations of March 1960 and, under Philip Kgosana, marched to Cape Town to protest against subsequent arrests.

These upheavals occurred against a background of economic difficulty. Cape Town harbour was affected by the global decline in shipping and international sanctions took their toll. By the time influx control was lifted in 1986, unemployment was rife, especially in new townships like Mitchell's Plain and Khayalitsha. Nevertheless, despite a high crime rate, Cape Town has suffered less from township violence than other cities.

(E B van Heyningen)

Carnarvon was Secretary of State for the Colonies from 1866 to 1867, and again from 1874 to 1878 (Transvaal Archives TAB 34471)

Capital Punishment

Widely employed in South Africa, in African chiefdoms in the past and by Dutch and British rulers at the Cape, as well as by governments this century. In the early nineteenth century in the Cape, the British greatly reduced the number of crimes which could attract the death penalty, limiting them to murder, treason and rape. Between 1910 and 1989, 4 278 people were hanged in South Africa, not including the Bantustans. In his speech of 2 February 1990 President de Klerk announced a moratorium on capital punishment, and since then no one has been put to death as a result of judicial murder.

Carnarvon, Henry Howard Molyneux Herbert, Fourth Earl of

LONDON, 1831 — LONDON, 1890

Imperial statesman. Twice Secretary of State for the colonies (1866–1867 and 1874–1878), Carnarvon became devoted to the idea of South African federation. He sought to guide South Africa in the path that Canada had taken with the British North America Act of 1867. He got the British Parliament to pass permissive legislation for a South African federation but his attempt to bring about federation helped provoke opposition which prevented it from being realised. A conference he organised in London was not a success. He hoped that Sir Bartle Frere would, as High Commissioner, act purposefully to create a federal South Africa, but before Frere had been long in South Africa, Carnarvon resigned as Colonial Secretary on an unrelated issue.

Carnegie Commission (1929–1932)

Set up to investigate poor-whiteism in South Africa on the initiative of the Dutch Reformed Churches, the Commission found that some 300 000 whites were 'very poor', of whom Afrikaners constituted some 90 per cent. The five volume report dealt with rural impoverishment, the psychology of poor-whiteism, and the educational, health and social aspects of the problem. The report's stress on the importance of social care led the Hertzog government to establish a Department of Social Welfare in 1934. In the 1980s a second Carnegie Commission of Enquiry investigated the problem of poverty, this time mainly black poverty. The findings were summarised in a book by Francis Wilson and Mamphela Ramphele entitled *Uprooting Poverty, The South African Challenge* (Cape Town, 1989).

Cattle-killing (1856–1857)

On the basis of the prophecies of a young Xhosa girl called Nongqause, and on the advice of their chiefs, a large segment of the Xhosa people slaughtered their stock and destroyed their crops in the expectation of the provision of food from heaven and a resurrection of the ancestors. Though the movement drew on ideas taken from Christianity, it must be understood fundamentally as a reaction to the process of conquest and colonisation underway since the previous century. When the prophecies failed, a large population found itself starving and desperate. Tens of thousands in what was then known as British Kaffraria, now the Ciskei, died of starvation, and tens of thousands more fled westwards into the Cape Colony in a desperate search for work and food. The Cape Governor Sir George Grey exploited the situation to his own advantage, and the Xhosa paramount Sarili, himself a leading participant in the cattle-killing, was in its aftermath driven eastwards from his territory immediately across the Kei River.

Censorship

In the 1820s Lord Charles Somerset, Governor of the Cape, tried to stop publication of a newspaper and journal. But the widespread use of politically motivated censorship came with the advent of apartheid. Newspapers were banned in the 1950s under the Suppression of Communism Act (1950), which also prohibited banned people from being quoted or their writings being published. Then in 1963 a Publications Control Board was created with wide powers to ban publications and films considered offensive, harmful to public morals, blasphemous or prejudicial to state security or good order. This board was replaced by another under the Publications Act of 1974, from which no appeals were allowed. Tens of thousands of publications were banned for possession or distribution under the Act. Though newspapers were exempt from the Act, they imposed upon themselves a system of internal censorship, knowing that the alternative was the control of a government-appointed statutory body. In 1985 the government imposed a total news black-out of what was happening in the townships when it banned journalists and photographers from areas affected by the state of emergency. With the unbanning of the political organisations in 1990, censorship eased considerably, and large numbers of formerly banned publications became available for the first time within the country.

Cetshwayo

ZULULAND, *c.* 1826 — ESHOWE, 1884

Zulu ruler (1872–1879). Cetshwayo was the last great king of the independent Zulu state. His strong military leadership and political acumen restored the power and prestige of the Zulu nation which had declined during the reign of his father Mpande. As head of a rigidly disciplined army of 40 000 men, Cetshwayo was considered a threat to British colonial interests. That threat was removed by the Anglo-Zulu War (1879), which led to Cetshwayo's exile at the Cape, and the subsequent destruction of Zulu power in the Zulu Civil War, in the course of which Cetshwayo died soon after his return to Zululand.

Cetshwayo was the last ruler of the independent Zulu state
(Transvaal Archives TAB 6699)

Chamberlain, Joseph

LONDON, 1836 — BIRMINGHAM, 1914

British Secretary of State for the colonies from 1895 to 1903, during which time South African affairs were his main concern. Aware of Rhodes's schemes for the invasion of the Transvaal, he was accused of complicity in the Jameson Raid of 1895 but was cleared and proof of his complicity did not come out until long after his death. After the Raid, he continued to take a hard line towards Kruger. In 1897 he sent Sir Alfred Milner to the Cape as High Commissioner, and supported Milner as he led British-Transvaal relations towards war. A firm believer in British supremacy, he seems to have expected, along with the rest of the British cabinet, that there would be a short war and relatively easy victory.

Joseph Chamberlain, British Secretary of State for the Colonies from 1895 to 1903
(Transvaal Archives TAB 32186)

Chamber of Mines

Formed in 1887, one year after the discovery of the gold-bearing reefs on the Witwatersrand, the Chamber was a central coordinating body to promote and protect the interests of its members. The mining houses realised the advantages of united action, and the Chamber was in effect an employers' organisation. It enabled the mining houses to achieve a uniform policy in the matter of labour recruitment and wages. To eliminate competition for labour and bring down wages, a centralised monopolistic recruiting organisation was established (1896) which supplied labour from non-British territories, chiefly Mozambique. Another organisation formed in 1912 handled recruiting within South Africa and the High Commission territories. The Chamber spoke for an industry which until the Second World War was the strongest pressure group in South Africa, whose members were responsible

Miners in Pilgrim's Rest. The Chamber of Mines enabled the mining houses to achieve a uniform policy in matters of labour recruitment and wages
(South African Library)

for the production of nearly all South Africa's gold, uranium, diamonds and coal.

Champion, Allison Wessels George

TUGELA RIVER MOUTH, 1893 — NATAL, 1975

Trade unionist and political leader, first active in the Industrial and Commercial Workers' Union in the 1920s. From 1925 he organised the ICU from his base in Durban, and it soon had more members in Natal than anywhere else. He became a member of the African National Congress Executive (1927–1930 and 1937–1951), its Natal President (1945–1951), and its Acting President-General (1946–1947). He exerted a powerful conservative influence within the ANC, opposing its Youth League in the 1940s and demands for radical activism.

Chinese

Between 1904 and 1906 over 63 000 Chinese indentured workers were imported on three-year contracts to work on the gold mines in the Transvaal where they were housed in compounds. This scheme, the brainchild of Sir Alfred Milner, was prompted by the critical labour shortage on the mines after the South African War, and the need to bring them back into full production as quickly as possible. To appease whites who were afraid of economic competition, the Chinese workers were not allowed to hold skilled positions, they could not buy land nor trade, and on expiry of their contracts they had to return to China. They played a crucial role in the post-war recovery of the mines but by 1910 the last of these Chinese had been repatriated.

The first Chinese junk to appear in British waters. She rounded the Cape of Good Hope on 28 March 1848, 477 days from Canton
(Africana Museum)

The present South African Chinese community, estimated to be under 9 000 in 1980, are descendants of those who had come as traders in the nineteenth century. Over one third live in Johannesburg, others live mostly in Pretoria, Port Elizabeth, East London, Cape Town, Kimberley and Durban. The majority are Christians.

In the Transvaal, the early immigrants suffered the same trading and immigration restrictions as Indians. In 1907 the Chinese Association, led by Dr Leung Quinn, joined Indians in resisting the registration law and many went to jail.

Under apartheid laws the Chinese have had an ambiguous status. In terms of the Population Registration Act of 1950 they were considered coloured and under the Group Areas Act of 1950 separate Chinese areas had to be demarcated for them. Only three such group areas were proclaimed at Port Elizabeth, Kimberley and Uitenhage. However, they were allowed to live and trade in white areas under permit, attend white cinemas and restaurants and travel on white buses. Chinese children attended white private schools and could, by permit, attend white government schools. For immigration purposes, the Chinese were regarded as Asians and faced the same restrictions as Indians. In 1976 they were excluded from the restrictions applicable to Asians in terms of the Liquor Act of 1928, and so were permitted to drink in 'white' bars.

The Chinese Association of South Africa was formed in 1981 in opposition to the appointment of a Chinese to the President's Council. As a small minority group, however, neither white nor black, the Chinese have remained largely apolitical.

(U S Mesthrie)

Christianity

The origins of Christian influence in South Africa are traditionally associated with the Portuguese explorers commanded by Bartolomeu Dias, who erected a limestone pillar, capped by the Christian cross, at Kwaaihoek near Bushman's River Mouth, on the southern Cape coast, on 12 March 1488. Further brief intermittent landings on the South African coastline by European traders and sailors who adhered to the Christian faith ensued during the sixteenth and early seventeenth centuries, before the Dutch East India Company (VOC) established its refreshment station at Table Bay in 1652. This marked the beginnings of a permanent European and Christian presence in southern Africa.

The subsequent history of Christianity is deeply intertwined with the economic and political ambitions and fortunes of the early Dutch settlers, later immigrants from Europe and their white descendants. The VOC established the Dutch Reformed Church as the only authorised religious body at the Cape. No other religious organisation could function legally in public until 1778, when Lutherans were permitted public worship. The VOC was formally committed to the promotion of Christianity among the indigenous inhabitants of the Cape and the imported slaves, but in practice missionary activity before the end of the eighteenth century was isolated, sporadic and superficial. The rate of conversions was negligible, particularly out-

Chinese miners played a crucial role in the post-war recovery of the Transvaal gold mines
(Africana Museum)

The origins of Christian influence in South Africa are traditionally associated with the Portuguese explorer Bartolomeu Dias, who raised the cross on the southern Cape coast in 1488. Painting by Charles Bell, 1850
(South African Library)

The Lutheran Church, Strand Street, Cape Town, by Thomas Bowler. Lutherans were permitted public worship in 1778
(Africana Museum)

Revd Robert Moffat preaching to the Bechuana, by Charles Bell. Moffat was sent out by the London Missionary Society and established a mission station at Kuruman
(Africana Museum)

Georg Schmidt, the first Moravian missionary at the Cape who started work among the Khoikhoi in 1737
(South African Library)

side of Cape Town. Whites appear to have used their identity as 'Christians' as one key attribute to distinguish themselves from and elevate themselves above, other groups, and did not consider conversion of others to be a priority. This stance was never challenged by the official church establishment.

By contrast, the nineteenth century was characterised by determined Christian mission endeavour, which coincided with a period of British colonial and commercial conquest. In 1792, shortly before the first British occupation of the Cape, Moravian missionaries restarted work abandoned in 1744 by Georg Schmidt, while the London Missionary Society — whose two most famous missionaries were Johannes van der Kemp and John Philip — inaugurated its activities at the Cape in 1799. They were followed by French, German, Scandinavian and American missionaries. Mission stations were established throughout southern and south-eastern Africa, and

'Mr Archbell's congregation at Thaba 'Nchu, 1834', by Charles Bell. The Wesleyans (Methodists) pioneered mission work among the Barolong
(Africana Museum)

were frequently the focus of both religious and secular colonisation: indigenous societies and African beliefs were weakened. Evangelical and theological concerns were conspicuous ingredients of the message of the missionaries, but these were closely coupled to other factors: the advance of literacy and European concepts of education and civilisation, as well as the promotion of trade, commerce and British political and military hegemony.

While the influence of missionaries naturally varied from region to region, so too did the response of Africans to the Christian gospel. The primary reaction, particularly in the eastern Cape, was one of resistance, expressed either through direct hostility or, more commonly, through disregard: chiefs realised that missionaries represented a threat both to the social order in their communities and to their own personal power. Many chiefs were not averse, however, to utilising missionaries for their own purposes. They exploited them for the material and technological benefits they brought, such as irrigation, the plough, firearms and ammunition. Military advantage derived from European weapons, which conferred the ability to offer protection and attract followers, was particularly significant on the Cape northern frontier. On the material as well as the cultural, spiritual and symbolic levels, therefore, missionaries and Africans found themselves in deep confrontation. Only after the political and economic collapse of African societies — in which missionaries often played an important role — in the second half of the century were significant numbers of conversions to Christianity achieved.

Missionaries formed the vanguard of Christian activity in the nineteenth century, but various denominations founded institutional structures and congregations during this period. The majority were Protestant, and they are conventionally classified according to language. Despite different historical and cultural origins, they often shared similar values in their outlook on society. There were three Dutch (later Afrikaans) churches for whites. The Nederduitse Gereformeerde Kerk (NGK), which traced its history back to the VOC period, had the largest following, but experienced some rivalry from the smaller Nederduitsch Hervormde Kerk (established 1853) and the Gereformeerde Kerk (established 1859) in the Transvaal and Orange Free State from the mid-nineteenth century. Racially separate Dutch Reformed churches were established for coloureds — the Sendingkerk in 1881 — and for Africans — the NGK in Afrika in 1910. Among the English-speaking churches, Methodists after the 1820s and Anglicans after 1847 became the largest and most powerful groupings, but Presbyterians, Congregationalists and Baptists were other prominent denominations. The first Roman Catholic bishop arrived in 1838.

Enormous expansion in Christianity occured during the twentieth century, the era of industrial capitalism, rapid urbanisation and far-reaching social change. Christianity grew from its status as a mainly white, minority, imported faith to one embraced by the majority of South Africans, although in a wide variety of styles and expressions. By 1980, almost 77 per cent of the population claimed some form of Christian allegiance. Although most denominations experienced considerable growth in the number of black adherents, to the extent

The Zionist Church celebrated its 75th anniversary in 1985 (South African Communication Service)

that whites became a numerical minority within churches, the surge in Christianity can chiefly be ascribed to the independent African churches. By 1990, there were some 5 000 such denominations, with a following of perhaps eight million people. The Thembu Church, founded by Nehemiah Tile in 1884, and the Ethiopian Church, founded by Mangena Mokone in 1892, were the first Christian structures of significance independent of white control. Zionist and Apostolic Churches became prominent from the early twentieth century. These often focused black protest against the dispossession of land and labour, and provided a focus of identity for impoverished people in the towns and cities. A vast range of religious, ritual, faith-healing and prophetic expressions characterise these churches.

Christianity has been used in numerous ways to sanction different political and economic interests during the past century. It has been used by the white Protestant churches to justify apartheid and Afrikaner nationalism. Anglicans and Methodists in particular, with their membership that crosses the social and racial spectrum, have often experienced deep tension on sociopolitical issues. Various forms of liberation and black theology have been used to legitimate the struggle of black people against political and economic oppression.

In the process of assuming indigenous forms and becoming the most dominant religion in South African society, Christianity has both shaped and reflected the contested nature of that society, its complexities and its ambiguities.

(ND Southey)

Christian National Education (CNE)

Drawing on Calvinist ideas, and closely associated with Afrikaner nationalism, CNE aimed to prepare each child to occupy a niche in a segregated society. It evolved in the 1870s in the Transvaal and the Orange Free State where the Dutch language and religious instruction were reinstated in the schools. After the South African War, with the backing of the Dutch Reformed Church, CNE schools were established in opposition to Lord Milner's Anglicisation policy. CNE later became the official educational policy of the National Party.

Ciskei

A Bantustan created by the National Party's segregationist programme between 1961 and 1982, Ciskei shares the land between the Fish and the Kei Rivers with the so-called 'white corridor', stretching from East London to Queenstown. The population of Ciskei in 1990 was approximately 750 000. Only 15 per cent of its 8 300 sq km was suitable for cultivation. By 1980, 39 per cent of Ciskei was overgrazed, and 47 per cent categorised as moderately to severely eroded.

Ciskei is not identical to the Crown

'Members of Sandile's tribe', by T J Lucas. Most of these Rharhabe Xhosa were dispossessed of their land
(Africana Museum)

Colony of British Kaffraria (1847–1866): parts of British Kaffraria are not included in Ciskei, and parts of Ciskei were not included in British Kaffraria. The political dynamics were also very different. Whereas the purpose of British Kaffraria was to assimilate the Xhosa to European culture, the purpose of Ciskei was to re-segregate and retribalise them.

Present-day Ciskei is heir to both the Frontier Wars and the intense missionary activity of the nineteenth century. Most of the indigenous Rharhabe Xhosa were dispossessed of their lands, which were given out to white settlers and to black auxiliaries of the colonial forces. The most notable of these were the so-called Mfengu, who were refugees from the Shakan wars in Natal. In 1835 they swore a great oath to obey the government, accept Christianity and educate their children. The Ciskei area was home to many notable educational institutions such as Lovedale, Healdtown and Fort Hare.

Innovative governors such as Sir George Grey (1855–1861) deliberately interspersed white farmers among black landowners to promote 'civilisation by mingling'. The process of acculturation proceeded apace with hereditary chiefs giving way to elected headmen, communal land tenure to individual title, and traditional African religion to Christianity. Peasant agriculture flourished as black entrepreneurs invested in ploughs and waggons to maximise production for the market. Political leaders such as J T Jabavu and W B Rubusana mobilised black voters to elect liberal white politicians to the Cape Parliament. The philosophy known as Cape liberalism found its most concrete expression in the region which later became known as Ciskei.

Women students at Lovedale College
(Mayibuye Centre)

The mineral discoveries of the late nineteenth century brought this liberal era to an end. The Glen Grey Act of 1894 broke with the tradition of treating blacks and whites on an equal legal footing as citizens of a colour-blind British Empire. It created a special type of land tenure for Africans, which limited their holdings to four morgen each and abolished their franchise rights. The twentieth century saw the region decline from peasant prosperity to its present state, in which impoverishment mixes with education to produce a high degree of politicisation.

Fighting in the Amatolas, the stronghold of Chief Sandile. Painting by Thomas Baines, 1851 (Africana Museum)

Nearly 100 years after the last Frontier War, the Ciskei region again became the scene of massive population relocation. Pictured here, the notorius resettlement camp of Sada (Mayibuye Centre: photo by John Seymour)

The assimilated and integrated condition of Xhosa-speakers west of the Kei River contrasted sharply with that of their fellow-Xhosa on the other side of the river. The 'trans-Keian territories', as they were called, had been annexed to the Cape rather more gently, and they had retained their traditionalist political and intellectual structures. The term 'cis-Kei' became increasingly used to denote an area which white South Africa no longer wished to assimilate, but which was, at the same time, already too assimilated to amalgamate with the more traditionalist Transkei.

It was only in 1923 that the Department of Native Affairs, mindful of the 'chaotic state of affairs ... as regards Native administration in the Ciskei', appointed a Chief Commissioner with the specific brief of 'bringing the Ciskeian districts more or less into line with the Transkeian system of administration'. A Ciskeian General Council was instituted in 1934. Chieftainship was revived under the Bantu Authorities between 1957 and 1959, and the Ciskeian Territorial Authority was established in 1961.

The Verwoerd government which prepared Transkei for independence did not even consider incorporating the Ciskei Xhosa. Ciskei then consisted of no fewer than nineteen distinct fragments of black-owned land. The government solution, expressed in the euphemistic phrase, 'consolidation of the Ciskei', was two-pronged. On the one hand, about 300 000 hectares of white farmland were to be added to Ciskei. On the other hand, fourteen 'awkwardly situated Bantu areas' were to be forcibly removed from the 'white corridor' to the new Ciskei. Nearly one hundred years after the last Frontier War, the Ciskei region again became the scene of massive population relocation.

White farmers sold their land to the South African Development Trust, but before the land was handed over to the Ciskei authorities, it was involuntarily packed with Xhosa-speaking people forcibly removed from 'white' South Africa. Most came from small rural towns in the eastern Cape such as Middleburg and Hofmeyr. At least 40 000 were refugees from Herschel and Glen Grey, Ciskeian districts transferred to Transkei in 1975. The worst affected area was the district of Hewu (Whittlesea), home to the notorious resettlement camps of Sada, Thornhill and Zweledinga. It is estimated that over 300 000 people were forcibly removed to Ciskei between 1970 and 1982.

Ciskei was declared a self-governing territory in 1972. The first Chief Minister was Justice Mabandla, but he was soon superceded by his Agriculture Minister, Lennox Sebe. Sebe, who was a Rharhabe Xhosa, rallied ethnic support against Mabandla, a Mfengu, and became Chief Minister in 1973. Sebe failed to get King William's Town incorporated into Ciskei, but he was compensated when the South African government built a whole new city, Bisho, to serve as the Ciskei capital. He also built a 'National Shrine' at Ntaba kaNdoda in a vain attempt to inspire Ciskei nationalism.

In December 1982, Ciskei accepted 'independence' from South Africa. The government was faced with the task of policing a heavily politicised and unionised population. Sebe exercised control initially through the efforts of his energetic brother Charles, the ruthless head of the Ciskei Central Intelligence Service. After Charles fell from grace in 1983, Sebe became increasingly unable to maintain his authority. Matters came to a head in February 1990, when the release of Nelson Mandela provoked riots in Mdantsane. Sebe was overthrown in a bloodless military coup, apparently sponsored by the South African government. Ciskei's new ruler was hitherto unknown Brigadier Oupa Gqozo, a native of Kroonstad in the Orange Free State.

(J B Peires)

Civil Cooperation Bureau (CCB)

In 1986 approval was given — at what level remains unclear — for the establishment of a covert organisation operating under the Special Forces of the South African Defence Force and linked to Military Intelligence. Its main objective was maximum disruption of South Africa's enemies, perceived as the African National Congress, Pan Africanist Congress, South African Communist Party and Swapo. It was not until 1990 that the public learned of the existence of the CCB, when news of some of its secret projects leaked out. These had included attempts at intimidation, arson, bombing and the assassination of left-wing activists. The government announced that the CCB would be disbanded in August 1990, but its activities continued and in late 1992 some of its projects had not yet been wound up. Some commentators saw the CCB as a product of the P W Botha securocrat era, and argued that De Klerk had acted to the best of his abilities to end covert operations against his main negotiating partner; others believed that such operations had been allowed to continue because weakening the ANC served the interests of the National Party government.

Ciskei gained 'independence' from South Africa in December 1982
(Rapport Library)

Civilised Labour

The Pact Government of General Hertzog (1924–1933) adopted a policy of so-called Civilised Labour to assist the absorption of poor whites, the great majority Afrikaners, who were fleeing from the land into industrial occupations. In terms of this policy black workers were to be replaced as far as possible with poor whites at wages that ensured a 'civilised' standard of living. As a result, unskilled and semi-skilled whites were employed in the public sector and in parastatals, and on the railways, effectively solving the 'poor white problem'.

Codesa (Convention for a Democratic South Africa)

Negotiations on a new constitution for South Africa began at a multi-party meeting outside Johannesburg in December 1991, attended by representatives of the main political parties, organisations and administrations of the country, including the Bantustans but excluding the Conservative Party, the Pan Africanist Congress and the Azanian People's Organisation. The three main participants

ANC delegates at Codesa: Cyril Ramaphosa, Nelson Mandela and Jacob Zuma (South African Communication Service)

Bishop Colenso. His courageous support for the Zulu made him unpopular among Natal's white settlers (Transvaal Archives TAB 13174)

were the African National Congress, the South African government and the Inkatha Freedom Party, whose leader, Chief Minister Mangosuthu Buthelezi, did not attend. Codesa's aims were the formulation of a constitution for a united, democratic, non-racial state, with universal adult suffrage, and a justiciable bill of rights. These aims were expressed in a declaration of intent which was endorsed by seventeen of the nineteen delegates at Codesa. Five working groups were set up which met prior to a second meeting of Codesa in May 1992, held at the same venue.

Negotiations at Codesa II were marred by recriminations between the main participants over responsibility for the violence in the country, and eventually broke down over the issue of the percentage needed for approval of a new constitution in a Constituent Assembly.

Coetzee, John M

CAPE TOWN, 1940—

Author and academic. Educated mainly in South Africa, Coetzee spent ten years in Britain and America as a student and lecturer. He returned to South Africa in 1971 and became a lecturer in English at the University of Cape Town, where he still teaches. His first novel, *Dusklands*, was published in 1974. In 1976 he published *In the Heart of the Country* and his acclaimed *Waiting for the Barbarians* appeared in 1980. *The Life and Times of Michael K* followed in 1983. His more recent novels are *Foe* and *Age of Iron*.

Colenso, Bishop John William

ST. AUSTELL, CORNWALL, 1814—
PIETERMARITZBURG, 1883

Church of England Bishop of Natal, Zulu linguist and defender of the Zulu. Colenso arrived in Natal in 1853, after a varied career including the publishing of an arithmetic book for schools, editing journals and teaching. As Bishop of Natal, his liberal theological ideas were rejected by other white clergy and his energies were consumed by the demands of his Zulu friends and students. Not only did he find himself rejected by his church, but missionary societies withdrew their grants and he became even more unpopular among Natal's white settlers when he championed Langalibalele and Cetshwayo. As a result his friendship with Theophilus Shepstone was broken, and his courageous support for the Zulu alienated him further from most whites.

Colour Bar

Term used to describe a policy of job reservation based on colour in which the most skilled and more highly paid jobs were designated for whites, while the more menial jobs were given to blacks. White workers felt threatened by the attempts of capitalists to lower production costs by paying lower wages, as the politically powerless black workers were forced to accept whatever payment was offered. One of the only means white workers had to protect themselves was the colour bar.

Much of the key legislation implementing the colour bar was passed in the Botha-Smuts era. The Industrial Disputes Prevention Act (1909) and the Native Labour Regulation Act (1911) disallowed any bargaining or strike procedures for blacks, making them more exploitable and thus more of a threat to white workers. The Mines and Works Act of 1911 implemented what was an already existing colour bar in the Transvaal. The Status Quo Agreement of 1916 between the Chamber of Mines and the mining unions guaranteed that no more blacks would be given positions reserved for whites. The mineowners, however, constantly tried to dismantle the colour bar in their attempts to lower production costs on the mines, and the result was the 1922 strike by 20 000 white workers. The strike failed, but the Mines and Works Amendment Act (1926) or 'Colour Bar' Act protected white workers from competition by the issuing of certificates for skilled jobs to whites and coloureds only.

The Apprenticeship Act (1922) introduced a colour bar by ensuring that entry into apprenticeship was based on minimum age and maximum educational qualifications. This favoured whites, for whom primary education was compulsory. The 1924 Industrial Conciliation Act protected unionised white employees from competition. The Pact Government of 1924 was concerned about poor whites in the towns who were competing with blacks for jobs. The 1925 Wage Act established a Wage Board which regulated wages for unskilled workers who were not unionised. Payment determined by the 'type' of job was an effective and subtle form of colour bar. The Fusion government of the 1930s implemented the 1924 Act through industrial councils which entrenched a Civilised Labour Policy.

During the Second World War the need for labour in the manufacturing and engineering industries meant that black and coloured workers were employed in skilled capacities, but the job colour bar was entrenched further after 1948 by the Malan Government, which was especially concerned with the interests of white working-class voters. Strijdom carried job reservation further by amending the Industrial Conciliation Act (1956 and 1959), giving the Minister of Labour the power to reserve particular job categories for certain race groups in particular areas.

The expansion of the South African economy in the 1960s made inroads into the job colour bar system. The gold mining industry, faced with a white labour shortage, reached an agreement with the white unions allowing blacks to occupy positions originally reserved for whites in return for productivity payments and guarantees against retrenchments for white workers. In 1979 the Wiehahn Commission recommended not only that black trade unions be recognised but that job reservation based on colour be abolished. The implementation of these recommendations was met by resistance from white mineworkers but within a decade the last remnants of the colour bar had gone.

The general strike being declared at the Trade's Hall, Rissik Street, Johannesburg, 1922 (South African National Museum of Military History)

Coloured Labour Preference Policy

State policy that coloured labour should be employed in the western Cape in preference to African labour. Though its roots lie in the 1920s, it became official policy in 1954, and after that Africans were barred from a wide range of jobs in the area west of the so-called Eiselen line. The historical justification advanced for it was that Africans had only recently entered the western Cape, which was 'traditionally' the home of whites and coloureds. It was also a way of trying to win coloured support for apartheid policies. Many coloureds, however, were opposed to it, and by the early 1980s it broke down as Africans entered the western Cape in large numbers. In 1985 the government announced that CLP had been abolished.

Coloureds

Contrary to international usage, in South Africa the term 'coloured' does not refer to black people in general. It instead alludes to a phenotypically diverse

This church is all that remains of the former District Six, which, ostensibly in the interests of slum clearance, the Government demolished and proclaimed a white area
(Mayibuye Centre)

group of people descended largely from Cape slaves, indigenous Khoisan peoples and other blacks who had been assimilated to Cape colonial society by the late nineteenth century. Being also partly descended from European settlers, coloureds are popularly regarded as being of 'mixed race' and hold an intermediate status in the South African racial hierarchy, distinct from the dominant white minority and the numerically preponderant African population.

There are approximately three million coloured people in South Africa today. Constituting less than 10 per cent of the population and lacking significant political or economic power as a result of a heritage of slavery, dispossession and racial oppression, coloureds form a marginal group in South African society. There is, moreover, a marked regional concentration of coloured people, with approximately 85 per cent resident in the Cape Province, fully two-thirds in the western Cape and 30 per cent in the greater Cape Town area.

Although coloured identity crystallised in the late nineteenth century, the process of social amalgamation within the colonial black population at the Cape that gave rise to coloured group consciousness dates back to the period of Dutch colonial rule. It was, however, in the decades after the emancipation of slaves in 1838 that the various components of the Cape Colony's heterogeneous black labouring class integrated rapidly and developed an incipient shared identity based on a common socio-economic status. The emergence of a fully fledged coloured identity was precipitated in the late nineteenth century by the sweeping social changes that came in the wake of the mineral revolution. It was especially the incorporation of large numbers of Africans into Cape society that drove acculturated colonial blacks to assert a separate identity in order to claim a position of relative privilege to Africans on the basis of their closer assimilation to Western culture and being partly descended from European colonists.

Because of their marginality and the determination with which the state implemented white supremacist policies, the story of coloured political organisation has largely been one of compromise, retreat and failure. The most consistent feature of coloured political history has been the continual erosion of the civil rights first bestowed upon blacks in the Cape Colony by the British Administration in the mid-nineteenth century. The process of attrition started with the franchise restrictions of the late nineteenth century, and continued with the failure of the British government to extend the franchise to coloureds in the ex-Boer Republics at the end of the South African War. All blacks were denied the right to be elected to Parliament in the Union constitution of 1909.

During the 1920s and 1930s the economic status of coloureds, especially the petty bourgeois élite stratum, was undermined by the state through the Pact Government's Civilised Labour Policy and a number of laws designed to favour whites over blacks in the competition for employment. Furthermore, in the early 1930s the value of the coloured vote was more than halved by the enfranchisement of white women as well as all white males over the age of eighteen; only coloured males over the age of twenty-one, who met stipulated literacy and economic qualifications, remained eligible to vote.

It was during the apartheid era, however, that coloureds suffered the most severe violations of their civil rights. The most important of these measures were their classification under the Population Registration Act of 1950, the prohibition of mixed marriages, their removal from the common voters' roll in 1956, the forced relocation of tens of thousands of coloured families under the Group Areas Act and the segregation of public facilities under the Separate Amenities Act.

Because their primary objective was to assimilate into the dominant society, politicised coloureds initially avoided forming separate political organisations. However, by the turn of the century intensifying segregation forced them to mobilise politically in defence of their rights. Although the earliest coloured political organisations date back to the 1880s, the first substantive coloured political body, the African Political Organisation, was established in Cape Town in 1902. The APO subsequently dominated coloured protest politics for nearly four decades, becoming the main vehicle for expressing this community's assimilationist aspirations as well as its fears at the rising tide of white racism. The failure of the APO's moderate approach resulted in the emergence of a radical movement inspired by socialist ideology amongst the urban educated élite in coloured politics during the 1930s. The National Liberation League founded in 1935 and the Non-European Unity Movement established in 1943 were the most important of these organisations. Prone to fissure and unable to bridge the racial divisions within the society, the radical movement failed in its quest to unite blacks in the stuggle against segregation. Extra-parliamentary opposition amongst coloured political organisations was effectively quelled by state repression following the Sharpeville massacre of 1960 and only re-emerged in the wake of the Soweto uprising of 1976.

The nature of coloured identity has since become an extremely contentious issue as increasing numbers of educated and politicised people who had been classified 'coloured' under the Population Registration Act rejected coloured identity. They viewed it as an artificial categorisation imposed upon the society by the state as part of its 'divide and rule' strategies. The controversy was intensified by the growth of a mass, non-racial democratic movement in South Africa through the 1980s, most notably under the direction of the United Democratic Front, together with political conflict over the participation of coloureds in the Tricameral Parliament of the Botha government from the early 1980s onwards. In spite of this, coloured identity has endured, as demonstrated by political parties across the ideological spectrum continuing to appeal to coloured identity for support. In 1992 for example, Nelson Mandela urged the ANC to recognise 'coloured ethnicity' as a political reality.

The Separate Representation of Voters Act, which the Nationalist Government steamrollered through Parliament, removed from the Cape coloureds the franchise which they had had for almost 100 years
(Cartoon by Abe Berry)

Dr Abdullah Abdurahman, President of the APO from 1905, acquired considerable political leverage and public credibility through his efforts to resist segregation
(Africana Museum)

(M Adhikari)

Commandos

Mounted militia units. From the 1670s official commandos of Dutch East India Company soldiers, free burghers and company servants went out on punitive expeditions against the San. By the beginning of the eighteenth century very few regular soldiers participated in these commandos and from 1715 onwards they were composed entirely of burghers and their servants under burgher leaders. The company increasingly left the burghers a free hand to deal with the indigenous peoples as they saw fit, merely supplying the commandos with guns and ammunition. As the frontier farmers encroached on their pasture land, and the livestock diminished, so the pastoralists and hunter-gatherers, and later Bantu-speakers as well, retaliated by attacking the new settlers. Over the years the conflict intensified and commando duty became a way of life for white men.

Between 1715 and 1862 commandos hunted the San like vermin, killing thou-

'A Boer commando', painted by H Egersdörfer. Commando service was obligatory in both Voortrekker Republics and republican commandos fought against the British in the South African War
(Africana Museum)

sands. Captive children were commonly taken home to be brought up as farm servants. Indeed the demand for servants was probably one of the reasons for commando expeditions against the San. Although the commando system proved adequate on the northern frontier against the Khoisan, it was much less effective on the eastern frontier against the Bantu-speakers. Here British aid was necessary to dislodge the Xhosa from the Zuurveld and to establish white supremacy. From 1836 Voortrekker commandos clashed with blacks north of the Orange River. Commando service was obligatory in both Voortrekker Republics, and republican commandos fought against the British during the Anglo-Transvaal War (1880–1881) and the South African War (1899–1902). During the Rand Rebellion (1922) striking miners were organised into commandos across the Witwatersrand. Today the commando is a military unit of part-time soldiers in the South African Defence Force.

Jan Smuts airport. Crowds await Dr Verwoerd's return after South Africa lost her membership of the Commonwealth
(Rapport Library)

Commonwealth

Historically the Commonwealth is an evolutionary outgrowth of the British Empire. In 1917 Smuts referred to a 'British Commonwealth', and at an Imperial War Conference that year he carried through a resolution affirming the existing powers of self-government of the dominions and their status as 'autonomous nations'. It was chiefly Hertzog who, at the Imperial Conference of 1926, saw to it that the independent and equal status of the dominions was recognised. In 1961 South Africa asked the other Commonwealth countries whether it could become a republic while remaining within the Commonwealth. Because of its apartheid policies, there was opposition to this, as a result of which Dr Verwoerd withdrew South Africa's application to remain within the Commonwealth. That body continued to take a keen interest in South African developments, and especially in the years after the Soweto uprising (1976), the South African issue featured very prominently in its meetings and came close to destroying it.

Communist Party, *see* South African Communist Party

Compounds

Closed compounds were introduced in 1885 on the Kimberley diamond fields to house black migrant mine workers for the duration of their time at the mines. The migrants were not allowed to leave the compounds while in Kimberley, and when their contracts expired they were searched thoroughly to ensure that they were not secreting diamonds. Compounds were later used on the Witwatersrand gold mines, the Cape Town docks and elsewhere. They varied greatly: most were not closed and they were sometimes merely a rough collection of huts, housing a small group of workers. On the Witwatersrand they were commonly a complex of barracks accommodating several thousand migrant workers, who often had to sleep on concrete slabs, one row above the other. There the system was clearly a means of control, to prevent workers breaking their contracts, and a way to keep labour as cheap as possible. In 1920 and again in 1946 striking workers were isolated in their compounds, and the strike consequently broken. Despite government regulations of 1905 which laid down standards regarding compound construction, many compounds, and the hostels which took their place, remained into the 1990s unsanitary and overcrowded places.

Mine workers' compound, 1950s. In the Witwatersrand compounds commonly accommodated several thousand migrant workers, who often had to sleep on concrete slabs (Mayibuye Centre)

Concentration Camps

Set up in 1900 during the South African War (1899–1902) by the British military authorities to prevent guerrillas from being assisted by civilians. Boer women and children whose menfolk were on commando were interned, together with families of Boers who had surrendered and needed protection. Forty-four camps were set up, mostly in the Transvaal and the Orange River Colony. Conditions in the camps were extremely poor, resulting in the outbreak of epidemics and a high mortality rate. Official estimates of the number of Boer men, women and children who died in the camps vary between 18 000 and 28 000. The camps left an ineradicable scar on the Afrikaner consciousness. Blacks too were interned in large numbers in twenty-nine camps, and the official figure for black deaths in these camps was 14 154.

Confederation

The idea that the various white-ruled states should be joined together in some kind of federal union was first mooted by Cape Governor Sir George Grey in 1858, but nothing came of it at that time. Lord Carnarvon, British Colonial Secretary in the 1870s, wished to promote confederation in Britain's strategic interests, and he appointed Sir Bartle Frere Governor of the Cape in order to carry out his federation schemes. To this end Frere successfully destroyed Zulu military power, but the defeat at Isandlwana, and opposition to British rule within the Transvaal and to the idea of federation at the Cape, meant that by mid-1880 the British government had to accept that federation was not a viable policy. When political union was eventually achieved in 1910, it was not a federal union.

Congress Alliance

A united front formed in 1953 to oppose the apartheid state, comprising the African National Congress (ANC), the South African Indian Congress (SAIC), the Coloured People's Congress, the Congress of Democrats (whites) and after 1955 the

Washing day at a concentration camp in Aliwal North. During the South African War many thousands of Boer men, women and children died in camps such as this (Africana Museum)

Above:
Congress of the People, Kliptown 1955. Delegates march with their demands
(Mayibuye Centre)

Above right:
In 1982 Dr Andries Treurnicht broke away from the National Party to form the Conservative Party
(Rapport Library)

South African Congress of Trade Unions (SACTU). Led by the ANC, the alliance convened the Congress of the People in 1955 at which the Freedom Charter was adopted. The alliance sought to advance its policies in other campaigns, but in the face of state repression these achieved little. In 1956 one hundred and fifty-six prominent figures in the alliance were arrested and subsequently charged with treason. Opposition to the Congress Alliance strengthened the black nationalists in the ANC, who broke away in 1958 and the following year formed the Pan Africanist Congress.

Conservative Party (CP)

In the late 1970s the far right-wing of the National Party (NP) became increasingly dissatisfied with the ideas of power sharing promoted by P W Botha, who told his supporters they must 'adapt or die'. In 1982 the break came when Dr Andries Treurnicht, then the Transvaal leader of the NP, refused to support a motion of confidence in the Prime Minister. He was expelled from the NP and formed the CP. In the 1987 general election the CP, with support drawn from the rural constituencies of the Orange Free State and Transvaal, emerged with twenty-two seats and became the official opposition. In 1989 it increased its representation to thirty-nine seats, representing just over 30 per cent of the total number of votes cast, and breaking the traditional hold of the NP on the Afrikaner. After the formation of the CP Treurnicht consistently criticised the government for failing to represent any longer the true interests of the Afrikaner people, though he also sought support among right-wing English-speakers. The CP was a notable absentee from Codesa, which it called 'a recipe for conflict, bloodshed and domination through numbers', but it participated in the multi-party forum in 1993.

Constitutional Change

The constitution of the new Union of South Africa in 1910 was embodied in an Act of the British Parliament, the South Africa Act of 1909. This provided for a unitary, highly-centralised, Westminster-type political system. A central Parliament comprised a House of Assembly, initially consisting of 121 members — all white by law — directly elected by the voters of the Union, and a Senate of forty, partly indirectly elected and partly appointed. The leader of the majority party in the House of Assembly became Prime Minister and appointed a cabinet. A Governor-General, representing and appointed by the British monarch, was the formal head of the executive. The constitution could be altered by a simple majority, except for the entrenched clauses protecting the voting rights of coloureds and blacks in the Cape, and defining the equal status of the English and Dutch languages. The entrenched clauses could only be amended by a two-thirds majority of both Houses of Parliament in a joint sitting. Elected provincial councils had limited powers only.

Legislation introduced in 1951 to abolish the coloured franchise marked the beginning of a serious constitutional crisis. After the government had enlarged the Senate, the coloured franchise was eliminated by a two-thirds majority at a joint sitting of both Houses in 1956.

On 31 May 1961 the Union of South Africa became a Republic outside the Commonwealth. The constitution remained basically the same, except that the Governor-General was replaced by a State President elected by the legislature. In September 1984 a new constitution came into force which provided for three legislative chambers: a white House of Assembly, a coloured House of Representatives, and an Indian House of Delegates elected on separate voters' rolls. The cabinet and ministers' councils were chosen by the State President. The constitution greatly extended the powers of the State President, entrenched apartheid and ensured white domination. The African population, then over 75 per cent of the whole, had no say in the new dispensation, and the introduction of the constitution sparked off a major insurrection, in the course of which the government began to speak of further constitutional change. Negotiations for a new constitution became government policy in early 1990, and steps were then taken to create a climate for negotiation on such a new constitution.

Cosatu (Congress of South African Trade Unions)

The largest and strongest trade union federation in South Africa, with more than one million members. Cosatu was established in 1985, after four years of negotiations, to fight apartheid and capitalism. It refused to accept that it should restrict its activities to trade union rather than political issues, and strongly supported the sanctions and disinvestment campaign against South Africa. In 1990 Cosatu was formally included as the trade union arm of the African National Congress/ South African Communist Party alliance, but remained a separate organisation and pursued independent tactics.

Elijah Barayi, President of Cosatu, is hoisted aloft at the Cape launch of that organisation in 1986
(Mayibuye Centre)

Cradock, Sir John Francis
DUBLIN, IRELAND, 1762 — GRIMSTON, IRELAND, 1839

Soldier, governor. After a successful career in the army, during which time he served in Ireland, Cradock was appointed Governor of the Cape Colony. He used the British army and conscripted local burghers to drive the Xhosa over the Fish River in 1811–1812; he ordered the circuit court to investigate allegations of settler ill-treatment of the Khoikhoi people (1812–1813); he replaced the loan farm with a perpetual quitrent system, and sought to ensure that farm size was limited and that farms were surveyed; he created new magisterial districts; and he promoted education for white children in the colony.

Sir John Francis Cradock, Governor of the Cape Colony from 1811 to 1814
(Cape Archives AG 5813)

Creswell, Frederic Hugh Page
GIBRALTAR, 1866 — KUILSRIVIER, 1948

Mining engineer, labour leader and cabinet minister. A champion of the interests of white labour, Creswell became leader of the South African Labour Party (1910) and was from 1910 a Member of Parliament. He was appointed by Hertzog Minister of Labour and Defence in the Pact Government of 1924. Differences within the Labour Party led to his ousting as leader in 1928, but he remained a member of the cabinet until 1933.

F H P Creswell, founding member of the South African Labour Party
(Cape Archives AG 13921)

Cronjé, Pieter Arnoldus (Piet)
COLESBERG, 1836 — VENTERSDORP, 1911

Boer general. Cronjé played an active part in the attempts by Transvaal Boers to gain their independence from the British in 1880–1881. Then in January 1896 he and a commando of Boers forced Jameson and his invaders to surrender. In the South African War (1899–1902) he was sent from Mafeking, where he was besieging Baden-

Portrait of General Piet Cronjé by Willy Martens, 1904
(National Cultural History Museum)

The Crossroads squatter camp on the Cape Flats
(Mayibuye Centre)

Powell, to reinforce the Transvaal commandos. With De La Rey he set a trap for the British at Magersfontein by digging a trench line at the base of the kopies, and on 11 December 1899 almost 1 000 British lives were lost to the 255 lost on the Boer side. After the relief of Kimberley, Roberts, with his mounted troops, caught up with Cronjé at Paardeberg where more British troops were killed than at Magersfontein. In February 1900, with 4 000 men, women, children and servants, Cronjé surrendered. His surrender was a severe blow to Boer morale and its effects reverberated through to the end of the war.

Crossroads

A squatter camp on the Cape Flats, close to Cape Town's main airport, which grew up in the mid-1970s. Government attempts to destroy Crossroads by bulldozing squatters' shacks failed, as the people refused to move elsewhere. Their resistance became international news, and eventually the minister responsible agreed to settle permanently those with residential rights at New Crossroads. In the 1980s fighting erupted over control of Crossroads, ending with Ngxobongwana and his supporters brutally establishing complete hegemony.

Cuito Cuanavale, Battle of (1987–1988)

The battle of Cuito Cuanavale followed an attack by Angolan government forces on the forces of the Unita rebel movement, which Unita repulsed with the aid of South African troops. The Angolan government troops retreated to the strategic town of Cuito Cuanavale, where they were reinforced by Cuban forces. Battles continued until March 1988, but the town did not fall, and eventually the 3 000 South African troops withdrew to Namibia. Many saw this as a defeat for the South African forces and an important reason why the South African government agreed to withdraw from both Angola and Namibia.

D

Da Gama, Vasco
PORTUGAL *c.* 1460/69 — INDIA, 1524

Indian Viceroy and explorer. Under the Patronage of Manuel I of Portugal, he followed the route of Bartolomeu Dias around the southern coast of Africa. His ships rounded the Cape of Good Hope on 22 November 1497. He stopped and traded at Mossel Bay, where a stone cross *(padrão)* was erected. A skirmish developed with the Khoi over a misunderstanding concerning permission to take water, and the Khoi fled after having been fired upon. The Infante River — the point at which Dias had turned back — was passed in December 1497, and the Pondoland coast which was sighted a week later was given the name Natal. Another *padrão* was erected, probably at the mouth of the Quelimane River, before Da Gama continued to India.

Portrait of Vasco da Gama by Charles Gow, *c.* 1840. Following the route of Bartolomeu Dias, his ships rounded the Cape of Good Hope on 22 November 1497
(William Fehr Collection)

Dart, Raymond Arthur
BRISBANE, AUSTRALIA, 1893–1988

Discoverer of the Taung child. Professor of anatomy at the University of the Witwatersrand in the early 1920s, Dart examined a skull found at a lime quarry near Taung and concluded that the hole in the skull was made by a sharp, possibly man-made instrument. Later, in the same quarry, another skull was found, which in 1925 earned Dart world renown. He named it *Australopithecus africanus*, and it became known as the 'Taung child'. The endocranial cast revealed hominid features, despite the small brain size. Dart suggested the Taung child should be considered as an intermediate primate. Later, after other specimens had been found in the Transvaal, it became clear that *Australopithecus* was indeed a type of hominid. Dart had in fact found the skull of a member of the family of early man, confirming Darwin's prediction that the African continent was in all likelihood the cradle of the human race.

Professor Raymond Dart, discoverer of the Taung child
(Africana Museum)

Day of the Covenant

Prior to the battle of Blood River (16 December 1838), the Voortrekker leaders Andries Pretorius and Sarel Cilliers made a covenant to the effect that if God granted

The Day of the Covenant celebrates the Voortrekker victory over the Zulu in the Battle of Blood River (Africana Museum)

them victory over the Zulu, they would build a church and observe the day as a sabbath and a day of thanksgiving. But 16 December was given significance only when attempts were made to mobilise Afrikaners for the nationalist cause. By the 1930s it had become the high point of the 'civil religion' of the Afrikaners, a day of great emotional significance and the central day on which the *volk* were mobilised to the nationalist cause. Oddly, however, the National Party continued to call the public holiday on 16 December Dingane's Day for decades until it was renamed Day of the Covenant, and more recently, the Day of the Vow.

De Beers Consolidated Mines, Limited

The world's largest producer and distributor of diamonds. It was named after Nicholaas de Beer, owner of the farm near present-day Kimberley on which diamonds were first discovered. In 1873 Cecil Rhodes bought a claim to the De Beers mine, and later formed a company named after that mine. In 1888 he formed De Beers Consolidated Mines, and by 1891, after buying out rival mining companies, he had gained effective control of the industry. Ernest Oppenheimer, founder of the Anglo American Corporation, purchased a controlling interest in De Beers in the 1920s.

Diamond mining in Kimberley, *c.* 1875, on what was originally the farm of Nicholaas De Beer (South African Library)

Defiance Campaign (1952)

A civil disobedience campaign which was launched by the African National Congress (ANC) and the South African Indian Congress (SAIC) in June 1952. It was hoped to bring about changes in government policy relating to pass laws, livestock limitation, Bantu authorities, Group Areas, separate representation of voters and the suppression of communism. Mainly in the Transvaal and the Cape, large numbers of volunteers deliberately courted arrest by disobeying minor regulations, hoping that their actions would succeed in disorganising the state by filling the prisons and courts to capacity. By the time the campaign had ground to a halt in November, 8 326 people had been arrested and in nearly all cases convicted of an offence. Harsh punishment was introduced for such defiance, and the Public Safety Bill and the Criminal Law Amendment Bill effectively brought an end to the campaign. Its main achievement lay in gaining widespread popular support for the ANC, as a result of which it could claim that its membership had risen to 100 000.

De Klerk, Frederik Willem

JOHANNESBURG, 1936 —

Politician and State President of South Africa from 1989. Born into a political family in the Transvaal, De Klerk received an early training in politics through his membership of the Jeugbond (youth league of the National Party). After graduating from Potchefstroom University, he practised as an attorney in Vereeniging from 1961 until entering Parliament in 1972. He became a cabinet minister in 1978 and leader of the Transvaal National Party (NP) in 1982. He succeeded P W Botha as leader of the NP in 1989 and as State President six months later. Formerly considered a conservative, De Klerk on coming to power quickly aligned himself with those attempting to reform

Far left:
F W de Klerk. His reform initiatives put the country onto a new political path
(South African Communication Service)

Above:
Launch of the Defiance Campaign on Freedom Square, Fordsburg, 26 June 1952
(Mayibuye Centre)

Above left:
'The Delagoa Bay duck hunt'. Ownership of the Bay was contested by the Portuguese, the Dutch, the British and the Boers of the Transvaal
(Transvaal Archives TAB 22808)

the country's apartheid system. His decision to release Nelson Mandela and other African National Congress (ANC) leaders from jail, his unbanning of the ANC, Pan Africanist Congress and South African Communist Party, and his opening of negotiations with blacks on the future of South Africa, put the country onto a new political path.

Delagoa Bay

Close to the north-eastern border of South Africa in Mozambique, Delagoa Bay is the best natural harbour on the southeast coast of Africa. In the late eighteenth and early nineteenth centuries, the port served as an outlet for ivory and slaves exported from areas now in South Africa. Ownership of the bay, contested by the Portuguese, Dutch, English and eventually also the Boers of the Transvaal, was in 1875, as a result of international arbitration, awarded to the Portuguese, who had traded with African chiefdoms living in the vicinity from the early sixteenth century.

After the discovery of gold, Kruger built a railway line to the port to avoid having to use lines under Cape or Natal control, and the port became an important entry-point to the Rand. Large numbers of blacks from the Delagoa Bay hinterland entered South Africa to work on the diamond fields and then on the gold mines. Before the independence of Mozambique in 1975, many white South Africans holidayed in the bay at Lourenço Marques, now Maputo, but after independence most contact between South Africa and the bay was broken.

De la Rey, Jacobus Hercules
ORANGE RIVER SOVEREIGNTY, 1847 — JOHANNESBURG, 1914

Boer general and politician. De la Rey achieved fame in the South African War as a general who displayed exceptional military acumen. He was elected to the Transvaal Parliament as a member of Het Volk (1907), was a Transvaal delegate to the National Convention (1908), and then a Union senator (1910–1914). With the outbreak of the First World War, he was not prepared to support Louis Botha's policy, and planned an uprising in an attempt to restore republican independence. En route to Potchefstroom to start the rebellion, he was shot dead by a police patrol.

General De la Rey, whose military acumen won him honour during the South African War
(Transvaal Archives TAB 5984)

Delville Wood, Battle of (1916)

During the First World War a South African brigade landed in France as

After the Battle of Delville Wood, not a leaf or twig remained on any of the trees which had been stripped bare by the heat of canon fire
(Rapport Library)

part of the Imperial Army and became involved in fierce fighting during the Somme offensive of 1916. At the Battle of Delville Wood (15–20 July) South African troops won great military distinction by taking and then holding a stretch of forest on an exposed salient of the British line. Of the 3 433 men in the brigade, only 750 survived the battle.

Democratic Party (DP)

Public pressure for the creation of a unified parliamentary party to the left of the government led to talks between the Progressive Federal Party (PFP), the National Democratic Movement (NDM) and the Independent Party (IP), and the subsequent formation of the DP in April 1989. Initially Dennis Worrall, who had resigned as ambassador in London to oppose his erstwhile National Party (NP) colleagues as leader of the IP, Wynand Malan, who had left the NP caucus on the issue of reform and established the NDM, and Zach de Beer, leader of the PFP, were joint leaders of the new party. In the 1989 general election the DP increased the number of its seats from twenty to thirty-three, and in 1990 De Beer was elected the party's sole leader. It played an important mediating role at Codesa. A liberal democratic party, it saw itself as occupying the middle ground between the NP and the ANC, and as the custodian of liberal democratic principles.

In 1990 Zach de Beer was elected sole leader of the Democratic Party
(Rapport Library)

Demography

In 1991 the population of South Africa, including the Bantustans, was 38,5 million. Africans comprised 76 per cent (29 million) of the total, Asians 3 per cent (992 600), coloureds 9 per cent (3,2 million) and whites 13 per cent (5 million). Eighty-nine per cent of Asians, coloureds and whites were urbanised, as opposed to 50 per cent of Africans. More than half of the African population was under the age of nineteen years. The white population had dropped from 21,9 per cent of the total in 1921 to 13 per cent in 1991, while the African population had risen from 66 per cent of the total in 1911 to 76 per cent in 1991.

Depression

The economy of the Cape during the seventeenth and eighteenth centuries suffered periodic crises of overproduction and years of crop failure and drought. The increased economic activity in the nineteenth century which resulted from British occupation was punctuated by depressions of varying intensity, sometimes the result of depression in England, sometimes of drought in the colony. The failure of the wheat crop in 1821 led to a depression lasting five years, and a slump in the price of wool, the major export, after the end of the American Civil War, resulted in a depression in the 1860s.

The diamond discoveries of the late 1860s transformed the country's economy, but the 'diamond crisis' of 1881 was followed by a general depression in South Africa from 1882–1886, the most severe of the century, which ended only with the gold discoveries on the Witwatersrand. The South African War (1899–1902) was followed by a short boom, after which recession set in from 1903–1909, as a result of the disruption of gold mining and the destruction of farming areas during the war.

'General view of the Glencairn Gold Mine, Johannesburg 1896', by Melton Prior. The general depression from 1882 to 1886 ended with the gold discoveries on the Witwatersrand
(© The Brenthurst Press)

The Great Depression of 1929–1933 severely affected both South Africa's major economic sectors, agriculture and gold mining. The government's determination not to follow Britain in abandoning the gold standard intensified the impact of the depression by encouraging the outflow of capital and accentuating the decline of exports. Finally in 1932 South Africa left the gold standard, as a result of which the price of gold jumped immediately and the downward trend in the economy was reversed. A long period of economic growth followed.

The Sharpeville massacre in 1960 created a loss of confidence by investors and a large outflow of capital, but that was short-lived. After the oil-price increase of 1973 the country entered another period of recession, which gained added depth from 1981 with the collapse of the gold price. Political instability and a continuing low gold price helped fuel the recession through the 1980s and early 1990s. A very severe drought in 1992, and the recession in the world economy, threatened to turn the recession into a general depression.

Destabilisation

Part of P W Botha's total strategy, South Africa used its military superiority to restrain neighbouring states from pursuing anti-apartheid policies and assisting the African National Congress (ANC). From 1981 South African commandos raided or carried out undercover operations against every one of South Africa's neighbours. The South African government also offered covert support to resistance movements in southern African states, notably Angola, Mozambique and Lesotho. It cooperated with the National Union for the Total Independence of Angola (Unita) in its civil war against the Angolan government, and provided arms and financial and technical assistance to the Mozambique National Resistance (MNR or Renamo) in Mozambique. Promises by South Africa to stop aiding these movements were not honoured. According to a British Commonwealth committee report, South Africa's destabilising tactics led to the deaths of one million people between 1980 and 1989, made a further three million homeless, and caused twenty billion pounds worth of damage to the economies of neighbouring states.

Detention without Trial

Following the Sharpeville crisis and the formation of Umkhonto we Sizwe and Poqo, B J Vorster, who was appointed Minister of Justice in 1962, introduced draconian security legislation which included detention without trial. Step by step police officers were empowered to detain persons in solitary confinement, without charging them, initially for 12 days (1962), then 90 days (1963), then 180 days (1965), then for an unlimited period if authorised by a judge (1966), and eventually for an unlimited period even without such authorisation (1976). Thousands of people were detained, without anyone knowing where they were or why they had been detained. Allegations of torture were commonly made, and deaths in detention occurred regularly (seventy-two people died in detention between 1963 and 1990). In 1991 the consolidated act (the Internal Security Act) providing for indefinite detention without trial on the authority of the police was amended. Detention for a period of more than ten days then required authorisation by a judge.

De Wet, Christiaan Rudolph

LEEUWKOP, 1854 — KLIPFONTEIN, 1922

Volksraad member, Boer general, cabinet minister, rebel leader. A commandant in the Anglo-Transvaal War (1880–1881), De Wet was a protagonist of closer union between the Transvaal and Orange Free State Republics. He became a Boer Commander-in-Chief of the western frontier of the Free State in the South African War (1899–1902) and his guerrilla tactics were so costly to the British army that several 'De Wet hunts' were launched in an effort to capture him (1900–1902). As Acting President, he was a reluctant signatory of the Treaty of Vereeniging, which brought the war to an end (1902). He was elected Member of Parliament when the Orange River Colony became self-governing (1907), and was a delegate to the National Convention. He helped Hertzog form the National Party in 1914. He led the rebellion against Botha's policy to invade German South West Africa, and was sentenced for his complicity, but was released in the amnesty of 1915.

Diamonds

Alluvial diamonds were discovered near the confluence of the Orange and Vaal Rivers in 1867. Further discoveries in 1870, in what was later to become Kimberley, revealed diamondiferous pipes that extended below the earth's surface and contained the world's greatest diamond deposits. By 1872, 50 000 people had converged on the area. Individual diggers acquired small claims and worked the surface with pick and shovel, helped by three or four assistants. Most of the diggers were white, their assistants black. As advanced technology took over, small properties and individual diggers were superseded by larger holdings and highly capitalised organisations, until by the mid-1880s only three mining companies were left, and by the end of the decade De Beers Consolidated, owned by Cecil Rhodes, had established a monopoly over the diamond fields.

The diamond discoveries led to conflicting land claims between the Orange Free State, the Transvaal, and the Griqua chief, Nicholas Waterboer. In 1871 the fields were awarded to Waterboer and were included in the new Crown Colony of Griqualand West proclaimed by Sir Henry Barkly, Governor of the Cape.

Patterns of labour begun on the farms

'General De Wet breaking though', by Fütz Neum. His guerrilla tactics were so costly to the British army that several 'De Wet hunts' were launched in an effort to capture him (National Cultural History Museum)

were consolidated at Kimberley, South Africa's first industrial community. The permanent and increasingly professional white diggers were served by an ever-changing population of unskilled blacks, who laboured on the mines for a new rifle, often paid in lieu of wages. In 1872 an all-white diggers' committee eliminated black diggers. Blacks were liable to body searches, had to carry passes and from 1885 were housed in closed compounds. The northern Cape became a wealth generating region; colonial ports flourished with the increased trade brought by the mines, railways from the ports raced inland to Kimberley, and new markets were created for farmers. The diamond fields also unlocked capital which was available for the opening of the gold mines twenty years later.

Dias, Bartolomeu (Dias de Novaes)

PORTUGAL, *c.* 1450 — SOUTH ATLANTIC, 1500

Portuguese navigator. On his epoch-making voyage around the Cape, during which he unwittingly rounded the African continent, Dias dropped anchor in 1488 in what was to be named Mossel Bay, where in their search for fresh water, crew members clashed with the Khoikhoi herdsmen they encountered. Continuing eastwards, the caravels reached Algoa Bay before the crews, exhausted by their arduous voyage, demanded that they retrace their course and return home. On entering False Bay during the return voyage, Dias bestowed the name of *Cabo da Boa Esperança* – ironically, it was off this Cape of Good Hope that he was to die in a storm at sea on a subsequent voyage in 1500.

Dias' greatest feat was his rounding of Africa and the discovery of the sea route to the Indian Ocean. The information which he charted on the trade-wind system of the South Atlantic and the best course across it to round the continent, was subsequently used by Vasco da Gama.

Difaqane, *see* **Mfecane**

Dingane

NATAL, *c.* 1795 — SWAZILAND, 1840

Zulu king. Dingane assumed power in 1828 after murdering his half-brother, Shaka. He promised Piet Retief a large part of Natal in return for the recovery of a stolen herd of cattle. Seeing the trekkers as a threat, Dingane had Retief and his party murdered and his impis then fell on the other trekkers east of the Drakensberg (1838). The trekker deaths were avenged by Andries Pretorius at the battle of Blood River (December 1838) when 3 000 Zulu warriors were killed. Early in 1840 he was defeated by his half-brother, Mpande, and he fled to Swaziland, where he was murdered.

A nineteenth century engraving entitled 'The diamond washing'. Alluvial diamonds were discovered near the confluence of the Orange and Vaal Rivers in 1867
(The Brenthurst Library)

Dingiswayo

LOWER UMFOLOZI VALLEY, NATAL, *c.* 1770 — NONGOMA DISTRICT, NATAL, 1818

Chief of the Mthethwa. Dingiswayo initiated trade with the Portuguese at Delagoa Bay and imposed his authority on a large number of the people living between the Pongola and Tugela Rivers, absorbing them into a loose confederacy. Shaka, whom he granted refuge, became a military commander in the Mthethwa confederacy and Dingiswayo's chosen suc-

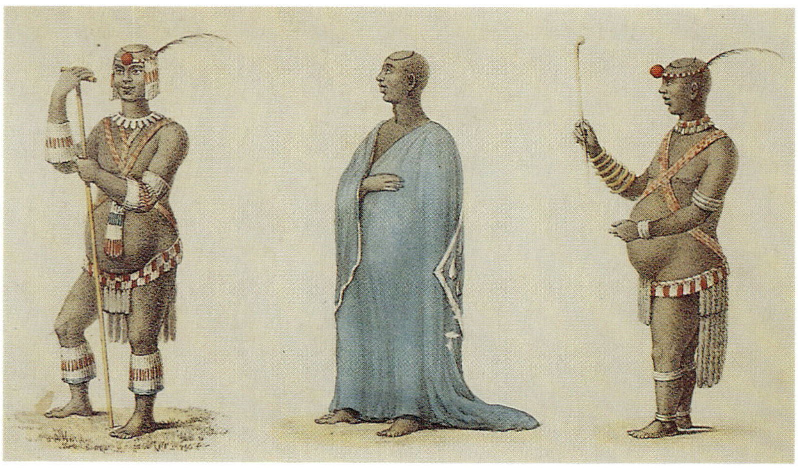

'Dingana in his ordinary and dancing dresses', an illustration from Allen Gardiner's *Narrative of a Journey to the Zoolu Country*, 1836
(Local History Museum Collection, Durban)

Dingiswayo, chief of the Mthethwa
(Africana Museum)

cessor. In 1818 Dingiswayo was captured and killed by Zwide of the Ndwandwe, his greatest enemy, and the Mthethwa were subsequently incorporated into Shaka's Zulu empire.

Dinuzulu

ZULULAND, *c.* 1870 — MIDDLEBURG, TRANSVAAL, 1913

Pretender to the Zulu throne, son and heir of Cetshwayo. Dinuzulu was fifteen years old when his father died (1884). In a bitter conflict with his father's chief rival, Zibhebhu, Dinuzulu sought aid from the Boers who, in return for land, agreed to recognise him as Zulu king.

When Britain in 1887 annexed Zululand, Dinuzulu went into rebellion, and was exiled to St Helena for ten years. On his return his attempts to win recognition as Zulu king failed and his official status remained that of a minor chief. Implicated in the Bambatha Rebellion (1906), he was found guilty of harbouring rebels and sentenced to four years imprisonment. He was released by Louis Botha in 1910 and spent the rest of his days on a government farm.

King Dinuzulu who was exiled to St Helena for ten years for his part in the rebellion against Britain's annexation of Zululand in 1887
(Africana Museum)

District Six

Part of what became popularly known in the twentieth century as Distict Six, it was the sixth district in the municipality of Cape Town. The larger District Six extended from Table Bay to the slopes of Devil's Peak, and there a vibrant, cosmopolitan community developed. Many of the properties were by the mid-twentieth century owned by whites, but the bulk of the population was coloured. The majority were poor, and the district was in part a slum, but it was perhaps the most lively part of Cape Town. In 1966 the National Party government proclaimed the area white in terms of the Group Areas Act (1950) and its coloured residents were forced to move out. The buildings they had inhabited were then demolished, ostensibly in the interests of slum clearance. Because of the protests against this forced removal, it took a long time before the ground was built on again, and only in the late 1980s and early 1990s was the large area of cleared ground enchroached on by new development.

Dithakong, Battle of (1823)

The significance of this battle lies in the fact that it prevented the disruption of the 'Time of Troubles' (Mfecane) from spreading further west into the lands of the western Sotho. There is much controversy about exactly where the tens of thousands who attacked Dithakong in June 1823 had come from. The settlement, north-east of present Kuruman, was defended by its local Tlhaping populace and an armed and mounted Griqua commando of one hundred. Griqua guns and horses prevailed, perhaps 500 of the invaders were killed and the remainder fled.

Dominion Party

Opposing the new United Party, and especially its flexibility on constitutional change, Colonel C F Stallard and a

Residents protested bitterly against the demolition of District Six, but to no avail
(Mayibuye Centre)

handful of supporters formed the Dominion Party in 1934 with the aim of preserving the Union's ties with Britain. Its main strength lay in Natal. In 1939 Stallard became a member of Smuts's war cabinet. After that its supporters moved over to the United Party, and by 1948 the party had ceased to exist.

In 1934 Colonel C F Stallard formed the Dominion Party with the aim of preserving the Union's ties with Britain
(Die Burger)

Dominion Status

Between 1917 and 1923 Smuts affirmed the powers of self-government of the dominions and their status as 'autonomous nations'. Then General Hertzog, his successor as Prime Minister, tackled the question of dominion status, asserting South Africa's right to full international sovereignty. He contributed substantially to the Balfour Declaration (1926) which recognised the autonomy of members of the Commonwealth and their equality with one another. The Status of the Union Act of 1934 finally confirmed the independent status of South Africa within the Commonwealth.

Dönges, Theophilus Ebenhaezer (Eben)

KLERKSDORP, 1898 — CAPE TOWN, 1968

An important intellectual figure in Afrikaner nationalism from the 1930s, Dönges served in Malan's cabinet from 1948, and in 1950, as Minister of the Interior, introduced the Group Areas Bill in Parliament, which enabled the government to set aside both business and residential property for certain race groups. He justified the bill on the grounds that whites had petitioned him to stop Indians and coloureds from buying residential properties in their areas for fear of property devaluation. He therefore hoped to 'remove the points of contact' between the groups. He also introduced the Separate Representation of Voters Bill into the House of Assembly in 1951, which initiated a constitutional crisis.

He succeeded Malan as Cape leader of the National Party in November 1953, but was considered too young to follow Malan as Prime Minister. Furthermore his reputation had been damaged in the crisis over the coloured franchise. After Strijdom died in office it was Verwoerd who succeeded, and Dönges had to be content with the ministry of finance in Verwoerd's cabinet.

T Eben Dönges, an important intellectual figure in Afrikaner Nationalism from the 1930s
(Africana Museum)

Drought

South Africa is particularly subject to droughts as rainfall in much of the country is sparse and unreliable. About 21 per cent of the country receives less than eight inches of rain annually; another 47 per cent is semi-arid, receiving eight to twenty-four inches annually. Droughts have varied in range and intensity; some have been so severe and widespread that famine has ensued. Rarely has the country been totally drought-free in any particular year. Until the late nineteenth century, stock farmers could escape the ravages of drought by trekking with their animals, but during the present century people who were impoverished as a result of drought increasingly left their farms and sought refuge in the cities. Legislation to assist farmers affected by drought was introduced in 1916, 1924 and 1927, and a drought commission was appointed in 1919 to report on the extent of the drought problem. The most severe droughts which are known occurred in the early 1800s (the Madlathule famine in Zululand), the early 1930s and the early 1990s, the latter affecting large areas of the eastern Cape and the northern Transvaal.

John L Dube, first President-General of the South African Native National Congress, later renamed the ANC
(Africana Museum)

Dube, John Langalibalele
INANDA, NATAL, 1871 — UMHLANGA, NATAL, 1946

Teacher, minister and politician. Dube was educated in Natal and the United States of America, where he was strongly influenced by the ideas and achievements of Booker T Washington of the Tuskegee Institute. On returning to South Africa, Dube established a school, the Ohlanga Institute (1901), and he launched Natal's first black newspaper, *Ilanga Lase Natal* (1903), which he continued to edit until 1915. He was elected first President-General of the South African Native National Congress (later the ANC) in 1912 and served in that office for five years, but was compromised by his support for segregationism. Thereafter he remained an influential, if idiosyncratic political leader in Natal, but did not play an important role at the national level.

Duncan, Sir Patrick
SCOTLAND, 1870 — PRETORIA, 1943

Politician, cabinet minister and Governor-General of the Union of South Africa. Under Sir Alfred Milner, Duncan was Colonial secretary for the Transvaal, a key position which he held from 1903 to 1907. After Union he became a member of Parliament and then a cabinet minister. He was also legal adviser on Bechuanaland to the British High Commissioner, and from 1936 the first South African to be appointed Governor-General. He supported national unity and tried to reconcile English and Afrikaner. As Governor-General, he played a crucial role in September 1939 in the events leading to South Africa's participation in the Second World War. He died in office in 1943.

Right:
Sir Patrick Duncan, Governor-General of the Union of South Africa
(South African Library)

Durban

The most important port city in South Africa situated on the Indian Ocean. White settlement on this large natural harbour began with a band of traders from the Cape Colony led by Lieutenant Francis Farewell and James King. They received a cession of land at the harbour from the Zulu ruler Shaka in 1824 and named the site Port Natal. The tiny trading post grew as more people arrived, mainly from the Cape, and in 1835 it was renamed Durban after Sir Benjamin D'Urban, then Governor of the Cape Colony.

In 1837 a large group of Voortrekkers under Piet Retief arrived, on their way to meet Dingane, Shaka's successor, and for a time Durban was part of the Trekker Republic of Natal. After Natal was annexed by Britain in 1843, large numbers of British immigrants began to arrive and the city grew in size and importance. It became

Far right:
'Birth of Natal', by R Canton Woodville. Farewell and his settler party are shown conferring with Shaka for a grant of land at Port Natal
(Local History Museum Collection, Durban)

'Durban from Currie's Residence', by Thomas Baines, 1873
(Local History Museum Collection, Durban)

Governor of the Cape Colony in 1833, Sir Benjamin D'Urban, after whom the city of Durban was named
(Transvaal Archives TAB 12910)

even more prosperous after the completion of the railway line to the Transvaal goldfields in 1895, and with the improvement of the harbour. From a commercial point of view, what mattered as much as, or even more than, inland communications was the conquest of the sandbar obstructing the mouth of the harbour, which allowed only very small vessels to enter, and then only at high tide. Work on the harbour, begun in 1849, was completed in 1904, when the first steamer entered the harbour.

In the 1980s Durban handled more cargo than any other South African port. The city had experienced a tremendous growth in manufacturing industry, was the headquarters of the country's sugar industry, and enjoyed a large tourist trade, much of it from the Witwatersrand. One of the three largest cities in the country, it was said to be the fastest growing city in the southern hemisphere, with a population of three million people; the majority Africans, the second largest group Indians, who had arrived mainly as indentured labourers for the sugar plantations from the 1860s, and thirdly the white population, which occupied all the most desirable parts of the city and dominated its government and economy.

D'Urban, Sir Benjamin

HALESWORTH, SUFFOLK, 1777 — MONTREAL, CANADA, 1849

General and colonial Administrator. D'Urban fought in the Napoleonic Wars with distinction, and after fifteen years as Governor in the West Indies, he was appointed Governor and Commander-in-Chief of the Cape Colony in 1833. He had to deal with the emancipation of the slaves (1834), the outbreak of the Sixth Frontier War (1834–1835) and the start of the Great Trek (1835–1836). His governorship ended in 1837, but he continued as Commander-in-Chief at the Cape until 1846.

Dutch East India Company

The Dutch East India Company, or the VOC (named after the initials of its Dutch title — *de Verenigde Ooste-Indische Compagnie)* was established on 20 March 1602 for the purpose of coordinating Dutch trading expeditions to the East Indies. Merchants of the United Provinces of the Netherlands convinced their government, the States General, that unless it intervened to curb the rivalry between individual companies the competition between them would destroy profits and allow foreigners to force the Dutch out of the lucrative spice trade with the East. The States General therefore presided over the drawing up of a charter which merged the various companies into one and granted the new company — the VOC — a monopoly of all Dutch trade east of the Cape of Good Hope. The VOC was to be governed by a board of seventeen directors, known as the Heren XVII (or Council of Seventeen), and under the guidance of these merchant capitalists it became the most powerful company in the world.

A large part of the Company's success was due to the fact that, from the very beginning, it represented the interests of both Dutch merchants and the Dutch government. In effect the VOC became an arm of the Dutch state, empowered by the States General to wage war and conduct diplomacy in pursuit of both mercantile and military objectives. A mixture of ruthless force, financial weight and aggressive competitiveness enabled the VOC to establish Dutch trading supremacy in the East and, by the second half of the seventeenth century, the Company wielded unprecedented political and commercial influence.

In 1652, at the height of its power, the VOC established a settlement at the halfway mark of the Cape in order to facilitate the voyages of its ships to and from the East. Although the Cape was never regarded as anything but a refreshment post by the Heren XVII it developed, in time, into an extensive colony and as such required government. Thus it was that until the British conquest in 1795 the Cape was administered by officials of a trading company.

The most obvious feature of Company rule at the Cape was that the colony was governed for the benefit of the VOC rather than for the benefit of the inhabitants. Since the primary concern of the Heren XVII was to maximise profits and reduce expenses, a self-serving style of government evolved, characterised by corruption and inefficiency amongst Company officials. Foremost amongst these officials was the Governor, supposedly responsible to the Heren XVII but able to exercise almost unlimited local power. He was assisted in his legislative functions by seven other Company appointees who together constituted the

Batavia, capital of the Dutch Colonies in the East Indies
(Africana Museum)

Fleet of Dutch Indiamen at anchor in Table Bay, *c.* 1760
(Africana Museum)

Seal of the Dutch East India Company, 1775
(Cape Archives AG 1540)

Council of Policy. The Governor was also president of the Court of Justice, a judicial body which consisted of six appointed Company officials and six appointed free burghers. These institutions were both repressive and unrepresentative, whilst the society over which the Company presided was hierarchical and marked by extreme inequalities.

At the bottom of the rung were the slaves, convicts and exiles, who entered the Cape under the VOC's auspices. They were kept in their place by brutal punishments and harsh restrictions. Only slightly more fortunate were the many sailors and soldiers in Company employment at the Cape who suffered from a crippling combination of low wages and rigorous discipline. Increasing numbers of Khoisan fell under the jurisdiction of Company law as the colony's borders expanded, but it would be wrong to suppose that this afforded them much protection. The Company was not strong enough to prevent the colonists from subjecting the indigenous people of the Cape interior to their will and exploiting their land, labour and livestock. Indeed, it usually assisted colonial commandos in crushing Khoisan resistance without, however, being able to guarantee the security of the colony's frontiers.

The free burghers — those who left the service of the Company to settle at the Cape or those who had immigrated of their own accord — were better off than other groups but were particularly unhappy about the economic restrictions which the Company had erected to protect its own interests. The Company, for instance, reserved for itself the right to purchase the produce of Cape farms and to set the prices it would pay. It also had a monopoly over the sale and importation of goods from elsewhere and over shipping. In practice these restrictions were not as complete as might be supposed, for bribery and corruption created many loopholes in the system. VOC control over the import and export market did, however, hamper economic development in the colony. Burghers complained about the low prices offered for their produce and the restricted market. Despite this, there was continuous growth in the production

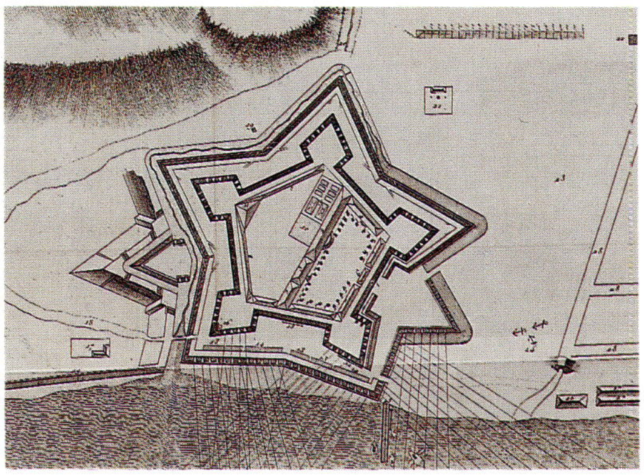

Plan of the Castle of Good Hope, 1795
(The Brenthurst Library)

One of the Company farms at the Cape *c.* 1795. The VOC reserved for itself the right to purchase the produce of the Cape farms and to set the price it would pay
(Africana Museum)

of wheat, wine and meat thanks to the demographic expansion of the colony and hence an increase in the number of local consumers.

A frequent complaint was that Company officials used unfair and illegal means to feather their own nests at the expense of the colonists. As early as 1705, with free burgher opposition to Governor W A van der Stel, it could be seen that local producers resented both Company corruption and competition. Regulations which forbade officials from simultaneously being producers did not prevent strategically placed Company servants from abusing the system. Nor did they prevent well-connected free burghers from exploiting their contacts with the government at the expense of poorer colonists. The Barbier Rebellion of 1738 demonstrated the type of resentment felt by frontier farmers against perceived inequalities and, as the colony expanded, such discontent grew. The clearest expression of burgher grievances came in 1779 and 1782 with petitions from the so-called Cape Patriots. Their requests were primarily for economic reforms although they also sought greater political influence in order to safeguard their interests.

By this date, however, the Company as a whole was in a process of irreversible decline. The VOC had been losing ground to its two greatest trading rivals, Britain and France, throughout the eighteenth century. The unwise intervention of the Netherlands against Britain during the American War of Independence led to the Fourth Anglo-Dutch War (1780–1784) and re-

Dutch East India Company shipyard, Amsterdam
(Africana Museum)

sulted in great losses for the VOC — ten million guilders in shipping alone. In 1783 the Company was obliged to ask the States General for a massive loan in order to ensure its survival. This loan was conditional on the Company putting its house in order but it was only in 1792 that circumstances in Holland permitted the dispatch of a Commission of Enquiry into the affairs of the VOC in the East. This Commission stopped at the Cape in order to investigate the sorry state of the colony. So abuse-ridden was the Cape that the Commissioners were detained for fifteeen months, during which time they amassed a welter of depressing evidence and proposed a handful of hopeless reforms. The Commission was still busy with its work in Batavia when, in 1795, the revolutionary events in the Netherlands transformed the Company itself.

In March 1796 the new Dutch government, the Batavian Republic, took the VOC under direct state control. A widespread European war was raging and the Cape had fallen to British forces in 1795. Company debts now amounted to 112 million guilders and its ships were being swept from the seas by the Royal Navy. In these circumstances there was little the government could do to rescue the Company. Thus it was that when the VOC's charter came up for renewal in 1804 it was simply allowed to lapse. The most powerful company in the world was no more.

(N G Penn)

Dutch-Khoi Wars (1659–1660 and 1673–1677)

These wars arose as a result of land disputes between the Khoikhoi and the Dutch settlers. The Peninsular Khoikhoi were the first to find their grazing land under pressure. Doman, who had been trained as an interpreter by the Dutch, turned rebel and with his followers attacked the free burghers in the vicinity of the Fort in 1659. The Dutch retaliated in a war which lasted for one year. Peace was eventually negotiated (April 1860) but the Khoi had failed in their attempt to force the Dutch to leave the Cape.

The Dutch gradually moved further inland to the Hottentots Holland, and in 1673 attempted to subjugate the Cochoqua leader, Gonnema. He and his followers escaped to the mountains but lost almost 900 sheep and 800 cattle to their attackers. Gonnema and the Cochoqua were not supported by neighbouring Khoikhoi groups who sided with the Dutch. They were attacked again in 1674 and lost a large number of cattle and sheep as well as weapons. Finally in 1677 Gonnema submitted to the Dutch Governor and agreed to pay a tribute in cattle every year. After that, an increasing number of white settlers encroached on Khoikhoi pastures.

Dutch Language

The Dutch of seventeenth century Holland was introduced to the Cape by the first settlers, and was the official language of the Cape until 1822, when it was replaced by English. After the second British occupation of the Cape (1806) Dutch was gradually superseded by English in government, schools and the law courts, and English became the sole language of the legislature. The Trekker Republics of the Orange Free State and the Transvaal had Dutch as their official language. The 1870s saw a revival of the Dutch language with 'Onze Jan' Hofmeyr (1845–1909) campaigning for equal rights for Dutch and English. On his initiative the use of Dutch in Parliament was allowed (1882) and Dutch became the medium of instruction in certain schools. Dutch acquired full equality with English in the Union established in 1910, being recognised as an official language, and the relevant clause in the constitution (the South Africa Act of 1909) was entrenched, that is it could only be amended after a special procedure. In 1925, the meaning of 'Dutch' in the constitution was extended to include Afrikaans, which then replaced Dutch as the second official language.

Dutch Reformed Churches

The Reformed Church was brought to the Cape from Holland by the first Dutch settlers and was the official church in the Cape Colony under the Dutch East India Company. The church at the Cape was subordinate to the Company and the mother church in Holland until Britain's occupation of the Cape, after which all links with Amsterdam were severed. In 1843 the Dutch Reformed Church was given virtual self-government by the state, and adopted the official name of the Nederduitse Gereformeerde Kerke (NGK). NGK congregations were established by the Voortrekkers in Natal, the Orange Free State and Transvaal. In the latter, schism and conflict led to the formation of two separate Dutch Reformed Churches, the Nederduitsch Hervormde Kerk and the Gereformeerde (Dopper) Kerk. Today more than half the white population are members of one or other of these Dutch Reformed churches. In 1857 the Cape NGK authorised the separation of coloured from white congregations, which led to the creation of separate mission churches for col-

De Groote Kerk, Church Square Cape Town, 1854, by Thomas Bowler
(Cape Archives M 952)

Totius, one of the best-known Afrikaans poets, whose name will always be associated with the Afrikaans translation of the Bible
(Transvaal Archives TAB 34443)

S J du Toit, an ardent champion of the Afrikaans language, who founded Die Genootskap van Regte Afrikaners
(Transvaal Archives TAB 34507)

oureds, Africans and Indians. Attempts were made in the 1980s to unite the mission churches and the main NGK, but they were not successful.

Du Toit, Jacob Daniel (Totius)

PAARL, 1877 — PRETORIA, 1953

Theologian and one of the best-known Afrikaans poets, more commonly known by his *nom de plume*, Totius. During the South African War he joined the Boer forces as a military chaplain and took part in the battle of Magersfontein (11 December 1899). After furthering his studies abroad, he was inducted as minister of the Potchefstroom congregation (which included most of the Western Transvaal) in 1903. He made a significant contribution to the clerical life of the Gereformeerde Kerk and enjoyed great popularity as a preacher, and in 1910 became Professor of the Theological school in Potchefstroom. Totius played an important role in the development of Afrikaans poetry and produced moving, lyrical work. His name will always be associated with the versification of the Psalms in Afrikaans and with the Afrikaans translation of the Bible.

Du Toit, Stephanus Jacobus

DAL JOSAFAT, NEAR PAARL, 1847 — DAL JOSAFAT, 1911

Protagonist of Afrikaans, Dutch Reformed Church minister, author. Du Toit was the most ardent early champion of Afrikaans as a language in its own right. He founded Die Genootskap van Regte Afrikaners (1875), the aim of which was 'to champion our language, our nation and our country'. He established and edited the first newspaper published in Afrikaans, *Die Afrikaanse Patriot* (1876), and he wrote the first Afrikaans grammar (1876) and history (1877). In 1879 he founded the Afrikaner Bond, the first organised party in the Cape Parliament. From 1882 to 1888 he was superintendent of education in the Transvaal Republic.

E

Eastern Cape Separatism

From the 1820s colonists in the eastern Cape felt that they were dominated and discriminated against by the west, and whenever their frustration reached a sufficient pitch, the cry for separatism was raised. This meant a great variety of things. To some few it meant the establishment of a completely separate colony or government for the eastern districts of the colony; to others it signified the removal of the seat of government to the eastern districts where it could be directly influenced by them; and to yet others it represented the beginning of a federal system within the colony. A powerful Separation League grew up in Port Elizabeth and Grahamstown in 1860 and used the easterners' indignation over seemingly unfair allocation of public funds to press for total political separation of east and west. The movement lost much of its drive with the new prosperity of the diamond era in the early 1870s which saw increasing commercial competition between towns in the eastern Cape.

Economic Development

The concept of an economy is essentially modern. Its modern meaning has developed in the twentieth century, with the idea of sectors, so that today it is common to talk about the primary sector, the secondary sector and the tertiary sector. The primary sector is concerned with the production of natural things, that is things which are not manufactured. Included in this sector are agriculture, mining, forestry and fishing. In the secondary sector is manufacturing and in the tertiary sector all the services that contribute to the production of goods by the primary or secondary sectors.

The total value of everything that is produced, both goods and services, makes up the Gross National Product, or GNP. The GNP has the same value as the Gross National Income. The Gross Domestic Product or GDP is the value of GNP minus payments to foreigners.

While economic activities existed long before the arrival of the Europeans, it would be untrue to talk of a South African economy in the sixteenth century or earlier. In fact it is not really accurate to talk of a South African economy before 1910, when the union of the four provinces was established. The discovery of gold in the Transvaal had dragged the South African Republic, as the Transvaal was then called, into the era of modern capitalism. The development of the Kimberley diamond fields had had a similar effect upon the Orange Free State and the northern Cape province.

In the distant past when only the San lived in what is today South Africa, there was no economic development of any recognisable kind. Amongst these hunter-

'Graham's Town 1833, the metropolis of the Eastern Division of the Cape of Good Hope'. Grahamstown saw the growth of a powerful separation league in 1860 (Africana Museum)

Sorting fish, the Bluff, Durban, at the turn of the century. Fishing is part of the primary sector of the economy
(Local History Museum Collection, Durban)

gatherers not even agriculture was developed and there were certainly no sectors to measure. The unending rhythm of nature dominated the life of early man. Change began with the Khoikhoi, who introduced animal husbandry and maintained a pastoral, nomadic way of life, until Bantu-speaking peoples began to drive them further south and west.

The Bantu speakers brought with them new developments in what we call the primary sector. They introduced agriculture of a shifting variety as, when the soil was exhausted, they abandoned it and moved on. They also introduced mining, both for iron and for copper. The former was important for cooking and for war purposes; the latter was for decoration. Since neither spears nor bracelets are made out of iron ore or copper ore, these developments required metal smelting and working up into useful articles. In this way developments in the secondary sector entered South Africa. They were accompanied by leather working and wood carving, but a tertiary sector in the modern sense did not exist; surpluses were not built up and stored and life remained precarious, with both man and beast always at the mercy of the elements in a land prone to regular droughts.

The coming of the Europeans changed all this. They were representatives of a highly developed capitalist society, which was in the throes of raising productivity throughout all sectors of the economy. The Netherlands boasted the world's most advanced economy in the seventeenth century, and with the arrival of the Dutch in the Cape came major advances in the tertiary sector, in commerce, in banking, in transport, in religion and in the provision of government services of all kinds. Modern money and methods of accounting entered South Africa, for the Dutch East India Company was the grandest capitalist institution in the world in the middle of the seventeenth century.

Yet the changes that occurred in the seventeenth and eighteenth centuries were limited. The Dutch East India Company did not permit much immigration and tried to suppress private trade. Modern agricultural methods were not introduced. Nor was modern manufacturing, as the servants of the Company maintained a semi-subsistent style of life. Their *raison d'être*

'Korah Hottentots preparing to remove', by Samuel Daniell. The Khoikhoi introduced animal husbandry and maintained a pastoral, nomadic way of life
(Africana Museum)

Above left:
Scene on a Boland farm in the early 1700s entitled, 'The method Cape Europeans take to destroy moles'. Modern agricultural practices had not been introduced at the time
(National Cultural History Museum)

Above:
Sale of sugar at the Durban market. Sugar-cane provided Natal with a valuable cash crop
(Cape Archives E 2142)

was to supply provisions for Dutch ships on the way home from the East. This was only partially modified by the introduction of viticulture and wine making. Meanwhile, outside the western Cape the old order continued, based on a pastoral, semi-nomadic existence.

Modern development of a far-reaching kind began with the first British occupation of the Cape in 1795 and was only temporarily interrupted by the return of the Cape to the Netherlands at the Treaty of Amiens. Great Britain, in the full vigour of the industrial revolution, controlled the world's oceans with her navy and dominated the trans-oceanic commerce of the world. All at once the Cape was brought into an expanding international economy. Commerce was freed from the suffocating grip of the Dutch East India Company and a new flow of immigrants entered the country who were to effect far-reaching changes upon agriculture, commerce, banking, transport and government services. These changes culminated, in the second half of the nineteenth century, in a mining bonanza, first with diamonds and then with gold.

In the nineteenth century a modern economy took shape. The primary sector led the way with the expansion of sheep farming that followed the arrival of the 1820 settlers and the British occupation of the eastern Cape. This development of commercial farming was the driving force behind the growth of Port Elizabeth. For half a century the eastern Cape provided the dynamism behind the growth of a modern economy. Had agriculture continued to be the engine of growth, the eastern Cape would have continued to lead the way; but the discovery of diamonds in Kimberley changed the situation and pulled the economic centre of gravity back to the western Cape and Cape Town.

About the same time that diamonds were accelerating the pace of economic development, sugar-cane growing was being introduced into Natal, thereby providing that colony with a valuable cash crop. The two Afrikaner Republics remained locked into a semi-subsistence economy. The discovery of gold on the Witwatersrand changed the situation abruptly. Growing urban markets placed pressure on the agricultural sector to provide fresh fruit and vegetables, dairy produce and meat, throughout the territories that were to form the Union in 1910.

Mining did not make great strides until the discovery of diamonds at Kimberley, but the profits flowing from the development of the diamond fields helped to pay for the first important railways in the Cape and provided the capital accumulations that financed the early development of the gold mines. Both Cecil Rhodes and Barney Barnato financed their moves into gold mining with the profits made in the Kimberley diamond fields. The exploitation of the country's coal reserves followed hard upon the heels of the railways, so that, by the time of Union, South Africa had a well organised and highly profitable mineral extraction industry.

The growth of a modern secondary sector occurred much more slowly. Before the opening up of the gold fields, it was virtually non-existent in the Transvaal and the Orange Free State and confined to the processing of a few agricultural products in the two British colonies. Gold mining, when it became deep level, led to growing demands for electricity and the products of mechanical engineering; but in 1910 South Africa relied on imports for both consumer and producer goods.

The tertiary sector had made greater progress than the secondary sector. Trading, both retail and wholesale, increased steadily throughout the nineteenth century

Men at work on the property of the Republic Gold Mining Company in Barberton. The gold mining industry led to significant growth in the secondary sector of the economy
(National Cultural History Museum)

The morning market, Johannesburg Market Square *c.* 1895. Once Johannesburg had begun to develop, commercial, financial and transport services progressed rapidly
(National Cultural History Museum)

and was accompanied by the creation of a banking system. Long distance transport was revolutionised with the opening of the Suez Canal and the arrival of the steam ship, while from the 1870s onwards inland transport began to be transformed by the development of railways to the diamond fields from three different ports, Cape Town, Port Elizabeth and East London. This development of the tertiary sector's commercial services was paralleled by the growth of governmental services. The British colonies benefited from an uncorrupt bureaucracy and an effective legal system. The colonial service of the nineteenth century was a model of nineteenth century government. It was accompanied by the provision of educational services, along with a free press and modern universities, and the beginnings of modern health services, with piped water and sanitation. It is not possible to put a price on these developments; but they were clearly vital to the economic well-being of the emerging societies.

Services took a longer time to evolve in the Boer Republics. The Orange Free State was more progressive than the more remote Transvaal and had a functioning distributive system long before the Transvaal. Its governmental services were also more developed. Political conflicts and growing nationalist feelings probably hindered the growth of a modern professional bureaucracy in the Transvaal before the South African War (1899–1902). Commercial, financial and transport services, of course, made rapid progress once Johannesburg had begun to develop, and war only temporarily broke the continuity of these developments. By 1910 a recognisably modern economy was taking shape in all four provinces of the Union

Outside this modern economy lay the African reserves, where the bulk of the population lived. Already a migratory pattern was developing, before the impact of the sustained demand for labour created by economic growth in the white areas. Already, too, there were signs of overcrowding and soil erosion in parts of the eastern Cape. In many of these African areas little development had taken place and a pre-capitalist way of life continued, until the voracious appetite of the gold mines for labour dragged them into the modern world of the late nineteenth century. In parts of Natal, where African reserves co-existed side by side with white farmland, the modernised sector had begun to exert an impact upon traditional agriculture. Elsewhere, communal ownership of the land accompanied by measuring wealth in the form of animal ownership formed a barrier to local economic development.

With the coming of Union, South Africa entered the age of modern statistics. Not only did the economy grow, but so too did the measurement of it. As a result, we have figures for the growth of the national income and the domestic product that tell us precisely how the economy has changed in the twentieth century. Figures start in 1912 and, if we compare the structure of the economy in that year with the structure in 1990, we can form a picture of how significant the changes have been. If we also select a year in the middle, say 1951, halfway between 1912 and 1990, we shall be able to form an even clearer picture of the changes that have taken place in the twentieth century.

Tables 1 and 2 show clearly the wealth of the economy and its structure in 1912. The relatively low size of the per capita incomes

'Natives going down to work in the New Primrose Mine, Johannesburg 1895', by Melton Prior. The voracious appetite of the gold mines for labour, destroyed the pre-capitalist way of life in African rural communities
(© The Brenthurst Press)

is the result of dividing the national income by the total population, at a time when a large proportion of the population was outside the modernised sector of the economy and still engaged in semi-subsistence agriculture. Accurate figures of all per capita incomes supported by the modernised sector of the economy should include not only those blacks working in the modernised sector, but the people they supported back home. Dividing the national income by the total population consequently provides us with a rough and ready way of measuring the growth of wealth in the economy.

At just over six million, the population was not yet pressing upon resources; but probably not much more than half were in the modernised capital sector of the economy. The base of the economy was broadening, but mining still dominated it. Mining was half as valuable again as agriculture and its output was worth more than four times that of manufacturing. Agriculture still employed more people than mining, but productivity was low, particularly in the African reserves, with the result that South Africa had become an importer of foodstuffs, such as wheat. In 1912 the future of the gold mines and of Johannesburg was not yet secured and, with a fixed gold price at a time of rising prices, the profitability of the gold mines was under pressure. Since the capital costs of deep level mining were considerable and permanent, the only way the mining companies could economise was to try to hold down wages, for the dividends they were paying were not particularly large. This pressure on wages lay behind the labour unrest of both the pre-war years and the immediate post-war years, culminating in the Rand Revolt of 1922.

By modern standards, of course, the most striking feature of the 1912 economy was the relatively small role played by the government. Government services of all kinds contributed just over a third of the national income. These services, moreover, included the work of central government, the four provinces and of all the municipalities of the country. Clearly in 1912 the government did not play a major role in the economy.

Fuelled by the expansion of the gold mines and stimulated by the benefits of

TABLE 1
THE POPULATION, THE NATIONAL INCOME AND PER CAPITA INCOMES IN 1912

Population	National Income	Per Capita Incomes
6 103 000	£132 900 000	£21,8

TABLE 2
THE STRUCTURE OF THE ECONOMY IN 1912

Primary Sector				Secondary Sector		Tertiary Sector			
Agriculture		Mining		Manufacturing		Commerce		Public Sector	
£million	%	£million	%	£million	%	£million	%	£million	%
23,1	17,4	36	27,1	8,9	6,7	18	13,5	46,9	35,3

Union and two world wars, the South African economy grew rapidly after the difficulties of the 1920s were overcome. Not all sectors shared equally in this growth.

The agricultural sector began to experience severe problems in the 1920s as a result of soil erosion and population growth. The land could not support the number of people trying to gain a living from it and a serious poor white problem developed. The world depression of 1929–1932 made this worse and it was not until the 1930s that the beginnings of a solution were found. In practice this meant that the state had to step in and take control of output and prices in a wide variety of agricultural products. The method adopted was the marketing board, which was producer and not consumer dominated. In this way the market mechanism in agriculture was undermined. It was replaced by management by politicians. Producer dominated marketing boards could force up prices, but they did not introduce widespread technological progress in the 1930s or 1940s, notwithstanding the stimulus given by the Second World War. Agriculture, however, had become moderately prosperous by 1950 and had increased its proportion of the gross domestic product. The foundations had been laid for the transformation of the 1950s and 1960s.

Mining underwent fewer changes in these years and declined in relative importance. New gold fields were opened up in the East Rand in the 1920s and the gold field of the Orange Free State was discovered in the 1930s, while the devaluation of the South African pound at the end of 1932 triggered a boom in the gold mining industry. Its expansion helped to make the South African economy one of the world's fastest growing economies in the 1930s. Diamonds, coal, iron ore, asbestos, copper and tin continued to be exploited. In 1951 the primary sector continued to dominate the economy.

There had, however, been rapid growth in manufacturing, which had benefited enormously from the two world wars and the interruption of the normal flow of imports into the country. The number of persons employed in manufacturing quadrupled in this period, as the food processing industries expanded, modern textile industries were developed and the beginnings of a modern iron and steel industry were established. Engineering steadily increased in importance. The secondary sector more than trebled its weighting in the economy in these years. It was the pace setter of economic growth.

In the tertiary sector there was no fundamental transformation in wholesaling or retailing, but in transport the impact of the motor vehicle was enormous and threatened the profitability of the railways. At sea there were few changes and in the skies the age of mass movement by plane still lay in the future. Communications were efficient, with the telephones increasingly supplementing the postal service. In the financial sector major changes had occurred at the time of Union, with the amalgamation movement in banking that had reduced the number of banks to two by 1920.

TABLE 3
THE POPULATION, THE GROSS DOMESTIC PRODUCT AND PER CAPITA INCOME IN 1951

Population	Gross Domestic Product	Per Capita Income
12 708 000	£1,241 million	£105,6

TABLE 4
THE STRUCTURE OF THE ECONOMY IN 1951

Primary Sector				Secondary Sector		Tertiary Sector			
Agriculture		Mining		Manufacturing		Commercial Services		Government Services	
£million	%	£million	%	£million	%	£million	%	£million	%
245,5	18,3	167,5	12,5	254	18,9	528,5	39,4	205,5	7,9

Thereafter, the main new developments were the founding of the Reserve Bank in 1920 and the takeover of the National Bank by Barclays DCO in 1925. Despite the enhanced role of the government during the two world wars the private sector of the economy grew faster than the public sector, which in 1951 accounted for only 33 per cent of the national income — less than in 1912. Tables 3 and 4 provide the details.

Major changes occurred in all the sectors of the economy in the years between 1951 and the 1990s. The position of agriculture, which had increased its weighting in the economy in the period 1912–1951, underwent a steady decline. This was clear evidence of the emergence of a modern economy. By 1990 mining had also experienced a relative decline, after the sharp upward movement following the rise in the gold price. Further evidence of this is seen in the growing importance of manufacturing, which, by 1990, was responsible for over a quarter of the Gross Domestic Product.

In the four decades after 1950 agriculture was transformed, the maize triangle emerged and the landscape became dotted with huge grain silos. Tropical, deciduous and citrus fruits all experienced rapid growth. Egg and poultry production were revolutionised and large-scale forestry projects were commenced. Agriculture was becoming increasingly specialised and capital intensive. Mining was not transformed; but base minerals, led by coal, increased steadily in importance. The latter accounted for 20 per cent of mineral exports in 1990. In the secondary sector, the industrial base broadened and deepened, both in the field of consumer goods and in the vital area of producer goods. Yet it was in the tertiary sector that the changes were the most far reaching. Transport, on land, on the sea and in the air, changed out of all recognition after 1950. So did retailing, with the growth of supermarkets, hypermarkets and large chains. In 1951 the country's banking was dominated by the imperial banks based in London, and there was no local money market. By 1990 a vibrant local money market existed, the banks had become South African and their functions had been transformed. Four of the big five were controlled by even larger life insurance companies and on top of all this there was big government, as Pretoria increased its influence on the economy ever more and more.

Threading wool in a loom at a textile factory. After the Second World War, the number of people employed in manufacturing quadrupled
(Cape Archives AG 3617)

TABLE 5
THE POPULATION, THE GROSS DOMESTIC PRODUCT AND PER CAPITA INCOME IN 1988

Population	Gross Domestic Product	Per Capita Income
35 934 000	R198 957 000	R6 718

TABLE 6
THE STRUCTURE OF THE ECONOMY IN 1990

Primary Sector				Secondary Sector		Tertiary Sector			
Argiculture		Mining		Manufacturing		Commercial Services		Government Services	
R million	%	R million	%	R million	%	R million	%	R million	%
11,886	5,1	25,079	10,7	60,018	25,6	107,177	45,7	32,147	13,7

South Africa was moving in the direction of a service economy too. The provision of commercial services that had accounted for 39,4 per cent of the Gross Domestic Product in 1951, had climbed to 45,6 per cent in 1990, while government services had risen to 13,7 per cent. Proportionately they had grown the most, with an increase of 73,4 per cent, a trend that was world-wide in the second half of the twentieth century. Tables 5 and 6 give the details.

In these respects the South African economy assumed a remarkably modern shape; but this picture conceals major differences from a Western European economy, for the South African economy still contained within it a large semi-subsistence sector in the African homelands. By 1990 this sector threatened to bring economic growth to a halt as a result of the increasing cost of providing the essential basic social services of a modern economy, in education, health and old age pensions. Since 1960 the population has grown by 40 per cent every decade, which made the provision of Western style social services for all impossible.

Moreover, the engine of growth that had driven the South African economy for much of the past century was failing. Mining was no longer the leading sector and any future growth was likely to occur only in the secondary and tertiary sectors.

(S Jones)

Education

The history of education in South Africa is often associated solely with the development of schooling along Western European lines. It is easy to pinpoint a date when the first person was employed as a 'teacher' in an area, when the first 'school' was opened or the first school building constructed and to claim that this was the beginning of the history of education in the area. Such an approach disregards completely previous patterns of education that may have existed, implying that whatever was learned in the school was inherently superior to any other form of education.

Anyone wishing to study the history of education should begin by considering the family, community and religious life of South African societies as archaeologists, anthropologists and historians have been able to reconstruct it. The education of children until the introduction of schooling often took place informally through, for example, the proverbs used in a language, story-telling and singing, games and dancing, and induction into rituals and ceremonies. But there was also more formal instruction involved in the learning of crafts such as iron smelting and forge work, pottery making and herbalism, in addition to instruction which adolescents might have received through rites of puberty.

The development of schooling in the Western tradition runs parallel to the history of the Christian church and missions in South Africa and has been strongly influenced by prevailing ideas of how close the relationship between the state and the church ought to be and who should supply the funds for schools. The other dominant characteristic of educational provision in South Africa has been the historical movement towards the segregation of races, language, and cultural, religious and class groups. Until very recently the development of education has almost always been in the direction of increased segregation. Schools have also been segregated in terms of their function: academic and vocational schools, commercial and technical, and a variety of 'special' schools. One conspicuous exception has been co-education. Segregated schools for girls and boys have only been popular in the English-speaking community, and are largely restricted to those schools which were established in the nineteenth century. A third important aspect of South African schooling has been the degree to which schools have been linked to the local community. In some places the first schools were community schools, and at times community schools have been established as an alternative to, or in protest against, the existing state or church schools. State policy towards community control in schools has also fluc-

A missionary and his family posing with black scholars and their teachers. The development of schooling in the Western tradition is linked with the history of Christian missionary activity in South Africa (National Cultural History Museum)

tuated between giving the community almost no say at all in the provision of state-aided schooling and regarding communities as being the joint providers of education.

Until the end of the eighteenth century almost all schooling at the Cape was under the control of the Dutch Reformed Church. Intentions were often more worthy than what was achieved in practice and the period of the VOC is chiefly significant for its Protestant pattern of schooling, which would determine to a considerable extent the type of schooling thereafter. The first school in the settlement — a school for slaves, to make them more useful to the colonists — was established in 1658.

The first proposals to secularise the provision of education and place it under the state were made during the administration of the Batavian Republic, but little was achieved before the Cape was handed to the British in 1806. British innovations in the provision of education at the Cape were the Anglicisation of schools and the establishment of a Department of Education under a Superintendent General in 1839. There were then two groups of state maintained schools, the 'first class' schools in the larger areas and the 'second class' schools providing primary education in smaller areas. Soon afterwards the idea of subsidised state-aided schools developed, whereby mission and farm schools received financial help, but the community retained a measure of control.

Schooling in Natal and the Orange Free State was not organised on any systematic basis before the advent of British control in 1843 and 1848, respectively. In both colonies a British pattern of schooling was introduced. In the former there was a clear policy of Anglicisation, together with undenominational state schools (which were opposed by those who favoured denominational education, and who established their own private schools). Despite the influence of the Dutch Reformed Church in the Orange Free State, the Dutch language and influence was neglected in its schools for most of the century. In the Transvaal the pattern was different, as schooling was based on a Dutch model, with teachers recruited from the Netherlands. After the Anglo-Transvaal War (1880–1881), education in the Transvaal was organised on a Christian national basis.

Mission education in the nineteenth century was generally of poor quality and often restricted to elementary schooling.

Pupils of Schietfontein farm school in the district of Pretoria, 1893
(Transvaal Archives TAB 32158)

'Vocational' and manual education played a much larger role than it did in other schools. Only in the Cape and to some extent in Natal could the beginnings of modern schooling for blacks be discerned, though by 1900 the (largely unmet) demand for schooling was clearly growing.

After the South African War (1899–1902), Britain attempted a policy of Anglicisation in the schools of the Transvaal and Orange Free State, which prompted the establishment of community-controlled Christian National Education (CNE) schools by Afrikaners. Although the restoration of self-government to the former Republics soon removed the necessity for these schools, the CNE ideal remained alive and became the policy of the National Party, and that of the government after 1948. Provincial control over white and coloured schools was maintained by the Act of Union in 1910, and the Cape, Orange Free State and Transvaal also kept elements of local control over their schools.

The Eiselen Commission (1951) paved the way for the National Party's policy of complete apartheid in schooling: 'Bantu education', 'coloured education', 'Indian education' and CNE-based white education. Until 1953 education for Africans had been under the control of churches and missions, then it became the responsibility of a government department, with the aim of educating more children than before, within their own culture and for a separate, unequal and inferior place in society.

The uprising of Soweto schools in 1976 was a turning point in the history of South African education. It was the start of an era of black student resistance to apartheid education and also a spur to the state to consider reforming the education system. The De Lange Commission (1981) abandoned reference to racially based educa-

The Soweto uprisings in 1976 proved to be a turning point in the history of South African education. Pupils took to the streets protesting against their second-rate schooling
(Mayibuye Centre)

tion. Immediate reforms did not follow, however, as the tricameral constitution of 1983 entrenched education as an 'own affair' of the three houses of Parliament. It was only ten years after De Lange that white schools began to be 'opened', initiating a process of transition to non-racial schooling.

(R F Siebörger)

Eiselen, Werner Willi Max

MIDDELBURG, TRANSVAAL, 1899 — TZANEEN, 1977

Administrator, academic. Professor of Bantu Studies at the University of Stellenbosch, Eiselen was also Chief Inspector of Native Education for the Transvaal Education Department (1936), and from 1949 Secretary of Native Affairs. He chaired the Native Education (Eiselen) Commission (1949) which recommended separate education and mother tongue instruction for black pupils. The Bantu Education Act (1953) implemented these recommendations. He was also the architect of the policy which sought to make the western Cape a Coloured Labour Preference area.

End Conscription Campaign (ECC)

The End Conscription Campaign, formed at the end of 1983, found a support base in the English-medium universities and some churches. It was dedicated to resisting conscription and general militarisation in South Africa. In 1985 its membership swelled in the wake of increasing opposition to troops being stationed in the townships. The ECC encouraged the growth of an anti-war culture. Under the 1986 state of emergency, ECC members experienced increasing state harassment and it was eventually banned in August 1988 after it had publicly given its support to conscripts who refused to do military service.

English-speakers

When the British first occupied the Cape in 1795, there were few English speakers in southern Africa. Their numbers subsequently grew steadily, particularly after 1806, and reached approximately 4 000 by 1820. In that year, a further 4 000 English-speaking settlers (about 1 000 men and 3 000 women and children) arrived at Algoa Bay, and were located by the Cape authorities in the Albany district on the eastern frontier of the colony. Despite this numerical boost, English-speakers formed a small minority of the white population (Dutch-speakers totalled some 43 000 people), but the English soon dominated the Cape colonial economy and society.

Considerable myth surrounds the 1820 settlers, who have come to symbolise English culture and tradition in South Africa. In reality, they were a socially and politically divided group, and the majority of males were artisans and tradesmen, though farmers, soldiers, teachers and a few professional people also emigrated. Few of the settlers were people of means, and none of them, as far as is known, owned any land in Britain. They were ill-equipped to survive as successful agricultural smallholders, as envisaged by the colonial authorities, whose primary motive in supporting the settlement was to secure the cheap defence of the eastern frontier against the Xhosa. By 1824, almost two-thirds of the settlers had abandoned their small farms and moved to Grahamstown and other emerging small towns in the eastern Cape.

Many of those who remained on the land were thereafter to prosper, particularly after the introduction of merino sheep farming by the settlers. Wool became the principal export of the Cape by the late 1830s. English-speakers in the towns quickly established themselves in a variety of commercial activities, and completely dominated Cape commercial life by the 1840s. Legal and illicit trade with black communities across the frontier became a

The landing of the British settlers in Algoa Bay as depicted by Thomas Baines in 1874. Despite the arrival of an additional 4 000 settlers in 1820, English-speakers formed a small minority of the white population (William Fehr Collection)

major source of wealth for many English settlers. English-speaking shopkeepers and merchants also penetrated the interior, and small centres which were established in the Boer Republics after the Great Trek frequently had a strong English-speaking presence.

The growth of English influence in the eastern Cape, which was consolidated by new immigrants from Britain throughout the century, was aided by the sympathetic colonial authorities in Cape Town. During the 1820s, an Anglicisation policy was pursued by the autocratic Governor, Lord Charles Somerset, who sought to replace the use of Dutch in public life by English. English became the sole language of government from 1825, and of the courts from 1827. Anglicisation was pursued less aggressively after 1827, but schools and churches experienced considerable pressures regarding the use of English for much of the nineteenth century. English-speakers dominated Cape politics during the century, though their position was strongly challenged by the Afrikaner Bond after the 1880s.

Natal differed from the Cape in the composition of its white population, as the majority were English-speaking. The earliest permanent white settlers in 1824 were English-speaking, but English preponderance was only secured after the annexation of Natal by the British in 1843. British immigrants thereafter arrived in considerable numbers, particularly between 1849 and 1852, when just under 5 000 English and Scottish people arrived in Durban. Their economic activities were diverse: many settled in Durban, Pietermaritzburg and other towns, while others farmed. Sugar and fruit crops, indigenous timber, wattle cultivation and cattle and sheep farming became the most profitable land-based economic activities in Natal.

Large numbers of English-speaking immigrants were attracted to South Africa after the discovery of diamonds and gold in the interior. Their presence caused considerable tension in the Transvaal, particularly after the Jameson Raid in 1895. The South African War (1899–1902), and Lord Milner's attempts at Anglicisation thereafter, deepened divisions between English-speakers and Afrikaners. With the

Cartoonist George Cruikshank imagined a cruel fate for the settlers. In reality, they were ill-equipped to survive as agricultural smallholders and by 1824 almost two-thirds had abandoned their farms (Cape Archives E 3058)

Top:
'The embarkation', an etching from the *Illustrated London News* of 6 July 1850. Between 1849 and 1852, just under 5 000 English and Scottish settlers arrived in Durban
(Local History Museum Collection, Durban)

Above:
A settler's homestead in Natal, in the mid-nineteenth century. Agriculture, wattle cultivation and stock farming became the most profitable land-based economic activities in Natal
(Local History Museum Collection, Durban)

Right:
Among whites, the strongest critics of apartheid were English-speaking. Here Helen Joseph, Lilian Ngoyi and Sophie Williams deliver petitions against the pass laws to the Prime Minister in Pretoria, 9 August 1956
(Mayibuye Centre)

formation of Union in 1910, a measure of reconciliation was achieved between the two white groups, and the status of English as an official language was enshrined in the constitution alongside Dutch (later Afrikaans). English-speakers were outnumbered by Afrikaners in the Union, despite continual immigration before 1948, and their political influence was thus restricted. During this period, the majority of English-speakers gave their political allegiance to the South African Party, which was committed to reconcile the interests of the Afrikaners and English-speakers, and later to the United Party. The more jingoistic Unionist and Dominion parties, which relied exclusively on English-speaking support, never became significant political forces.

Despite their political weakness, English-speakers continued to dominate commerce, business, industry and banking. English was also the principal language of South African urban life, even in places such as Bloemfontein and Pretoria, until Afrikaners began to urbanise during the inter-war years. Considerable economic inequalities between English and Afrikaans-speaking whites in towns persisted during the 1950s and 1960s.

After 1948, the political influence of English-speakers declined markedly. Initially most gave their allegiance to the white supremacist United Party, which slowly lost support and direction until its final demise in 1977. The National Party won the backing of an increasing number of English-speakers after the mid-1960s, after it had achieved its goal of a Republic in 1961 and toned down its more aggressive Afrikaner nationalism. More liberal English-speakers found their political home in the Progressive Party (called the Progressive Federal Party after 1977). Among whites, most of the strongest critics of apartheid were English-speaking: people such as Helen Suzman, who fought within the structures of Parliament, Alan Paton and Helen Joseph, as well as many English-language newspapers, won international renown for their anti-apartheid campaigns.

English-speaking settlers and their descendants have lived in close proximity to other language speakers for almost two centuries, and a form of English that is easily recognisable as 'South African' has emerged. Many words from Afrikaans, Khoisan and Bantu languages have been adopted, and South African English has many distinctive pronunciations, adaptations and constructions. A rich literature has developed in the last century, and much has won international acclaim, evidenced most notably in the award of the Nobel Prize for Literature to Nadine Gordimer in 1991.

English is the first language of approximately 39 per cent of whites, 15 per cent of coloureds, and 95 per cent of Indians. These three million people comprise about 8 per cent of South Africans, but English is currently preferred as the chief medium of communication between people of different backgrounds. Proficiency in English is regarded by many as essential, and English is certain to retain its place as a key language in South Africa.

(N D Southey)

Esau, Abraham

KENHARDT, CAPE COLONY, *c.* 1856 — CALVINIA, CAPE COLONY, 1901

Martyr. A blacksmith in Calvinia, Esau identified culturally and politically with the English and when war broke out in 1899 he rallied coloured support for the war effort and raised a force of coloured men to repel the invading Boers. Prominent throughout the war, Esau consequently became a marked man among the Boer rebels. After Calvinia fell to the Orange Free State commandos in 1901, Esau was rounded up and brutally murdered.

Ethiopianism

African independent church movement. The first such church was the Thembu Church established by Nehemiah Tile in the Transkei in 1884. In 1892 Mangena Mokone founded the first true Ethiopian Church, and the first to bear that name, in Pretoria. James Dwane joined him and established links between Mokone's church and the American Methodist Episcopal Church, before joining the Anglican Church as head of a separate Order of Ethiopia. Soon there was a proliferation of independent churches, based on a rejection of the fact that the mainline churches were run by whites, and asserting black religious autonomy. The process of fragmentation has continued this century. 'Ethiopian' churches are usually distinguished from 'Zion' churches on the basis of the fact that they largely continue to observe the practices and methods of worship of the main Christian churches.

Abraham Esau, murdered by Boer rebels because of his support for the English in the South African War
(South African Library)

F

Judge Henry A Fagan, Chairman of the Natives Laws Commission in 1946
(Cape Archives AG 15905)

Fagan Commission (Native Laws Commission — 1946–1948)

The large influx of Africans into the towns during the Second World War showed clearly that the government's policy of Africans being 'temporary sojourners' in the urban areas needed revision. In 1946 Smuts appointed a commission under the chairmanship of Judge Henry Fagan to inquire into the laws relating to urban Africans. The Fagan Report, published in February 1948, acknowledged an African urban population as an irreversible fact. Its recommendations included a revision of the pass laws, a Union-wide system of labour bureaux, and the stabilisation of a certain proportion of African labour in the towns. This added up to a considerable change in African policy. The Smuts government accepted the conclusions of the report, which was published a few months prior to the white general election of 1948. The changes in policy proposed held little attraction for most white workers and farmers, who found greater security in the National Party's (NP) policy of apartheid. The Fagan Report was therefore a factor in the NP's election victory.

John Fairbairn fought press censorship and was a staunch anti-slavery campaigner
(Cape Archives E 365)

Fairbairn, John

SCOTLAND, 1794 — CAPE TOWN, 1864

Journalist and member of Parliament. With Thomas Pringle, Fairbairn edited the *South African Journal*, but he is best known as editor of the *South African Commercial Advertiser*. He fought attempts to censor the press and was a staunch anti-slavery campaigner. His support for the London Missionary Society's attitude to the Frontier Wars angered many colonists. He opposed the expulsion of the Xhosa from the Ciskei by D'Urban in 1835, but supported the Stockenström treaties (1836) which gave a certain independence to the chiefs. After the War of the Axe (1846–1847), he advocated the subordination of the Xhosa. A radical leader of the Cape Town anti-convict movement (1849), he supported representative government at the Cape and as a member of the Legislative Council (1850) he was instrumental in drawing up a draft constitution for the colony. He represented Swellendam in the Legislative Assembly (1854–1864), and continued to take an active interest in the commercial affairs of the Cape.

Faku

PONDOLAND, 1780 — PONDOLAND, 1867

Paramount chief of the Mpondo from about 1820 until his death. After the 'Time of Troubles' (Mfecane) Mpondo power was consolidated under Faku, who allowed a Wesleyan mission to be established among his people. This gave him a line of communication with the Cape government and he later received protection from the Cape Governor Napier against the Voortrekkers. Once Natal was annexed, the British saw Faku and his Mpondo as a useful buffer, and a treaty was signed with him (1844) which made him responsible for a large area of land. Various conflicts over land followed with the British authorities and neighbouring peoples, and after the Xhosa cattle-killing his position with the British authorities was weakened further. In his later life he handed over the rule of eastern Pondoland to his son Mqikela and of western Pondoland to his eldest son Ndamase.

Federasie van Afrikaanse Kultuurvereniginge (FAK) (Federation of Afrikaner Cultural Organisations)

An association for the coordination of Afrikaner cultural societies in South Africa, the FAK came to play a vital role in the history of Afrikaner nationalism. Established in 1929 on Broederbond initiative, it had, by 1937, over 300 affiliated organisations. Its main task was to stimulate interest in Afrikaans literature and the arts, but it also promoted Christian National Education and assisted Afrikaners trying to enter more fully into the business life of the country.

Federation of South African Women (FSAW)

A non-racial federation formed in 1954 by leading women in the Congress Alliance, such as Lilian Ngoyi, Florence Mkhize, Ray Alexander and Helen Joseph. A mainly black, urban movement, it aimed to bring women's organisations together in the struggle for women's rights, and to get women to participate more actively in the broader liberation struggle. FSAW began a campaign against the extension of the pass system to women, the high point of which was a march of 20 000 women to the Union Buildings in Pretoria on 9 August 1956, a day subsequently designated South African Women's Day. At the end of 1956 the main leaders of FSAW were arrested and charged with treason alongside other activists of the Congress Alliance, which FSAW had joined in 1955. The organisation was subject to further state repression in the 1960s, although it was never formally banned.

Fingo, *see* Mfengu

FitzPatrick, Sir James Percy

KING WILLIAM'S TOWN, 1862 — UITENHAGE, 1931

Author, politician, agriculturist. Best known as the author of the famous novel *Jock of the Bushveld*, which records his experiences on the Barberton goldfields, FitzPatrick was a prominent leader of the uitlanders in their campaign against the Kruger government of the Transvaal in the 1890s. In 1896 he was imprisoned and fined for his part in the Jameson Raid. An influential employee of the mining house Wernher, Beit-Eckstein, he urged Milner, the High Commissioner, to take a strong stand against Kruger, even at the cost of war. After the war he threw his energies into reconstruction and unification, working for reconciliation between Boer and Briton.

Flag Question

The Hertzog government's proposal in 1926 to adopt a new national flag which contained neither the old republican colours nor the Union Jack, aroused great feelings of emotion among many whites, and the issue was highly contentious. After talks between Hertzog and Smuts, a compromise was reached: the flags of the former Republics as well as the Union Jack were included in the centre of the new flag, and the Union Jack was to fly alongside the Union flag on certain occasions.

Forced Removals

The resettlement of black South Africans was carried out on a massive scale from 1950 onwards in accordance with the apartheid regime's Bantustan and Group Areas policies. In the interests of Bantustan consolidation, an estimated 3,5 million blacks who were considered redundant to South Africa's labour needs were removed from their homes between 1960 and 1982, often by force, and resettled in the Bantustans. Most were labour tenants repatriated from white farms, others were the aged and the unfit, those (mainly women and children) who did not qualify to live in town in terms of the influx control measures, and residents of areas known as 'black spots' surrounded by white areas. Such people were typically dumped in the veld in prefabricated huts with rations and little else. Overpopulation and overgrazing of farm land together with few opportunities for employment led to the Bantustans developing into vast rural slums.

The FSAW march against the extension of the pass system to women, 9 August 1956. Sophie Williams, Rahima Moosa, Helen Joseph and Lilian Ngoyi lead protestors up the stairs of the Union Buildings
(Mayibuye Centre)

The squatter camp on Modderdam Road outside Cape Town was demolished by government bulldozers in 1977
(Mayibuye Centre)

Relocation of people for political reasons resulted in great distress and bitterness, and sometimes in resistance, as in the case of squatters living on Modderdam Road outside Cape Town who refused to leave the area, and whose camps were demolished by government bulldozers in 1977–1978. Forced removals were also carried out in conformity with the Group Areas Act. Possibly the most publicised of these was the displacement of 40 000 coloureds from District Six in central Cape Town, after it had been proclaimed a white area in 1966; those people were removed to the Cape Flats on the outskirts of the city. By 1985, 83 691 coloured families had been moved in terms of Group Areas, 40 067 Indian families and 2 418 white families. Although removals as a result of Bantustan consolidation ceased by 1990, the removal of labour-tenants from white-owned farms continued.

In 1898 Kruger sent Dr W J Leyds to Brussels as Envoy-Extraordinary to represent the South African Republic's interests in Europe (Transvaal Archives SAB 2955)

Foreign Relations

The official relationship since Union between the South African government and other countries or international organisations, and the conduct of these relations, has been the task of the staff of the Department of Foreign Relations, acting on the instructions of the government of the day. South Africa's domestic policies have crucially influenced its foreign relations.

After the Sand River (1852) and Bloemfontein (1854) Conventions, the Boer Republics could in theory establish full relations with other countries, but the foreign interests of the British colonies of the Cape and Natal were represented by the British government in London. In practice, the South African Republic (SAR) and Orange Free State governments' foreign relations were almost exclusively conducted with Britain. Representatives of the SAR did travel to France, Germany and Holland to raise funds for the building of the Delagoa Bay railway in 1884, and in 1898 Kruger sent Dr W J Leyds to Brussels as Envoy-Extraordinary to represent the Republic's interests in Europe. During the South African War (1899–1902), a deputation from both Republics visited various European capitals and Washington, and at the end of 1900 Paul Kruger was received by the Dutch and Swiss governments as an exiled head of state.

Kruger during his tour of Europe. After 1900 he was received by the Dutch and Swiss governments as an exiled head of state (Transvaal Archives TAB 3791)

After the Treaty of Vereeniging, the foreign interests of all four British colonies were represented by the British government and although the Act of Union (1910) gave South Africa self-government, its foreign relations remained under British control. When the First World War was declared, South Africa was automatically at war with Germany, but Parliament had to decide whether or not to send forces to German South West Africa. South Africa's participation in the war entitled it to send a delegation to the Paris Peace Conference (1919). It was awarded a 'C' mandate over South West Africa and was a founder member of the League of Nations.

The Balfour Declaration of 1926 recognised the British dominions' right to conduct their own foreign relations and in 1927 the South African Department of External Affairs was established. Ambassadors were sent to several countries and South African foreign policy often clashed with Britain's, for example over the continuation of League of Nations sanctions against Italy in 1936.

When Britain declared war on Germany in September 1939, the South African Parliament had to decide what South Africa would do, showing that it now had complete control over its foreign relations. South Africa played its part in defeating Germany, but in 1946 found that its segregationist policies were beginning to affect its international standing adversely. Smuts had attended the United Nations' founding conference in San Francisco and had written the preamble to the UN Charter, but India attacked South Africa's Asiatic Land Tenure and Indian Representation Act at the second session of the UN General Assembly, and Smuts's request that South Africa should be permitted to incorporate South West Africa was firmly rejected.

After the Second World War, world public opinion turned strongly against racism and the newly independent states of Asia and Africa were deeply hostile to apartheid. More than forty years of increasing international pressure and iso-

Left:
General Smuts and Winston Churchill during the Second World War. Although South Africa played its part in defeating Germany, from 1946 its segregationist policies affected its international standing adversely
(National Cultural History Museum)

Above:
General Hertzog outside 10 Downing Street, London
(Rapport Library)

lation were to follow the National Party's election victory in 1948. In the 1950s, this focused chiefly on South West Africa and policy towards South African Indians, but after Sharpeville (March 1960), apartheid became the main focus of international action against South Africa.

United Nations sanctions intended to force South Africa to change its policies included the recommendation that members sever diplomatic relations with South Africa (1962), and a voluntary arms embargo (1963). In 1974 the South African delegation was expelled from the UN General Assembly and South Africa also lost its membership of most UN agencies. South Africa argued that the UN had no right to interfere in the domestic affairs of its members, but the international community believed that apartheid was a threat to international peace and thus legitimately a matter for concern.

South Africa responded to decolonisation in Africa in a number of ways. In the 1950s, there was little response to D F Malan's African Charter, which proposed that South Africa should play a leading role on the continent. The members of the Organisation of African Unity, established in 1963, pledged not to enter into relations with South Africa until apartheid had been destroyed, though many of them did so for economic reasons. John Vorster (1966–1978) tried to make friends with African states by offering them technological assistance. He opened diplomatic relations with Malawi (1967), while maintaining the customs union with Botswana, Lesotho and Swaziland. Vorster and Zambia's Kenneth Kaunda also attempted to mediate between the Smith government and its opponents in Rhodesia.

South Africa's position in Africa deteriorated when Mozambique and Angola became independent in 1975 and it was soon intervening militarily in Angola and supporting the anti-Marxist movements of Unita (Angola) and Renamo (Mozambique). P W Botha's policy of a Constellation of Southern African States, and the Nkomati Accord signed with Mozambique in 1984, showed that South Africa intended to play an active role in the region. Despite South Africa's undertaking at Nkomati to cease its support for Renamo, it continued to destabilise the governments of Mozambique and other states such as Botswana, Zimbabwe and Zambia, on the grounds that they were acting as bases for the ANC. It also continued direct military action in Angola until 1988.

After 1945, South Africa saw Britain, the Commonwealth, Europe and the United States as its most important international partners. It tried to persuade them that it was an essential ally against the Soviet Union because of its control of the Cape sea route and its rich mineral resources. However Britain gave up its naval base at Simonstown in 1955 and no alliances were ever concluded with South Africa. In 1961, South Africa had to resign from the British Commonwealth and although diplomatic relations with Britain, the EC countries and the USA were not broken off, trade and other relations were reduced to a minimum. In the 1980s, the American gov-

Above:
When P W Botha toured Europe in 1984, he found that even the Thatcher government was largely unsympathetic to his limited reforms
(South African Communication Service)

Above right:
P W Botha and Samora Machel shake hands after signing the Nkomati Accord in 1984
(South African Communication Service)

ernment's policy of Constructive Engagement was intended to persuade South Africa to abandon apartheid but this more gentle approach ended in 1986 when Congress passed the Comprehensive Anti-Apartheid Act. When P W Botha toured Europe in 1984, he found that even the Thatcher government in London was largely unsympathetic to his limited reforms. His 'Rubicon' speech of 1985 and the states of emergency of the mid-1980s further damaged South Africa's international standing. In May 1986, the Commonwealth's Eminent Persons Group visited South Africa to see if it could help bring about negotiations but was forced to leave after South African airforce raids on Lusaka, Harare and Gaborone.

South Africa was therefore extremely isolated by the mid-1980s. It had diplomatic relations with less than 30 of the world's more than 170 independent states and its trade, cultural, sport and other relations were also very limited.

South Africa's foreign relations entered a new era after the release of Nelson Mandela in February 1990. The prospect of a democratic South Africa encouraged many Asian and African countries to begin to conduct open relations with South Africa. The collapse of the Soviet Union led to the reopening of relations between South Africa, Russia and East European states after nearly fifty years.

(S Pienaar)

Fort Hare

James Stewart, principal of the Lovedale Missionary Institute, persuaded the Lagden Commission (1905) of the need for an institution of higher learning for blacks, increasing numbers of whom were going abroad to be educated. In 1916 the South African Native College opened on land given by the Church of Scotland at the site of a military post, Fort Hare, that had figured prominently in the frontier history of the eastern Cape.

Fort Hare College became the cradle of African political leaders, counting among its past students Nelson Mandela, Oliver Tambo, Seretse Khama, Kaiser Matanzima, Mangosuthu Buthelezi and Robert Mugabe. It was affiliated with Rhodes University in 1949, but in 1959 control of the college passed to the Department of Bantu Education, and it became an ethnic university for Xhosa-speaking students. In the late 1960s it was one of the main centres of the Black Consciousness movement, and like many universities in South Africa, it experienced repeated student unrest in the 1970s and 1980s. In the early 1990s it again became a respected university, with Oliver Tambo its Chancellor until his death in 1993 and a number of returned exiles joining its staff.

Franchise Policies

From 1854, the Cape had a colour-blind franchise with relatively low qualifications. In 1887 and 1892 qualifications were raised at a time when African and coloured voters could affect the result in almost a quarter of the Cape constituencies. Natal paid mere lip-service to black suffrage: though in theory a colour-blind franchise existed there as well, in 1865 all Africans who had not been exempted from customary law were disfranchised.

Dr James Stewart, principal of the Lovedale Missionary Institute, and Lovedale students (Mayibuye Centre)

The Orange Free State and Transvaal from the start limited the franchise to white males. The Peace of Vereeniging allowed the two conquered Republics to decide the issue of black suffrage after the introduction of self-government, and there the franchise remained the exclusive privilege of white men. After Union each state retained the franchise system existing before Union, but only whites could become members of the House of Assembly or senate. The extension of the vote to white women in 1930, and the removal in 1931 of the income and property qualifications applicable to white male voters in the Cape, added a significant number of white voters to the common roll, while reducing the black proportion of voters in the Cape Province.

In 1936 African voters were removed from the common voters' roll in the Cape, and after a bitter struggle so were the coloureds in 1956. Both groups were placed on a separate roll and allowed to elect whites to represent them in Parliament. Such representation for Africans was abolished in 1959, and for coloureds in 1969. The racially-based tricameral constitution of 1983 provided for three legislative chambers, for whites, coloureds and Indians, elected on separate voters' rolls and constituted so that the white assembly was larger than the other two together. The African majority remained totally excluded from representation in the institutions of central government.

Free Blacks

Blacks who were not slaves, the free black community at the Cape comprised some descendants of Asians sentenced by the Dutch East India Company to serve terms of imprisonment at the Cape, Prize Negroes (those freed from slave-ships; sometimes called Liberated Africans) after they had served their terms of apprenticeship, and those emancipated from slavery. Most free blacks lived in Cape Town itself and were poor and often Muslim. Ordinance 50 of 1828 removed restrictions on the freedom of movement of such 'free persons of colour'. They became part of the coloured community.

Free Burghers

Term used for former officials of the Dutch East India Company who were given land to farm. The Company wished to substitute limited private farming for state production, in order to reduce expenditure. The free burghers were to produce cattle, corn and wine for the Company at prices which the Company itself laid down. The first free burghers were settled on farms in the Liesbeeck valley on the eastern side of Table Mountain in 1657. That the land they were given was Khoi grazing land helped provoke the first Dutch-Khoi war.

Freedom Charter

A manifesto adopted by the Congress of the People at Kliptown in 1955. It was based on ideas widely canvassed from supporters of the Congress Alliance, but its exact authorship has remained controversial, some claiming that members of the banned Communist Party had a major role in drafting the final version. It began by af-

The Freedom Charter was adopted by the Congress of the People at Kliptown in 1955
(Mayibuye Centre)

firming that South Africa belonged to all its inhabitants, black and white. It called for a non-racial, democratic system of government, and equal protection of all people before the law. It also demanded equal work and educational opportunities, nationalisation of banks, mines and heavy industry, and redistribution of land. The Charter was endorsed by the African National Congress in 1956, though there were those who opposed it, most of whom left to join the Pan Africanist Congress and a few to join the Liberal Party, which had opposed the Charter mainly because of the clauses about nationalisation, which suggested a socialist future.

Freedom of the Press

The struggle for press freedom began with the publication of the first independent newspaper in South Africa, the *South African Commercial Advertiser* in 1823, which Governor Lord Charles Somerset first censored and then suppressed. In the twentieth century, and especially from 1948 onwards, press freedom has been curtailed by a battery of restrictive legislation. Newspapers were restricted in what they could print, especially information relating to the military, prisons, police and state security. Newspapers were not only charged or threatened with prosecution; some were even closed down (*The Guardian* (1963), *The World* (1977), *The Post* (1981), and, for brief periods in 1988 and 1989 *The Weekly Mail, New Nation, South, Grassroots* and *New Era*). Journalists and editors were detained and banned, and foreign journalists were expelled or forbidden to enter the country.

Comprehensive restrictions on the press were introduced under the states of emergency of the 1980s; they went so far as to forbid any reporting of violence in the townships. These regulations were lifted in 1990–1991, and the press was very much freer then than it had been in previous decades, but many laws restricting freedom of the press remained on the statute book.

Frere, Sir Henry Bartle Edward
WALES, 1815 — LONDON, 1884

Sir Bartle Frere was appointed Governor of the Cape and High Commissioner in 1877
(Local History Museum Collection, Durban)

Governor of the Cape Colony and High Commissioner. After a highly successful period as Colonial Administrator in India (1842–1867), Frere was appointed Governor of the Cape Colony and High Commissioner (1877) specifically to carry out Carnarvon's plans for the confederation of South Africa. This Frere was determined to effect. His mission, however, was beset with insurmountable obstacles. He was determined to tame the Zulu power, and brought on the Anglo-Zulu War, which opened with the defeat of the British at Isandlwana (January 1879). Once it was realised that federation was out of the question, Frere's usefulness at the Cape ceased and he was recalled to London (1880), where he died a broken man.

Frontier Armed and Mounted Police (FAMP)

Created by Sir George Cathcart in 1853 by amalgamating the rural police forces into a single unit, the FAMP under Sir Walter Currie, its first commandant, consisted of approximately 500 men, scattered at nineteen stations within the Cape Colony and three in the Transkei, then still under African rule. The duties of these men included the apprehension of marauders and the protection of property. In subsequent years the FAMP came increasingly to perform military duties, undertaking military campaigns for the Cape government and being sent to areas of unrest. In 1878 the FAMP was reorganised and renamed the Cape Mounted Riflemen.

Frontiers

For many people the term 'frontier' conjures up certain images, often highly romanticised, perhaps shaped by the tales of colonial pioneers or American western movies. In South African history the term is most readily associated with the eastern Cape frontier and the century of conflict that occurred in that region from the late eighteenth century (thus a recent book dealing with the history of this particular region at that time is simply entitled *Frontiers*). But these are superficial images and connotations which miss the complexities of the 'frontier' concept. For historians of South Africa the term has given rise to a range of issues and debates which have come to take on a broad significance in analyses of the country's history.

The complexity begins when one tries to define a frontier. As scholars have come to show, there have been many different types of frontier. So distinctions are drawn between the missionary, trading and hunting frontiers; between the opening and closing frontier, or between the pioneering and settled frontier. These distinctions tell us that frontiers vary from region to region, and that they pass through different phases. But one does need a broad, general definition. Such a definition has been provided by Lamar and Thompson, who regard 'a frontier not as a boundary or line, but as a territory or zone of interpenetration between two previously distinct societies. Usually, one of these societies is indigenous to the region or at least has occupied it for many generations; the other is intrusive. The frontier "opens" in a given zone when the first representatives of the intrusive society arrive; it "closes" when a single political authority has established hegemony over the zone.' Built into this definition are the two key defining characteristics of a frontier: first, the existence in close proximity to each other of communities with different histories, cultures and social structures; and second, the absence of a political authority that is able to exercise effective control over the zone occupied by these communities.

In South Africa several frontiers 'opened' in a period of about 200 years from the early eighteenth century. By the end of the nineteenth they had all 'closed'. The process of 'opening' began as white trekboers started to expand eastwards and northwards away from the Cape Town area in the early 1700s. As they did so they pressed against Khoisan herding, hunting and gathering communities. The eastward expansion of the trekboers was particularly devastating for these Khoisan communities as they lost cattle and access to land and game. The northward expansion of the trekboers had different consequences, giving rise to the emergence, north of the Orange River, of mixed-blood communities such as the Griqua.

By the last quarter of the eighteenth century the eastward expansion of the trekboers had brought into being a new frontier zone in the eastern Cape. There the trekboers began to press against the southernmost settlements of Xhosa-speaking communities in the land between the Bushmans River and the Fish River. So began a century of intermittent warfare, as the Xhosa strove to defend their long-occupied territory against the force of colonial expansionism.

A common difficulty in frontier zones was the absence of clearly defined or mutually acceptable boundaries. This was for long a problem on the Cape eastern frontier. The very notion of a defined boundary was generally alien in precolonial Africa. Thus the attempts by successive colonial governments in the Cape to impose such a boundary on the eastern frontier were invariably rejected or ignored by black communities. In 1780 the Dutch East India Company administration proclaimed the Great Fish River as the boundary line. But it was not until the Fourth Frontier War of 1811–1812 that the

The Frontier Armed and Mounted Police was created by Sir George Cathcart (top) in 1853 and was placed under the command of Sir Walter Currie (bottom)
(South African Library)

'Gonaqua Khoikhoi of the eastern Cape'. The eastward expansion of the trekboers was particularly devastating for the Khoisan communities as they lost their cattle and access to land and game (The Brenthurst Library)

'The Second Waterkloof Offensive', by Thomas Baines. In October 1851 the 74th Highlanders and their allies among the Mfengu took action against the Xhosa ruler Maqoma (Africana Museum)

Xhosa were driven beyond this line. Subsequent wars were to be followed by further colonial expropriation of Xhosa-occupied land. This was a moving frontier that gradually came to be closed, as successive colonial governments were able increasingly to impose their will on the region, through conquest and the extension of colonial rule.

From the 1830s several other frontier zones were opened in South Africa. These were largely the result of the Great Trek, which led to the establishment in the interior of many Boer communities in areas which impinged upon the territory of African chiefdoms or states. Thus a number of new frontiers were created in zones where there was no effective, recognised authority, where boundaries were not defined, and where territorial claims were disputed. Many such frontier zones came into being: in the eastern Free State where Boers pressed up against the Basotho state; between Boer settlements in the western Transvaal and adjacent Tswana chiefdoms; in the northern and north-eastern Transvaal where the Venda and the Pedi felt the pressure of Boer expansion; in the eastern and south-eastern Transvaal the Swazi and the Zulu neighboured uneasily upon colonial settlements; the Tugela River ran through the heart of a frontier zone between Natal and the Zulu state.

In most of these frontier zones tensions and conflicts arose. There was intermittent warfare between the Free State and the Basotho in the 1850s and 1860s. In the 1880s there was turbulence on the western Transvaal-Tswana frontier. There were conflicts between the Transvaal Boers and both the Venda and the Pedi from the 1850s until the Venda were finally conquered in 1898. Land disputes were common in the Transvaal-Swazi and Transvaal-Zulu frontier zones from the 1860s.

All this might create the impression that conflict and warfare were perhaps the defining characteristics of frontier zones. This was not the case. Many forms of interaction occurred in these zones. White missionaries and traders were often active — so much so that historians often refer to the 'missionary frontier' or the 'trading frontier'.

The missionary frontier penetrated far and wide. Some missionary societies were

'Missionary house and church at Groenkloof', by C Latrobe. Some missionary societies were able to gain a foothold in established African states and chiefdoms
(National Cultural History Museum)

able to gain a foothold in established African states and chiefdoms, especially among the Basotho and Tswana. In other areas, such as the eastern Cape and Natal, their greatest impact was upon African communities or groups who had been displaced or subjected to severe social dislocation.

Frontier historiography has also generated the notion of the 'transfrontiersman'. Such a person was a white colonist who moved away from colonial society, crossed a frontier and lived among indigenous people, adapting to their lifestyle and culture. Two examples of transfrontiersmen stand out in South African history. One was Coenraad de Buys, who in the late eighteenth century lived among the Xhosa and took Chief Ngqika's mother as a lover, later fleeing northwards and living among the Tswana. Another was John Dunn. In the second half of the nineteenth century he abandoned white colonial society in Natal and went to live in Zululand. There he adopted an African lifestyle, married forty-nine wives, and became a gun-runner and adviser to King Cetshwayo.

The history of the South African frontier has given rise to extensive debate among historians and other scholars. The debate has centred around certain fundamental questions: how can one best capture the essential character of the South African frontier? Was it a frontier of conflict, or one of cooperation? What is the place of the frontier era in the broad sweep of South African history? Can the origins of racism, segregation and apartheid in any way be traced back to forms of consciousness that developed on the frontier?

These questions have been approached from varying perspectives and have therefore produced some very different answers. For Afrikaner nationalist and other pro-colonist historians the frontier era was characterised essentially by the arduous, heroic white struggle for survival, a struggle which was ultimately won, albeit with great sacrifices. According to this view, it was a struggle waged by whites against barbaric blacks who launched indiscriminate attacks against white communities, massacred white women and children, stole white-owned cattle, and encroached on white-owned land. It was a stuggle in which whites drew upon their resilience, energy and technological superiority, ultimately subjugating the 'barbarous hordes' and bringing order where there was once chaos. Thus, for these historians the frontier era symbolised the positive, heroic achievement of the white minority in the face of hostile forces. The frontier both highlighted the contrast between white civilisation and black barbarism, but also revealed the remarkable white capacity for survival, a capacity that came to be carried over into the twentieth century.

It was in reaction to this view that a number of historians, who can be labelled loosely as liberal, offered a more negative interpretation of frontier history. One such historian was Eric Walker. Writing in the 1930s, he saw in the frontier era trends and behaviour patterns that influenced the course of South African history for the worse. It was the trekkers in particular who rode roughshod over black communities,

John Dunn abandoned white colonial society in Natal and went to live in Zululand, where he adopted an African life-style and became adviser to King Cetshwayo
(Africana Museum)

'Muster of colonial volunteers in the High Street, Graham's Town', from the *Illustrated London News* of 24 November 1877 (South African Library)

grabbing their land, exploiting their labour, ever eager to take up arms against those who stood in their way. Thus it was in the frontier environment that racist attitudes among whites became widespread. Such attitudes took root especially in the Boer Republics in the nineteenth century. And they came to be carried over into the twentieth century, providing the basis for the policies of segregation and apartheid.

This view was taken further a few years later by a psychologist, I D MacCrone, who stressed the isolation of frontier life. Cut off from civilising agencies and rational influences, white frontier society became imbued with a sense of rugged individualism and lawlessness, and with a strong racial consciousness and accompanying hostility towards other racial groups. Thus MacCrone traced the roots of segregation back to the frontier era.

One of the features of this writing was the tendency to view a frontier zone as comprising two monolithic, racially distinct, mutually exclusive blocs, the one white and other black. Moreover it was also assumed that these blocs were invariably in conflict with each other. For pro-colonist historians it was a clash between civilisation and barbarism. For most liberal historians the roots of conflict lay in competition for land and cattle.

In the past two decades or so this dichotomised model of frontier history has been shown, as a result of new research and reinterpretation, to be oversimplified. Frontier communities were not monolithic blocs; rather were they divided by internal stratification and cleavages. White society on the frontier was often scattered and fragmented, with few institutions or symbols to bind groups or families together. Black frontier communities might also be stratified or divided: perhaps between those who controlled cattle, access to land, and firearms, and those who did not. Chiefdoms might split over succession disputes or other dynastic rivalries.

These internal divisions often gave rise to a further tendency in frontier society — a tendency for cross-cutting interracial alliances to develop. The trekkers, in particular, were adept at exploiting divisions between black factions. In the late 1830s, for instance, the trekkers in Natal formed an alliance with Mpande against his half-brother, Dingane, the Zulu king. In the 1840s the Swazi ruler formed an alliance with a Boer neighbour in an effort to strengthen his power in the divided, unstable Swazi state. The neighbouring Boer community was itself divided, so on each side of the frontier there were opportunities to build strategic alliances or to play off one faction against another. A similar pattern occurred on the western Transvaal-Tswana frontier in the 1880s. There land-hungry Boers formed alliances with one Tswana faction against another. These were alliances of mutual convenience. The particular Tswana faction forming the alliance might be able to gain the upper hand in the struggle with its rival faction. The Boers would claim Tswana land as the pay-off for their support rendered in that struggle.

So while many conflicts did occur in frontier zones, they were rarely straight conflicts between black and white. Indeed, as Lamar and Thompson have observed, 'power during the open frontier period was conceived of in terms of allegiance rather than political territory or racism'. Moreover, it is a mistake to perceive conflict as the essential feature of frontier society. The idea that forms of cooperative interracial interaction occurred in frontier zones was promoted by some liberal scholars in the 1930s. It was developed further in the *Oxford History of South Africa* which viewed frontier zones as arenas of conflict and cooperation, the latter occurring mainly in the trading, labour and missionary spheres.

The cooperative forms of frontier interaction and black-white frontier alliances came to be stressed by radical Marxist scholars from the 1970s. Indeed, frontier history became an area of contention in the race-class debate that raged at that time. Radicals were particularly concerned to demonstrate that racism, segregation and apartheid were largely the products of the modern era of industrial capitalism in South Africa. Thus earlier forms of white racism were played down. Whereas writers like Walker and MacCrone had closely associated white racism with the frontier mentality, radical writers like Legassick argued that a strong race consciousness did not develop among whites in frontier communities.

The frontier debate died out in the 1980s and there have been few new contributions to it in the past ten years. As a result of this debate the frontier era of South African history has come to be looked at in new ways. The old idea that two sharply contrasting, often conflicting black and white communities squared up to each other in frontier zones is no longer acceptable. Such zones gave rise to complex forms of interaction, and to shifting, cross-cutting allegiances. Certainly conflict and warfare represented one form of interaction, as is indicated by the numerous frontier wars that occurred, but other more peaceful exchanges also took place in frontier zones. However, evidence for interracial cooperation does not necessarily prove the absence of racism in frontier zones. Thus, while South African frontier historiography has raised some interesting questions, it has as yet produced few conclusive answers.

(P R Maylam)

Fugard, Athol

MIDDELBURG, TRANSVAAL, 1932 —

Leading South African dramatist, actor and director. Fugard sustained a theatre group in Port Elizabeth that defiantly produced plays indicting the government's apartheid policy. His international reputation was established with his play *The Blood Knot* (1963) which was produced for stage and television in both London and New York. His later plays include *Hello and Goodbye, Boesman and Lena, Sizwe Bansi is Dead, The Island, Dimetos, A Lesson from Aloes, Master Harold and the Boys, The Road to Mecca* and *Playland.*

'King William's Town, 1864', by Thomas Baines. In 1847 this frontier town became the capital of British Kaffraria
(Africana Museum)

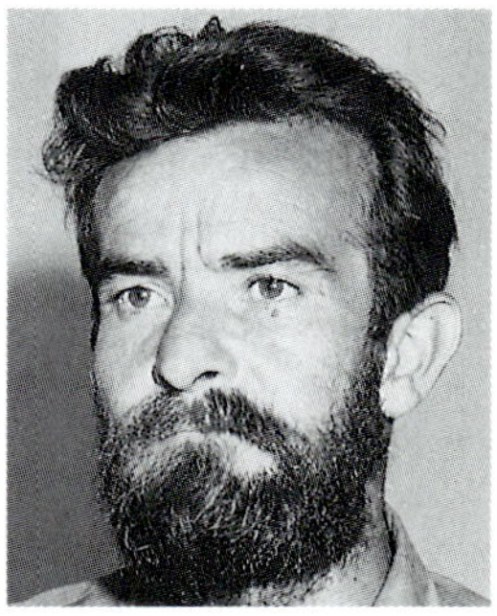

Above:
Athol Fugard
(South African Library)

Fusion

Against a background of economic depression and a desire for white unity, a coalition in 1933 between Hertzog's National Party and Smuts's South African Party was followed by the fusion of the two parties into the United Party in 1934 and the formation of what was known as the Fusion Government. Dr D F Malan and his supporters went into opposition as the Purified National Party. Fusion ended in 1939 when Smuts broke with Hertzog and took South Africa into the Second World War.

Below:
The Fusion cabinet, 1933. Hertzog (front row, third from left) was Prime Minister, and Smuts (front row, third from right) was Minister of Justice
(Transvaal Archives SAB 3028)

G

After spending nearly 20 years of his adult life in South Africa, Gandhi returned to India in 1914 to lead the struggle there for independence from the British
(Local History Museum Collection, Durban)

Gandhi, Mohandas Karamchand

PORBANDAR, INDIA, 1869 — DELHI, INDIA, 1948

Indian political leader. Gandhi trained as a lawyer in England and came out to South Africa (1893) to act in a law suit. He was shocked at the racial discrimination he found and became an advocate for Indians being accorded equal status. He undertook a series of challenges to the government that led eventually to his being jailed, and he won only minor concessions for his people.

After spending nearly twenty years of his adult life in South Africa, during which time he developed his philosophy and methods for achieving social and political reform — *satyagraha*, or non-violent resistance — Gandhi returned to India in 1914 to lead the struggle there for independence from the British.

Gazankulu

A self-governing but non-independent Bantustan established by the National Party government for Shangaan and Tsonga people in the north-eastern Transvaal, many of whom had close links with people in Mozambique. Its creation involved the mass removal of hundreds of thousands of non-Shangaan and Tsonga people in the late 1960s and 1970s. By the end of the 1970s its population was almost 900 000 and 80 per cent of its income was earned outside its borders. Hundreds of thousands of people fled across the border into Gazankulu from Mozambique as a result of the civil war there in the 1980s, further aggravating the poverty of the area.

Genadendal

Originally called Baviaan's Kloof, Genadendal, situated in the district of Swellendam, is the oldest mission station in South Africa, founded in 1737 by Georg Schmidt of the Moravian Missionary Society. Six years later, encountering opposition to his work amongst the Khoi from white colonists and local church authorities, Schmidt had to close down the mission. It was re-established in 1792 and flourished from then on, despite hostility from white farmers who regarded it as an undesirable refuge for potential workers.

Gencor Limited

The General Mining Union Corporation Limited was formed in 1980 when Union Corporation and General Mining and Finance Corporation merged. Gencor is a mining house with interests in gold, coal, minerals, platinum and ferro-alloy products, as well as in energy (oil and gas) and manufacturing industry. It has in-

Interior of the church at Genadendal during a service, by C Latrobe, 1818
(Africana Museum)

vestments in paper and packaging, engineering and construction, medical care and international freight. In the early 1990s it had over 170 subsidiary and associated companies, which together employed almost a quarter of a million people.

German Immigrants

German immigrants were brought out to the Cape by the Dutch East India Company in accordance with the Company's policy of encouraging white settlement in the latter part of the seventeenth century. They formed a significant element of the white population, and during the eighteenth century more Germans than Dutch entered the colony. German, however, played no part as an everyday language, as the newcomers, mainly single men, were absorbed into the local Dutch population through marriage.

In the nineteenth century, German settlers immigrated to South Africa with their families or in larger parties. Impressed by the diligence shown by German settlers at New Germany in Durban in 1848, colonial governments promoted German immigration on a large scale. In 1857 Sir George Grey brought out 2 400 members of the disbanded Anglo-German Legion and their families, settling them in British Kaffraria. They were followed by a group of 4 000 north German peasants. German settlers established communities at places like Stutterheim, Potsdam, Berlin and Hanover. By 1991 there were some 33 000 German-speaking whites in South Africa.

Glen Grey Act (1894)

What Cecil Rhodes called his 'Bill for Africa', this Cape Act was applied initially to the Glen Grey district in the eastern Cape and later extended to the Transkei. It facilitated acquisition of land by Africans under individual tenure, but contained a provision preventing land acquired under the Act from counting for the franchise qualification. It also contained provisions for local governing councils in the territories, and for the imposition of a tax intended to force Africans to enter employment as migrant labourers.

Gold

Gold, mined in the Transvaal by blacks in pre-colonial times, began to be mined by whites from the 1870s. However, the discovery of the Witwatersrand main reef in 1886 overshadowed all other goldfields in wealth and importance. The richest in the world, the Transvaal gold mines were also the most difficult to work. The extensive gold-bearing reef lay hundreds of metres deep and the gold content of the ore was exceptionally low. Surface mining by diggers soon gave way to shaft mining and later to deep level mining, which required large amounts of capital and the necessary technical expertise. The invention of the cyanide process in 1891 made deep level mining possible, thereby greatly increasing gold production. The diamond magnates made their way to the Witwatersrand after 1886 and they poured considerable sums into the gold mining industry. At the same time overseas capital was invested in the mines.

As a result of the gold discovery in 1886 the South African Republic was transformed from an impoverished, rural society into a wealthy industrial state, and became the single largest gold producer in

A family gathering of German settlers with their farm staff
(Cape Archives AG 6357)

Witwatersrand gold miners pose in front of a 30-stamp battery, of the type used on the Californian goldfields. Each stamp weighed 1 250 pounds and the tappets which were raised by the revolving cams are seen above the cross timbers
(National Cultural History Museum)

the world. Gold was to play a major part in bringing about both the South African War (1899–1902) and the Union of South Africa in 1910. It has remained the backbone of the South African economy, contributing massively to state revenue and earning substantially in foreign exchange. South Africa's prosperity has to a large extent been dependent on the price of gold. This was pegged at $35 an ounce from 1933–1970, but was then freed from the dollar and in 1980 it reached a record $850 an ounce, yielding a revenue of R3,6 billion from the gold mines. By June 1982, however, it had dropped to below $300 and for long periods thereafter it failed to reach the $400 mark.

Goldstone Commission

A standing Commission on public violence under the chairmanship of Judge Richard Goldstone, established by the Prevention of Public Violence and Intimidation Act of 1991. The Commission grew out of the signing of the National Peace Accord in September 1991. Its aim was to investigate the causes of violence and make recommendations for the prevention of further violence. The Commission was empowered to establish regional committees, and to refer evidence to the Attorney-General and the Special Criminal Courts for further investigation. In the course of 1992 it acquired further powers, and in November 1992 it announced that some of its investigators had uncovered a secret Military Intelligence operation designed to carry out 'dirty tricks' against Umkhonto we Sizwe.

Gool, Zainunnissa ('Cissie')

CAPE TOWN, 1897 — CAPE TOWN, 1963

Political activist. Daughter of Dr Abdullah Abdurahman, Gool came to play a leading role in the struggle against segregation and is best remembered for her sustained efforts to improve the lot of blacks. For many years she was the only female member of the Cape Town city council, on which she acted as chairperson of the health committee. She was arrested and cautioned by the authorities a number of times, and was restricted under the Suppression of Communism Act.

Gordimer, Nadine

SPRINGS, TRANSVAAL, 1923 —

Novelist and writer of short stories. Gordimer began writing at an early age, publishing her first story in a magazine at the age of fifteen. A series of novels written over more than three decades reflect the changing political scene as seen from a liberal, radical perspective. In her later work, her major theme has been exile and alienation. She is a determined opponent of apartheid, and her stories concern the devastating effects of apartheid on the lives of individual South Africans. She has won a number of literary awards, the most prestigious of which was the Nobel Prize for Literature (1991).

Graaff-Reinet

A town on the Sundays River in the Cape midlands, it was founded in 1786 on what was then the Cape's eastern

Right:
Judge R J Goldstone, Chairman of the standing commission on public violence
(Rapport Library)

Far Right:
Nadine Gordimer signing copies of her latest book at the annual book fair held at the Johannesburg public library, 3 August 1993
(Beeld)

frontier, a vain attempt by the Dutch East India Company to retain some control over the advancing frontiersmen. It was named after Governor Cornelis Jacob van de Graaff and his wife Cornelia Reynet. In 1795 colonists dissatisfied with Company policy on the frontier went into rebellion and set up a republican government, but they were forced to accept British authority in 1796. Further minor rebellions took place in 1799 and 1801.

Opening of a session of Parliament, Grahamstown, 1864 (Cape Archives M 581)

Grahamstown

Town in the eastern Cape, founded in 1812 by Colonel John Graham in the disputed Zuurveld as a garrison post to prevent the Xhosa retaking their lost land. In April 1819 the Xhosa attacked the fledgling town and were repulsed. Seat of the magistracy for the district of Albany, Grahamstown grew rapidly as a result of trade, both amongst the people from Britain who settled in the Albany district in 1820 and with blacks living east of the Fish River. From a garrison town and administrative centre for the British settlers, Grahamstown had by the mid-nineteenth century become the principal town in the eastern Cape Colony, second only to Cape Town, and the centre for a movement for eastern Cape separatism. The Cape Parliament met there in 1864, after which the separatist movement declined. When railways were built into the interior, Grahamstown was bypassed, and in the twentieth century it became rather a backwater, though renowned as an educational centre, home of Rhodes University, and known also for the struggle over the Fingo village, close to the centre of the town, which, despite the efforts of the state to clear it, remained a black residential area.

Gray, Robert

DURHAM, ENGLAND, 1809 — CLAREMONT, CAPE, 1872

First Anglican bishop of Cape Town, Gray was consecrated in Westminster Abbey in 1847. With his wife Sophia and their four children, he arrived in Cape Town in 1848, where he established Bishopscourt as his residence. He founded Zonnebloem as a school for the sons and daughters of African rulers, and the Diocesan College, which became known as 'Bishops', for boys. Gray was a tireless

Grahamstown, division of Albany, 1852. By the mid-nineteenth century it had become the principal town in the eastern Cape and second only to Cape Town in the colony (Africana Museum)

traveller throughout his large diocese, campaigning energetically for improvements. He was also strongly opposed to convicts being settled at the Cape. Having proved that the task of evangelising his vast territory could not be managed from Cape Town, he divided the diocese, ensuring that bishops were consecrated for Grahamstown and Natal. In 1853 he formally resigned his Letters Patent for a new appointment as Metropolitan (Archbishop) of Cape Town. He became a strong opponent of Bishop Colenso and lost a legal battle concerning the juridical foundations of the Church of England in the colonies, as a result of which the Anglican Church in South Africa became a separate Church of the Province.

Robert Gray, the first Anglican bishop of Cape Town, consecrated in Westminster Abbey in 1847
(South African Library)

Great Trek

The organised migration of Afrikaners from the Cape Colony into the interior of South Africa. By the mid-1830s there was wide-spread dissatisfaction and insecurity amongst the Afrikaners of the eastern districts of the Cape Colony. Cape Ordinance 50 of 1828, which made the Khoi and free blacks equal before the law with whites, was thought to have disturbed the 'proper' relations between master and servant, and the frontier farmers suffered heavy losses as a result of the frontier wars. Land hunger helped prompt the idea of trekking out beyond British colonial limits. By 1836 reconnaissance expeditions had revealed the existence of fertile and apparently unpopulated land on the highveld beyond the Orange River and south of the Tugela River. During the next few years, several large, organised groups under prominent leaders trekked out of the colony with their wagons, cattle and sheep. By 1840 about 15 000 Afrikaners had migrated, one-tenth of the Cape Afrikaners.

Most were pastoral farmers from the eastern districts of the colony, and they took with them perhaps an equal number of servants. They were rebelling against a government whose interference in their lives they regarded as intolerable. During the 1820s and 1830s the people of large areas of the highveld and Natal had been dislocated and devastated in the Mfecane or 'Time of Troubles', giving the impression that the land was unoccupied. In reality, these areas were inhabited, and dominated by the Zulu chief Dingane, and Mzilikazi, the chief of the Ndebele. When the first groups of Voortrekkers spread out

The Afrikaner Great Trek, 1836–1854

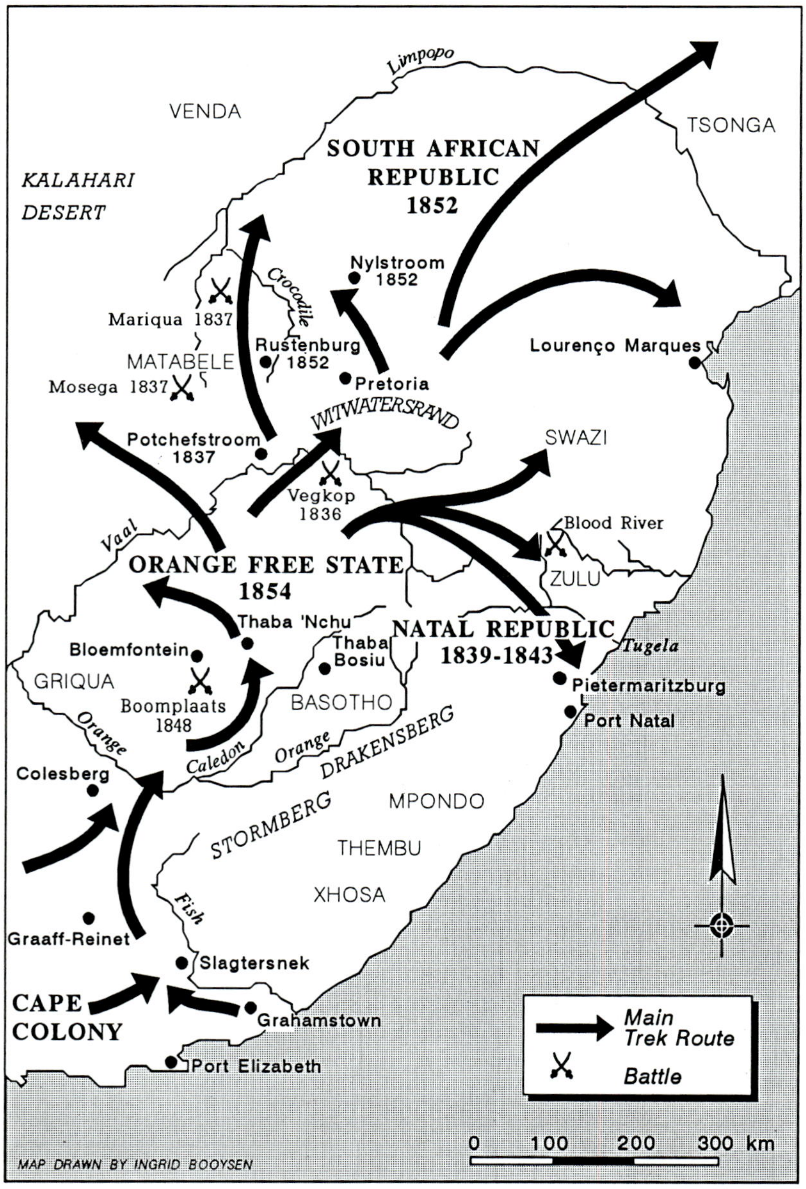

on either side of the Vaal River they came up against the Ndebele. Other trekkers under Piet Retief, anxious to secure an outlet to the sea, went to Natal where they clashed with the Zulu. In 1843 after Britain had annexed Natal, most of the trekkers there recrossed the Drakensberg to join their compatriots on the highveld. In 1852 and 1854 Britain recognised the independence of the trekkers across the Vaal and Orange rivers respectively.

Grey, Sir George

LISBON, 1812 — LONDON, 1898

Colonial administrator. Appointed Governor of the Cape and High Commissioner of South Africa in 1854, Grey was required to try to make the colony self-sufficient and able to defend itself. During his term of office, the first Cape Parliament was inaugurated. When the Xhosa cattle-killing occurred, he seized upon it as a way of promoting his goal of subordinating the African peoples on the eastern frontier, and he ruthlessly pursued his aim of advancing what he called British civilisation. He was the first British administrator to regard South Africa as an entity, and to work for federation. His federation plan came to nothing, but most colonists viewed his administration of the Cape as a success. In 1859 he was dismissed for insubordination, but was reinstated in 1860 by a new government in Britain. He finally left the Cape in 1861 to become Governor of New Zealand.

Griqua

Pastoralists of Khoi and mixed origin, who settled on the Cape's northern frontier and beyond and formed their own statelets. By the latter part of the eighteenth century, Griqua communities possessing guns and horses were becoming dominant along the middle Orange River. In the 1800s two independent Griqua chiefdoms were established north of the Orange: Griquatown, founded with missionary encouragement in 1804–1805, and ruled by the Waterboer family; and Philippolis, established in southern Transorangia in 1826 by Adam Kok II. In 1813 missionaries of the London Missionary Society persuaded the Griqua to change their name from Bastards to Griqua, after the original Grigriqua from whom they were in part descended. In the 1820s predatory Griqua raiding groups with firearms attacked African groups in a wide area of the interior. White penetration of the Transorangia area from the 1830s led to increasing pressure on Adam Kok III's Griqua in what became the Orange River Sovereignty and then the Orange Free State. In 1861 they sold all their lands to the Orange Free State and trekked across the Drakensberg mountains to the country known as 'Nomansland' on the eastern side of the Drakensberg, which then became known as Griqualand East. There the Griqua community began to lose land to whites after Kok's death in 1875. After an unsuccessful rebellion in 1878 the community began to disintegrate, and in 1879 Griqualand East was incorporated in the Cape Colony. The Griqua of Griqualand West under Nicholas Waterboer met no serious challenge to their land rights until the discovery of diamonds in the area in the late 1860s. Rival claims to the diamond fields resulted in the fields being awarded to Waterboer in 1871; Griqualand West was then annexed by Britain, and finally incorporated into the Cape colony in 1880. Most Griqua had by then sold their farms to whites, and by the end of the century few remained as landholders and the majority were sunk in poverty.

Sir George Grey, Governor of the Cape from 1854 to 1861
(Cape Archives E 362)

Philippolis, capital of Griqualand in 1834, by Charles Bell
(Africana Museum)

Griqualand East

In 1861–1862 Adam Kok III led a mass migration of Griqua from Philippolis in the Orange Free State over the Drakensberg mountains to what had been called 'Nomansland' and which then became known as Griqualand East. Kokstad was founded as the main Griqua settlement, and the first Cape colonial official was stationed there in 1874. The following year Kok was killed in a road accident, after which the Cape government lifted its ban on the sale of liquor and land in the territory. By 1878 the community had largely disintegrated and in 1879 Griqualand East was formally annexed to the Cape Colony. A century later, after the neighbouring

Encampment of the Griqua chief Adam Kok, near the Riet and Modder Rivers, by Charles Bell, 1835
(Africana Museum)

Transkei had been led to independence, Griqualand East was transferred from Cape administration to Natal.

Griqualand West

Territory north of the Orange River in which diamonds were discovered. In the early nineteenth century the Griqua under Cornelis Kok and Barends were persuaded by London Missionary Society missionaries to settle down with their followers at what became Griquatown. The Griqua chiefs fought a losing battle against whites purchasing the farms of their subjects. In 1871, a few years after diamonds were found in the area, the British formally annexed what it termed Griqualand West, land which the Orange Free State claimed and for which it was paid £90 000 compensation. After the territory was incorporated into the Cape Colony in 1880, it was represented in Parliament by Cecil Rhodes.

Group Areas Act (1950)

The instrument by which the government implemented residential segregation on the basis of race in urban areas. The Act set aside residential and business areas in towns and villages for the ownership or occupation of particular race groups. In terms of the Act, and its many amendments, large numbers of families were uprooted from their homes and businesses were relocated, usually very much further away from the city centres and their places of work. Between 1960 and 1983 about 860 000 people were moved, and the Act was the cause of immense suffering and generated much bitterness. The coloured community suffered most severely, Indians substantially and whites hardly at all. Africans had long been segregated in urban areas. In 1991 the Act, along with other legislation providing for the segregation of residential areas, was repealed. By then the social geography of such major cities as Cape Town and Durban, and even small towns and villages, had been transformed as a direct result of the Group Areas Act.

Archie Gumede, Natal Secretary of the ANC from 1951 to 1960
(Mayibuye Centre)

Gumede, Archibald Jacob
PIETERMARITZBURG, 1914 —

Anti-apartheid activist. An active member of the African National Congress in Natal from the 1940s, Gumede was its Natal Secretary from 1951 to 1960. His involvement in the Congress of the People campaign led to his being charged with treason in 1956, and in 1963 he was banned for five years under the Suppression of Communism Act. He became an attorney in 1967 after a period as an articled clerk in Pietermaritzburg, and later set up a legal practice of his own. He worked closely with the Natal Indian Congress, particularly on education issues, and was involved in community issues such as health and commuter problems. He played an active part in the creation of the United Democratic Front in 1983, and he was one of its first presidents. Threatened with detention in 1984, he and six others sought refuge in the British Consulate in Durban. On leaving the Consulate, they were charged with treason, but the charges were withdrawn in June 1986. In 1988 Gumede was again banned, but in 1990 he was one of the ANC delegates who met with representatives of the South African government at Groote Schuur in Cape Town.

H

Hani, Martin Thembisile (Chris)

COFIMVABA, TRANSKEI, 1942 — BOKSBURG, TRANSVAAL, 1993

Charismatic politician. A devout Christian in his youth, who joined the African National Congress (ANC) while at school in 1957, Hani attended the University of Fort Hare, where he was influenced by Marxist ideas and became a lover of Latin and of literature. He left South Africa in 1963 to undergo military training and fought in Rhodesia. From 1974, based in Lesotho, he worked to create a political structure for the ANC in the eastern Cape. He rose through the ranks of Umkhonto we Sizwe to become Chief of Staff in 1987. After the ANC and Communist Party (CP) were unbanned, he returned to South Africa and soon became a very popular speaker in the townships. Long an active member of the CP, he was elected its General Secretary in 1991. In the last year of his life he urged militant youth to work for peace. His assassination in April 1993 sent shock waves through South Africa. A massive funeral was held and in the aftermath of the assassination violence increased markedly and racial tensions grew.

Herstigte Nasionale Party (HNP) (Restored National Party)

Dissident members of the National Party broke away in 1969 and reconstituted themselves as the HNP under the leadership of Dr Albert Hertzog. They felt that any modification of Verwoerd's policy was a betrayal, they opposed Vorster's Outward Policy, and they objected to mixed race sport and the appointment of black ambassadors from foreign states. In subsequent elections the HNP failed to gain a single seat in Parliament, but continued to snipe at the government from the far right. After the establishment of the Conservative Party in 1982, there was speculation that the two parties might merge, but this did not happen. They worked together at times, as in the white referendum in March 1992, but more frequently opposed one another.

Nationwide protests and demonstrations erupted after the assassination of Chris Hani
(The Argus)

Hertzog, James Barry Munnik

WELLINGTON, CAPE, 1866 — PRETORIA, 1942

High court judge, Boer general and Prime Minister of the Union of South Africa. Hertzog entered politics as leader of the Orangia-Unie Party in 1906. A member of the Union's first cabinet under Louis Botha, his strong nationalist views led to his exclusion from government in 1912. He then formed the National Party (1914) and with the support of the Labour Party became Prime Minister in 1924. His party joined with Smuts's South African Party during the Depression and a new United Party was born, but he remained Prime Minister and only lost office when he opposed South Africa's entry into the Second World War in September 1939.

A staunch segregationist, he was responsible for some of the key legislation which oppressed blacks, including the Act, passed in 1936, which removed Cape Africans from the common voters' roll and offered them instead the opportunity of participating in an advisory Natives' Representative Council.

J B M Hertzog, Prime Minister of the Union of South Africa
(Transvaal Archives TAB 9295)

Het Volk (The People's Party)

A political organisation founded by Louis Botha in the Transvaal Colony in 1904. Its aims were conciliation and unification of the whites in South Africa, self-government for the Transvaal, equal status for English and Dutch, and an end to further importation of Chinese labourers for the mines. After it gained an outright victory in the 1907 elections, Botha became Prime Minister of the Transvaal. In 1910, at the time of Union, it was absorbed into the new South African Party.

Right:
Portrait of Emily Hobhouse by Hugo Naudé. During the South African War she visited the concentration camps and brought the plight of the Boer inmates to the attention of the British public
(National Cultural History Museum)

High Commissioner

The office of High Commissioner was developed in 1846 and added to that of Cape Governor. The High Commission gave its holder vague authority beyond the Cape's frontiers. Gradually the high commissionership became an informal and inexpensive means of extending British sovereignty in southern Africa. British Kaffraria (1847) and the Orange River Sovereignty (1848) were established under the High Commission, and Basutoland (1868) and the Diamond Fields (1871) were annexed to Britain in terms of the High Commission. Sir Bartle Frere and Sir Alfred Milner used the High Commission to full effect, and thanks to it they were able to act as imperial proconsuls for the region as a whole. After the British defeat at Isandlwana in 1879 a separate High Commissioner for South East Africa was appointed. Basutoland, Bechuanaland and Swaziland were long known as the High Commission territories because they fell directly under the High Commissioner, who from 1910 was also Governor-General. As those territories moved towards independence, the office of High Commission was abolished in 1964.

Hintsa, chief of the Gcaleka and Xhosa paramount from 1804
(Africana Museum)

Hintsa

TRANSKEI, *c.* 1790 — TRANSKEI, 1835

Chief of the Gcaleka and Xhosa paramount from 1804. Believing in his complicity in the Xhosa invasion of the colony in December 1834, the British in turn invaded his territory beyond the Kei and persuaded him to enter their camp to negotiate the return of cattle. When he realised that he had been made a hostage, he attempted to escape and was shot, after which his body was mutilated. His death made him a martyr among the Xhosa.

Hobhouse, Emily

CORNWALL, 1860 — LONDON, 1926

British philanthropist, active in South Africa during and after the South African War (1899–1902). In 1901 she visited the British concentration camps, in which a high incidence of disease and poor organisation were claiming an appalling number of lives among the Boer inmates.

When she returned to England, her revelations of the conditions prevailing in these camps shocked many and led the Liberal Party to criticise the Tory Government's

'methods of barbarism'. After the war she set up home industries for impoverished Boer girls.

Hofmeyr, Jan Hendrik (Onze Jan)

CAPE TOWN, 1845 — LONDON, 1909

Journalist, champion of the Dutch language and Cape political leader. Hofmeyr derived much of his political strength in the Cape Parliament (1879–1895) from his leadership of the Afrikaner Bond. Until 1900 no man assumed the premiership without consulting him. His alliance with Rhodes, of mutual advantage, ended with the Jameson Raid, which Hofmeyr condemned strongly. He worked hard to prevent war, and in the aftermath encouraged reconciliation between Boer and Briton.

Hofmeyr, Jan Hendrik

CAPE TOWN, 1894 — PRETORIA, 1948

Politician. Brilliant classics scholar, Principal of the University of the Witwatersrand (1919–1924), and Administrator of the Transvaal (1924–1929), Hofmeyr entered politics as the South African Party member of Parliament for Johannesburg North in 1929. Smuts's more liberal deputy, he held a number of cabinet posts in United Party governments, most notably finance and education, and he acted as Prime Minister several times during the war years. An able debator and hard-working administrator, many saw him as Smuts's successor.

Far left:
Onze Jan, champion of the Dutch language and leader of the Afrikaner Bond
(South African Library)

Left:
Crossroads squatter camp. In 1991 the housing shortage nationwide was estimated at 1,3 million units
(Mayibuye Centre)

Homelands, *see* **Bantustans**

Hottentots, *see* **Khoikhoi**

Housing

The massive influx of both Africans and whites into the towns early this century, the almost complete cessation of building activity as a result of the First World War, and the conspicuous neglect of African housing by local authorities, resulted in an acute housing shortage by the 1920s. After 1923 the compulsory residential segregation of Africans helped prompt some local authorities to begin to provide housing for Africans, but few municipalities made use of the facilities available for borrowing funds for sub-economic housing. Until 1937 Africans in the Cape could acquire freehold property in towns. Thereafter, like Africans elsewhere, they had to rent government housing in locations, or build houses on land acquired on thirty-year lease. Rapid African urbanisation after 1939 exacerbated the housing shortage, and spawned a large number of squatter settlements in the major urban centres.

After 1948 the National Party government encouraged 'site and service' schemes and cleared the squatter settlements, and its influx control policies helped reduce the housing shortage in the towns. As it was government policy to build homes in the Bantustans, municipal housing was cut back, producing a severe, contrived shortage of housing. Slums appeared and reappeared in urban areas. After 1982 the government shifted responsibility for provision of housing to the private sector, providing land and as many serviced sites as possible where individuals could erect their own homes financed with loans from banks and building societies. In 1991 the housing shortage was estimated at 1,2 million units, and it was thought that there were approximately seven million people living in squatter settlements, the majority of which lay outside Johannesburg, Durban and Cape Town.

Huguenots

French refugees, some 200 of whom were brought to the Cape by the Dutch East India Company between 1688 and 1700. Many French Protestants had already left France before the Edict of Nantes was repealed by Louis XIV in 1685. The removal of the last guarantee of immunity from the persecuted Calvinists resulted in a flood of refugees, some of whom were attracted by

Above:
'Bushman Hottentots armed for an expedition', by Samuel Daniell, 1804. The men hunted with bows and poison-tipped arrows, and used a variety of snares and traps
(Africana Museum)

Above right:
Hut tax collecting, Natal
(Local History Museum Collection, Durban)

the offer from the Dutch East India Company of a passage to the Cape and a chance to begin a new life there. The new arrivals settled mainly in the Stellenbosch district at De Fransche Hoek (the French corner), present-day Franschhoek. The Huguenots were a cohesive group and might have developed into a distinct community, had not Governor Simon van der Stel interspersed them amongst the Dutch free burghers, and required them to learn, worship and communicate with the authorities in Dutch. By the mid-1700s use of the French language had died out.

Hunter-gatherers

The earliest people to live in southern Africa were hunters and gatherers. Speaking a variety of languages characterised by clicks, these yellow-skinned people lived either along the coast, where they collected shellfish, or inland, where they relied on their knowledge of the foods and waterholes of the semi-desert regions, or lived in mountainous areas, living off game, plant-foods, wild honey and such small animals as caterpillars, termites and locusts.

The men hunted with bows and poison-tipped arrows, and used a variety of snares and traps. The women gathered the plant foods, using a digging stick and a skin cloak, which also served as a bag. Those who lived in the more mountainous areas fished in rivers with harpoons made of bone. Other equipment included stone knives, bone and stone tools, and ostrich eggs used for storing water. Organised in small, loosely knit bands, of which the family was the basic unit, the hunter-gatherers roamed seasonally within a defined area, following the game and available vegetation. Some were prolific artists, painting and engraving on stone and ostrich eggs.

As the population of the country increased and the wild game diminished, hunter-gatherers were forced to resort to stealing domestic stock. As a result, white settlers and Khoi made war on them, driving them from one mountain range to another, hunting them like animals, and capturing their children for use as farm servants. Only in the Kalahari Desert regions of Botswana and Namibia have the few remaining communities been able to maintain a semblance of their old way of life.

Hut Tax

A tax imposed by colonial authorities on African communities throughout the country and used as a means of forcing Africans to enter the labour market and to serve as a source of revenue. The South African Republic introduced a hut tax in 1870 in response to a labour shortage; the British imposed a hut tax on the Sotho after annexing Basutoland in 1868; hut tax was collected in Griqualand West from 1879. In Natal a tax of seven shillings per hut introduced in 1849 yielded the considerable income of over £10 000 per year for the colonial treasury. From 1888 a hut tax was imposed on the whole of Zululand by the British and was the major source of revenue for the territory. Many Africans were forced to sell their cattle to pay the tax, and larger numbers entered the wage labour market to raise the necessary cash. In this way the imposition of hut tax contributed to the creation of a migrant labour force.

I

Immigration

Thirty-six years after a victualling station had been established at the Cape, the first organised immigration scheme was undertaken when the Dutch East India Company brought out 225 French Protestant refugees between 1688 and 1700. During the early eighteenth century the free burghers at the Cape opposed immigration, and when the Council of Seventeen attempted to pursue a more active immigration policy in the latter half of the century, they had little success.

The nineteenth century was an era of vast emigration from Europe. Relatively few immigrants were attracted to South Africa, however, for the country offered insufficient opportunities for employment and low rates of pay. Under a scheme sponsored by the British government, 5 000 British immigrants were settled in the eastern Cape in 1820, and over 6 000 German military and civilian immigrants and their families were settled in British Kaffraria by Sir George Grey in 1858. Five thousand British settlers arrived in Natal between 1849 and 1852.

From 1860 Indian labourers were recruited on contract to work on Natal's sugar cane plantations, railways and coal mines. Mainly male Hindus from Madras, most of these labourers chose to remain in South Africa after the expiration of their contracts. After 1913 Union legislation prevented the entry of new immigrants from India.

The mineral discoveries of the 1870s and 1880s started the first large rush of immigrants to South Africa from all over the world. Skilled workers and artisans, many from Britain, came out to work on the mines. The last two decades of the nineteenth century saw a large influx of Jews from Eastern Europe, particularly Lithuania. This immigration was cut off by the Quota Act of 1930. However, immigration of German Jews continued, 7 000 of whom fled to South Africa in the 1930s before the Aliens Act of 1937 closed the door to further German Jewish immigration. Attempts to encourage immigration in the early twentieth century failed due to economic depression and the lack of scope for unskilled white labour. After the Second World War, Smuts started a large-scale state-organised immigration scheme to alleviate the shortage of skilled labour. In 1947–1948, 64 000 immigrants arrived, 88 per cent of whom were British. When the National Party came to power in 1948 it ended the scheme. However, by 1961, with the establishment of the Republic, the Nationalist government overcame its fear of foreigners and significant immigration from Europe accompanied the economic recovery which followed Sharpeville.

With the decolonisation of Africa, immigration of whites to South Africa from other African countries greatly increased, especially from Mozambique and Angola in the mid-1970s, and from Rhodesia/Zimbabwe as that country moved to independence.

Indian family, Umzinto, Natal. Between 1860 and 1911, 152 184 indentured workers from India arrived in Natal on five-year contracts
(Cape Archives J 1421)

Immorality Act

The first Immorality Act passed in 1927 forbade extra-marital sex between whites and blacks. An amending Act (No. 21 of 1950), passed shortly after the Mixed Marriages Act, which forbade inter-racial marriages, extended the prohibition by forbidding extra-marital sex between whites and any people of colour. Further amendments in 1957, 1967 and 1969 extended the scope of the Act to include immoral or indecent acts and increased the maximum penalty for offences to seven years imprisonment. The Act led to sensational court cases, and many instances of suicide. Its effects were vividly shown in Alan Paton's novel *Too Late the Phalarope*. Eventually the government repealed the Immorality Act, along with the Mixed Marriages Act, in 1985.

Imvo Zabantsundu (Opinions of the People)

An influential weekly Xhosa newspaper established in King William's Town in the eastern Cape in 1884. Its founding and best-known editor, John Tengo Jabavu, established the newspaper with capital guaranteed by R W Rose Innes and J W Weir, liberal white businessmen. *Imvo* became the recognised mouthpiece of Xhosa opinion and Jabavu a leading political figure in the Cape. In its columns, which were in both English and Xhosa, Jabavu tried to persuade those Africans who qualified for the vote to become involved politically. *Imvo* was shut down by government order in August 1901 after Jabavu, whose political sympathies were with Hofmeyr's Afrikaner Bond, had blamed Milner for starting the South African War. It appeared again in October 1902 and has continued to be published since, though it never regained the importance it enjoyed in its early days.

The Zion Christian Church, the largest independent church by the mid-1980s, invited State President P W Botha to its 75th Anniversary celebrations in 1985 (South African Communication Service)

Independent Churches

The African independent church movement, which began in the latter part of the nineteenth century, was an expression both of black religious autonomy and of political opposition to white colonial rule. Disillusioned with the paternalistic control of white missionaries, who either tended to frustrate Africans' ambitions by closing off opportunities for leadership within the mission churches, or who caused offence by denouncing African culture and customs, African church leaders began to secede. In 1884 Nehemiah Tile, a Wesleyan Methodist preacher, set up his Thembu Church in the Transkei, and in 1892 Mangena Mokone's Ethiopian Church was founded in Pretoria. In 1896 Mokone's Church became affiliated to the African Methodist Episcopal Church, an American foundation which spread rapidly throughout South Africa under the leadership of James M Dwane, and which claimed 10 000 members by 1898. The Revd Pambani Mzimba broke away from the Presbyterian Free Church of Scotland Mission to set up a Bantu Presbyterian Church, and Simungu Shibe seceded from the American Board's Zulu Mission to form the Zulu Congregational Church. The Lutheran Bapedi Church and the Africa Church had been established in the South African Republic in 1889.

The movement, which spread rapidly throughout South Africa, so that by 1990 there were nearly five thousand different churches claiming the allegiance of thirty per cent of the African population, at first gained adherents at a time when African political independence was largely destroyed and access to land was severely curtailed. Some of the early independent churches were millenarian in character, such as the Israelite sect, founded by Enoch Mgijima at Bulhoek in the eastern Cape in 1918, and that founded in the Transkei in the 1920s by Dr Wellington Buthelezi. While leaders such as Tile, Mzimba and Dwane were active and articulated black dissatisfaction with white rule, the independent church movement was predominantly an alternative channel for Africans to political activity, and many of the churches were highly conservative, as demonstrated when the Zion Christian Church, the largest independent church by the mid 1980s, invited State President P W Botha to its annual celebrations in the northern Transvaal.

Indians

The first Indians to come to South Africa were slaves who were brought to the Cape in the seventeenth century by the Dutch. The origin of the Indian community of today, however, lies in two streams of migration which began in the second half of the nineteenth century. Between 1860 and 1911, 152 184 indentured workers from south and north-eastern India arrived in Natal on five-year contracts. White sugar farmers on the coast had requested such labour, but Indians were also employed on up-country farms, the wattle estates, the coal mines and the railways. Others served as cooks, waiters and laundrymen. Close to 80 per cent were Hindus, others were Muslim and Christian. Their languages included Tamil, Telugu, and varieties of Hindi and Urdu. At the end of their contracts, workers could reindenture for a further term, remain in Natal as free Indians or return to India on a free passage after ten years. Over half remained in Natal and became market gardeners, hawkers and fishermen. Others went to the diamond-fields at Kimberley and to the Transvaal.

The second group of migrants were Gujerati-speaking Muslim and Hindu traders from the west coast of India, though some came from Mauritius. A few were Christian teachers and priests. They were known as 'passenger' Indians because they paid their own passage to Natal. Indian merchants also migrated directly to the Transvaal, the Orange Free State and the Cape.

By 1911 the Indian population in South Africa numbered 149 791 (89 per cent in Natal, 7 per cent in the Transvaal, 4 per cent in the Cape and only 106 Indians in the Orange Free State). In 1980 of the 821 320 Indian South Africans, 82 per cent lived in Natal, 14 per cent in the Transvaal and 4 per cent in the Cape. Sixty-two per cent were Hindu, 19 per cent Muslim and 12 per cent Christian. Although Indians have never constituted more than 3 per cent of the total South African population, since 1904 they have outnumbered whites in Natal.

Various South African governments placed restrictions on Indians once they began to compete economically with whites. In the Transvaal, Law 3 of 1885 denied Asians citizenship rights and restricted ownership of property only to specially demarcated areas; in 1907 all Asians had to carry registration certificates; and new immigration was almost closed in 1908 since immigrants were required to pass a test in a European language. In the Orange Free State, Indians were denied the right to purchase or rent fixed property in 1885 and in 1890 they could not settle there for longer than two months or pursue any business without permission. In Natal, a £3-tax was imposed on ex-indentured workers to encourage them to return to India or to re-indenture; Indians were denied the franchise in 1896; in 1897 a Dealers' Licences Act was passed to restrict the growth of Indian traders and the Immigration Restriction Act of 1897 required immigrants to know a European language. This provision was also adopted by the Cape Colony in 1902, although Indians suffered the least discrimination there.

The earliest Indian political organisations, the Natal Indian Congress (1894) and

Cutting sugar cane, Natal 1888. Sugar farmers on the coast made extensive use of indentured Indian labour
(Cape Archives J 1445)

Indians landing at the Durban docks
(Africana Museum)

Above:
Gandhi as a barrister of law in Johannesburg, 1900
(Local History Museum Collection, Durban)

Right:
The Great March, 29 October 1913. Gandhi led 200 striking miners of the Natal collieries from Newcastle towards the Transvaal in protest against the legal restrictions on Indians and the £3-tax. The march was the climax of the Passive Resistance Campaign
(Local History Museum Collection, Durban)

the Transvaal British Association (1903) presented petitions to the colonial and imperial governments to protest against these laws. In 1907 Mohandas Gandhi launched a *satyagraha* (the force of truth) campaign, which led to Indians courting imprisonment by breaking the registration and immigration laws of the Transvaal. In 1913 this struggle culminated in a strike of 20 000 workers in Natal against the £3-tax which was then abolished. The government also accepted the validity of Indian marriages which had become an issue in the campaign. Most of the restrictive laws against Indians, however, remained.

Mosque in Durban's Indian quarter, 1923, by Elizabeth Drake
(Local History Museum Collection, Durban)

The Immigrants' Regulation Act of 1913 prohibited new Indian immigration except for the wives and children of domiciled Indians. In 1953 even this was stopped. Indians did not enjoy freedom of inter-provincial movement until 1975. From 1914 successive South African governments also tried to repatriate Indians by offering free passages to India and cash bonuses. The Indian government gave its assistance according to the Cape Town agreement of 1927. These schemes failed to significantly reduce the Indian population, although over 40 000 Indians left the country. In 1961 the Nationalist government accepted Indians as a permanent part of South Africa, and the inducements to leave the country were removed in 1975.

South African governments also attempted to segregate Indians for both trade and residential purposes. The intervention of the Indian government and the Cape Town agreement stayed such legislation until the 1940s. Moderate Indian politicians in Natal undertook to dissuade Indians from buying in predominately white areas. After two commissions of inquiry in 1941 and 1943 had investigated the extent of acquisition of property by Indians, the Smuts government passed the Pegging Act of 1943 which prohibited the transfer of property in Durban from whites to Indians except by permit. In 1946 this was replaced by the Asiatic Land Tenure and Indian Representation Act, which divided Natal into exempted and controlled areas where Indian purchases would be restricted. As a result, India withdrew its High Commissioner to South Africa, imposed trade sanctions, and put the treatment of Indian South Africans before the United Nations.

Indian radicals who had taken over the Natal Indian Congress in 1945 launched a passive resistance campaign (1946–1948). Effective segregation of Indians throughout the country was ultimately ensured by the Group Areas Act of 1950. By 1972, 27 694 Indian families had been removed and relocated; by 1975, 1 277 traders had been displaced.

In 1964 a government-nominated advisory body, the National Indian Council, was established, which became the South African Indian Council in 1968. It eventually became an elected body but in the first elections of 1981 only 10 per cent of voters went to the polls. In terms of the South African constitution of 1983, Indians elected members to a House of Delegates, while Indian ministers had responsibility for 'own affairs' such as education, health and housing. Of the registered voters, only 20 per cent voted in the 1984 elections.

Tensions between Indians and Africans in Natal erupted in riots in 1949 and 1985. On the other hand, Indian Congress leaders forged alliances with the African National Congress and in 1952 participated in the Defiance Campaign. Some Indian leaders willingly participated in government structures, while others joined the United Democratic Front in 1983. Today there are Indian members of the African National Congress, the Pan Africanist Congress and the Azanian People's Organisation.

(U S Mesthrie)

Industrial and Commercial Workers' Union of South Africa (ICU)

A trade union formed by Clements Kadalie in 1919, the ICU grew into the first mass movement of blacks in South Africa. Kadalie, a mission-educated Malawian, formed a small trade union among coloured dockworkers in Cape Town in 1919, and organised a moderately successful strike of these workers in the same year. In the 1920s, as national secretary, he built up the ICU into a massive movement, which expanded especially in the rural areas of Natal, Transvaal and the Orange Free State. In 1927 it claimed a membership of 100 000, the majority rural Africans.

The ICU voiced a broad range of popular grievances. In the towns its main success was in organising workers in the docks, railways and municipal services. In the countryside, it played on black grievances relating to the issues of land, wages and the pass laws. Kadalie consistently sought to win recognition for the ICU as a legitimate union and voice for black workers. Failing to win acceptance by white-led unions in South Africa, he went abroad in 1926 in a bid to secure international recognition for the ICU. William Ballinger, an adviser sent out by the British Labour movement in 1928, found the affairs of the ICU in chaos. Kadalie fell out with both Ballinger and A W G Champion, leader of the Natal ICU, who broke away in 1928 and established a rival ICU *yaseNatal*. Conflict, together with financial misdealings, destroyed the ICU from within, while the government and employers both acted to suppress the organisation. By 1929 the ICU was in rapid decline. Kadalie established an Independent ICU which had an organised following only in East London. By 1933 the ICU had virtually disappeared. It had won few advances for its members, and achieved very little for them except giving them a brief 'taste of freedom'.

Dr G M Naicker (right), President of the Natal Indian Congress, addresses the crowd at a Passive Resistance rally, 26 June 1946
(Mayibuye Centre)

Influenza Epidemic (1918)

In September 1918 South Africa was overwhelmed by the worst single natural disaster in its history to date, when it was struck by the world-wide Spanish Influenza epidemic. By the time the epidemic had abated in November, probably more than a quarter of a million South Africans had died. South Africa sustained one of the highest per capita death rates in the world, particularly among Africans and coloureds, those in the Cape being particularly hard hit. The epidemic served to draw attention to the squalid conditions in which black people lived in the towns, but in the aftermath little was done to ameliorate the situation.

Influx Control

Control over the movement of Africans into the urban areas. Smuts's Natives (Urban Areas) Act of 1923 imposed a system of segregation and influx control on the African population. Africans were to be allowed into the towns only to serve white labour needs, and in strict proportion to the availability of work. All African people, except for domestic workers, would be housed in locations outside the towns. Towns would thus be kept 'white', and a steady supply of African labour to the white farms would be maintained. In 1937 male labourers from the reserves were given fourteen days in which to find work in the towns, or return to the reserves. From 1938 influx control regulations were applied systematically, chiefly by means of the pass laws, amendments to the 1923 Act and subsequent related legislation. In 1952 the notorious 'Section Ten' legislation was enacted. This denied the right to any African person, male or female, to live in an urban area unless he or she had lived there continuously for fifteen years or served under the same employer for ten years. It also reduced to seventy-two hours the time allowed Africans for finding employment in an urban area.

From 1958 all African men, and from 1963 all African women, had to carry passes which showed whether they were legally entitled to be in the towns. If not, they were sent back to the homelands. Failure to carry the necessary document was in itself a punishable offence. Despite all these measures the number of Africans in the towns grew. Influx control caused immense social distress — husbands and wives were separated, homes were broken up — and the administration of the system led to the growth of a vast and corrupt bureaucracy. In 1986 influx control was abolished by the P W Botha government.

Inkatha

A national cultural liberation movement, Inkatha yeNkululeko yeSizwe, was established by Chief Mangosuthu Buthelezi in 1975. He claimed to be reviving a body with the same name which had had a short-lived existence in the 1920s. Inkatha grew rapidly in the late 1970s, gaining support almost exclusively among Zulu-speakers. It had close connections with the KwaZulu Bantustan. In 1979 Buthelezi went to London for discussions with the African National Congress. These failed and after that the two organisations became bitter rivals. By the end of the 1980s Inkatha claimed more than 1,5 million signed up members. In 1990 it was transformed by Buthelezi into a political party — the Inkatha Freedom Party — open to all races. The IFP seeks a multi-party, non-racial democracy, supported by a free market system, and rejects violence as a mechanism for change. In mid-1991 it was revealed that Inkatha had received state funding.

Right:
Inkatha supporters brandishing cultural weapons
(Mayibuye Centre)

Iron Age

Sometime around AD 200, the first farming communities moved southwards across the Limpopo River into what is today South Africa. These people lived in small villages, grew crops such as sorghum and millet and (where conditions were suitable) kept livestock: sheep, goats and cattle. In physical type and, probably, in the language that they spoke, these early farmers were the direct ancestors of the majority of modern South Africans. Because they smelted and forged ore to make iron tools, these communities are grouped together as the 'Iron Age'.

Searching out soils that were best suited to cultivation, the first Iron Age farmers lived in the river valleys of the eastern Transvaal, Mozambique, Natal and Transkei. For many years, hunter-gatherers continued to live in the high grasslands and mountain foothills, sometimes trading with their new neighbours, and representing them in their rock paintings.

Relatively little is known about the way of life of these first farmers. Because houses were made of wood and thatch, they have not survived the passage of time. Probably, men and women made a variety of everyday objects out of wood, leather and other

Far left:
Excavations of an Early Iron Age site in Natal's Thukela River Valley. Decorated pots, such as those shown here, are distinctive markers of the sites of earlier villages
(UCT Archaeology Department)

Left:
A lowveld archaeological site before excavation. Places such as these preserve rich evidence of the way of life of South Africa's first farmers
(UCT Archaeology Department)

organic materials — these, too, have invariably failed to survive. However, Iron Age people also fired clay pots, adorning the sides of these vessels with distinctive decorations. Broken sherds of these pots mark the locations where villages once stood. In addition, burnt wood (as well as some other material) from excavated sites has been used by archaeologists to estimate the ages of some villages using the technique of radiocarbon dating. Based on this evidence, a fairly detailed outline of where and when people lived has now been worked out

Between about AD 800 and AD 1200 Iron Age patterns of settlement, and of social and economic organisation, began to change. Farmers continued to live in the low-lying river valleys, but at the same time they also moved up onto the high grasslands, taking into use virtually all parts of South Africa that receive regular summer rainfall. It is probable that this change was related to the increasing importance of cattle in everyday life.

In many parts of the Transvaal highveld, the Orange Free State and the foothills of the Drakensberg mountains the foundations of stone villages have been found, originating in this period of expansion. Complex arrangements of livestock enclosures have left ornate designs impressed on today's landscape, best seen from aerial photographs. These settlements are often concentrated along the low ridges that break the monotony of the high grasslands. Often, they are collected together — the homes of hundreds of people. Archaeological excavations have provided a considerable amount of detail about the ways of life practised.

Such expansion brought the need for more specialised economies. In particular, the high grassland areas did not have the timber resources essential for iron smelting. Consequently, networks of trade developed, sometimes across considerable distances. Iron was smelted in large quantities in the wooded valleys of Natal and Zululand, and in the ore-rich lowlands of the eastern Transvaal, and was exchanged on the highveld, probably for cattle and grain. In other areas, salt was precipitated and traded, and it is probable that other commodities, which have not survived on archaeological sites, were also exchanged.

By AD 800 there were also opportunities for trade in exotic goods, particularly glass beads, made beyond Africa's shores. Arab traders, taking advantage of seasonal winds and currents, had certainly set up camps on the Mozambican coast by this time. As with the gold and ivory that southern Africa offered Europe and Asia, glass beads had immense value because they were not made locally, and they became a form of currency.

It was probably on the basis of this new form of wealth that some Iron Age farmers became considerably more wealthy than others. The results were dramatic. Early in

Great Zimbabwe, looking from the Hill towards the Great Enclosure. These stone-walled buildings, marking the status of their occupiers, were the centre of a large town
(UCT Archaeology Department)

Artwork from the Early Iron Age. One of the seven Lydenburg Heads which were modelled in clay, fired and decorated (UCT Archaeology Department)

the twelfth century South Africa's first town was built close to the south bank of the Limpopo River. Mapungubwe — as the hill at its centre is known today — is believed to have had a population of more than 10 000 people. People of rank and status lived on the flat top of Mapungubwe Hill, and were buried there with ornate grave goods. Lesser residents of the town lived in more cramped quarters in the valley below. Within a century or so, Mapungubwe was abandoned, probably because it had been eclipsed by the rise of a new town to its north — Great Zimbabwe.

Mapungubwe was the first in a series of early South African towns. Some of these, such as the nineteenth century Zulu royal settlements of Ondini and Mgungundlovu, are quite well known from excavations, oral tradition and early travel accounts. Others await detailed study. But at the same time, the majority of South Africa's people lived in smaller villages, continuing long-established ways of tilling the soil and tending livestock. As a result, there are direct connections between the present day and the movement south of pioneer farmers some 2 000 years ago.

The Iron Age ended with the beginning of the colonial era — when new stock farmers pressed across the high grasslands of the South African interior, and when new trade settlements were established on the Mozambican and Natal coasts. New economic demands — for land, trade profits and migrant labour — broke up old ways of living, and new mythologies were introduced. It was claimed that Bantu farmers had only occupied some parts of the land for a few centuries, and that other areas had never been taken into use. But archaeological and historical research has clearly demonstrated that South Africa has a long and varied history which pre-dates colonial settlement.

(M Hall)

Iron and Steel Corporation of South Africa (Iscor)

After bitter controversy, Iscor was established by an Act of Parliament in 1928 as a public utility corporation in which the government held the controlling power. The iron and steel mills at Pretoria came into production in 1933 and provided a source of raw materials for the metal engineering industries which expanded rapidly. With the creation of Iscor the foundations were laid for rapid industrial development, and a successful policy was initiated to combat white unemployment.

Isandlwana

The site in Zululand of the first major battle in the Anglo-Zulu War (January 1879). The British failure to defend their encampment led to the obliteration of an imperial force of about 1 700 men by more than 20 000 Zulu who advanced unnoticed. Although the Zulu lost three or four thousand men, this battle was regarded as a crushing defeat for the British, and Sir Bartle Frere's policy of confederation received a setback from which it never recovered.

Islam

The first Muslims at the Cape were political exiles, convicts and slaves, brought from south-eastern Asia by the Dutch East India Company in the seventeenth century. By far the largest of these groups, and the most important as far as the establishment and growth of Islam at the Cape is concerned, was the slaves. Some came from Indonesia, others from Bengal and India. The Indonesians, who constituted about half the slave population

Death of Lieutenants Melville and Coghill of the 24th Regiment. This episode in the Battle of Isandlwana was painted by C E Fripp, special artist to *The Graphic* throughout the Zulu campaign
(Africana Museum)

Far left:
'Malay girl'. The name 'Cape Malay' was erroneously applied to the entire Cape Muslim population, only some of whom had come from the Malay Archipelago
(Africana Museum)

Left:
'Mahometan priest'. Muslim Imams performed marriages and funerals which the slave population at the Cape could not obtain in Christian churches
(Africana Museum)

of Cape Town itself, were skilled artisans, spoke Malay and retained some Malay customs. In time the name 'Cape Malay' was erroneously applied to the entire Cape Muslim population, only some of whom had come from the Malay Archipelago. Islam made greater strides than Christianity among the Cape slave population. Slaves were virtually excluded from Christianity, whereas Muslim imams identified with the black population and performed marriages and funerals which the slaves could not obtain in Christian churches.

From 1770 Islam spread rapidly at the Cape when legislation was passed prohibiting the buying and selling of Christian slaves. No such prohibition applied to Muslim slaves, and an added boon to white slave-owners was that Muslim slaves did not drink. By the turn of the nineteenth century there was a flourishing Muslim community in Cape Town which included both slaves and Free Blacks. During Britain's first occupation of the Cape, Muslims were allowed the right of public worship for the first time, praying in stone quarries and houses until the first mosque was built. Cape Muslims are Sunni; most belong to the Shafi sect, and a minority adhere to Hanafi beliefs. After 1860 Indian

Muslims arrived in South Africa to work on the Natal sugar plantations, and their descendants constitute the majority of the almost half a million Muslims in South Africa in the early 1990s.

Israelites

An African religious sect which drew upon Jewish as well as Christian ritual and doctrines, and tried to imitate the Israelites of the Old Testament in dress. The preachings of their leader, Enoch Mgijima (1868–1928), were strongly millenial: the world would soon come to an end and only God's chosen people, the Israelites, would be saved. Their main centre was in the eastern Cape near Queenstown, and they became well known through the Bulhoek massacre of 1921, a tragic incident in which the Israelites defied government attempts to remove them and were massacred by police. Their church remains active in that area today.

Bulhoek, November 1921. The temple of the Israelites
(Africana Museum)

J

Jabavu, John Tengo

HEALDTOWN, CAPE, 1859 — FORT HARE, 1921

Newspaper editor and spokesperson for the Xhosa people. The son of Mfengu Methodists, Jabavu qualified as a teacher at Healdtown. In 1884 he became editor of *Imvo Zabantsundu* ('Opinions of the People'), a weekly newspaper published in King William's Town. He used his influential position to argue against anti-black legislation and to influence African opinion. His paper was the voice of the newly emergent black petty bourgeoisie of the eastern Cape.

Jabavu was instrumental in establishing Fort Hare University for African students (1916) and became the most prominent Xhosa-speaking layman in the Methodist Church.

Jameson, Leander Starr

EDINBURGH, 1838 — LONDON, 1917

Politician and physician. After qualifying as a medical doctor he accepted a partnership in Kimberley where he was involved in a court case after wrongly diagnosing cases of smallpox amongst black mine workers. He later became invaluable to C J Rhodes in the latter's attempts to open up Matabeleland in Southern Rhodesia to white settlement. He was arrested in the western Transvaal for his part in what became known as the Jameson Raid, a conspiracy to topple the Kruger government. Soon released, he entered Cape politics in 1900 and was Prime Minister until 1908, when he resigned at a time of severe financial depression. He opposed Louis Botha in the Union elections of 1910 and became Leader of the Opposition.

Jameson Raid (December 1895)

An abortive attempt to overthrow the government of the Transvaal Republic. Kruger's government was the chief obstacle to Cecil Rhodes's plans for a South African federation under British control, and so the Prime Minister of the Cape secretly

John Tengo Jabavu (front row, second from right) and the promoters of the Inter-State Native College Scheme, *c.* 1908. Jabavu was instrumental in the establishment of Fort Hare University
(Cory Library)

Dr Jameson opposed Louis Botha in the Union elections of 1910
(Africana Museum)

plotted, with his close friend Dr Leander Starr Jameson and Uitlander leaders of the Transvaal, to overthrow Kruger. Jameson was to invade the Transvaal from Bechuanaland with an armed party, which was to link up with an Uitlander uprising on the Rand. The scheme was bungled, the uprising did not materialise, and Jameson and 500 men were forced to surrender by republican troops on 2 January 1896. The Kruger government imposed heavy fines on the Uitlander ringleaders after they had been tried and sentenced to death. Jameson himself, who was sentenced to fifteen months imprisonment, was released after a few months. The fiasco of the Raid ruined Rhodes's political career, for he had to resign as Prime Minister. It also destroyed the alliance which he had constructed between English and Afrikaners in the Cape. The fact that the British Colonial Secretary, Joseph Chamberlain, was party to the affair

'Dr Jameson's famous march – attack by the Boers'. The bungled Uitlander uprising against the Kruger government had heavy political costs (Africana Museum)

was suppressed by a Committee of Inquiry held in London in 1897, and evidence of his involvement was not proved until many decades later.

Jewish Community

South Africa's Jewish community, predominantly of Lithuanian origin, is mostly orthodox, with some 20 per cent supporting Reform Judaism and an unknown number not committed to religious observance. In the early 1990s the community numbered about 118 000, which represented 0,5 per cent of the overall population. A survey in the late 1980s indicated that South African Jews were generally perceived as part of the privileged white community, not as a separate minority. Jews have made notable contributions to South African society, out of proportion to their numbers, in commerce, politics and the professions, and many radical whites have been of Jewish origin.

Job Reservation

One of the earliest ordinances implementing job segregation was that passed by the British in the Transvaal which restricted Chinese labour to unskilled positions. In 1907 white mine workers went on strike over attempts by mineowners to give African and Chinese labourers jobs which had previously been held exclusively by white workers. The Mines and Works Act (1911) was a crucial landmark in officially sanctioned job reservation in South Africa. It secured skilled positions in the mines for white workers only.

In 1916 a Status Quo agreement was reached between the Chamber of Mines and the unions which guaranteed no further deviation from job segregation but which allowed those Africans who had already been placed in skilled jobs to remain there. However the fixed price of gold and the increase in production costs for mines meant a reduction in profitability. As a result mineowners attempted to lower production costs by dismantling the colour bar which reserved particular jobs for more highly paid white workers. Although in 1919 the mineowners wished to do away with job segregation, they were happy to keep the wage bar which kept black wages at a minimum. In 1920, after mineowners had asked the government for subsidies for marginal mines, a government inquiry suggested that the colour bar be dissolved. After the 1920 strike by black mine workers, mineowners were more determined than ever to abolish job reservation. In 1922 however, over 20 000 white workers went on strike partly to counter the attempts made by mineowners over the years from 1920 to 1922 to erode the job colour bar. The strike failed but the Pact Government which came to power in 1924 adopted a 'Whites First' policy to protect white workers in all sectors of the economy from black competition. An amended Mines and Works Act was passed in 1926 and it was not until the mid-1980s that job reservation in the mines was finally discarded.

Johannesburg

The largest city in South Africa, and centre of the gold mining industry, manufacturing and commerce, Johannesburg emerged from the barren veld in 1886 with the discovery of gold in the Witwatersrand area of the Transvaal. The farms from Driefontein in the east to Roodepoort in the west were proclaimed public diggings, and gold mining operations began. By November 1886 a Goldfield's Diggers Committee was elected, which became the city's first local government authority. Johannesburg was named after Johannes Rissik, the Acting Surveyor General, and Christian Johannes Joubert, Head of the Mines Department of the South African Republic, who had been appointed as commissioners to investigate mining.

By 1887 mining syndicates had begun to operate in Johannesburg, and houses, churches, shops, bars and brothels were springing up amongst the tented diggers' camps. For five years, until the railway from Cape Town reached Johannesburg in 1892, every article of food and clothing, and every piece of machinery or building material had to be transported by wagon from Kimberley or from the coast. The pursuit of wealth led to a very rapid increase in population, from 3 000 in 1886 to 120 000 in 1899. By 1914 the city boasted over a quarter of a million inhabitants, excluding those blacks living illegally on the outskirts of the town. To accommodate people and buildings, municipal boundaries were pushed out from five square miles in 1901, to eighty-two square miles in 1903.

By the mid-twentieth century, Johannesburg had become the centre of the South African business world and the hub of the largest industrial and commercial complex in the country. Many of the gold mines on the Witwatersrand were worked out by the early 1970s, but most of the business and administrative headquarters of the gold mining companies were still located in the city.

One of the earliest ordinances implementing job reservation restricted Chinese labour to unskilled positions in the gold mines
(Cape Archives J 2064)

This etching of Commissioner Street, the main street in Johannesburg, appeared in *The Graphic* of 8 August 1891
(The Brenthurst Library)

Piet Joubert, Commandant-General of the Transvaal Republic's forces during the Anglo-Transvaal War of 1880–1881
(National Cultural History Museum)

Joint Councils

Joint Councils of Africans and Europeans were established in 1921 to promote interracial cooperation and to investigate and make representations on matters affecting the welfare of Africans. These Councils provided a form of white-black contact, and helped lead to the founding of the South African Institute of Race Relations in 1929, which continued the task of promoting such contacts. Some Joint Councils continued in existence, but by the 1950s few remained active.

Joubert, Petrus Jacobus

DAMASKUS, NEAR PRINCE ALBERT, 1831 — PRETORIA, 1900

Military and political leader. The son of Voortrekkers, Joubert began a public career in 1860 as member of the Transvaal Volksraad, became Chairman in 1873 and acted as Vice President when President Burgers visited Europe (1875–1876). As Commandant-General, he assumed command of the Republic's forces during the Anglo-Transvaal War (1880–1881), gaining victories at Laing's Nek, Ingogo and Majuba Hill. Until 1898 he was a regular candidate for election to the presidency, but never succeeded in obtaining a majority over Kruger, his lifelong ally and rival.

K

Kadalie, Clements

NKHATA BAY, MALAWI, 1896 — EAST LONDON, 1951

Trade unionist. A teacher from Malawi, Kadalie settled in Cape Town where in 1919 he launched the Industrial and Commercial Workers' Union of South Africa (ICU), becoming its first secretary. During the 1920s he built the ICU into the first modern mass movement of blacks in South Africa. By 1929, however, the ICU had disintegrated and Kadalie spent his remaining years in East London in futile attempts to revive and reunite it.

Clements Kadalie launched the Industrial and Commercial Workers' Union of South Africa in 1919
(Africana Museum)

KaNgwane

A non-independent Bantustan created in 1977 in the eastern Transvaal for the Swazi people. Comprising two separate pieces of land, KaNgwane abuts on Swaziland, and is part of the traditional land of the Swazi. All Swazi people in South Africa became citizens of KaNgwane, which in 1989 had a population of 583 535. South African government attempts to cede KaNgwane, along with the Ingwavuma portion of KwaZulu, to Swaziland, to give that country an opening to the sea, were blocked by the courts in 1982.

Karoo

The name, derived from the Khoi, means 'hard', 'dry'. The Karoo is a semi-desert region encompassing more than half of the Cape Province, and occupying about one-third of the total area of South Africa. Bounded by the Langeberg mountains in the south, and extending northwards into the southern Orange Free State, it is a region of flat-topped hills and open treeless plains, its vegetation giving it a unique character. By the 1740s white trekboers had crossed the Langeberg and entered the Karoo. San hunters, resentful of alien intruders who shot game on their hunting grounds, attacked their cattle. Bantu-speaking mixed farmers did not settle in the Karoo in any numbers prior to the nineteenth century because of its aridity. In the past century much of the Karoo has been given over to sheep farming and poor farming practices have caused the deterioration and sometimes destruction of the indigenous vegetation, resulting in an enlargement of the Karoo, especially eastwards.

Kat River Settlement

In terms of Cape Ordinance 50 of 1828 the right of Khoi and 'other free persons of colour' to own land was affirmed, but the Cape government only initiated one experiment in granting land to such people. In 1829 land in the Kat River valley in the eastern Cape, from which the Xhosa chief Maqoma had been expelled, was made available to 250 families. The settlement, on a military frontier, was intended to serve as a buffer between colonists and the Xhosa. The settlers supported the colony in two frontier wars, but saw their settlement devastated, and increasingly threatened by encroaching white settlers. Some decided to go into rebellion against the colony in 1851, at the time of the Eighth Frontier War. The rebels lost their land, but the settlement survived and some of the descendants of the original settlers were forced from the Kat River in the 1970s and 1980s after the land had been incorporated in the Ciskeian Bantustan.

Khoikhoi (Khoekhoe or Hottentots)

Indigenous herding people of the Cape, and the first South Africans encountered by Portuguese explorers (Bartolomeu Dias in 1488 and Vasco da Gama in 1497) seeking a sea route to India. Contemporary descriptions of the Khoikhoi in the fifteenth to seventeenth centuries indicate they had large herds of cattle and sheep which they

Prime specimens of the Ripplemead stud flock. Much of the Karoo has been given over to sheep farming and poor farming practices have contributed to an enlargement of this semi-desert area
(Cape Archives AG 9601)

'View of a Bushman kraal', by W J Burchell. The huts were made of decorated mats laid over a wooden structure, and were easily dismantled and transported on the backs of oxen
(The Brenthurst Library)

traded with the Europeans for metals. Because their stock were considered as both wealth and food, they ensured that the reproductive capacities of their herds took precedence. This meant that only older animals beyond breeding age were either exchanged or ritually killed.

Since their animals needed pasture and water, they constantly moved their camps. This was not a random movement: in the western Cape they would winter near the coast around Saldanha Bay, utilising coastal foods, like shellfish and seals. As the pasture diminished they moved inland across the Swartland towards the mountains and the Berg River. On the south coast, summer rains allowed a different mobility pattern: wintering in the Little Karoo, and returning to the coast in summertime.

The tools and shelter of the Khoikhoi were designed for mobility. They made containers of wood and leather, as well as clay pots with handles, and carried spears and knobkerries. Their huts were decorated mats laid over a wooden structure which were easily dismantled and carried on the backs of oxen.

The origins of the Khoikhoi are somewhat obscure, but both linguistic and archaeological information supports the idea that they developed some 2 000 years ago out of the Khoe-speaking hunting people (San) of the area where Angola, Botswana, Namibia and Zambia have common borders today. How the hunters became herders is not known. One suggestion is that they intermarried with incoming black Iron Age farmers, obtaining stock as well as acquiring the necessary social organisation to nurture and breed the animals.

Entry to the Cape may have been down the Atlantic coast. Archaeological evidence of their passing indicates that they only had sheep at this time. Once they entered the Cape they encountered local hunting people called Soaqua (another form of San). Several archaeological sites in the Cape have produced evidence of early herding activity. One major site, Kasteelberg, north of Saldanha Bay, has produced the bones of animals eaten between 1 800 and 800 years ago. Although many sheep bones were found, the dominant mammals represented were seals. Residues sticking to the outside of potsherds from the site show that the people boiled seal carcasses to render the fat. In the same area are small caves. One of these, Witklip, was occupied by people at the same time as Kasteelberg was being used. Witklip produced almost no sheep or seal bones, but many bones of little buck, as well as different kinds of tools and smaller ostrich eggshell beads than those found at Kasteelberg. These finds provide archaeological support for the existence of both hunters and herders in the area.

As the Khoikhoi expanded around the south coast, they ultimately came into contact with African farmers in the eastern Cape and Transkei. It is probable that it was this second association with such farmers that allowed the exchange of cattle which were later seen by the first Europeans.

The Khoikhoi were socially organised into different groups under a chief, each with its own pasture territory. There was constant raiding between groups, mostly for cattle. Pasture and water rights were strictly controlled and it was the Portuguese lack of understanding of this that led to conflict on the first encounters between the Khoikhoi and Dias's crew when the latter had the 'bad manners' to try to fill their water casks without permission. Land was used communally on a need and pasture availability basis, another area foreign to the private ownership concept

'A group of San, frying locusts', by G Ferrario
(The Brenthurst Library)

prevailing in Europe at the time. When the Dutch landed in Table Bay, the fact that there was no one there was taken to mean that the land was empty. But the Khoikhoi had merely moved inland, and expected to return to Table Bay when their pasture schedule demanded it.

The Dutch frequently accused the Khoikhoi of stealing their goods, but ownership of personal property (other than cattle) was not recognised among them. They shared their personal possessions on a need basis without asking, and by taking

Left:
Hottentots, 1687. Fat or seal-oil mixed with a red pigment was rubbed onto their bodies to keep their skin supple
(Cape Archives M 1048)

Left:
N J Merriman's depiction of a Hottentot man and woman
(Africana Museum)

from the Dutch, the Khoikhoi accorded them the status of patrons or wealthy people.

Fat or seal-oil mixed with red pigment was rubbed onto their bodies, both as a sign of wealth (only a person with many animals could afford to do this) and to keep their skin supple. This produced a strong odour which repelled the Europeans, although some of the Dutch admitted that the fynbos herbs (such as buchu) mixed with the fat had quite a pleasant smell.

Pressures on Khoikhoi lands, as well as on the Khoikhoi to trade their stock with the Dutch colony, increased steadily. Their initial reluctance to part with their breeding stock meant that unscrupulous colonists went out and stole the animals. This was one reason for the wars between the Khoikhoi and the Dutch of 1659–1660 and 1673–1677. The last conflict forced the Khoikhoi to recognise that the Dutch were there to stay. Loss of lands and livestock meant that many herders continued to retreat as the colony expanded. For the Khoikhoi of the southwestern Cape, the final blow occurred in the years 1713 to 1720 when first a devastating smallpox epidemic killed many of their number, and then stock diseases and drought decimated their herds. After this the Khoikhoi at the Cape virtually disappeared as independent food producers, and became Dutch dependents.

Land continued to be lost to white farmers, and it was only during the nineteenth century that the mission stations of Namaqualand (Leliefontein, Kommagas, Steinkopf and Richtersveld) gave the Khoikhoi some measure of security of tenure. These were taken over by government administration in 1909 and designated 'coloured Reserves'.

(A B Smith)

General view of the diggings at Kimberley c. 1871. One year after the discovery of diamonds, Colesberg Koppie was well on the way to becoming the 'Big Hole'. As the diggings went deeper, each claimant set up his own pulley to extract the diamond-bearing ore (National Cultural History Museum)

Kimberley

Principal diamond mining centre of South Africa, and commercial centre of the northern Cape, Kimberley grew out of a mining camp which developed after the discovery of diamonds in the area in 1869–1870. The 'big rush' commenced in 1871 after the sensational discovery of a diamond-bearing pipe at a hill called the Colesberg Koppie. By the end of 1871 approximately 50 000 people had flocked to the diamond fields and Kimberley was second in size only to Cape Town on the sub-continent. The diamond fields were annexed by the British Colonial Secretary, the Earl of Kimberley, in 1871 and the town, along with the rest of what was known as Griqualand West, was incorporated into the Cape Colony in 1880. By 1877 Kimberley had become the centre of an enormous gun trade: large numbers of black migrant labourers worked on the mines long enough to earn a rifle before returning home. During the South African War (1899–1902) Kimberley was besieged by Boer forces for four months (November 1899– February 1900) until relieved by General John French. The town remained the headquarters of De Beers Consolidated Mines until the early 1990s.

Kindergarten

Collective nickname for a group of brilliant young men from Oxford, who were attracted by Milner's reputation and came out to assist him in his administration of the Transvaal and Orange River Colony after the South African War (1899–1902). They included G Dawson, P Kerr, L Curtis, R H Brand, P Duncan, L S Amery and E Grigg. Inspired and coordinated by Milner, they provided the Transvaal with an excellent administration, and many went on to distinguished careers in later years.

Kitchener, Horatio Herbert

COUNTY KERRY, IRELAND, 1850 — OFF ORKNEY ISLANDS, 1916

Soldier and Administrator. Appointed Chief of Staff to Lord Roberts, he arrived in South Africa in 1900. It was under his supreme command that an unsuccessful attack was launched on Cronjé at Paardeberg, in which many British soldiers died. As Commander-in-Chief he attempted unsuccessfully to end the war, instituting a series of blockhouses and using a scorched earth policy to try to end the guerrilla fighting. He was responsible for the establishment of concentration camps in which many Boer women and children died. He left South Africa in 1902.

Kok, Adam III

GRIQUALAND WEST, 1811 — NEAR KOKSTAD, 1875

Griqua chief. In 1837 Kok became chief of the Griqua at Philippolis in what became the Orange Free State. Pressed seriously by Boer expansion, he sold all his lands to the Free State government (1861), and led 2 000 Griqua on a two-year trek across the Drakensberg mountains to what was called Nomansland, later renamed Griqualand East. There he considered himself an independent ally of the British, but in 1874 a colonial official began the process of imposing colonial rule, and Griqualand East was formally annexed to the Cape after Kok's death in 1879.

Korana

Khoi pastoralists distinguished from other Khoi groups such as the Nama and Cape Khoi by their separate language, Korana. By the nineteenth century Korana were living both north and south of the Orange River. Some had moved into Griqua territory, and others had settled in the valleys of the Vaal and Hart Rivers. By the mid-nineteenth century Korana clans, possessing firearms and horses, dominated the middle Orange, from Griqualand West to Kakamas. Increasing resentment over white and coloured encroachment of Korana pasturelands south of the Orange led the Korana to engage in cattle-stealing from farmers living on the Cape's northern border. Two northern border wars were fought between Korana and the Cape government (1868–1869 and 1878–1879), resulting in the defeat of the Korana. Their chiefs were imprisoned on Robben Island, and most of the Korana men, women and children were sent into service in the Cape Colony. Koranaland was renamed Gordonia and opened to white and coloured settlement.

Kruger, Stephanus Johannes Paulus

BULHOEK, CRADOCK, 1825 — CLARENS, SWITZERLAND, 1904

President of the South African Republic. The son of Voortrekkers, with a reputation as a brave soldier, Kruger became Commandant-General of the Transvaal Republic in 1863. When Britain annexed the Transvaal (1877) he successfully led his people in the struggle to regain independence. In 1883 he was elected President of the restored Republic and won further elections in 1888, 1893 and 1898. He resisted Milner's more extreme demands and decided to launch war against the

Kitchener was appointed Chief of Staff to Lord Roberts when he arrived in South Africa in 1900
(Transvaal Archives TAB 21285)

Above:
Griqua chief Adam Kok
(Transvaal Archives TAB 20995)

Left
'A Korah Hottentot village on the left bank of the Orange River', by Samuel Daniell c. 1800. After losing their land, many Khoikhoi migrated north and settled in the Orange River area
(Africana Museum)

Right:
President Paul Kruger. He died in exile in Switzerland after the South African War
(Cape Archives AG 13918)

Above:
King Goodwill Zwelithini of KwaZulu (second from left) and Chief Minister Mangosuthu Buthelezi celebrate Shaka Day in Pietermaritzburg, 29 September 1988
(Mayibuye Centre)

British pre-emptively in October 1899. He was forced to flee from his country in 1900 and died in exile.

KwaNdebele

A non-independent Bantustan in the central Transvaal for Transvaal Ndebele, who are of Nguni origin. KwaNdebele was established in 1979 when several Transvaal Ndebele were expelled from nearby Bophuthatswana as a result of ethnic tensions. KwaNdebele became a self-governing Bantustan in 1981. A tiny, impoverished state of 516 300 people, KwaNdebele functions as a dormitory and labour reserve for the Pretoria-Witwatersrand-Vereeniging industrial area.

KwaZulu

KwaZulu is the largest and most populous of the Bantustans, as well as the most fragmented, comprising twenty-nine major and forty-one minor fragments of land, scattered throughout Natal and Zululand, most of which are surrounded by South Africa. KwaZulu became self-governing in 1977, under its king, Chief Goodwill Zwelithini Bhekuzulu. Its leader, Chief Minister Mangosuthu Buthelezi, was able, with the backing of Inkatha, to gain control of the KwaZulu legislature and use it to resist independence. His efforts to unite Bantustan leaders in opposition to political fragmentation failed when the leaders of Transkei, Bophuthatswana, Venda and Ciskei all accepted independence between 1976 and 1981.

In 1980 the Buthelezi Commission was launched by the KwaZulu Legislative Assembly to investigate the possibility of reconstituting KwaZulu and Natal as a self-governing unit. In 1982 the commission reported in favour of the political unification of KwaZulu and Natal under a form of consociational democracy. Buthelezi's constitutional initiatives attracted considerable liberal support but were rejected by the government, which in 1986 turned down a further proposal for a joint Natal-KwaZulu legislature. In parts of Natal and KwaZulu there was a major outbreak of violence from 1985 onwards, between Inkatha and United Democratic Front/African National Congress supporters. The conflict slowly escalated into virtual civil war and included elements of gangsterism and criminality.

In the early 1990s KwaZulu was an impoverished Bantustan with a population of 5,2 million people, of whom (in 1986) 439 000 commuted daily between their homes and places of employment outside KwaZulu, and a further 333 000 were employed outside the region as migrant workers. Migrant and commuter income together contributed 71 per cent of Gross National Product. KwaZulu accounts for 66 per cent of the population of the Natal/KwaZulu area and contributes only 6 per cent to the Gross Domestic Product of the area. As leader of the single largest group in South Africa, Buthelezi demanded recognition as an equal partner together with the government and the African National Congress in negotiations over a future government.

L

Labour Party (Coloured)

The Labour Party (LP) was formed in 1965 in anticipation of the establishment of the Coloured Persons' Representative Council (CRC). It used its participation in that body as a springboard for coloured resistance. The LP decided in 1983 to participate in the government's tricameral parliamentary system, breaking the unity of the Black Alliance and creating a credibility problem for the party. The LP was the majority party in the coloured House of Representatives from its establishment until 1992, when so many of its members left to join the National Party that it consequently lost that position. LP spokesmen claimed that the party played a major role in the tricameral system in bringing about reform. Many coloureds, however, rejected the LP as collaborationist, and LP candidates were often returned to Parliament in elections in which very few people voted.

Labour Party (White)

Formed in 1910 under the leadership of Colonel F H P Creswell, by the amalgamation of two smaller labour parties in the Cape and the Transvaal, the Labour Party (LP) championed the interests of white workers in the cities, seeking their protection against African, coloured and Asian competition. From its establishment, therefore, the LP proposed segregationist policies. It formed a pact with Hertzog's National Party before the 1924 general election, and the Pact Government formed after that election marked the high point in the party's fortunes. Thereafter it slowly declined; it split in 1928 and by 1958 had ceased to exist.

Lagden Commission (1903–1905)

To achieve uniformity in 'native policy' in the four South African colonies which he hoped would unite, Sir Alfred Milner appointed a South African Native Affairs Commission in 1903 to make recommendations on 'native policy' to the governments of the four colonies. The chairperson, Sir Godfrey Lagden, had been appointed Commissioner for Native Affairs in the Transvaal by Milner after the South African War (1899–1902). The Commission proposed the permanent separation of Africans and whites politically and territorially, and the segregation of races in the towns. Many of its proposals were enacted into law after Union in 1910.

Langa

The oldest African township on the Cape Flats outside Cape Town, Langa was established in 1927 to replace the Ndabeni location, which was to be demolished so that the land could be used for industrial purposes. The majority of Langa's inhabitants became single male workers, for from 1954, in line with its influx control policy, the government refused to sanction the building of any more family accommodation. In 1960 anti-pass law demonstrations resulted in three deaths and numbers of wounded in Langa. As late as the early 1980s there was talk of moving the residents of the township further away from the city, but instead the residents of Langa were able to buy their own houses and the township was upgraded and enlarged in the early 1990s.

Langalibalele

UTRECHT DISTRICT, NATAL, 1818 —
PIETERMARITZBURG, 1889

Chief of the Hlubi. By 1873 Langalibalele was one of the most powerful hereditary chiefs still independent in Natal. In that year he refused to register his people's rifles as required by law. He was

Colonel F H P Creswell, leader of the Labour Party which was formed in 1910
(South African Library)

Above:
Cartoon of Sir Godfrey Lagden, chairman of the Lagden Commission
(Africana Museum)

Left:
Chief Langalibalele and his sons
(Local History Museum Collection, Durban)

C J Langenhoven, author of *Die Stem van Suid-Afrika* (Transvaal Archives TAB 34490)

deposed by Shepstone, who sent a military force against him. His people subsequently lost their land and cattle, and Langalibalele, who tried to flee, was arrested and brought to trial. In a travesty of justice, he was found guilty of murder, treason and rebellion, was banished for life and imprisoned first on Robben Island and then on the Cape Flats.

Langenhoven, Cornelis Jacob

LADISMITH DISTRICT CAPE, 1873 — OUDTSHOORN, 1932

Writer, politician, promoter of the Afrikaans language. Langenhoven was a lawyer and practised in Oudtshoorn in the southern Cape. He was a strong advocate of the cause of the Afrikaans language, wishing it to be taught in schools and officially recognised. As a senator in Parliament in the 1920s he saw the latter goal obtained in 1925. He wrote a regular column for *Die Burger*, and a number of books, poems, plays and essays in Afrikaans. He also wrote *Die Stem van Suid-Afrika* which became the national anthem.

Law

In South Africa the constitution embodied in the South Africa Act (1909) and the Republic of South Africa Constitution Act (1961) vested the power to make law in four bodies: Parliament, provincial councils, city councils and the law courts. Law made by the first three bodies was referred to as 'statute law' or 'legislation'. Once passed in Parliament, legislation could be repealed or amended only by Parliament, and the law courts (including the Supreme Court) enforced the 'will of Parliament'. Provincial councils made laws providing for white school education, hospitals, local authorities, roads, etc. City councils made local by-laws and regulations governing social amenities, traffic and health services.

Law made in the law courts, 'common law', was based on Roman Dutch and English law, and evolved by 'precedents' — the interpretation of law in relation to specific test cases. A judge made law only if no precedent existed. Minor offences were dealt with in magistrates' courts, or sometimes the courts of chiefs and headmen. Disputes could also be settled by arbitration or tribunal; but if proceedings failed, appeal had to be made or action instituted in a division of the Supreme Court, presided over by a judge. Conflict between the interests of common law and the bureaucratic state gave rise to professional bodies such as Lawyers for Human Rights, which attempted to monitor discrimination in the administration of justice. The South African Law Commission Act (1973) provided a channel for recommendations on reform and improvement in all branches of the law.

The Houses of Parliament, Cape Town

Lebowa

A non-independent Bantustan in the central northern Transvaal for northern Sotho people, including the Pedi and Lobedu. Comprising several detached pieces of land, Lebowa became self-governing in 1972, but like the other Bantustans remained heavily dependent on Pretoria for money to balance its budget. In 1978, 54 per cent of South Africa's northern Sotho lived in Lebowa; the remainder continued to live in other parts of South Africa. Gross maladministration had drained the Bantustan's coffers by the early 1980s and caused unrest, especially in the schools.

Le Fleur, Andrew Abraham Stockenström

HERSCHEL, 1867 — KRANTZHOEK, PLETTENBERG BAY DISTRICT, 1941

Visionary; Griqua leader. The son of an advisor to Adam Kok III, Le Fleur married into the Kok family. In the late nineteenth century, he represented the Griqua in their land claims. After spending time in prison for sedition, he was barred from returning to Griqualand East and worked with coloureds in Cape Town, attempting to set up self-help schemes. The agricultural settlements he established at De Doorns and Touws River (1913–1915) failed, but the one founded near Plettenberg Bay under his direction flourished and became the main Griqua establishment in South Africa.

Leipoldt, Christiaan Frederik Louis

WORCESTER, 1880 — CAPE TOWN, 1947

Afrikaans poet, writer and educator. Leipoldt trained as a medical doctor and was an eminent paediatrician. From 1926, he was for many years the editor of the *South African Medical Journal*. As a journalist of note he wrote numerous articles in Dutch, Afrikaans and English. One of his most well-known volumes of Afrikaans poetry was *Oom Gert Vertel en Ander Gedigte* (1911), and as a dramatist, his major work was *Die Heks* (1923). These and other works made a substantial contribution to the development of Afrikaans as a written language. His English works include *The Ballad of Dick King* (1949) and his autobiography, *Bushveld Doctor* (1930). Despite his circle of largely English friends, he identified strongly with Afrikaner aspirations.

Lembede, Anton Muziwakhe

GEORGEDALE, NATAL, 1914 — 1947

A leading intellectual, Lembede was the first President of the African National Congress Youth League, established in 1944, and the originator, with A P Mda, of an Africanist ideology. Born into a family of Zulu labourers in Natal, Lembede trained as a teacher and then a lawyer in Johannesburg. He rose rapidly in the African National Congress and became a leading advocate of more militant tactics, and a foe of the communists, who were the most articulate opponents of his Africanist philosophy. His early death was widely acknowledged to be a tragedy.

Liberalism

The political philosophy of liberalism champions the freedom of the individual against political, social and economic domination. Essentially a humanist philosophy, with its roots in the eighteenth century Enlightenment, liberalism cherishes certain 'democratic rights' as essential: freedom of conscience, speech and of the press, and equality before the law. Unrestrained 'freedom', it believes, leads to anarchy, and most liberals therefore argue for a political system that offers maximum individual liberty while maintaining social stability and political and economic security.

Griqua leader Andrew Le Fleur and a group of his followers outside the Kokstad prison, 1898
(Cape Archives AG 1545)

C Louis Leipoldt. His writings made a substantial contribution to the development of the Afrikaans language
(Cape Archives AG 4590)

In South Africa, liberalism developed in relationship to white minority rule, and was thus preoccupied with two issues: race relations and the rule of law. Though some liberals thought for a time that segregation could be just, after the National Party's election victory in 1948 led to the promulgation of extensive legislation designed to entrench apartheid, liberals opposed these measures strongly, particularly as they set the government and its agents beyond the bounds of law, thus eroding the 'rule of law' (based on the constitution and an independent judiciary), and replaced it with 'rule by the law' (measures introduced apart from the constitution to give the power of law to party policies).

Liberalism tended to oppose both nationalism (white or black) and communism, as both seemed to require authoritarian forms of government that curtail democratic liberties. Liberals thus spent much time advocating a constitution that enshrined a bill of rights, and contained 'checks and balances' to prevent any group (whether majority or minority) from dominating the society as a whole.

Liberal Party

Founded in 1953 as a result of dissatisfaction among a small group of whites with the racial policy of the United Party (UP), the Liberal Party, initially led by Margaret Ballinger, one of the Native Representatives in the House of Assembly, called for the elimination of all racial discrimination. At first it advocated a qualified franchise, but later adopted the principle of political equality for all and adult suffrage in a democratic South Africa. The party was strongly anti-communist and opposed the Freedom Charter, rejecting the clauses in that document which called for nationalisation as illiberal. In 1963–1964 the party was hard hit when a few of its members were involved in sabotage. Consequently the Minister of Justice, B J Vorster, identified it with communism and used strong-arm tactics against it. Over forty of its leading members were arrested or banned, and a number of others went into exile. With the passage of the Prohibition of Political Interference Act (1968), which made multiracial parties illegal, the Liberal Party decided to dissolve itself. At that time, it had an estimated 3 000 supporters, half of whom were black, and its leader was the internationally known writer Alan Paton, himself a founder member. Some of its white members had stood for Parliament, but none even came close to winning a seat. After its dissolution, some became active in the Civil Rights League, the Black Sash and other extra-parliamentary organisations.

Above:
Early prose-writing was largely non-fictional. The letters and diaries of Lady Anne Barnard provide great insight into life at the Cape during the years of British Occupation
(Africana Museum)

Above:
Henry Rider Haggard's romances enjoyed great popularity towards the end of the nineteenth century
(Transvaal Archives TAB 14132)

Above:
Pauline Smith's *The Little Karoo* transfers into English the speech structures of the Afrikaners who are her subject
(South African Library)

Literature in English

Literature in English in South Africa first appeared as a result of immigration from Britain in the eighteenth and nineteenth centuries. Early prose-writing was largely non-fictional — comprising journalism, travellers' tales, diaries such as that of Lady Anne Barnard, and hunting romances — which gave rise to a strong tradition of fictional realism which would persist into the twentieth century. At the end of the nineteenth century the imperialist romances of Henry Rider Haggard, such as *Allan Quatermain* (1887), were popular. This tradition resurfaced in the twentieth century with Laurens van der Post's mystic travelogues and romance narratives like *Venture into the Interior* (1952).

A parallel pastoral tradition developed. Olive Schreiner's *The Story of an African Farm* (1881) was to become renowned. Pauline Smith's *The Little Karoo* (1925) transfers into English the speech structures of the Afrikaners who are her subject. Herman Charles Bosman continued the pastoral tradition, fusing it with an ironic vision as in his *Mafeking Road* (1947).

In the twentieth century, while still following the pattern of social realism, literature has become increasingly politicised. This trend had in fact begun with the 'liberal' and socially aware poetry of the 1820 settlers — Thomas Pringle and Andrew Geddes Bain. William Plomer's *Turbott Wolfe* (1929), with its theme of miscegenation, was the first novel to use social realism as a mode of protest against racialism. Miscegenation is also the theme of Sarah Gertrude Millin's *God's Step-children* (1924), a novel which has been excoriated for its apparently racist tendencies. Writing from a liberal humanist standpoint in *Cry the Beloved Country* (1948), Alan Paton continued the tradition of protest literature. This novel is also an example of a genre, dubbed 'Jim comes to Jo'burg', dealing with the evils of the social dislocations caused by labour control. Peter Abrahams's *Mine Boy* (1946) is a further example of this type. Dan Jacobson's early novellas — *The Trap* (1955) and *A Dance in the Sun* (1956) — combine social realism and political awareness with the pastoral vision of earlier writers.

After the Nationalist government's institutionalisation of apartheid, awareness of the indignities suffered by the blacks fuelled a committed literature among both black and white writers. It has been difficult for white English-speaking writers to find an idiom to express their abiding sense of alienation and marginalisation, trapped between the opposing nationalisms of Afrikaners and Africans. Nadine Gordimer has created a mode of urban realism that from *The Lying Days* (1953) to *My Son's Story* (1990) provides an exploration of, and comment upon, the years of apartheid.

Before the 1950s writing by blacks in English had been sparse, mainly nurtured by mission schools and drawing heavily on English models. Sol Plaatje's *Mhudi* (1930) follows the romance tradition and R R R Dhlomo's *An African Tragedy* (1928) that of social realism. During the 1950s the magazine *Drum*, centred in Johannesburg, encouraged black writing, and a hugely influential generation of young black writers including Nat Nakasa, Lewis Nkosi, Can Themba and Ezekiel Mphaphlele wrote fiction which was impressionistic, racy, readable and strongly based on American models. In the 1950s and 1960s, when political protest and black writing was suppressed, many writers committed suicide or were hounded into exile, where they produced mainly poetry — the leading names were Dennis Brutus, Arthur Nortje, Mazizi Kunene, Mongane Wally Serote —

or autobiographical or semi-autobiographical work — such as Mphaphlele (*Down Second Avenue*, 1959) and Alex La Guma (*A Walk in the Night*, 1967).

Poetry of the early period was largely based on English models, although poets struggled to come to terms with the concept of Africa. The outstanding poetic voice of the beginning of the century was that of Roy Campbell. He spent most of his life in Europe, but his early epic *The Flaming Terrapin* (1924) and the lyrics of *Adamastor* (1930) are influenced by African themes and images. After the Second World War, Guy Butler, Sydney Clouts and Ruth Miller were in the forefront of a strong local tradition of poetry. Poets of the early 1990s still working largely in a European mode, included Douglas Livingstone, Patrick Cullinan and Stephen Watson. Since the 1960s poets like Wopko Jensma, and much more recently Kelwyn Sole, Jeremy Cronin and Ari Sitas write socially committed and often technically experimental poetry.

Oswald Mbuyiseni Mtshali's collection, *Sounds of a Cowhide Drum* (1971) and Serote's *Yakhal'inkomo* (1972) signalled the flowering of black poetry during the 1970s and the creation of an authentic South African idiom, mainly under the influence of the Black Consciousness movement. 'Soweto Poetry' as it came to be called, encouraged by *Staffrider* magazine during and after the 1980s, often employed a new version of English, influenced by *tsotsi-taal* (the *lingua franca* of the townships), Afrikaans, African vernacular languages and Americanisms. This has remained a feature of black poetry to the present day in the work of poets like Farouk Asvat, Sipho Sepamla and Essop Patel, and it has become for them, as for many white poets, a new rhetoric of resistance. Until recently little use was made of the African oral tradition, but, as practised by Mzwakhe Mbuli it is now a popular form of community expression.

South African drama developed late, although during the 1950s Guy Butler and Lewis Sowden had written plays on the theme of the clash between Afrikaner and Englishman or black and white. Athol Fugard in such plays as *The Blood Knot* (1961) and *My Africa! My Children!* (1990) has pioneered a new type of non-racial and politicised theatre, based on American models and relying heavily on improvisation. Since the non-racial Market Theatre opened in 1976, this type of drama has flourished and an indigenous dramatic form has been developed by white as well as black writers, drawing on traditions of black community theatre and providing a voice for the oppressed.

Drum **magazine actively encouraged black writing, and a hugely influential generation of young writers emerged, among them Lewis Nkosi**
(Mayibuye Centre)

Mongane Wally Serote, one of the leading names among black protest writers
(Mayibuye Centre)

During the 1980s Cavafy's motif 'waiting for the barbarians' became a controlling image in fiction as well as poetry, figuring social upheaval and a potentially cataclysmic confrontation between black and white. The novels of J M Coetzee (*Waiting for the Barbarians*, 1980 and *Foe*, 1986) have been pre-eminent in showing a direction outside the Anglo-African tradition. The use of post-modernist structures, particularly in fiction, has recently become an increasingly popular literary device.

(M I Leveson)

London Missionary Society (LMS)

The most important missionary society active in South Africa in the early nineteenth century, the LMS was an interdenominational Protestant society foun-

Jan Tzatzoe, Andries Stoffels, Revd James Read (Snr), Revd James Read (Jnr) and Dr Philip, all of the London Missionary Society, give evidence before the House of Commons Select Committee
(Cory Library)

ded in 1795. It came into conflict with the government of the Cape over policy towards the Khoi and the slaves. One of the first missionaries sent out by the LMS to the Cape, Johannes van der Kemp, arrived in 1799 and a few years later established what became the best-known LMS mission in South Africa at Bethelsdorp, today part of Port Elizabeth. Other prominent LMS representatives in South Africa included James Read, who worked with Van der Kemp at Bethelsdorp and was later missionary in the Kat River Settlement, Robert Moffat, who worked at Kuruman, the missionary/explorer David Livingstone, and John Philip, who was superintendent of the society in South Africa from 1819 to 1849. In the first half of the nineteenth century the LMS had more missionaries in the field, scattered over a wider area, than any other missionary society.

Luthuli, Albert John

BULAWAYO, ZIMBABWE, *c.* 1898 — STANGER, NATAL, 1967

Zulu chief, teacher and President-General of the African National Congress (ANC). A teacher by vocation, Luthuli spent seventeen years as chief of his people at Groutville. In 1952 he was elected President-General of the ANC and soon came into conflict with the government, suffering a succession of banning orders. A deeply religious man, Luthuli was awarded the Nobel Peace Prize for 1960 in recognition of his non-violent struggle against apartheid. He recalled his life in a moving autobiography entitled *Let My People Go.* He died when knocked down by a train in mysterious circumstances.

Albert Luthuli in Oslo, 1960, where he was awarded the Nobel Peace Prize
(Mayibuye Centre)

M

Madlathule Famine

A massive famine which occurred in the first decade of the nineteenth century and affected the entire northern Nguni area. It is thought that it was preceded by a steady decline in rainfall which reached its lowest point at about the time of the famine. The famine shattered the precarious balance between population and resources in Zululand, and is thought by some historians to be an important factor in promoting the process of political centralisation which climaxed in the creation of Shaka's Zulu kingdom.

Mafeking

The most northerly town in the Cape Colony, Mafeking was established in 1885 after the annexation of Bechuanaland by the British. Although outside the Protectorate of Bechuanaland, it was the headquarters of the administration for many years. Mafeking became famous when it was besieged by the Boers for seven months (October 1899 — May 1900) during the South African War. News of its relief was received with jubilation in London. In 1980 Mafeking was transferred to the Bantustan of Bophuthatswana and its name was changed to Mafikeng.

Above:
This photograph, taken by a Boer doctor, shows the Boers in action against the British at Magersfontein. In the pit beneath the awning, the Boers treated their wounded
(Transvaal Archives TAB 24011)

Magersfontein, Battle of (1899)

A key battle in the early part of the South African War. When British troops stormed Magersfontein on 11 December 1899, they were cut down by rifle fire from thousands of Boers in concealed trenches, so well disguised as to be invisible to reconnaissance. The British lost 948 men, the Boers 255. The severe defeat for the British in this battle meant that Lord Methuen's efforts to relieve Kimberley had to be postponed. With the news from Magersfontein, the British realised that the war would not be over by Christmas.

Left:
'The heroic defence of Mafeking by Colonel Baden-Powell'. The town was besieged for seven months during the South African War
(National Cultural History Museum)

Above:
Sketch plan of Majuba mountain
(Transvaal Archives TAB 30824)

Majuba, Battle of (1881)

In December 1880 Kruger, Joubert and Pretorius announced the restoration of the Transvaal Republic, beginning the Anglo-Transvaal War, otherwise known as the Transvaal War of Independence. Major-General Sir George Pomeroy Colley and the Natal Field Force, attempting to march into the Transvaal, occupied Majuba mountain in late February 1881. The British were sleeping when Boer volunteers stormed the mountain and forced them to retreat along the open plateau. British resistance collapsed and Colley was among those mortally wounded. There were many calls to 'avenge Majuba', but by the time the battle was fought the British government had already decided to withdraw from the Transvaal. An armistice agreement was signed on 6 March 1881 and by the Pretoria Convention of August 1881 the Transvaal became a self-governing territory.

Above:
Dr D F Malan, Prime Minister from 1948 to 1954
(Transvaal Archives SAB 2824)

Malan, Daniel Francois

RIEBEEK WEST, 1874 — STELLENBOSCH, 1959

Politician and theologian. A Dutch Reformed Church minister and champion of Afrikaans culture, Malan became editor of *Die Burger,* which supported the National Party, in 1915. He entered Parliament in 1918, and joined Hertzog's cabinet in 1924. With the formation of the Fusion Government (1934), he broke away and founded the Purified National Party, which then formed the official opposition. A reunited National Party won the 1948 elections and Malan became Prime Minister. His government then began to implement apartheid and acted in constitutional and unconstitutional ways to ensure that it remained in power. He retired from politics in 1954.

Mandela, Nelson Rolihlahla

QUNU, NEAR UMTATA, TRANSKEI, 1918 —

Leader of the African National Congress (ANC), for long the most famous prisoner in the world, then Deputy President and President of the ANC, Mandela, a man of great stature, is a member of the royal Thembu family. He became involved in student politics at Fort Hare University, from which he and his close friend and colleague Oliver Tambo were expelled for participating in a student strike. A prominent member of the ANC Youth League in the late 1940s and early 1950s, he became increasingly active in organising Congress resistance to government policies. In 1952 he and Tambo opened the first black law practice in the country. From 1956 he was one of those who stood trial for treason, a

Right:
Nelson Mandela, accompanied by his wife Winnie, leaves the Victor Verster Prison on 11 February 1990
(Mayibuye Centre)

trial which dragged on until he and others were acquitted in 1961. After Sharpeville, he was instrumental in the formation of Umkhonto we Sizwe, and became its first Commander-in-Chief. In 1962 he was arrested and in 1964 he was sentenced to life imprisonment with other leaders of Umkhonto on charges of sabotage and planning guerrilla war. He was then imprisoned, first on Robben Island and later in Pollsmoor prison on the Cape Peninsula. His release from incarceration was the subject of many campaigns, in South Africa and around the world. In the late 1980s he proposed to the government of P W Botha that the government and the ANC enter negotiations on the country's future. On 11 February 1990 he was released from Victor Verster jail near Paarl in the Cape. As Deputy President and later President of the ANC he then frequently held discussions with the government on matters of state.

Manufacturing

Prior to the mineral discoveries of the 1870s, some seventy small-scale manufacturing concerns were scattered throughout the Cape Colony, with Cape Town as the main manufacturing centre. Factories either processed agricultural products, such as distilling wine, or supplied a local need, building wagons and making bricks. The mineral discoveries and associated mining activities provided the necessary market for manufactured goods, and dynamite, mining equipment and miners' boots were made.

The development of the diamond and gold mines drew off capital and skilled labour, while the large earnings of foreign exchange from the export of diamonds and gold enabled the country to pay for cheap industrial imports. As a result, the development of manufacturing on a large scale only took place from the First World War onwards. In 1914 a protective tariff policy was introduced on a small scale, and then more markedly after 1925 when the Hertzog government provided manufacturing industries with tariff protection stipulating that they adopt a Civilised Labour Policy. This stimulated growth, and provided a new field of employment for whites, reducing white poverty.

Considerable economic growth followed South Africa's abandonment of the gold standard in 1932. The price of gold jumped and the high foreign exchange earnings helped to finance a major expansion in manufacturing industry. Clothing and textiles, metals and engineering, stone, bricks and clay all more than doubled their output. Further growth took place during the Second World War, and during the 1960s after the crisis of Sharpeville. By 1965 the contribution of manufacturing to Gross Domestic Product (GDP) exceeded that of mining and farming together. By 1990 manufacturing was responsible for 23 per cent of GDP, the largest single share, and employed 1,5 million people, about 13,2 per cent of the economically active population.

On the factory floor at the Lancashire Milling Company *c.* 1949
(South African Library)

Most of the country's factories are concentrated in the four main metropolitan areas: the southwestern Cape; Port Elizabeth and Uitenhage; Durban and Pinetown; and Pretoria, Witwatersrand and Vereeniging (PWV), the latter by far the most important region for manufacturing industry in the country.

Maqoma

BURNSHILL, CISKEI, 1798 — ROBBEN ISLAND, 1873

One of the greatest of the Xhosa chiefs, Maqoma was half-brother of Sandile and heir to the Rharhabe paramountcy. He

The warrior Maqoma. In three major Frontier Wars he attempted to counter the relentless white expansion into Xhosa territory
(© The Brenthurst Press)

Eugène Marais, owner and editor of *Land en Volk*, a newspaper which he used to launch a series of biting attacks on Kruger and his government
(Transvaal Archives TAB 7935)

Sammy Marks. He helped to lay the foundations of secondary industry in the Transvaal
(National Cultural History Museum)

was embittered when expelled in 1828 from the Ceded Territory along the Kat River, where the Kat River Settlement was subsequently established. In three major frontier wars he attempted to counter the relentless white expansion into Xhosa territory. Found guilty of complicity in the cattle-killing in 1857, he was exiled to Robben Island.

Marais, Eugène Nielen

PRETORIA, 1871 — PELINDABA, 1936

Poet, naturalist, journalist and advocate, Marais was particularly known for his writing skills. He produced articles for the *Observer* as well as for the London *Times* and Reuters. Locally, he contributed articles on the Volksraad (Parliament) to the *Transvaal Advertiser*, was editor of *Press* and editor and owner of *Land en Volk*, a newspaper which he used to launch a series of biting and frequently personal attacks on Kruger and his government. As a result he was repeatedly summonsed to court on charges of libel. Writing the editorials of *Land en Volk* in Afrikaans, he became, through both his prose and poetry, a leading figure in the development of Afrikaans language and literature.

In 1905 he sold his newspaper and devoted himself to naturalist studies in the Waterberg district, and it was there that he wrote his pioneering behavioural field studies *The Soul of the White Ant, The Soul of the Ape* and *My Friends the Baboons*.

Suffering periodically from fits of black depression, he waged a forty-four year battle against morphine addiction before finally shooting himself in 1936.

Maritz, Gerhardus Marthinus

GRAAFF-REINET DISTRICT, 1797 — LITTLE TUGELA, NATAL, 1838

Voortrekker leader. Unlike the majority of the Voortrekkers, Maritz had a settled, urban background, having worked as a wagon-maker in Graaff-Reinet where he also participated in local administration. Objecting to certain matters of government policy and concerned by the authorities' inability to secure peace and safety for the people of the eastern districts, he gathered together numerous members of prominent and influential families. His trek left Graaff-Reinet in 1836 and followed a route over the Orange to Thaba 'Nchu, where he was elected as chairman and head of administration in the newly formed Voortrekker government. He then moved north and across the Drakensberg to the Little Tugela in Natal. On occasions his trek converged with those of Potgieter and Retief. With Potgieter he led a campaign against Mzilikazi's Ndebele in 1837, but his party escaped the 'great massacre' which followed Dingane's killing of Retief in 1838.

Marks, Samuel

LITHUANIA, 1843 — JOHANNESBURG, 1920

Industrialist and financier. Marks came out to South Africa in 1868, attracted by news of the diamond discoveries. Together with his cousin and life-long partner Isaac Lewis, he founded a major business enterprise, Lewis and Marks, which was launched during the Barberton gold rush in 1885. Anticipating the rise of a vast consumer's market for manufactured goods on the Witwatersrand, he started numerous new industries, helping to lay the foundations of secondary industry in the Transvaal. His restored home, Zwartkoppies, outside Pretoria, is now a museum.

Mass Mobilisation

Part of African National Congress (ANC) strategy since 1984, which has been used together with the armed struggle and economic sanctions to isolate and attack the state, make apartheid unworkable and the black townships ungovernable. Since the lifting of the ban on the ANC in 1990, and the substantial falling away of economic sanctions and armed struggle, mass action became the ANC's principal weapon in its struggle for power. Other political organisations, notably the Pan Africanist Congress, the Azanian People's Organisation and the Inkatha Freedom Party, opposed the mass action organised by the ANC, while some feared it would strengthen the right wing, deter capital investment and heighten conflict and confrontation to the point where increasing anarchy made a slide into ungovernability inevitable.

Medicine and Health

One of the reasons for the Dutch East India Company establishing a refreshment station at the Cape was in order that sick sailors from Company fleets could be landed and nursed back to health. By 1656, Van Riebeeck, who was himself a trained surgeon, had established a per-

Mass mobilisation. Cape Town, 13 September 1989, where 25 000 people marched in protest against police brutality on election day when at least 20 were killed
(Mayibuye Centre)

manent hospital within the fort for Company servants. The three hospitals built before 1780 were staffed by Company ships' surgeons, some of whom went into private practice among the free burghers behind Table Mountain once their tour of duty had ended. Visiting fleets brought virulent epidemics such as smallpox and measles, which periodically spread like wildfire through the colony, taking their toll on white colonists and decimating the Khoisan population.

Gradually precautions were developed to control these epidemics; public health rules were applied, ships quarantined and inoculations carried out. In 1818 the first civilian (and privately built) hospital at the Cape, the Somerset Hospital, still operating, was opened for the destitute and the mentally ill. Prior to this no hospital existed for either civilians or slaves. From the mid-1800s other large hospitals were founded in the colony. In 1846 a general infirmary was established on Robben Island to which lepers, the chronically sick and the mentally ill were transferred from the overcrowded Somerset Hospital.

The mineral discoveries brought droves of doctors and enormous public health problems to the country. In the mining camps typhoid and malaria took their toll, necessitating the building first of Kimberley Hospital, and then the Johannesburg General Hospital, which within ten years of its foundation had become the largest hospital south of the Sahara. By the end of the nineteenth century, a rudimentary pubic health service existed in all four states. In 1918 the governmental Department of Health came into being, and South Africa's first medical school was established at the University of Cape Town.

From the late nineteenth century medical work was increasingly segregated on racial lines, with separate wards set aside in certain hospitals for people of different racial groups, or with entirely separate hospitals being built. Segregation intensified during the apartheid era, when even ambulances in some cases did not pick up dying people because they were the 'wrong' colour. Some doctors courageously tried to fight this segregation, and by the

Above:
Somerset Hospital, Cape Town, in 1900. It was the first civilian hospital at the Cape and was opened for the destitute and the mentally ill
(Cape Archives E 9361)

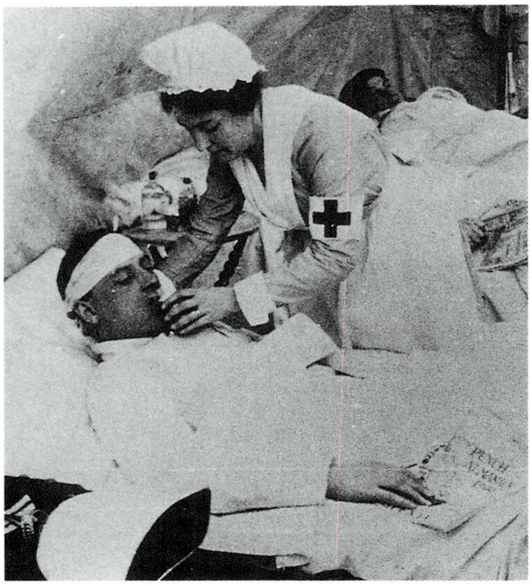

In a field hospital on the Tugela River
(Transvaal Archives TAB 1277)

end of the 1980s a number of the major hospitals had effectively desegregated themselves. Official policy remained that health should be segregated, however, and much money allocated to health in the budget was wasted through duplication of services and administration because of the continued existence of segregated health provision.

Mendi

A troopship which sank on the way to Europe in 1917, in which 615 blacks, members of the South African Native Labour Contingent, lost their lives. The men were among the 10 000 African troops requested by the British government to serve in labour battalions under British command in France. The loss of the *Mendi*, more than any other event of the First World War, impinged upon the consciousness of blacks in South Africa and was long remembered as a great tragedy.

Above:
John X Merriman
(Cape Archives AG 791)

Merriman, John Xavier

SOMERSET, 1841 — STELLENBOSCH DISTRICT, 1926

Politician and statesman. After completing his education in Britain, he returned to the Cape in 1862 and for a time worked as a surveyor. A man of great wit and a very lively mind, he became a minister in J C Molteno's government in the mid-1870s, at a time when the latter opposed the federation scheme of Lord Carnarvon. He returned to office in Rhodes's cabinet in 1890, being known as a rather idiosyncratic 'Cape liberal'. In 1896 he condemned Rhodes's part in the Jameson Raid, and he was opposed to the war which followed in 1899. He travelled to Britain in 1901 to plead for peace, and after the war he supported full self-government for the Transvaal and Orange River colonies. He played an important role at the National Convention of 1908–1909, realising that a compromise was necessary over the franchise with Smuts and those who refused to agree to any extension of the Cape system to the rest of the Union-to-be. Some thought of him as a possible first Prime Minister of the Union, but he was passed over because he came from the Cape and instead he became an elder statesman, living on his farm near Stellenbosch until his death.

Right:
The troopship *Mendi* sank on the way to Europe in 1917 and 615 members of the South African Native Labour Contingent lost their lives
(South African National Museum of Military History)

Mfecane

Mfecane was a term coined by historians to refer to a great 'Time of Troubles' in Natal/Zululand and on the interior highveld in the early nineteenth century. (Mfecane was the Nguni word for this dispersion of people, known in Sotho as the Difaqane.) The picture presented in numerous historical works was of a time of vast destruction, beginning with the rise of the Zulu state and leading to inter-state warfare and various forms of raiding, and a massive destruction of life and property in the 1820s and early 1830s.

In the 1960s historians sought to reverse this picture by emphasising not the destruction but rather the creation of new states, which was seen as a positive development. Then in the 1980s Julian Cobbing of Rhodes University decided to attack the concept altogether. His argument was that the upheaval itself had been greatly exaggerated by historians wishing to legitimate the subsequent white conquest, and that it must be disaggregated, for the causes of disruption varied from place to place, though all were related not to the rise of Shaka's kingdom but instead to the penetration of commercial capitalism. The influences of capitalism spread into the interior from Delagoa Bay, where slave trading was much more significant than previously imagined (though the evidence for this remains highly conjectural), and from the eastern Cape Colony and such cross-frontier raiders as the Griqua. The states which emerged in Zululand and in the interior were, Cobbing argued, defensive ones. Shaka was not the motor for violence throughout the region, and his Zulu state was not nearly as large or powerful as formerly thought. Refugees did not flee from his state to the eastern Cape and the western highveld. Rather, people had been brought into the Cape as forced labour, and called refugees from disorder in the interior to cover up what was *de facto* slave raiding.

This new interpretation is still under scrutiny by historians, many of whom are sceptical of the flimsy evidence on which many of the key arguments are based. The topic will remain controversial, for the evidence will never be conclusive and will always be open to different interpretations.

Left:
'Burgher Fingoes on the Frontier of the Cape Colony', *Illustrated London News*, 7 January 1852. The Mfengu served as allies of the colonists in three of the Frontier Wars
(South African Library)

Above:
Miners on the Witwatersrand. At first the labour needs of the mining industry were met haphazardly, by blacks making their way to the mining centres
(South African Library)

Mfengu (Fingo)

The origins of the Mfengu are controversial. They themselves believe that they were the descendants of those who during the 1820s fled Shaka's tyranny and sought shelter among the chiefdoms south of what is now Natal. Because they had no cattle or means of sustenance they were called Mfengu from the verb *ukufenguza*, meaning 'to wander about seeking advice'. They attached themselves to wealthy men as clients, and often worked as herdsmen. In 1835 Sir Benjamin D'Urban settled 17 000 Mfengu on land which had formerly been occupied by Xhosa, as a buffer between the colonists and the Xhosa to the east. The Mfengu served as allies of the whites in the frontier wars of 1846–1847, 1850–1853 and 1877–1878 and were rewarded with further grants of land, most particularly in the southern Transkei, further alienating them from the Xhosa. Even today ethnic rivalries between Mfengu and Xhosa remain important in the Ciskei and Transkei.

Migrancy

Migrancy meant regular, temporary, long-distance absence from home for the purposes of earning an income from wage labour. Migrancy occurs everywhere in the modern world, but only in South Africa did it evolve into a systematic, state-directed policy for the mobilisation, direction and employment of labour. In South Africa, as nowhere else, the system of labour migrancy formed a foundation stone of a racially defined economic and political order. Thus while migrancy to farms and towns occurred long before the mineral discoveries, it makes sense to define migrancy in its peculiarly South African context as a phenomenon and policy growing out of the particular needs of South Africa's mining economy. The needs of the mining industry — diamonds from the late 1860s and gold from 1886 — given the technology and the cost and pricing structure involved, were for a mass of low-cost, unskilled labour.

At first, labour needs were met haphazardly, by blacks making their way to mining centres to meet consumer needs. Many, such as the regiments of Pedi sent by Chief Sekonyela to Kimberley, were eager for guns, with which to fend off new military forces at work in the subcontinent, and as a result many chiefdoms became heavily armed. Others were after increments to their livestock wealth, or wished to acquire European manufactures and agricultural implements. Sometimes elders controlled the flow of labour; in other circumstances migrancy could be more a form of rebellion against the authority of elders in the lineage, enabling young men to acquire independence earlier by acquiring for themselves the cattle necessary to marry and set up their own homesteads. Migrancy could thus shore up or undermine the authority of elders or chiefs.

In early years income from migrancy facilitated investment in agricultural production for markets by blacks; but from the start, and increasingly, migrancy was also an index of impoverishment and loss of self-sufficiency. Some people, such as the Sotho, took to labour migrancy avidly, at the same time as they greatly increased production of grain crops for sale; others, such as the Zulu, maintained a determined isolation from the colonial economy for as long as possible, making their eventual economic and political incorporation all the more violent. The role of private recruiters was important in early years, most of them traders who benefited greatly from the wage money of migrants, and who had the great advantage of often being creditors of potential migrants, who could be pressured into selling their labour in payment of store debt. Cattle advances to potential migrants to be paid off from wages were also practised.

But from the start mine employers and the state were concerned to regularise recruitment and control conditions of employment, especially as labour supplies tended to fluctuate, and wages to rise, as economic activity intensified and the demand for labour increased. There were also considerable problems of desertion and resistance, and, on the diamond mines, the problem of diamond theft. The colonial states of the region, with greater or lesser degree of success, sought to extend control over labour supplies through pass and squatter laws and the extension of colonial rule over African peoples. The imposition of head or hut taxes was an important spur to wage earning. One way and another, greater regulation over the economic lives of African peoples was being exerted. At the same time, contracts and the regimentation of the closed compound, pioneered at Kimberley and elaborated on the Rand, secured compliance and work discipline at the place of employment. The efficiency of the state greatly increased after the South African War (1899–1902), when the British were able to coordinate policy and bring greater coercive power to bear through the sub-continent. The British administration extended the geographical scope of recruitment greatly through the Modus Vivendi treaty with the Portuguese authorities in 1901, which provided for payment of a capitation fee for each labourer recruited for the mines in Mozambique. South Africa's 'labour empire' has ever since been sub-continental in its reach. But labour supplies and wage levels continued to be volatile (despite resort for a few years to indentured Chinese), and in 1912 the Native Recruiting Corporation was established to coordinate recruiting for the Chamber of Mines in the reserves of South Africa, doing away with resort to private recruiters.

The De Beers compound, Kimberley. The regimentation of the closed compound secured compliance and work discipline at the place of employment
(Cape Archives AG 651)

Thus was established a uniquely pervasive system of labour mobilisation and control, built on the premise that migrant labour, still firmly tied through relationships to a pre-industrial, rural economy, was likely to be cheaper, more manageable and less of a drain on the treasury in terms of social spending requirements, than a labour force completely divorced from its rural farming base and pre-existing communal social system. The efficiency of the migrant system is revealed in the fact that real wages on the gold mines in the early 1970s were in fact lower than at the time of Union in 1910. A complex system of pass laws, influx control regulations, urban planning measures and labour bureaux was elaborated to maintain the migrancy system, long after the idea that wage migrancy was a supplement to family farming had become a fiction due to rural landlessness and overcrowding. Gradually during the course of the first half of the twentieth century, migrancy ceased to be partly discretionary, and became a way of life regimented by state law. The elaboration of the system was also fuelled by the segregationist idea that African cultural distinctiveness had to be preserved in the

face of westernising influences, and political rights had to be exercised separately through 'traditional' institutions. The definition and entrenchment of the reserve areas was part of this developing ideology.

However, countervailing pressures were evident early on. Permanent African populations were always present in urban areas. Employers' interests differed. Manufacturing industry, which grew steadily between the wars and rapidly in the 1940s, required a more skilled, stable and long-term labour force than migrancy could provide. Urbanisation became an unstoppable force. By the 1970s it had become apparent that black labour unionism could not be wished away, that black labour and political assertiveness could not be suppressed in the long term, and that bottlenecks in the availability of skills and restrictions in the growth of the black consumer market had made enforced migrancy counterproductive to further economic development. The lifting of restrictions on labour mobility and organisation as a major element in the process of bureaucratic reform initiated under P W Botha from the late 1970s, did not herald the end of migrancy (single-sex hostels are still common institutions in the cities of South Africa). But it did mean the beginning of the dismantling of the labour migrant system as a peculiarly South African institution.

(T Keegan)

Millin, Sarah Gertrude

LITHUANIA, 1888 — JOHANNESBURG, 1968

Writer. A prolific author of sociological fiction (some thirty novels) and an accomplished biographer (Rhodes and Smuts), Millin gained an international reputation with the novel *God's Stepchildren* (1924), but it was her book *The South Africans* (1926) which made her famous in South Africa. She is best known for her works reflecting the social and political opinions of her era, such as *King of the Bastards* (1959) and *Burning Man* (1952), and her austere, dramatic style dominated South African literature for many years. Her account of the Bulhoek massacre in *The Coming of the Lord* (1928), showed her revulsion for state violence, but she supported Smuts in the miners' strike of 1922, and later supported segregation in principle (miscegenation horrified her).

Milner, Alfred, First Viscount

HESSE-DARMSTADT, GERMANY, 1854 — CANTERBURY, ENGLAND, 1925

Imperial pro-consul and social engineer. An able administrator and ardent imperialist, Milner was appointed Governor of the Cape Colony and High Commissioner for South Africa in 1897. He was determined to break Kruger's power, thereby assuring Britain's political control of the Transvaal, and he was prepared to go to war to achieve his objective.

After the South African War (1899–1902) he took over the administration of the conquered Republics, tried to encourage economic growth, particularly through building up the gold-mining industry, resettling Boers on their farms and promoting the immigration of British settlers. He left South Africa in 1905 with his work at best half finished.

Mining

Mining has been the driving force behind the growth of the modern South African economy since the discovery of diamonds at Kimberley in the late 1860s. From that date until the 1980s, South Africa has experienced mining-led growth. This phase of the country's economic growth has ended, because of the failure to dis-

Above left:
The single-sex hostels are still common in the cities of South Africa
(Mayibuye Centre)

Above:
Workers from the Bantustans and townships wait for buses to take them home
(Mayibuye Centre)

Above:
Sarah Gertrude Millin, prolific novelist and accomplished biographer
(Africana Museum)

Above:
Sir Alfred Milner
(Transvaal Archives TAB 30562)

'Spectakel Mine, Cape Copper Mining Company', Namaqualand 1884. Modern mining began with the 'copper mania' of the Northern Cape in the 1850s
(South African Library)

cover significant new gold-fields in the second half of the twentieth century.

Mining in South Africa goes back a long way in history, to when Bantu-speaking peoples introduced the working of iron about 1 500 years ago. Copper mining for decorative purposes also developed and was highly valued by the time the Portuguese reached Africa at the end of the fifteenth century. Iron mines and primitive furnaces of the bloomery type have been found in many places of the highveld. Blast furnaces did not develop in Europe until the late Middle Ages, but from then on progress was rapid and by the time the Dutch reached South Africa, Europe was technologically ahead of the rest of the world.

Modern mining began in the middle of the nineteenth century with the 'copper mania' of the northern Cape in the 1850s. While this led to a permanent industry being established, it was part of a world-wide mining boom, and did not trigger economic growth comparable to that in Australia or California. Copper mining in Namaqualand was discontinued in the depression of the 1930s, but was resumed during the Second World War and is today a profitable industry.

Diamond mining followed hard on the heels of the copper mania. First discovered along the banks of the Vaal River in 1867, the centre of activity quickly passed to what was to become the Kimberley region in 1871, with its four diamondiferous pipes. Almost overnight the South African economy was transformed. Fortune hunters flocked to the mines and thousands of people had to be housed and fed. Trade of all kinds received a boost and the increased revenues flowing to the government of the Cape Colony at last enabled it to undertake serious railway building.

The government assumed ownership of the land on which the diamond pipes were found in 1875 and slowly brought order into a situation of great confusion and speculation. Inevitably, though, as the diamond diggings got deeper, so too did the costs grow greater, a process that was to lead to the elimination of the small man. Deeper mines with drainage problems required more capital to work them and very early on in its history concentration began to emerge in the ownership of the Kimberely diamond mines.

Cecil Rhodes took the lead in these developments, helped by his control over the pumping machinery that was essential in the deep level mines. It was this that provided him with the funds to buy up more and more claims until his De Beers Company came to tower over the diamond diggings. Once limits on the number of claims that could be owned by a single person were lifted in 1876, the way was open for a modern joint stock company to take control. It took Rhodes thirteen years to accomplish this; but by 1889 his victory was complete and Barney Barnato had conceded victory to the son of an English vicar.

Cecil Rhodes was the greatest of the nineteenth century entrepreneurs in South African history. It was his vision and determination that transformed the diamond speculations of Kimberley into a permanent industry. He did this by emulating the policy of the Dutch East India Company towards spices in the seventeenth century, that is by systematically acquiring a monopoly over production. This enabled him to establish price stability and to maintain profitability — a policy that has been pursued ever since by the De Beers Company and which was not altered by Sir Ernest Oppenheimer when he gained control of the company.

In the second half of the twentieth century, however, De Beers underwent a rev-

Early diggings at Kimberley as depicted in the *Illustrated London News* of 31 August 1872. The two 'big holes' were dug by hand
(Cape Archives M 657)

Far left:
Miners sorting and sieving gravel at the Kimberley diamond mines c. 1872
(Cape Archives AG 4190)

Left:
The first gold mine in Johannesburg, 1886
(South African Library)

Above:
Buffelsdoorn Mine in the late 1800s, by Melton Prior
(© The Brenthurst Press)

olution, as it converted itself from being a monopoly into a monopsony. When it was a monopoly, De Beers controlled most of the world's production of diamonds. As a monopsony, it no longer controls most of the production; instead it has established itself as the world's main buyer of diamonds and through the Central Selling Organisation controls the price of diamonds.

The importance of diamonds to South Africa may be seen in the fact that the market capitalisation of diamond shares on the Johannesburg Stock Exchange sometimes exceeds that of all the gold mines.

Kimberley's diamond diggings and the two 'big holes' that were dug by hand (one of which still exists today and contains South Africa's most exciting museum) were but a prelude to the even more important gold discoveries of 1886.

The discovery of the gold-fields of the Witwatersrand attracted attention in a way that not even the glitter of the diamond-fields had done, for gold was a solid store of value and represented real money in the nineteenth century. Like the diamond-fields, the first gold mines were financed from within South Africa; but when the deep level mines developed in the 1890s, large amounts of capital were necessary. This entered the country via London and the Stock Exchange, as investors in Britain, France and Germany rushed to buy the shares of gold mining companies. The Corner House Group of Werner, Beit and Eckstein led the way and rapidly built up the world's largest mining house that was to become famous as Rand Mines. Others followed: Cecil Rhodes founded Gold Fields, Barney Barnato set up Johannesburg Consolidated Investment Company, J B Robinson developed the Robinson Deep Gold Mine, and the Albu brothers the company that was to become General Mining. Political troubles overtook the gold mines with the notorious Jameson Raid of 1895 and the South African War of 1899–1902; but with the resumption of peace, renewed development took place on the gold-fields and the Edwardian era saw a permanent and moderately prosperous industry emerge.

New mines were opened and the industry spread out from its original central Witwatersrand base, as gold mines were opened along the line of the Reef in both the East Rand and West Rand. Sir Ernest Oppenheimer took the lead in opening up the East Rand in the 1920s, and in discovering the gold-fields of the Orange Free State in the 1930s. These were brought into production in the mid-1950s and were followed by the famous deep level mines of the far West Rand, the most celebrated of which is Western Deep Levels.

As a result, the gold mining industry continued to expand and to increase its production until the last third of the twentieth century. It also remained capital intensive and labour intensive, the former the result of the mines becoming ever deeper, and the latter the result of the primitive way of extracting the ore, which consists of blasting it with dynamite and then shovelling it by hand. Until the 1970s labour costs were low, which discouraged attempts at mechanisation. In fact for ninety years, the real wages of mine workers did not rise. The rising gold price in the 1970s changed this situation and in the 1980s the industry was faced with

Coal mining, Newcastle Natal c. 1880
(Local History Museum Collection, Durban)

rapidly rising labour costs and a static gold price. In the 1990s the future of the gold mines is once again in doubt.

The crucial importance of the gold mines is revealed in the growth of output. From a value of £32 million in 1910, the value had risen to £268 million in 1960. After having not risen at all in the 1920s it increased by 159 per cent in the 1930s. In the 1950s the value of output again rose rapidly: it increased by 85 per cent. By 1970 output had risen to over one million kilograms with a value of R831 million, which was a 55 per cent increase on the figure for 1960. Since then the value in rand terms has increased, but the quantity produced has declined.

In the years since 1960 gold has retained its importance for South Africa's balance of payments, as a result of the rise in the price of gold. In 1985 gold was relatively more important to the balance of payments than it had been in 1950; but in the post-war years it never reached the levels of the 1930s, when gold exports rose to over 70 per cent of total exports. Since 1985 the relative importance of the gold mines has declined.

The last of the great mining booms in South African history has been that associated with coal. This is a recent development and has been export-led. Coal fields exist in Natal and in many areas of the Transvaal. Diamond and gold mining and the associated railway developments created a growing demand for coal that before 1914 was provided both from abroad and from within the country. Mechanisation occurred early in the coal mines, keeping the price low by international standards. Railways and electricity generation created a buoyant demand for coal that held back the growth of exports in the 1950s and 1960s. Then a technological breakthrough helped to make South African coal more competitive in the overseas market for coking coal. The first Japanese contract followed in 1969. Between 1960 and 1985 coal output trebled and a new railway line to Richards Bay was built for exporting coal. In 1988 coal exports were second to gold exports, earning R2 800 million. They helped to make Italy South Africa's second largest export market.

Other minerals are important to South Africa, which has been blessed with abundant resources; but in the history of the country's economic development, diamonds, gold and coal have led the way. Each has created wealth on a large scale. Diamonds and gold were at one time each responsible for spear-heading mining developments. With the value of coal output now a third of that of the gold mines, the day may come when the black gold replaces its more famous predecessor as the great engine of growth.

(S Jones)

Miscegenation

Interbreeding between whites, slaves and Khoi occurred extensively from the time of the Dutch East India Company, and helped produce the so-called coloured

'Brakpan mines, No 1 Coal shaft, April 1901'. The value of South Africa's coal output rose to a third of that of the gold mines
(The Brenthurst Library)

people of South Africa. In the twentieth century various Acts — the Cape Morality Act (1902), the Immorality Act (1927), the Mixed Marriages Act (1949), and the Immorality Act (1950) — attempted to forbid sexual relationships and marriages between whites and people of colour. In 1985 the government repealed the bans on interracial sex and marriage.

Missionaries

Until 1799, when the first representative of the London Missionary Society arrived at the Cape, only a few (mostly short-lived) attempts had been made to evangelise the aboriginal and slave population of the colony. A hundred years later, the churches founded by the various missionary groups had become established, so closing the primary era of mission.

Nineteenth-century white missionaries occupied an ambivalent position during a period that witnessed tremendous social and political conflict and change. Often, like John Philip, they were resented by white colonists because they campaigned for human rights and equality before the law for blacks. On the other hand, traditional societies sometimes blamed them for introducing diseases, epidemics or drought. Whilst they sought to uplift Africans by tendering the Gospel, western medicine, schooling, modern agriculture and commerce, the missionaries were generally convinced of the superiority both of their culture and of colonial rule. They were responsible for hastening the decline of traditional culture as the Gospel gained acceptance. On the frontiers the missionaries were in varying degrees agents of the colonial authorities, recommending their interests to coloured and African people.

On the other hand, Moshweshwe, for instance, used 'his' missionaries for his own political advantage. Nor were all missionaries white. Ntsikana (converted in 1815) sought to lead his people to God within the structure of traditional Xhosa society. Tiyo Soga (1829—1871), converted and schooled by Scottish missionaries, used black evangelists and catechists to disseminate the Gospel. Some regard him as a founder of the Black Consciousness movement because of his sense of the unity of all black Africans. Nehemiah Tile (d. 1892), originally a Wesleyan catechist, broke away to form the Thembu Church, the forerunner of future African independent churches, which today claim the allegiance of some 30 per cent of black Christians.

Mixed Marriages

Marriages between whites and people of colour have never taken place on a large scale. One early example was the marriage between Eva, a Khoi woman, and Van Meerhof, a Dutch East India Company official, in 1664. Thereafter it was considered a disgrace for Christians, that is whites, to marry people of colour, even if they were free. In 1685 marriages between whites and slaves were prohibited by law. The Mixed

Genadendal, by G F Angas. It is the oldest mission station in South Africa, founded in 1737 by Georg Schmidt of the Moravian Missionary Society
(Africana Museum)

Robert Moffat, one of the best-known missionaries of the London Missionary Society
(Cory Library)

Sir John Charles Molteno, first Prime Minister of the Cape Colony
(Transvaal Archives TAB 34489)

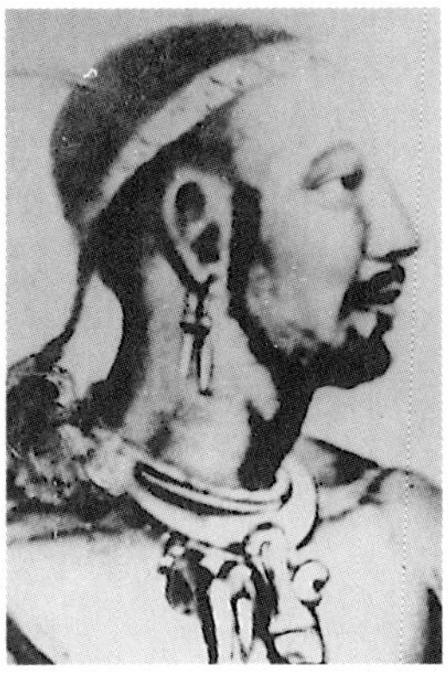

Moshweshwe, first paramount chief of the Sotho
(Transvaal Archives TAB 33358)

Marriages Act of 1949, repealed in 1985, forbade marriages between whites and people of colour, though there had been fewer than 100 mixed marriages a year in the years before it was passed.

Mlanjeni War (Eighth Frontier War, 1850–1853)

With the establishment of British Kaffraria (1847) the territories of the Ngqika and the Ndlambe were placed under British control. The resulting discontent was exacerbated by Mlanjeni, a Xhosa prophet from the Ciskei, who promised ancestral aid in total war against the whites, and who appeared to the government as a mouthpiece of the chiefs' resentment. The deposition of the Ngqika chief Sandile in 1850 was the spark which led to war. In December of that year the Ngqika destroyed three military villages in Victoria and the Eighth Frontier War, the longest and costliest thus far, began. Sir Harry Smith, whose policies had done much to cause the war, was recalled to London in disgrace, and it was not until 1853 that his successor, Sir George Cathcart, was able to bring the war to an end.

Moffat, Robert

SCOTLAND, 1795 — KENT, ENGLAND, 1883

Missionary. One of the best-known missionaries of the London Missionary Society, Moffat worked in Namaqualand and succeeded in converting the Nama chief, Jonker Afrikaner. He later set up his mission among the Tlhaping people at Kuruman (1824–1870) and the church that he built there became an educational centre and Christian retreat. He visited, and developed a long-lasting friendship with, the Ndebele ruler Mzilikazi. A talented linguist, he published, amongst other works, a translation of the New Testament in Sechuana and was responsible for Tswana being the first written African language in South Africa. He directed David Livingstone's interest toward Africa (1841), and his eldest daughter married the famous explorer.

Molteno, Sir John Charles

LONDON, 1814 — CLAREMONT, CAPE, 1886

First Prime Minister of the Cape Colony. Molteno began his career as a wealthy merchant, wool farmer and banker in the Beaufort district where he earned his nickname, 'the lion of Beaufort'. He later fought as commandant in the Sixth Frontier War (1846). As a member of the Legislative Assembly from 1854, he headed the movement for responsible self-government, and was the first Prime Minister of the Cape (1872–1878). His government benefited from an economic boom, and Molteno encouraged the building of railways, bridges and harbours. During his term of office great strides were also made in the field of education. He rejected imperial intervention in the affairs of the colony, in particular the proposed annexation of Griqualand West and the attempt to promote a South African federation. He clashed with the Governor Sir Bartle Frere over the use of British troops against the Xhosa in the Ninth Frontier War (1877) and was dismissed as a result in 1878.

Moroka II

LOTLHAKANE, NEAR MAFEKING, *c.* 1795 — THABA 'NCHU, 1880

Chief of that group of Sotho-speakers known as the Seleka Rolong (1830–1880). Under threat of attack by the Ndebele, and short of grazing land and water, Moroka and his people moved away from the marginal land they inhabited west of what is now the Transvaal, and in 1833 settled west of the Caledon River, establishing their headquarters, with Moshweshwe's permission, at Thaba 'Nchu (Black Mountain). Moroka became a friend and ally of both the Voortrekkers and the British, assisting the former in expeditions against the Ndebele and then supporting the latter at times against the Sotho.

Moshweshwe

MENKHOANENG, NORTHERN BASUTOLAND, *c.* 1786 — THABA BOSIGO, BASUTOLAND, 1870

Founder and first paramount chief of the Sotho. Moshweshwe won a reputation for leadership as a young man by conducting daring cattle raids. By employing superior military tactics and skilful diplomacy, he eventually united various small Sotho groups to form a new nation. Ruling from his impregnable stronghold Thaba Bosigo (Mountain of Night), he pursued a policy of peace and prosperity. From the 1850s he was involved in a major struggle for territory which continued to the end of his life. Anxious to preserve Basutoland against encroachments, especially from the

Boers of the Orange Free State, Moshweshwe sought British protection and in March 1868, when under serious threat from the Boers, Basutoland was annexed as a British colony.

Mpande

BABANANGO DISTRICT, NATAL, 1798 — NODWENGU KRAAL, NATAL, 1872

Zulu king, half-brother of Shaka and Dingane, and the father of Cetshwayo. Mpande joined forces with the Voortrekkers in 1839 and drove out his predecessor, Dingane, the following year. Thereafter he skilfully ruled his kingdom for thirty-two years and kept it intact and independent by playing off the British on his southern borders against the Boers on his western borders. Mpande conserved the Zulu military system intact, and avoided direct confrontation with white power.

Mrs Ples

Nickname given to the well-preserved cranium of a female of the genus *Plesianthropus transvaalensis* (Sterkfontein hominid 5) discovered by Dr Robert Broom and J T Robinson at Sterkfontein in 1947. It was considered to be 2,5 million years old, and was related to the Taung child but of a different subspecies. The discovery of Mrs Ples helped prove that southern Africa was the home of some of the very earliest hominids.

Muizenberg, Battle of (1795)

When the Dutch monarchy collapsed and was replaced by the Batavian Republic, the British decided to take action to protect their trade route to the East. British soldiers were therefore landed at Simonstown, and they marched towards Muizenberg, south of Cape Town, under the protective fire of their four sloops of war. The Dutch garrison was defeated by mid-September. The battle of Muizenberg effectively ended 150 years of Dutch possession at the Cape.

Mujaji (Modjadji II) (The Rain Queen)

BOLOBEDU, *c.* 1800 — BOLOBEDU, 1895

Mujaji succeeded her father King Mugodo ('the Outcast') as ruler of the Lovedu, who live on the edge of the

Zulu king Mpande, by G F Angas
(Africana Museum)

Mujaji, the Rain Queen
(South African Library)

Dr Connie Mulder, who was implicated in the Information scandal of 1978
(Transvaal Archives SAB 8835)

Revd Andrew Murray
(Transvaal Archives TAB 20482)

Mzilikazi transformed his band of fugitives into a powerful kingdom
(South African Library)

highveld near the Strydpoort mountains north of Tzaneen in the Transvaal. Since her reign, the Lovedu have always been ruled by a queen. Her special power was based on her position in the rain cult and in her control over the wife-exchange system. By 1879 she could command perhaps 10 000 warriors, and she claimed tribute from many of the tribes surrounding her chiefdom on the grounds of her power as a bringer of rain.

Mulder, Cornelius Petrus (Connie)

WARMBATHS, 1925 — JOHANNESBURG, 1988

Conservative politician. Author of a doctoral thesis on the influence of the Bible on the formation of the Afrikaner character, Mulder left teaching and local Randfontein politics to become a National Party member of Parliament (1958–1979). He served in a number of ministerial posts including Information, Social Welfare and Pensions, Immigration, and Plural Relations and Development. From 1974 he was leader of the National Party in the Transvaal, but his opportunity to become premier on Vorster's resignation was lost when rumours of maladministration of funds in the Information Department surfaced and R F (Pik) Botha's entry into the race split the vote in favour of P W Botha. What was called the 'Muldergate' scandal exposed the secret funding by the Department of Information of *The Citizen*, an English language newspaper, about which Mulder had lied to Parliament. Following the appointment of a judicial Commission of Inquiry, Mulder resigned his posts in the National Party, which expelled him after he refused to accept the Commission's conclusions. He later joined the Conservative Party.

Muldergate (1978)

The name given by the press to the scandal in the Department of Information headed by Dr Connie Mulder. In 1978 misuse of secret government funds, *inter alia* to buy control of the English-language press for the National Party, was revealed. The scandal forced Vorster to resign as Prime Minister. Mulder, who had been the main contender for the premiership, lost it to P W Botha and had to resign from office. Dr Eschel Rhoodie, Secretary of the Department of Information, was initially sentenced to twelve years' imprisonment, but won an appeal and finally settled in America.

Murray, Andrew

GRAAFF-REINET, 1828 — WELLINGTON, 1917

Dutch Reformed minister. Murray studied in Aberdeen in Scotland, and on his return to South Africa he was appointed to Bloemfontein where he had to travel constantly on horseback or by ox-wagon to cover his 80 000 sq km parish. For fifty-eight years Murray was a minister of the NG Kerk, serving as its first minister north of the Vaal. In 1860 he continued his mission work in the Boland and later was called to the Cape Town (1864) and Wellington (1871) congregations. Among the numerous religious and educational institutions he founded were the Young Men's Christian Association (1865), numerous seminaries throughout the country, the Bible and Prayer Union, the Student's Christian Association in South Africa (1896), and Grey College. He wrote over 250 inspirational works and was particularly known for *Blijf in Jezus* (1864), translated as *Abide in Christ* (1882).

Mzilikazi

ZULULAND, *c.* 1795 — INGAMA KRAAL, NEAR BULAWAYO, ZIMBABWE, 1868

Thought to have been one of Shaka's lieutenants, Mzilikazi rebelled and fled with a few hundred of his Khumalo people to the highveld of the northern Drakensberg. While in the Transvaal he transformed his band of fugitives into a powerful, centralised kingdom by incorporating local peoples. By 1829 he ruled some sixty to eighty thousand people. The superior firepower of the Voortrekkers, who clashed with his forces at Vegkop in 1838, and the threat from Griqua raiders, persuaded Mzilikazi to relocate his state, and so he trekked north from the western Transvaal, crossed the Limpopo River, and in what became known as Matabeleland in southwestern Zimbabwe, he re-established his kingdom.

N

Namibia

South Africa ruled Namibia from 1915 to 1990. South African troops conquered the territory known as South West Africa from the Germans during the First World War, and after five years of military rule, the territory was granted as a C-class mandate to South Africa by the League of Nations in 1920. South Africa continued many German practices, extended the system of reserves and introduced more white settlers from the Union. Resistance by the Bondelswartz and other indigenous people was put down harshly.

When the League dissolved, the South African government of General Smuts hoped to be able to annex the territory, and formally applied to the newly formed United Nations (UN) in 1946 to do this, but its request was refused, largely on the grounds that the indigenous people had not been adequately consulted. The UN instead asked South Africa to place the territory under its Trusteeship system, which provided for eventual independence for such territories. When South Africa refused to do this, a long drawn-out legal battle began, in which the International Court of Justice at the Hague handed down a series of judgements on the status of South West Africa. In 1966, however, the Court decided that it had no legal standing in a case which turned on whether South Africa was governing the territory in the spirit of the mandate. After the failure of the International Court to rule on that issue, the UN General Assembly in October 1966 terminated the mandate unilaterally, a decision which was, a few years later, ratified by the Security Council. In 1971 that ratification was in turn given legal validity by the International Court. In the same year a general strike of South West African workers posed a new threat to South African rule in the territory.

In the face of these developments, the South African government decided to abandon its policy of seeking to incorporate the territory to a greater and greater extent into its own administration, as a *de facto* fifth province. It decided instead that the territory should, despite the application there of a policy of Bantustans on the South African model, remain as one entity. An ethnically-based advisory council was established, and then in 1975 a conference of ethnic representatives was called together in the Turnhalle building in Windhoek. By that time it seemed possible that once Angola was independent, the People's Liberation Army of Namibia (PLAN), the armed wing of the South West African People's Organisation (SWAPO), would be able to operate from southern Angola, and so pose a much greater threat to the South African forces defending northern Namibia. A small South African expeditionary force advanced towards the Angolan capital in October 1975 to try to prevent the pro-SWAPO MPLA from taking power, but in the face of the arrival of Cuban forces and the failure of support from the West, the South African force had to withdraw, the MPLA became the governing party, and SWAPO was able to establish itself in southern Angola.

In 1977, when it seemed that the Turnhalle might produce an 'internal settlement', in which the South African government would give independence to a

Men of the Camel Corps, German South West Africa, 1914
(South African National Museum of Military History)

Katatura Township, Windhoek. SWAPO supporters celebrate Namibia Day, the anniversary of the formation of PLAN and the launch of the armed struggle
(South Light)

local client group, a so-called Western Contact Group was formed, consisting of the five western countries then members of the UN Security Council, to press for a form of independence which would mesh with the UN demand for a transfer of power to the people of the territory (UN Security Council Resolution 385 of 1976). By April 1978 a formula had been worked out providing for joint UN/South African administration during a transition period in which the UN would provide a monitoring team and a military force to keep the peace during the seven month period leading to an election and during the election itself. South African forces were to be greatly reduced, and then confined to bases in the north. The South African government accepted this plan in April 1978, probably without any serious intention of ever implementing it.

Numerous reasons were advanced in the following years by South African government spokesmen as to why the plan (embodied in UN Security Council resolution 435 of September 1978) could not be implemented: the alleged partiality of the UN; the composition of the UNTAG force to enter the territory during the transitional phase; the monitoring and location of SWAPO's military bases; and, from 1981, the presence of the Cuban forces in Angola. From northern Namibia South African forces, and, from 1980, South West African forces under South African command, launched raids against SWAPO bases in southern Angola. Brutal repression was used in northern Namibia to try to destroy SWAPO, while at the same time the Democratic Turnhalle Alliance (DTA) and other groupings were built up in an attempt to form an anti-SWAPO alliance.

Voters queue at polling booths all over Namibia during the elections in November 1989
(South Light)

It was events in southern Angola — the military stalemate which developed at Cuito Cuanavale, . and the advance of Cuban forces into southern Angola in early 1988 — which did most to bring the South African government to decide that resolution 435 must be implemented. A series of negotiations was held with the Angolan and Cuban governments, under American mediation, from May 1988, and in December that year the three governments signed an agreement providing for the withdrawal of Cuban troops from Angola and the implementation of resolution 435, to begin on 1 April 1989. After an initial crisis, caused by the incursion of armed SWAPO forces into the north of the territory, the plan was carried out as envisaged in 1978, and in the election held in November 1989 a Constituent Assembly was chosen in which SWAPO held 41 of the 72 seats. SWAPO then agreed to abide by the constitutional principles it had approved in 1982, a liberal constitution was approved unanimously in remarkably short time, and on 21 March 1990 South African administration came to an end when the territory finally became independent.

The Western Contact Group had accepted that Walvis Bay, Namibia's main port, would not be included in the negotiations and that its status would be decided after Namibian independence. In November 1992 the Namibian and South African governments began a joint administration of the port. The two countries had been so integrated economically that it was clear that for a long time to come South Africa would continue to dominate the new nation economically.

(C C Saunders)

Natal

Lying between the Drakensberg mountains and the Indian Ocean, Natal was inhabited for centuries by small Nguni chiefdoms before the first white settlers founded a trading post in 1824 which they called Port Natal. By that time, the Zulu kingdom under Shaka was the dominant power in south-eastern Africa. The first large group of whites to enter Natal were the Voortrekkers, who crossed over the Drakensberg in 1837 and established the short-lived Republic of Natalia.

In 1842 Britain occupied Port Natal, largely for strategic reasons, and formally annexed it the following year. With the advent of British rule, many of the Af-

rikaner inhabitants left, and were replaced by immigrants, mainly from Britain, the first large group of 5 000 arriving between 1849 and 1851. Many of the new settlers moved into the towns, and under their influence Durban and Pietermaritzburg began to develop a more vigorous commercial and cultural life. By the mid-nineteenth century Natal was British in character, with a white population that was overwhelmed by a large black population. Under the paternalistic, segregationist policies of Theophilus Shepstone, most Africans were placed in reserves, leaving the rest of the colony available for white settlement. The Exemption and Native Franchise Laws (1865) made it extremely difficult for blacks to obtain the vote, despite the existence of a franchise which was nominally colour-blind.

From 1860 indentured Indian labourers arrived, destined for the sugar plantations along the sub-tropical north coast. Many stayed on after their contracts had expired, forming the nucleus of the present-day Indian community in Natal. In 1879 Zulu power was broken by the British, and Zululand was annexed and incorporated into Natal in 1897. The Bambatha Rebellion of 1906 contributed to a lack of confidence amongst Natal's whites in their ability to stand alone, and in 1910 Natal entered the Union. In the 1970s the Zulu Bantustan of KwaZulu was created from numerous pieces of land carved out of Natal and Zululand. From time to time Natalians have suggested 'going it alone', and in late 1992 a separatist option, this time by KwaZulu-Natal, was again suggested.

National Convention (1908–1909)

Thirty white delegates from the four South African states, representing both ruling and opposition parties, met in Durban, Cape Town and Bloemfontein from October 1908 to May 1909 to discuss the unification of South Africa and a new constitution. There was heated debate on such matters as where the capital of the new Union was to be and whether or not blacks should have the vote. In the end compromises were reached, and what was decided at the National Convention was embodied in the South Africa Act of 1909, the Union constitution. Blacks — none of whom were represented at the Convention — especially opposed the colour bar in the constitution.

Left:
Map of Natal and Kaffraria, engraved by J Rapkin, 1850
(Local History Museum Collection, Durban)

Above:
'HMS Southampton relieving Natal, 1842', by Thomas Bowler. Britain occupied Port Natal in 1842 and formally annexed it the following year
(Local History Museum Collection, Durban)

Below:
Mr Schalk Burger, one of the Transvaal delegates, arriving at the Town Hall to attend the National Convention which sat at Durban from 12 October to 5 November 1908
(Local History Museum Collection, Durban)

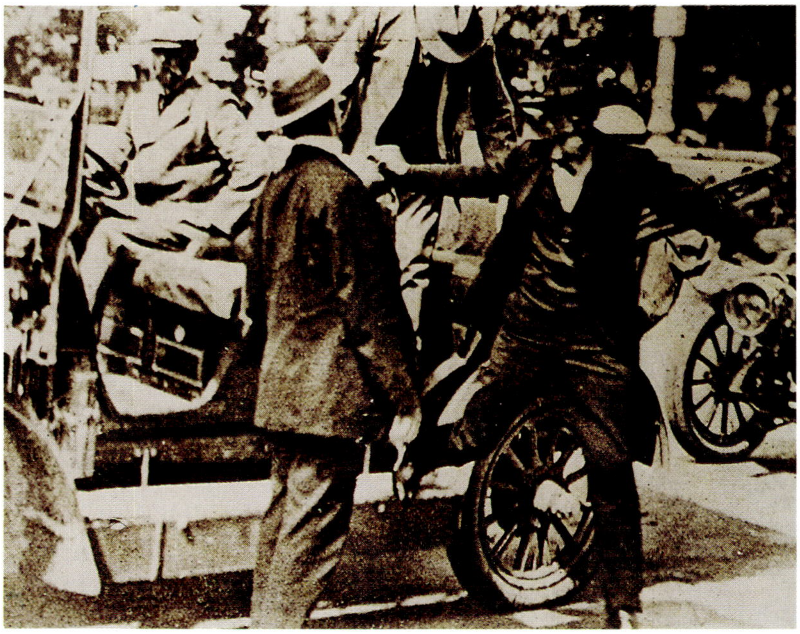

National Party

In 1914 General Hertzog broke away from the South African Party (SAP) of Botha and Smuts, to found a new political party, the National Party (NP). This was an exclusively Afrikaner party, and its support was initially mainly rural and agrarian. In 1924 the NP came to power with the support of the Labour Party and remained in power until its fusion with the SAP, which gave birth to the United Party in 1934.

Some Nationalists led by D F Malan rejected the idea of joining with the SAP and kept the NP alive, first as the Purified NP and then as the Reunited NP. It was the latter party which won the general election of 1948 on a platform of apartheid and white supremacy, and which has ruled the country ever since. Under successive NP prime ministers apartheid was rigidly imposed, and South Africa broke away from the Commonwealth and became a Republic (1961). From the premiership of Vorster, the NP attempted a more 'enlightened' form of apartheid, which eventually led to a right-wing break-away in 1982. Under Prime Minister F W De Klerk, NP policy shifted dramatically, the party rejected apartheid, opened its ranks to all and committed itself to a negotiated settlement based on a democratic form of power-sharing.

Some Nationalists led by D F Malan formed the Reunited National Party which won the general election in 1948 on a platform of apartheid and white supremacy
(Transvaal Archives TAB 544)

National Peace Accord

Formulated to combat the escalating level of political violence in the country, and to create a suitable climate for negotiation, the accord was signed in Johannesburg on 14 September 1991. Its twenty-nine signatories included the government, the African National Congress, the Inkatha Freedom Party and trade unions. It laid down codes of conduct for all concerned, provided for the establishment of local committees to resolve political disputes, and obliged all parties to refrain from violence for political ends.

While its provisions were often blatantly ignored in the years that followed, and violence continued at a high level, many of its local dispute resolution committees did useful work, and its monitors worked closely with, and facilitated the work of, other peace monitors from the United Nations, the European Community and the Commonwealth.

National Symbols

South Africa's best-known national symbols include the coat-of-arms (used on all coinage, official seals and stationery), the flag, the Springbok, and the anthem (*Die Stem van Suid-Afrika*, The Voice of South Africa). Although officially adopted at different dates, these symbols emerged around the time of Union (1910), a period of reconstruction after the ravages of the South African War.

The coat-of-arms combines emblems for each of the four provinces. The lion at the crest and the motto below (*Ex Unitate Vires*) are derived from a seventeenth century Dutch official device, and reflect the modifications of British influence on South Africa's Dutch heritage. Union did not eradicate tensions between Boer and British loyalties: controversy over the flag raged for two years before acceptance (1927) of the Prinsenvlag (used by Jan van Riebeeck), with the flags of the Boer Republics and the Union Jack superimposed in the middle. The Springbok became an emblem of national sporting achievement when it was adopted by the first South African Rugby team to tour abroad (1906). *Die Stem*, written by C J Langenhoven in 1918, was officially accepted as the national anthem in 1957.

Inevitably, these essentially 'European' symbols came to be associated internationally with apartheid, and with South Africa's return to international sport in 1992 pressure groups attempted to prevent sportsmen and sports bodies from using the Springbok emblem, the flag and the anthem.

With the formation of the Bantustans, flags and emblems symbolising their respective 'nationhoods' came into use. Besides exemplifying traditional values, most of these signalled aspirations towards peace and prosperity through development and progress. Enoch Sontonga's anthem, *Nkosi Sikeleli Afrika* (God Bless Africa, 1899), gained popular currency among black South Africans generally, and became a powerful symbol of African nationalism and pan-African unity in south-central Africa.

National Union of South African Students (NUSAS)

An umbrella student organisation formed in 1924 by students from nine English and Afrikaans-speaking white universities, aimed at promoting the interests of students. By 1945, when Fort Hare University became the first black affiliate of NUSAS, all the Afrikaans-medium universities had withdrawn. An outspoken opponent of government policy, NUSAS came under increasing attack from the government: eight of its leaders were banned in 1973 and it was declared an 'affected' organisation the following year, which meant it was prohibited from receiving foreign funds. In 1969 black students had broken away to form their own South African Students Organisation (SASO). In 1991 the two organisations decided to merge.

Natives Land Act (1913)

Crucial law passed by the Botha government in 1913, which imposed a policy of territorial segregation. Prior to Union in 1910 Africans were legally able to buy land in all of the provinces except the Orange Free State (OFS), where the purchase or lease of land by blacks was forbidden by law. In the Cape and Natal, blacks could buy or lease land without any discrimination, and in the Transvaal they could acquire land for which the government acted as trustee. The 1913 Act was an attempt to establish a uniform land policy by restricting African occupancy to 10,4 million morgen (7 per cent of the country), with the promise of more land in the future. Africans were prohibited from purchasing or leasing land in white areas; African land ownership was limited to the demarcated reserves. Similarly whites could not acquire land in the African areas.

With the rise in land values in the late nineteenth century, and the increasing commercialisation of farming, white farmers sought to exclude competition from black peasant farmers and squatters, and at the same time provide themselves with plentiful cheap labour. The Act achieved this for them, by reducing black squatters and sharecroppers in the white-owned rural areas to tenant and wage labourers. African squatters in Natal and the Transvaal were spared eviction from white farms until Parliament 'made other provisions '. However, in the OFS, where similar provisions were already in force, the Act prompted the sudden eviction of large numbers of African squatters from white-owned farms, movingly described by Sol Plaatje in his classic *Native Life in South Africa* (1916).

The Cape was excluded from the 1913 Act as its application there would have affected black franchise rights entrenched by the South Africa Act. In 1936 those franchise rights were removed and a new Land Act provided for uniformity throughout the country and authorised the provision of more land for black occupation, but fifty years later all the land had in fact not been granted.

Natives Representative Council (NRC)

An advisory body established in 1936. The African National Congress and the All African Convention (until 1943) hoped it might serve as a platform. Between 1937 and 1946 it passed moderate resolutions calling for the redress of black grievances; these were consistently ignored by the government. By 1946 relations with the government had broken down. The last straw was the government's handling of the mine workers' strike in 1946. The Council decided to adjourn indefinitely. In 1951 the government abolished the NRC.

New Republic

A Boer republic established in 1884 from lands which Boer volunteers received from Dinuzulu after they had helped him to defeat his rival Zibhebhu.

The New Republic was established in 1884 from lands which Boer volunteers received from Dinuzulu
(Transvaal Archives TAB 4130)

The New Republic comprised the districts of Vryheid, Wakkerstroom and Utrecht in northwestern Zululand. In 1887 Britain annexed the remainder of Zululand, by agreement with the Boers, and the following year the New Republic was incorporated into the Transvaal.

Newspapers

In 1800 *The Cape Town Gazette and African Advertiser*, a government gazette, began appearing weekly. This was the only regular publication until 1824, when George Greig's *South African Commercial Advertiser*, the first independent newspaper in South Africa, appeared. Governor Lord Charles Somerset first attempted to censor and then suppress the *Advertiser*, and when it resumed regular publication in 1828, subject only to libel laws, press freedom in South Africa had been established. The *Advertiser* was followed by the appearance of the bilingual *Zuid Afrikaan* (1830) and the *Graham's Town Journal* (1831). Thereafter numbers of English and Dutch newspapers began publication.

It was in the second half of the nineteenth century that most of the leading English language dailies were established, such as *The Cape Argus* (1857), the East London *Daily Dispatch and Frontier Advertiser* (1872), *The Cape Times* (1876), *The Natal Witness (1881)*, and *The Star* (1889). The first Afrikaans newspaper was *Die Afrikaanse Patriot* (1876), a vehicle for the Afrikaner political and cultural revival of the 1870s.

In the late 1800s and early 1900s the small politically conscious black educated class began to found newspapers to serve their interests. The most prominent of these were *Imvo Zabantsundu* (1884) started by J T Jabavu, and *Ilanga Lase Natal* (1903) edited by J L Dube. Gandhi's weekly newspaper, *Indian Opinion* (1903), advocated the cause of South African Indians. By the early twentieth century a large free press existed, reflecting and influencing the different group, race and class interests in South Africa. In 1915 the Nasionale Pers was established, which started publishing *Die Burger*, mouthpiece of the National Party; it was edited initially by D F Malan. Some years later another daily espousing the National Party cause was begun in Johannesburg, *Die Transvaler* (1937) owned by the Voortrekker-Pers and edited by H F Verwoerd. Stringent censorship laws restricting press freedom from 1950 on, resulted in the suppression of various newspapers, among them the Communist Party organ, *The Guardian* (1952), and *The World* (1977) and *The Post* (1981), both of which had a large black readership. The single greatest blow came with the shutting down of the *Rand Daily Mail*, Johannesburg's main English newspaper, allegedly because it was losing money for the mining house which owned it. It was succeeded by the *Weekly Mail*, the leading alternative newspaper in the early 1990s.

Meeting between Ngqika, paramount chief of the Western Xhosa, and General Janssens at the Kat River, June 1803 (Africana Museum)

Ngqika

CISKEI *c.* 1775 — BURNSHILL, 1829

Paramount chief of the western Xhosa (Rharhabe). At the age of eleven he became chief of the Rharhabe in what became known as the Ciskei. Ngqika clashed with Ndlambe, his uncle and rival, who had acted as regent during his minority, and sought colonial aid, as a result of which his people lost considerable stretches of land. In 1818, after Ngqika had been defeated by the combined forces of Ndlambe and Hintsa (paramount chief of the Gcaleka) at the battle of Amalinde, colonial troops came to his aid and invaded the lands of Ndlambe and Hintsa, capturing 23 000 cattle. Ndlambe was then defeated in the Fifth Frontier War (1818–1819), and Ngqika was recognised by the Cape government as paramount chief and permitted to establish himself along the Tyhume River, but had to accept the loss of much of the former territory of the Rharhabe. His accession to this demand lost him what remaining support he had amongst his people and he died a bitter and lonely man.

Far left:
'Zulu kraal', by George Duff. The beehive-shaped dwellings of poles and thatch, arranged in a semi-circle around the cattle kraal, are a hallmark of the Nguni
(Local History Museum Collection, Durban)

Left:
P W Botha and Samora Machel at the signing of the Nkomati Accord
(South African Communication Service)

Nguni

Linguistic term for Bantu-speaking people living in the south-eastern region between the interior plateau and the Indian Ocean, stretching from the Ciskei to Swaziland. The northern Nguni comprise the Zulu and Swazi, the southern Nguni include the Xhosa, Thembu, Mfengu, Mpondo and Mpondomise. The Nguni people were never united politically, but comprised many small-scale communities, each enjoying political and economic autonomy. They lived in relatively small chiefdoms, some only a few villages. Their scattered homesteads, beehive-shaped dwellings of poles and thatch, were arranged in a semi-circle around the cattle kraal. Their economy centred on herding, cultivation and hunting. The Nguni languages are unique among Bantu-languages in that they have clicking sounds, which were absorbed into the language through intermarriage with Khoisan-speaking people whose languages were characterised by such clicks.

Nkomati Accord

A formal non-aggression treaty between South Africa and Mozambique signed at Nkomati on the border between the two countries in March 1984. According to the agreement both sides undertook to refrain from interference in each other's affairs, to resolve their differences peacefully, and to prohibit the operation of terrorist organisations from their territories. The Accord meant little, for Renamo (the Mozambique National Resistance) continued to be supported from South Africa, and the mysterious death of Mozambican President Samora Machel in a plane crash over South African territory cast another major shadow over relations between the two countries.

Non-European Unity Movement (NEUM)

Created in 1943 in Cape Town at a meeting which brought together members of the All African Convention (AAC) and the Anti-CAD (Anti-Coloured Affairs Department), a coloured organisation. Its aim was to build unity among the oppressed in South Africa. The NEUM, strongly anti-racist, in fact drew support largely from coloured intellectuals in the western Cape. Its policy was non-collaboration and boycott of racist institutions. In the face of state repression, it disintegrated in the early 1960s when a number of its leaders were banned or forced into exile. It was reconstituted as the New Unity Movement in the 1980s.

Nongqause (Nongqawuse)

KENTANI DISTRICT, TRANSKEI, 1841 — GLEN SHAW, ALEXANDRIA DISTRICT, 1898

Prophetess. Nongqause's prophecies spelled catastrophe for the Xhosa in

Nongqause (right) *c.* 1858. The young woman's prophecies spelled catastrophe for the Xhosa nation in the late 1850s
(South African Library)

the late 1850s. An adolescent girl in the custody of her uncle Mhlakaza, she reputedly saw a vision of her ancestors at the Gxara stream who advised the Xhosa to slaughter their cattle. According to her vision, if they obeyed an army of their ancestors would rise from the dead to aid them against the British, who had recently defeated them in the Eighth Frontier War. Sarili, paramount chief of the Gcaleka, ordered his followers to slaughter their cattle. The date set for the resurrection of the Xhosa ancestors passed, and almost one-third of the Xhosa population died of starvation or fled to the Cape Colony. Nongqause was captured in Bomvanaland and later lived under official protection on Robben Island, then under a false name near what is now Alexandra in the eastern Cape.

Ntsikana, an early Christian among the Ngqika of the eastern Cape
(Africana Museum)

Nuclear Programme

At Pelindaba, near Pretoria, site of the National Nuclear Research Centre, two small nuclear reactors went critical in 1965 and 1967. Then in 1971 the government announced a breakthrough in the process of enriching uranium, an important nuclear fuel. In 1984 the Koeberg nuclear power station near Cape Town, came into production.

It was not until 1992 that it was revealed that the government had embarked on a secret programme to build nuclear weapons in the mid-1970s. By 1989, when the programme was abandoned, six weapons had been produced. In 1991 the government agreed to sign the Nuclear non-Proliferation Treaty.

Ntsikana

CISKEI, *c.* 1760 — CISKEI, 1820

Seer and hymn-writer. An early Christian among the Ngqika of the eastern Cape, he was converted after meeting Van der Kemp of the London Missionary Society. Ntsikana came to reject certain customs such as polygamy, and he opposed the anti-white stance of his rival Nxele. As councillor to Ngqika, he warned him of the consequences of war with Ndlambe. The Ngqika were defeated at the battle of Amalinde (1818), but Nxele was crushed the following year. Ntsikana became influential as a mystic and visionary and was revered for the hymns he composed, and for his prophetic utterances.

O

Oppenheimer, Sir Ernest

HESSE, GERMANY, 1880 — JOHANNESBURG, 1957

Financier, founder of Anglo American Corporation. Oppenheimer arrived in South Africa in 1902 as a representative for a London-based diamond company. He soon became involved in both municipal and commercial concerns, and was instrumental in the amalgamation of the South West African diamond fields under the control of the De Beers diamond group and then the Anglo American Corporation. Although the target for anti-German feeling, he attended the Versailles Peace Conference in 1919 as an observer. In a series of bold financial manoeuvres during the depression years, Oppenheimer was able to keep the diamond market a profitable monopoly.

Sir Ernest Oppenheimer
(The Brenthurst Library)

Orange Free State (OFS)

An independent Voortrekker Republic between the Orange and Vaal Rivers which came into being after gaining its independence from Britain in the Bloemfontein Convention of 1854. A constitution combining elements of the Cape colonial system of administration and the United States constitution was drawn up, and a government was elected consisting of a uni-cameral Volksraad and a directly elected President. All whites who had lived in the Republic for six months were citizens, and the franchise was restricted to all white male citizens who had registered for military service.

White Free State society was mainly Afrikaans-speaking, rural and was thinly scattered across the land, most of which was in the hands of some 15 000 commercial farmers. Blacks, who were forbidden by law to acquire land in the Republic, provided labour, or were squatters and sharecroppers on white-owned farms. Griqua owned land in the south, but in 1861 Adam Kok sold his remaining land rights in the Free State to whites and trekked across the Drakensberg. Competition for the fertile lands along the Caledon River valley between Moshweshwe's Sotho and Free Staters led to war in 1858 and 1865, and ended with the Boers in possession of the 'conquered territory' when Britain annexed a truncated Basutoland in 1868. With the acquisition of Rolong farms at Thaba 'Nchu (Black Mountain) in the 1880s the white monopoly of land ownership in the Free State was virtually complete.

Parade in Bloemfontein's Market Square during the annexation of the Orange River Colony in 1900
(National Cultural History Museum)

Centrally situated between the Cape Colony to the south and the South African Republic to the north, the OFS was initially drawn into the orbit of the Cape's market economy, exporting wool and increasing its agricultural production in response to the new demands after the mineral discoveries. In the 1880s it moved closer to the Transvaal, and an alliance with its sister

Republic to the north took it into the South African War in 1899. British forces occupied Bloemfontein in March 1900 and the OFS became the British Orange River Colony. It was incorporated in the Union in 1910 as the province of the Orange Free State. Bloemfontein became the national judicial capital.

Orange River Sovereignty (1848–1854)

Territory between the Orange and Vaal Rivers, proclaimed a British sovereignty by Sir Harry Smith in terms of his High Commission. Smith was concerned about stability on the Cape's northern border. Six year later, weary of the border disputes between white farmers and Moshweshwe's Sotho, and of bearing the burden of administering the sovereignty, Britain recognised the independence of the white colonists in the area in the Bloemfontein Convention, and the Orange River Sovereignty ceased to exist.

Ordinance 50 (1828)

Legislation which made 'Hottentots and other free people of colour' equal before the law with whites. All discriminatory restrictions on the Khoi were abolished — Khoi could legally own land and could move around freely without having to carry passes. The Ordinance was in part a response to a humanitarian concern for justice for the Khoi and in part a response to the demands for a more mobile labour force in the expanding labour market of the colony.

As South Africa's international isolation grew, Prime Minister B J Vorster attempted to maintain good relations with other states in Africa. In March 1967 Vorster and his Foreign Minister Dr H Muller, received a goodwill mission from Malawi
(Die Burger)

Ossewabrandwag (Oxwaggon Sentinels)

Initially a cultural organisation established in 1939 which grew out of the Great Trek centenary celebrations of the previous year. After the outbreak of the Second World War, the Ossewabrandwag (OB) became a national socialist, paramilitary body with its own stormtroopers under a new leader, J F J van Rensburg. It challenged Malan's National Party for control of the Afrikaner nationalist movement, and embarked on sabotage against the war effort. By the 1943 general election the National Party had clearly emerged as the dominant political mouthpiece of Afrikanerdom and the OB was a spent force.

Outward Policy

Also known as 'dialogue' or 'detente', the Outward Policy was an attempt to establish friendly relations with other states in Africa. Dr H F Verwoerd recognised the independence of Lesotho, Botswana and Swaziland in the 1960s and pledged to maintain good relations with them. This policy was continued by Verwoerd's successor B J Vorster as international pressure on South Africa, and her isolation, grew. But South Africa continued to be condemned by African states for its apartheid policies, and its involvement in the Angolan civil war (1975–1976) effectively ended the Outward Policy.

P

Pact Government (1924–1933)

An electoral pact was concluded in 1923 between Hertzog's National Party and Creswell's Labour Party, under which they agreed not to oppose each other in the next general election but to support each other's candidates against those of the South African Party. In the 1924 general election the Hertzog-Creswell Pact won, with Hertzog becoming Prime Minister and Creswell, Minister of Labour and Defence. The Pact continued until the Hertzog-Smuts coalition in 1933.

Painting

South African painting begins with the Bushmen many thousands of years before the arrival of Europeans. In the more mountainous areas of Southern Africa many rock shelters and large boulders contain images of the Bushmen people's religious beliefs. Although we know little about the details of individual painters, their images stand as a powerful historical and religious testament to a group of people exterminated by colonial expansion.

The first western painters were colonial officials, missionaries, travellers and naturalists. Few of them were professional artists, and their pictorial records of South Africa, while of great historical value, are of lesser artistic significance. Many of the earliest professional painters were British visitors or settlers, like Thomas Baines, George Angas, Frederick I'Ons and Thomas Bowler. They were primarily concerned with producing an accurate pictorial record, and ignored the country's wealth of rock art and the cultural traditions of the different black peoples whom they encountered.

Amongst the earliest South African-born painters were the landscapists J E A Volschenk (1853–1936) and Hugo Naudé (1869–1941). Other important South African painters are J H Pierneef, whose love of the Transvaal countryside is reflected in his landscapes, H Stratford Caldecott, the first South African painter to apply impressionist principles to the sun-scorched Cape landscape, and Walter Battiss. The influence of expressionism reached South Africa in the 1920s when Irma Stern and Maggie Laubser returned from studying in Germany. The paintings of Stern, probably South Africa's most widely celebrated painter, were derided for many years by a conservative public whose tastes had been moulded by Edward Roworth and others trained in the English academic tradition.

Gerard Sekoto, the first black painter of importance, concentrated on life in the now destroyed communities of Sophiatown and District Six. From the Polly Street Art Centre in Johannesburg in the 1950s

South African art begins with the Bushmen. This complex panel of shaded polychrome depicting eland superimposed on large shamans, was discovered in the Natal Drakensberg
(Wits Archaeology)

'The fishmonger', by Maggie Laubser. Returning from her studies in Germany, Laubser brought with her the influence of expressionism
(Pretoria Art Museum)

emerged the urban black artistic movement, led by Louis Maqhubela and Ephraim Ngatane. Township art reflected daily life in the black townships outside Johannesburg, from which the bulk of painting by black artists in the 1950s and 1960s emanated.

Pan Africanist Congress

Africanists in the African National Congress (ANC) broke away and established the Pan Africanist Congress (PAC) in 1959 under the leadership of Robert Sobukwe. Proclaiming 'Africa for Africans', the PAC aimed for the creation of a United States of Africa, and the achievement of an Africanist socialist democracy. In 1960 it pre-empted the ANC anti-pass law campaign, and on 21 March PAC demonstrations against the pass laws resulted in the shootings of Sharpeville and Langa. On 8 April the PAC was outlawed. With only a skeletal organisation and most of its leaders imprisoned, it was unable to organise effectively underground. It sponsored an underground insurrectionary movement, Poqo, and set up headquarters outside South Africa. Between 1964 and 1968 the PAC was expelled first from Maseru (Lesotho), then from Lusaka (Zambia), and its attempts to send saboteurs into South Africa via Mozambique in 1968 met with failure. Riven by internal dissension, the PAC struggled on in exile until 1990 when the ban imposed on it in 1960 was lifted. Its fortunes then revived under the leadership of Clarence Makwetu. At first it refused to enter into any negotiations with the De Klerk regime, but in 1992 it relented after the government had accepted the idea of a one person one vote Constituent Assembly.

Soweto, 9 December 1990. Clarence Makwetu was elected President of the PAC at the first congress of that organisation to be held in South Africa in 30 years
(Mayibuye Centre)

Pass Laws

Laws used to control the movement of people within the country, particularly into the towns. The origin of such laws is to be found in the eighteenth century, when slaves were obliged to carry documents signed by their masters when they were absent from their masters' homes. Black labourers on the diamond mines in Kimberley in the 1870s were required to carry passes, and in 1895 the Transvaal legislature enacted a pass law compelling a black man on entering the Witwatersrand to obtain a pass authorising him to seek employment. If he was found without a pass, he was liable to be arrested. The enforced carrying of passes by all African men, and from 1952 African women, over the age of sixteen, provoked many protests and demonstrations, one of which led to the Sharpeville massacre. The state's attempt to enforce the pass laws created a vast class of lawbreakers, for by the 1960s more than 100 000 blacks were arrested every year under these laws. But efforts to prevent the influx of Africans to the towns proved, in the end, futile. It was not until 1986, by which time they were hardly operative, that P W Botha's government repealed these hated laws. By then, it was estimated, over seventeen million blacks had been arrested under the laws this century.

Paton, Alan Stewart

PIETERMARITZBURG, 1903 — BOTHA'S HILL, NATAL, 1988

Writer and politician. First a teacher, Paton took charge of the Diepkloof Reformatory for delinquent black boys near Johannesburg in 1935. In 1948 his first and most famous novel *Cry the Beloved Country* was published. It made a tremendous impact and focused international attention on the plight of South African blacks. It was followed by *Too Late the Phalarope*, a novel exposing the immorality of the Immorality Act. His later writings included *Hofmeyr*, a biography of Smuts's deputy, and two volumes of autobiography. Always an active opponent of apartheid, Paton was a prominent figure in the Liberal Party, and its national President from 1960 until its enforced dissolution in 1968.

Petty Apartheid

As distinct from the 'grand apartheid' of the Bantustans, 'petty apartheid' was the term used for provisions for keeping the races segregated and protecting white privilege in a common area. These discriminatory measures extended segregation to such places as libraries, churches, trains, buses, beaches, restaurants and entrances to public buildings. Such provisions were all-embracing in the late 1960s and early 1970s. Thereafter, bans on interracial sports, recreation and entertainment came under attack and some provisions were relaxed or removed. It was not until 1991, however, that the Separate Amenities Act, under which these provisions were mainly enacted, was repealed.

Philip, John

SCOTLAND, 1775 — HANKEY, CAPE, 1851

Superintendent of missions. Philip came out to the Cape in 1819 to take charge of the missions of the London Missionary Society (LMS). He soon condemned the colonists for their harsh treatment of the Khoi, and took his campaign for improvement of their lot to London, where he lobbied the House of Commons. By the 1830s he was one of the best informed people at the Cape, and he continued to write voluminously in the cause of promoting peace on the frontier and justice in the colony. He remained superintendent of the LMS in South Africa until his resignation in 1849.

Pietermaritzburg

Capital of the province of Natal, situated in the Umsindusi River valley, at the base of an escarpment, seventy-seven kilometres inland from Durban, Pietermaritzburg was founded in 1839 after a Voortrekker victory over the Zulus at Blood River. It was named in honour of the Voortrekker leaders Piet Retief and Gerrit Maritz, and became the capital of the Boer Republic of Natalia, established in the same year. For five years the Republic was the main focus of Voortrekker settlement, and Pietermaritzburg was its seat of government. In 1843 the British annexed Natal, and established a garrison at Fort Napier on the edge of the town to reinforce their authority. In 1856 Pietermaritzburg became the capital of the Crown Colony of Natal. Whilst most of the Afrikaners were trekking back across the Drakensberg mountains to the highveld, new British immigrants were arriving in Natal, some 5 000 coming out between 1849 and 1852. Brought out to farm the land, many of them abandoned farming and settled in Pietermaritzburg and Durban. In 1887 Pietermaritzburg, with a white population of 9 251, was still a more important city than Durban, and enjoyed considerable trade owing to its favourable position en route from the port of Durban to the inland areas. Commercial prosperity was boosted by the completion of the railway line between Durban and Pietermaritzburg in 1880 and between Pietermaritzburg and the Transvaal in 1895.

In the twentieth century the city was far surpassed by Durban, both in size of population (in 1991 Pietermaritzburg had a

Alan Paton's *Cry the Beloved Country* focused international attention on the plight of South African blacks
(Local History Museum Collection, Durban)

John Philip, superintendent of the London Missionary Society
(South African Library)

Below:
'Fort Napier, 1852', by Edmund Tatham. In 1843 the British annexed Natal and established a garrison at Fort Napier
(Local History Museum Collection, Durban)

Above:
Townsend's 'Pietermaritzburg in the 1850s'. Many of the British settlers who were brought out to Natal between 1849 and 1852, abandoned farming and settled in Pietermaritzburg
(Local History Museum Collection, Durban)

population of 228 549) and importance. But Pietermaritzburg remained the seat of the provincial legislature and the Natal division of the Supreme Court, and lay at the centre of an important economic sub-region.

Pirow, Oswald

ABERDEEN, CAPE, 1890 — PRETORIA, 1959

Lawyer, politician and author. Pirow formed a law partnership with Tielman Roos in Pretoria in 1914, later supporting Roos as leader of the National Party in the Transvaal, and himself entered Parliament as member for Soutpansberg, in 1929 becoming Minister of Justice. He steered the Riotous Assemblies Amendment Act, the first major piece of anti-communist legislation, through Parliament in 1930.

A supporter of Hitler and his ideas, Pirow was sent to Germany in 1938 to try to dissuade the German chancellor from war. When war came the following year, he opposed South Africa's entry into the war, and founded a New Order, which aimed to create an Afrikaner socialist state in South Africa. After failing to achieve a closer liaison with the Ossewabrandwag and the Greyshirts, he withdrew from public life.

Far right:
Mr and Mrs Oswald Pirow, 1938. A supporter of Hitler and his ideas, Pirow was sent to Germany in 1938 to try to dissuade the German chancellor from war
(South African Library)

Above:
The Cato Manor Riots, 1959, one of the many instances of politically-related violence
(Photograph supplied by Tom Lodge)

Plaatje, Solomon Tshekisho
BOSHOF DISTRICT, ORANGE FREE STATE, 1875 — JOHANNESBURG, 1932

Journalist, politician, writer. The son of Christian Rolong parents, Plaatje put to good use his command of some eight languages in his various roles as interpreter during the South African War (1899–1902), editor of Tswana-English newspapers (1901–1915), Secretary General of the South African Native National Congress (later the ANC) and member of delegations to Europe. The author of *Native Life in South Africa* (1915), an indictment of the Natives Land Act of 1913 and its effects, Plaatje also translated a number of Shakespeare's plays into Tswana.

Far left:
Sol Plaatje
(South African Library)

Political Violence

Political violence has taken many forms in South African history, but the phrase acquired a new currency in the early 1990s, when politically-related violence reached new proportions. Whereas in 1976–1977 and again in 1984–1987 there had been full-scale revolts, the violence of the early 1990s was more random and sporadic, involving the occasional massacre, a number of attacks on commuters in trains, and a large number of individual shootings and murders. Beginning in Natal in the late 1980s, such violence moved to the Rand in 1990. In each year in the early 1990s on average almost 2 000 people were killed, though such statistics must be viewed with great caution. There was no doubt that criminal elements participated in the violence and some of what was called political violence was probably not politically motivated, but the product of an environment of poverty, unemployment and rightlessness and a consequent attitude that 'life was cheap', a breakdown of law and order in certain communities, and personal grudges and retributions. In Natal especially, local war-lords sought to retain control of particular areas, and one instance of violence often provoked another, producing a cycle of violence.

The political causes of this violence, which seemed to peak when negotiations reached sensitive phases, aroused great controversy. Some whites called it 'black-on-black' violence, and pointed to the conflict between the African National Congress (ANC) and Inkatha as the main cause. Members of the ANC and Inkatha each blamed the other for the violence. Some blacks, on the other hand, blamed apartheid and a 'third force', organised by whites, sometimes said to include members of the cabinet itself. Sensitive to this charge, the government appointed in 1991 a Commission of Enquiry Regarding the Prevention of Public Violence and Intimidation (the Goldstone Commission), which in its second interim report of April 1992 said it had found no evidence of a 'third force'. It was clear, however, that members of the security forces had played a role in instigating some of the violence, and very few of those responsible for this violence were ever brought to justice and charged with criminal offences.

(C C Saunders)

Poor Whiteism

Poor whites was a term used for whites without skills and education who were unable to obtain employment in competition with blacks. By the turn of the century, considerable numbers of such people were settling in towns as a result of land shortage, the rinderpest epidemic of 1896–1897, the burning of Boer farms by the British army during the South African War (1899–1902), and the drought of 1903–1908. By 1930 about one-fifth of the Afrikaner population could be loosely classified as poor white. A major commission of enquiry, funded by the Carnegie Corporation, investigated the 'problem'. State intervention on their behalf, and the revival in the economy after South Africa left the gold standard in 1932, together worked to reduce the numbers of poor whites drastically.

Population Registration Act (No. 30) 1950

By means of this Act a national register was compiled in which every individual was classified according to his race. Section 13 of the Act provided for the issue of an identity document to everyone on the population register over sixteen years of age, a document which clearly stated the race to which they belonged. As most apartheid laws were based on a racial definition, the Act was a cornerstone of apartheid. It was repealed in 1991.

Port Elizabeth

Situated on Algoa Bay in the Cape, Port Elizabeth's foundation dates from the arrival of the British settlers in 1820. It is named after the wife of the Acting Governor of the Cape at the time, Sir Rufane Donkin. The gateway to the settler colonies of the interior, Port Elizabeth became the chief outlet for the export of wool from the Cape Colony, and developed into an important commercial and industrial centre. From the 1920s to the late 1980s, a number of motor assembly plants were situated there.

Potchefstroom

Town on the Mooi River in the western Transvaal founded in 1838 by Voortrekker leader Andries Potgieter on land which Sotho-speakers had long occupied and which had come temporarily under the control of Mzilikazi's Ndebele. It served as the capital of the Transvaal Republic until displaced by the more centrally situated Pretoria in 1860.

Centre of a relatively rich agricultural district, Potchefstroom became an important ecclesiastical and educational centre for Afrikaners: both the Nederduitse Gereformeerde Kerk (Transvaal) (1842), and the Nederduitsch Hervormde Kerk (1853) originated there and one of the three Afrikaans theological schools in the country was established in the town, which was also the home of the Potchefstroom University for Christian Higher Education.

Potgieter, Andries Hendrik

GRAAFF-REINET, DISTRICT, 1792 —
SCHOEMANSDAL, SOUTPANSBERG, 1852

Voortrekker leader. Potgieter led his party from the Colesberg area to Natal. After successfully defending his party against the Ndebele at Vegkop, he combined forces with A W J Pretorius to defeat the Zulu. He then led his party to Potchefstroom and he set up a Republic in the western Transvaal before moving east to Andries-Ohrigstad and the Soutpansberg. He insisted on trekker independence and was prepared to sacrifice even trekker unity for this cause.

Pretoria

Established on the Apies River in the Transvaal in 1855 by Marthinus Pretorius, who named it after his father, Voortrekker leader Andries Pretorius. It became the capital of the Transvaal Republic in 1860, and the administrative capital of South Africa after Union in 1910. The Peace of Vereeniging which ended the South African War, was signed at Melrose House, Pretoria, on 31 May 1902. Pretoria became the main home of the country's civil ser-

Above:
'Southern view of Port Elizabeth, Algoa Bay'. The gateway to the settler colonies of the interior, Port Elizabeth developed into an important commercial and industrial centre
(Africana Museum)

Left:
Voortrekker leader, Andries Hendrik Potgieter
(Transvaal Archives TAB 5218)

Right:
'View of Pretoria, 1872', by Thomas Baines. Pretoria became the capital of the Transvaal Republic in 1860 and the administrative capital of South Africa after Union in 1910
(Africana Museum)

vice, as well as the headquarters of the South African Defence Force, the South African Police, and numerous other government bodies and parastatals. The buildings of the University of South Africa curve round one of the hills overlooking the city, and on another the Voortrekker Monument, opened in 1949, has been the venue each year for a gathering of nationalistic Afrikaners. Many of the blacks who work in the city commute to it from either the Bophuthatswana or KwaNdebele Bantustans.

Pretorius, Andries Wilhelmus Jacobus

GRAAFF-REINET, 1798 — GROOTPLAATS, PRETORIA DISTRICT, 1853

Voortrekker leader. Known particularly for his leadership in the battle of Blood River (1838), Pretorius negotiated a settlement with Mpande to expel his brother Dingane, and he was instrumental in the establishment of the Natal Republic. He was a staunch advocate of Voortrekker unity, attempting to unite the trekkers of Natal and Winburg-Potchefstroom (1840) and later to form a united Volksraad north of the Vaal. He was involved in battles with British forces in Natal in 1842, and when Britain annexed the Orange River Sovereignty in 1848, he led a Boer force against them which was defeated at Boomplaats. He represented the Boers at the Sand River Convention of 1852 at which the British recognised the independence of the trekkers north of the Vaal River.

Far right:
Portrait of Andries Pretorius, painted by Haufer two years after the Battle of Blood River
(National Cultural History Museum)

Pretorius, Marthinus Wessel

PRETORIUSKLOOF, 1819 — POTCHEFSTROOM, 1910

President of the Transvaal Republic and the Orange Free State. The son of the Voortrekker leader A W J Pretorius, Marthinus was old enough to be a leader himself during the Great Trek, yet he lived to the year of Union. He became a very young President of the Transvaal in 1855, and his greatest achievement was in reconciling the trekkers of the eastern and western Transvaal, and establishing a unified state by 1860. When he tried to unite the Orange Free State and the Transvaal Republics, he precipitated near war. He was elected State President of the OFS in 1859 and again of the Transvaal Republic in 1864. He hoped the Transvaal could gain access to an alternative harbour to that of Natal, but was again in that unsuccessful. He was, with Joubert and Kruger, one of the signatories of the Pretoria Convention at the end of the Anglo-Transvaal War in 1881.

Pringle, Thomas

SCOTLAND, 1789 — LONDON, 1834

Poet. Pringle emigrated to the Cape in 1820 and was appointed librarian of the South African Public Library in Cape Town. A staunch advocate of a free press, he clashed with the Governor, Lord Charles Somerset, on this issue, first when he and Revd A Faure began to publish the *South African Journal*, and then again when with Fairbairn he edited the *South African Commercial Advertiser* (1824). Facing censorship by Somerset, he played a leading role in calling for the freedom of the press. He is perhaps best known for his *African Sketches* (1834) and is regarded as the first poet of distinction in South African literature.

Progressive Party

Political party formed in 1959 after eleven liberal members of the United Party (UP) resigned over that party's decision to oppose further purchases of land by the government for African settlement. The Progressive Party (PP) advocated a qualified franchise and the abolition of racial discrimination. Its members were almost all whites, but there were some black members in its early years. For thirteen years it had only one parliamentary representative, Helen Suzman. Then in 1974 a further six PP candidates were elected to Parliament. In 1975 the PP amalgamated with the Reform Party to become the Progressive Federal Party, which was for a time the official opposition in Parliament and was succeeded eventually by the Democratic Party.

Marthinus Wessel Pretorius
(Transvaal Archives TAB 14145)

Poet Thomas Pringle
(Cape Archives M 448)

Q

QwaQwa

A non-independent Bantustan for the southern Sotho people, formerly known as Witzieshoek, QwaQwa is located on the edge of the Drakensberg mountains in barren territory bordering on Lesotho, Natal and the Orange Free State. Its population rose from 24 000 in 1970 to 453 100 in 1991, as people were cleared from Free State farms and forced to resettle in the Bantustan. QwaQwa offers few opportunities for farming or industrial employment, and most of its people live in poverty. Almost all its income is derived from migrant contract workers or from grants from Pretoria.

R

Railways

The first railway line was opened in Durban in 1860, and two years later a line from Cape Town to Stellenbosch was completed, which was extended to Wellington in 1863. By 1870 there was no more than seventy miles of rail in the whole of South Africa. With the discovery of minerals and the accompanying growth of towns, major construction of railways began. The coastal ports competed for the interior trade of the diamond-fields and the gold mines. By the end of 1895, the Rand gold-fields were connected by railway to the ports of Delagoa Bay (1894), Durban (1895), East London (1892), Port Elizabeth (1892), and Cape Town (1892), and much of the country's present railway network was completed. The creation of a single central South African Railways in 1903 helped bring about political unification of the country, as well as providing the essential infrastructure for the development of manufacturing industry.

Ramaphosa, Matamela Cyril

JOHANNESBURG, 1952 —

Trade unionist and politician. While a student at the University of the North (Turfloop), Ramaphosa was an active member of the South African Students' Organisation (SASO), the Student Christian Movement and the Black People's Convention. In the late 1970s, however, his allegiance shifted from Black Consciousness

Far right:
Cyril Ramaphosa, Secretary-General of the ANC
(Mayibuye Centre)

Right:
Robert Bristow Tatham's watercolour of the official opening of South Africa's first railway line in Durban, 26 June 1860. Bishop Colenso blessed the enterprise
(Local History Museum Collection, Durban)

to the African National Congress (ANC). A lawyer by training, he became legal advisor for the Council of Unions of South Africa, and then General Secretary of the newly established National Union of Mineworkers (NUM) in 1982. Three years later he was one of the founders of the Congress of South African Trade Unions (Cosatu). After organising a strike involving over 200 000 miners in 1987, he was instrumental in drawing up NUM's code of conduct for the mines. Active in the Mass Democratic Movement in the late 1980s, he served as a member of the National Reception Committee at the time of the release of Mandela in February 1990, and he took over from Alfred Nzo as Secretary General of the ANC in 1991.

Randlords

Mining magnates of the Witwatersrand, living in palatial homes in Parktown and other Johannesburg suburbs, the Randlords were of varied national and class origins. Some made quick profits at minimal cost from surface deposits; others, when it became known that the goldbearing reefs extended deep below the surface, made heavy investments for the long term. By 1895 the managements of most of the mining companies, whether French, German or British, had come to the conclusion that the republican government of the Transvaal was an obstruction to be removed. The Kruger government's inability to adequately create and coerce a labour force, and its liquor, railway and dynamite policies were especially irksome to the deep-level mineowners, some of whom were implicated in the Jameson Raid plot. The role of the Randlords in the outbreak of the South African War (1899–1902) remains controversial, though it is today thought that Alfred Milner did not act under any particular influence from them. There was no need for such influence, for the interests of British imperial policy and those of the mining companies coincided in the years prior to war.

Rand Revolt (1922)

An armed uprising by white mine workers on the Witwatersrand. During a period of economic crisis, the Chamber of Mines decided to cut costs by reducing the number of white workers, whose wages were fifteen times those of Africans able to perform the same semi-skilled operations. In November 1921 the Chamber announced its intention of abandoning the status quo agreement by eliminating the colour bar in semi-skilled work. White mine workers came out on strike in January and when the government supported the mineowners, they formed armed commandos across the Rand. In March negotiations broke down, Prime Minister Smuts backed the mineowners, a general strike was declared (7 March), and three days later Smuts proclaimed martial law. It took several days of bitter fighting in the suburbs of Johannesburg between the army and the commandos before the insurrection was put down (16 March). By then 153 people were dead and 687 were injured. The political costs were high: Smuts lost the 1924 general election to a Pact Government comprising Hertzog's National Party and the Labour Party.

Above:
Directors of the Consolidated Gold Fields Company. By 1895 the management of most of the mining companies came to view the Transvaal government as an obstacle to mining progress
(Transvaal Archives TAB 20828)

Below:
The Rand Revolt. Striking mine workers gather in the streets of Johannesburg, 1922. Several days of bitter fighting between the army and the miners ensued, in which 153 people lost their lives and 687 were injured
(Die Burger)

Reconstruction

Term used for the rebuilding of the Transvaal and Orange River Colony after their defeat in the South African War (1899–1902). Alfred Milner, Governor and Administrator of the new colonies, devoted much of his attention to the gold mines, and by 1904, despite a serious labour shortage, gold mining had returned to its pre-war production level and expanded steadily thereafter. Farms were restored and Boer prisoners of war repatriated. The administration spent over sixteen million pounds on relief and repatriation for whites and blacks. By the end of 1902 most of those displaced by the war were back on the land. In 1903 a South African-wide Railways and South African Customs Union was established.

In order to ensure the dominance of the British element in the Transvaal, Milner pursued an Anglicisation policy in the schools and tried to swamp the Afrikaners with British settlers. Both policies failed. Despite promises during the war, no serious attempt was made to change the racial policies of the conquered Republics.

F W Reitz, a signatory of the Treaty of Vereeniging (Transvaal Archives TAB 15089)

Below:
Crowds in front of the Town Hall, Natal Referendum, 10 June 1909. Posters on the left displayed by the Unionist Party illustrate the anticipated effects of Union and Isolation respectively on local industry (Local History Museum Collection, Durban)

Referenda

In 1909 the proposed Union constitution was submitted to the white electorate of Natal in a referendum; a majority voted in favour of Natal entering the new Union. In 1960 the Verwoerd government held a referendum in which all white voters were asked to decide the issue of whether or not South Africa should become a Republic; by the slim margin of 52 per cent the voters decided that it should, and South Africa duly became a Republic in 1961.

In a third referendum held in 1983 the issue before white voters was a new tricameral constitution for South Africa. That time there was a two-thirds majority in favour. In 1992 yet another referendum was held among white voters, who were asked whether they supported the reform initiatives made by President de Klerk since February 1990. A much higher majority than expected cast their votes in favour, and the vote boosted the confidence of De Klerk and the National Party, which then became more assertive in bargaining with the African National Congress.

Reitz, Francis William

SWELLENDAM, 1844 — CAPE TOWN, 1934

President of the Orange Free State. A lawyer, Reitz was the Beaufort West representative in the Cape Legislative Assembly when appointed President of the Free State Court of Appeal in 1873. He reformed the legal system there, establishing a circuit and a supreme court. As President of the Free State from 1889, he developed closer links with the Transvaal. A staunch Republican, he resigned from the Volksraad in 1895 and worked in the Transvaal as a judge. As State Secretary to the President of the Transvaal he drafted Kruger's ultimatum to Britain (1899) which triggered the South African War. A signatory of the Treaty of Vereeniging (1902) he was the first President of the Senate of the Union of South Africa (1910–1920).

Rembrandt Group

Conglomerate. The Rembrandt Tobacco Corporation (SA) Limited, formed by Anton Rupert in the late 1940s, changed its name to Rembrandt Group Limited in 1969. REMGRO is an investment holding company which by the early 1990s controlled over fifty subsidiary and associated companies with interests in tobacco, spirits, food and wine products, petrochemical products, medical services, printing and packaging, banking and life assurance, amongst others.

Republic

The South African War of 1899–1902 brought to an end the republican governments of the Orange Free State and the Transvaal. However the idea of an Afrikaner republic remained an ideal for many Afrikaners. The Afrikaner rebellion of 1914 was an attempt to restore republican independence by those who still hankered after the lost Boer Republics and wanted to be free of imperial domination. General Hertzog's National Party (NP) demanded complete independence for South Africa, and had a large republican following. In 1936 the NP converted itself into a fully-fledged republican party, and in 1948 came to power, dedicated to the creation of a Republic, but promising to remain within the Commonwealth. The government proceeded to take various steps to emphasise the sovereignty of the Union. A South African Citizen Act was passed (1949), and a single national anthem and flag were accepted (1957). In 1949 India became a Republic within the Commonwealth, which convinced many South Africans that the establishment of a Republic would not lead to isolation or cessation.

By the late 1950s the scene was set for the establishment of a Republic. In January 1960 Prime Minister Verwoerd announced that a referendum would be held on the issue. Harold Macmillan's 'wind of change' speech the following month made it clear to many English-speaking South Africans with pro-British feelings that they could no longer pin their hopes for the future on Britain, but both the United Party and the Progressive Party urged their supporters to vote against a Republic. In the referendum held on 5 October 1960 a narrow majority of whites voted in favour of a Republic (52,1 per cent for, 47,4 per cent against). Natal was the only province in which the majority was opposed to the establishment of a Republic. When Verwoerd went to London, he found opposition by the Commonwealth to South Africa remaining a member as a Republic, because of its apartheid policies, and on 31 May 1960 the country became a Republic outside the Commonwealth.

Retief, Pieter

WELLINGTON, 1780 — ZULULAND, 1838

Voortrekker leader. Unsuccessful as a business man in Grahamstown, Retief became the leading Voortrekker after he issued a manifesto, printed in the *Grahamstown Journal* in 1837, explaining the trekkers' reasons for leaving the colony. After trekking north of the Orange River, Retief was elected commandant of the trekker community at Thaba 'Nchu. With a small party, he then crossed into Natal, where he hoped the trekkers could settle. Having recently recovered cattle from Sekonyela for Dingane, Retief went to visit Dingane to ask for cession of territory. The Zulu ruler seemed to be about to cede land to the trekkers when he had Retief and his party brutally murdered.

Crowds on Church Square Pretoria, 31 May 1961, when South Africa became a Republic outside the Commonwealth (Transvaal Archives SAB 3047)

Rharhabe

TRANSKEI, *c.* 1722 — CISKEI, 1787

Xhosa ruler. Rharhabe and Gcaleka both claimed to be heir and successor to their father, Phalo. They clashed in battle and Rharhabe, who was defeated, took his followers to the west bank of the Kei River. The division of the Xhosa, thus begun, remained and helped weaken the Xhosa polity in the face of white intrusion into their traditional lands. Rharhabe built up his power base west of the Fish River, but increasingly clashed with trekboers in that region. He and his son and heir, Mlawu,

Below:
Piet Retief and his escort visit Dingane to ask for cession of territory. The Zulu ruler had the Voortrekker party brutally murdered (Africana Museum)

Far right:
Portrait of Cecil John Rhodes by C Marston
(National Cultural History Museum)

were killed in a skirmish with the Thembu in 1782. Another son, Ngqika, at the time eleven years old, became the new ruler of the western Xhosa, with Ndlambe as regent.

Rhodes, Cecil John

HERTFORDSHIRE, ENGLAND, 1853 — MUIZENBERG, CAPE, 1902

Mining magnate, politician, founder of De Beers Consolidated Mines, Prime Minister of the Cape Colony (1890–1896). Rhodes was the son of a vicar. He came out to South Africa in 1870 to join his brother, and they soon made their way to the Kimberley diamond-fields, where Rhodes gradually advanced from being a speculative digger to forming De Beers Mining Company (1880) and De Beers Consolidated Mines (1887). He also acquired a large stake in the Transvaal gold mines and formed the Gold Fields of South Africa Company (1887). In 1890, having entered Parliament in 1881, he established an alliance with the Afrikaner Bond. The imperialistic Rhodes engineered the disastrous Jameson Raid, as a result of which he was forced to resign. Much of his time in the years of his greatest influence was taken up with developing the territory north of the Transvaal, which was to bear his name for over eighty years.

Below:
The Rivonia trialists. The eight sentenced were: (top, from left) Nelson Mandela, Walter Sisulu, Govan Mbeki, Raymond Mhlaba, (bottom, from left) Elias Motsoaledi, Andrew Mlangeni, Ahmed Kathrada and Dennis Goldberg
(Mayibuye Centre)

Rivonia Trial (1963–1964)

Sensational political trial of Umkhonto we Sizwe leaders captured in 1963 at Rivonia, their headquarters near Johannesburg. The trial began in October 1963 and ended in June 1964. The eleven defendants included Nelson Mandela (arrested in 1962), Walter Sisulu, Govan Mbeki, Raymond Mhlaba, Denis Goldberg and Ahmed Kathrada. They were charged under the General Law Amendment (Sabotage) Act and the Suppression of Communism Act, after the state withdrew the original charge of treason. One defendant was released in exchange for testifying for the prosecution soon after the trial started. Mandela took the stand on 20 April 1964, and his five hours of testimony received wide publicity. Sentences of life imprisonment were handed out to eight of the ten accused; the sentences were strongly condemned at the United Nations, which two weeks later established a special committee on apartheid. Bram Fischer, the defence counsel in the Rivonia trial and a member of a prominent Orange Free State Afrikaner family, was subsequently revealed to have been a leading member of the South African Communist Party, and he too was sentenced to life imprisonment.

Road to the North

The missionaries' road was the route running up the eastern side of what became Bechuanaland (Botswana), and furnished the only access route other than through the Transvaal from the Cape to central Africa. The formation of the small

Boer Republics of Stellaland and Goshen straddling the road to the north, Rhodes's campaign for the annexation of Bechuanaland to the Cape Colony, and German colonisation in South West Africa in 1884, led Britain to secure the road to the north by establishing a protectorate over Bechuanaland in 1885.

Rock Art

Rock art represents Southern Africa's longest and most extensive artistic tradition. A painted stone recovered from a cave deposit in Namibia has been dated to about 27 000 years ago. The oldest known engraving is about 10 000 years old. Paintings are found in the more mountainous areas of Southern Africa, whereas the engravings tend to be on the central plateau. The subject matter of the paintings and the engravings differ markedly. The paintings depict large numbers of human figures involved in various activities, while engraved depictions comprise mainly animals and geometric patterns. Painted images are often found in complex panels with more than one layer. Engravings are more often isolated on small boulders.

Southern African rock art is associated with the trance experiences and beliefs of medicine people, or shamans. A central ritual for the Bushmen is the trance dance. At a dance women clap and sing medicine songs, named after animals believed to possess supernatural power. Men dance rhythmically around the women activating the supernatural power. Shamans harness this power to enter the spirit world to cure the sick, control the game and the rain, as well as to resolve social conflict. Shamans report experiencing a variety of visual, aural and physical hallucinations. These beliefs about and experiences of the spirit world are painted or engraved in the shelters and on boulders.

To communicate these esoteric experiences shamans used ideas of 'death' and being underwater as metaphors. For instance, Bushmen saw similarities between a shaman entering a trance and a dying eland. Both bleed at the nose, froth at the mouth, stumble about and eventually collapse unconscious. Further, being underwater and entering a trance state have certain physical similarities, such as a sense of weightlessness and altered vision and hearing. For these reasons shamans are sometimes depicted next to dying antelope or surrounded by fish and eels. Although these are the general beliefs that give meaning to the art, individual ideas, no matter how contradictory, are accepted as valid revelations of the spirit world. Bushman religion is idiosyncratic and personal ideas are highly valued by the community.

The paintings and engravings were probably done by shaman-artists after the trance dance as they would have lacked the physical control during the dance necessary to execute the often very delicate images. Notions of the spirit world, painted or engraved for all to see, were used to maintain shamans' privileged position in society. Because one of the main tasks of shamans was to alleviate both internal and external social tensions, the art does not simply reflect esoteric beliefs. As the arrival of pastoralists, farmers and Europeans affected Bushman communities, so too the shamans' position in their communities would have changed. The art, changing through time, documents the changes shamans and their communities experienced.

An engraving found in the northern Cape, depicting shamans dancing around an hallucinatory elephant
(Wits Archaeology)

A painting in the north eastern Cape of a 'dying' shaman surrounded by fish and eels
(South African Museum)

Rock art then is not just a cultural heritage to be preserved; these images help write Bushman history from a Bushman perspective.

(T Dowson)

Rolong

Sotho speakers, one of the leading groups among the Tswana-speaking people. The name is derived from Morolong, a legendary chief. The Rolong developed a powerful state in the seventeenth and eighteenth centuries in the northwestern Cape and southwestern Transvaal. They then split up into four chiefdoms: the Rratlou-Rolong, Seleka-Rolong, Tshidi-Rolong and Rrapulana-Rolong. All four Rolong groups suffered disruption in the 1820s and early 1830s, when many Rolong took refuge at Thaba 'Nchu in what became the eastern Orange Free State and, later, a portion of the Bophuthatswana Bantustan.

Roman Catholicism

Prior to an announcement of religious toleration in 1804, public practice of Catholicism at the Cape was forbidden. The first consecrated vicar of the Cape, Bishop Patrick Griffith, arrived in 1838. By 1850 there were two Catholic bishops in South Africa, at Cape Town and Grahamstown, and three or four priests. Catholic mission work amongst blacks was delayed until the late nineteenth century because of Protestant opposition. The most famous Catholic mission centre was Marianhill in Natal, inland of Durban, which was founded by Trappist monks and is still flourishing today. After 1948 the Catholic archbishops frequently took a strong anti-apartheid position in public statements.

Tielman Roos withdrew from political life in 1929 to become a Judge of Appeal
(Die Burger)

Roos, Tielman Johannes de Villiers

CAPE TOWN, 1879 — JOHANNESBURG, 1935

Politician and judge. Roos rose within Het Volk before Union, but he became a Hertzog supporter and helped found the National Party in the Transvaal. He was elected to Parliament as a National Party member in 1915. An outspoken republican, he issued an independence manifesto in 1919. His negotiations with the Labour Party led to Hertzog and Creswell's election agreement (1923) and to the National Party victory in 1924. Deputy Prime Minister and Minister of Justice (1924), he helped to resolve the issue of a national flag (1927) and inspired Hertzog's 'Black Manifesto' election campaign of 1929, but withdrew from politics that year to become a Judge of Appeal. With the country in crisis in late 1932, he attempted to return to active politics as the leader of a new government, but when Smuts and Hertzog agreed to form a coalition government, he was forced to admit defeat.

Rubicon Speech

Ironic name given the speech made by Prime Minister P W Botha to the Natal congress of the National Party in Durban on 15 August 1985. It was widely expected that major policy changes would be announced, and Botha himself spoke of his speech as marking the crossing of the Rubicon. But he ruled out significant concessions to South Africa's black population and rejected demands that apartheid be abandoned. The speech dashed reformists' hopes, created world-wide disillusionment and led directly to economic sanctions. There was an immediate flight of capital from the country, foreign banks led by Chase Manhattan refused to roll over their loans, and the rand fell sharply in value.

The speech which did mark a major change of direction, and hence a real crossing of the Rubicon, was that given by F W de Klerk on 2 February 1990 at the opening of Parliament.

Rural Change

Until the mineral revolution, rural South Africa was a patchwork quilt of more or less autonomous, although interdependent, societies and communities, black and white. The most commercialised areas were in the coastal colonies, whereas subsistence production, combined with sales of mainly animal products to pay for consumption needs characterised areas distant from the coast in the Boer Republics. Internal markets away from coastal ports were poorly developed. But in the more densely populated areas of Natal and the eastern Cape there were already by mid-century signs of differentiation in African society, and the development, linked with the adoption of Christianity and the beginnings of mission education, of a commercialised rural élite of larger-scale peasant producers investing in ploughs and wagons and producing grain surpluses

Left:
'Booshuana women manufacturing earthernware, 1805', by Samuel Daniell. Rural African communities made intensive use of family labour, including women and children (Africana Museum)

Left:
'Zulu kraal near Umlazi', by G F Angas. With the development of large-scale urban markets in the interior, rural society over a large area began to change substantially (Africana Museum)

successfully for local markets.

With the development of large-scale urban markets in the interior, first at Kimberley and then on the Rand, rural society over a large area began to change substantially. Those who lived in the drier, non-arable regions, and in those older areas of more specialised export production in the coastal colonies or provinces, were naturally not so radically affected as those in the arable staple-producing regions of the interior. Those who were most suited in the short term to meet needs for staple grain crops were black farmers, such as the Sotho people of the Caledon River valley, or blacks resident on white-owned farms on the arable highveld. African villages, consisting usually of large extended kin groups, turned to grain production by making intensive use of family labour (including women and children) and by pooling communal resources such as spans

'Klaas Smit's River', by Thomas Baines. Wagon transport became an important element in the rural economy
(National Cultural History Museum)

of oxen. The demand for European implements and manufactures increased greatly in such areas.

The whites by contrast were pastoral farmers who did not, by and large, have the capital, skills or labour to exploit the land intensively themselves. Thus there developed in the last decades of the nineteenth century and early twentieth century a short-lived but highly effective sharecropping economy, in which white landowners and rentiers would take a share of the crop, usually a half share. It was not uncommon in such relationships for patriarchs in black communities to be the economically dominant partner. Wagon transport became an important element in the rural economy from which many people made a good living before railway construction gradually squeezed it out. Out of these economic opportunities created by the growth of urban markets, there emerged a class of relatively educated people who were very active in the formative years of black politics in South Africa. Thus for a period of rapid intensification of rural production, black farming communities benefited greatly from new opportunities for profit, as did many white landholders.

But for black and white alike, the new economic forces at work could also mean impoverishment. Farms were subdivided and more intensively used, and many people could not compete. As some economic opportunities arose, older ones were undermined by the readier availability of manufactures and the gradual concentration of trade and transport in the hands of the more capitalised. Extensive and transhumant pastoralism, and hunting, declined and disappeared. Boers were particularly vulnerable, without the traditional farming skills and communal work ethic that enabled many blacks to take advantage of new farming opportunities. Growing indebtedness was not compensated by growing income, as Boer self-sufficiency eroded in the face of new economic forces. A wave of mortgage capital flooded the interior regions, as it had earlier in the century in the Cape wool districts; but mortgage debt for many white landholders inevitably meant eventual land loss, especially after the South African War (1899–1902) had devastated the productive capital of so many, and much land fell into corporate or speculative hands. For many it was only the enterprise of their black sharecroppers which enabled them to survive.

Often it was single Boer women who moved to the towns first in search of income, as their household work was not crucial in family survival on the land, whereas in black society field work by women (and children) became all the more crucial, both for cash crop production and to make up for the absence of male migrants. Thus it was, paradoxically, that rural black society initially showed more resistance to family breakdown, economic dislocation, and urbanisation than did Afrikaners; and hence the centrality of the 'poor white' question in the white politics of the first half of the twentieth century, and the fierceness of the state's efforts to undermine the self-sufficiency of more successful black farming communities in the same period.

Through much of the twentieth century, then, the South African state was concerned with reconstructing rural society along racial lines. It sought, through massive expenditure and intervention, to promote capitalist white farming. More dramatically, beginning with the seminal Natives Land Act of 1913, the state outlawed all forms of independent African farming outside defined reserve areas. This meant the outlawing of all forms of rent tenancy, sharecropping, and the granting of land rights in return for labour service (labour tenancy). This type of wholesale social-engineering legislation could never be fully implemented, given the ubiquity of such relationships and the dependence of so many white landholders on them. But its existence meant that countless rural blacks on the land led insecure lives, without any bargaining power, subject to legal sanction at any time, but often prospering despite the law. At the same time, the extension of master and servants legislation over all blacks living on white-owned farms meant that a wide range of acts of commission or omission, such as disobedience or desertion, became criminal acts, even for those not contracted to render labour.

As overcrowding and resource deterioration in the reserves gradually turned them into feeder areas of migrant labourers instead of functioning commercial farming areas, independent black farming declined radically through the century, as laws piled up against blacks. This process reached a climax in the 1950s and after, with a final assault on labour tenancy in those more extensive farming areas where it had survived — such as the Transvaal lowveld and the Natal interior — and the removal of the 'black spots' — those areas of communal African settlement outside of the reserves where Africans held title dating back to the time before 1913 when African land purchase was unrestricted. The extent of these removals was vast, running to 3,5 million people according to an authoritative survey, a programme of social engineering of extraordinary dimensions even by global standards. All restrictions on land ownership, occupancy and usage were repealed as part of F W de Klerk's retreat from legislative apartheid, and the question of land reform and restitution is high on the agenda in current debate on the future South Africa.

(T Keegan)

Forced removals, Magopa 1983. Many rural Africans led insecure lives under apartheid, and countless thousands were forcibly removed from 'black spots'
(Mayibuye Centre)

Above:
Train derailed by Boers *c.* 1900. The railway network was vital to the British troops during the South African War and the Boers sabotaged many bridges and railway lines
(National Cultural History Museum)

Above right:
Kalahari San man scraping an animal skin with an adze
(South African Museum)

Below:
San people drinking from ostrich eggshell water flask
(South African Museum)

Sabotage

Acts of sabotage were committed by members of the Ossewabrandwag in 1942 as a protest against South Africa's involvement in the Second World War. In the early 1960s Umkhonto we Sizwe and the African Resistance Movement sabotaged state installations as part of the campaign of violence initiated by the banned African National Congress after Sharpeville. The government reacted by passing the Sabotage Act in 1962, providing for detention without trial and harsh penalties for sabotage. Umkhonto we Sizwe began acts of sabotage again after 1977. Far-right splinter groups admitted to perpetrating a number of acts of sabotage in the early 1990s.

San

The term 'San' was used by indigenous herders at the Cape (themselves known variously as Khoikhoi or Hottentots) to describe their hunter-gatherer neighbours, although its origin is somewhat in dispute. In the Nama language, one of the few languages of herders to survive today, San is a proper noun used in the plural form to describe the hunter-gatherers others call Bushmen. The derivation is the word *sa* 'to inhabit, to dwell, to be located' and presumably reflects the idea that the San are the aboriginal people of southern Africa. The word *sab* means 'bush', allowing the possibility that San was almost literally translated as Bushman.

Some years after Van Riebeeck had arrived in the Cape he learned the names of local herding groups and from them heard of groups without domestic animals, hunter-gatherer communities his informants called *Sonqua* or some variant of this word. These Sonqua lived in the mountain areas north of the Cape and were encountered from 1660 on by soldiers sent out from the Castle. It is likely that the term Sonqua, like its counterpart San, was a general term for 'poor people', that is those without domestic stock, and that it was never a word used by people to describe themselves.

These Sonqua, first encountered in the Cape Fold Belt mountains by Van Riebeeck's soldiers, were in fact the surviving Later Stone Age hunter-gatherers for whom the inhospitable mountains represented a refuge area not attractive to local stock keepers. From archaeological excavations in caves and rock shelters in the mountainous regions, we know they lived by hunting, fishing, snaring small game and collecting plant foods. Like their predecessors, they made tools of bone, stone, wood, hide, reed, shell and sinew and they painted on the walls of the shelters in which they lived. Because the European soldiers only briefly encountered the Sonqua, they never saw the paintings and did not fully understand the relations between hunter-gatherers and herders. They did note that the Sonqua were small people.

By the 1680s the colonists had shifted to the use of the word 'Bosjiesman', or some variant, to describe the residual hunter-gatherers of the nearby mountains and the word Sonqua fell into disuse. Unfortunately the term Bosjiesman or Bushman was used indiscriminately to refer to any marginal community, including runaway slaves and dispossessed herders as well as surviving aboriginal hunter-gatherers. Thus, especially nearer the Cape, the term came to be used in the sense of 'bandit'. Further erosion of meaning through the history of the colony meant that Bushman — or Boesman, the Afrikaans version — acquired a distinctly pejorative tone and was no longer useful for historians or anthropologists wishing to refer to indigenous groups.

The growth of ethnographic studies of indigenous hunter-gatherer communities in the 1960s, and the recognition of the pejorative sense of 'Bushman' as a term, led to the resurrection of the word San. For some time it was felt to be a less pejorative, more meaningful description of pre-colonial hunter-gatherers as well as those who had continued to hunt and gather into recent times in isolated parts of the landscape. Hence rock art was referred to as San rock paintings and the !kung speaking Kalahari hunter-gatherers became the !kung San.

From the 1960s on there have been many good ethnographic studies of San people in various parts of the arid interior of southern Africa. Like the rugged mountainous regions of the Cape Fold Belt and the Drakensberg, the relatively waterless Kalahari has proved a barrier to the expansion of herding or agricultural groups, allowing hunter-gatherers to remain until recent times. Kalahari San have interacted for generations with Tswana-speaking herders and farmers but have never been fully integrated.

The fact is, of course, that indigenous hunter-gatherers probably had never required a word that distinguished themselves as a sub continent-wide group from their pastoralist or agriculturalist neighbours. The !Kung speakers at Dobe in the Kalahari referred to themselves as ju/wasi — people — but had no wider term. This realisation, along with the recognition that San is no better than Bushman, merely a translation and perhaps just as derogatory, has led to a reversion to the term Bushman for former hunter-gatherer groups. Outside the community of historians, archaeologists and anthropologists, the term Bushman is widely known and not necessarily pejoratively perceived. The ju/wasi now wish to be known as Bushmen rather than San.

(J Parkington)

Kalahari San woman making ostrich eggshell beads
(South African Museum)

Sanctions

Sanctions of different kinds were imposed by the international community after 1960 to try to force South Africa to abandon its apartheid policies. In 1963 the Security Council of the United Nations imposed a ban on the sale of arms to South Africa, and this was made compulsory in November 1977. An oil embargo was imposed by the Organisation of Petroleum Exporting Countries (OPEC) in 1973. In 1972 a disinvestment campaign was begun by a large number of American, British and European religious, academic and political groups, and it intensified after the Soweto riots of 1976 and the township revolt which began in 1984. By 1988 one-fifth of all British firms had withdrawn from the country. In 1986 the United States Congress enacted a Comprehensive Anti-Apartheid Act, which amongst other things banned

Right:
The apartheid system began to buckle under sustained international pressure. In 1986 the United States Congress enacted a Comprehensive Anti-apartheid Act, which banned new investment in South Africa and prohibited bank loans
(Cartoon by Abe Berry)

Above:
'Sandile's kraal in the Amathole', by Thomas Baines, 1849. The blanket conceals Sandile's withered leg
(William Fehr Collection)

new investment in South Africa and bank loans. The repeal of some of the major apartheid laws in 1991 led to the lifting of most sanctions and the repeal of the American Act, though state and city governments refused to repeal their sanctions legislation. The sanctions imposed in the cultural, academic and sporting fields had largely fallen away by the end of 1991 with the repeal of some of the major apartheid laws.

Sandile

CISKEI, 1820 — ISIDENGE FOREST, BUFFALO RIVER, 1878

Paramount chief of the Rharhabe branch of the western Xhosa from 1840, Sandile was about eight years of age when his father Ngqika died. His mother, Suthu, was then appointed regent. After Sandile succeeded to the chieftainship, the western Xhosa continued to try to resist the ever-growing pressure of white encroachment on their land. Sandile became involved in the Seventh, Eighth and Ninth Frontier Wars, and told his people to kill their cattle in 1856–1857. Each episode contributed to the undermining of his chieftainship. He died resisting the British forces in the last war in the Ciskei.

Far right:
Sarili, his wife and counsellor, by N J Merriman
(Africana Museum)

Sarili (Kreli)

TRANSKEI, *c.* 1814 — SHOLORA, BOMVANALAND, 1892

Paramount chief of the Xhosa, and head of the Gcaleka eastern branch from the death of his father Hintsa in 1835. He was persuaded to agree to a treaty of friendship with the Cape in 1844, but in 1846 found his country again invaded during the War of the Axe. In the following frontier war he and his people were accused by the colonial authorities of being implicated, and were forced to make reparations. His people suffered severely from their participation in the cattle-killing of 1856–1857 and in its aftermath they were expelled from their lands between the Kei and the Mbashe Rivers. In 1877 his people were involved in a skirmish with Mfengu who occupied land from which they had been ousted, and that led to war with the Cape Colony. Again Sarili was forced to flee, this time into Bomvanaland, where he ended his days in exile without power.

School People

Name given those Xhosa-speakers in the eastern Cape who were Christian converts, attended the mission schools and wore western-style clothing, as opposed to the pagan or 'red' people who continued to anoint themselves with red clay. The cleavage between conservative and radical, 'red' and school, and Xhosa and Mfengu (the latter more readily accepting Christian education), goes back to the mid-nineteenth century and is deeper among Xhosa-speakers than other African communities.

Schreiner, Olive Emilie Albertina

WITTEBERGEN, HERSCHEL, CAPE, 1855 — WYNBERG, CAPE, 1920

Writer and feminist. A woman of powerful intellect and advanced and passionately-held views on politics and society, Schreiner gained fame as the author of *The Story of an African Farm* (1883) which was an immediate success in Europe and the United States. She later wrote a number of political works attacking what she regarded as Rhodes's ruthless imperialism, and championing the causes of the Boers and the blacks. She was also one of the first eloquent champions of equal rights for women.

Segregation

The term 'segregation' can, in a loose sense, simply denote the practice or policy of racial separation. However, in the context of South African history the term has come to take on a more specific meaning. It refers to a set of ideas and policies which evolved in the early years of the twentieth century and gradually gained institutional and legislative expression in the period 1910–1948. This policy of segregation is generally viewed as the precursor of apartheid. Indeed apartheid essentially amounted to the systematisation, entrenchment and more rigorous enforcement of segregationist principles.

It is not possible to locate a single source of origin for segregation in South Africa. But a basic segregationist framework was first outlined by the South African Native Affairs Commission (1903–1905), which had been appointed by the post-war Milner administration to investigate 'native policy' with a view to achieving some kind of uniformity among the four British colonies. Among the principles proposed in the commission's report were those of territorial separation, urban segregation and political differentiation — in other words, Africans could not expect to enjoy normal citizenship rights in terms of access to land, to urban residential space, and to the franchise. None of these principles represented significant new departures, as each had been in operation in one form or another at various times in either the British colonies or the Boer Republics. What was new was the attempt to formulate a coherent segregationist framework. And it is interesting to note that this was done by a commission largely composed of English-speakers.

The legislative framework. During the thirty years after Union successive governments — South African Party, National Party and United Party — passed measures realising these principles and others. These measures, in varying degrees of rigour and compulsion, enacted segregation in four main spheres: politics, land, urbanisation and labour.

Political segregation was to a large extent built into the Act of Union. Although the Union constitution preserved the Cape's qualified non-racial franchise, it maintained a racially exclusive franchise in the three other provinces. The notion that Africans should be subjected to differential political treatment was taken further in the 1920 Native Affairs Act, and even more so in the 1927 Native Administration Act which effectively enabled the white government to exercise or delegate enormous political and judicial power over African territories. The delegation of power was to be especially important, as the government was at this time moving more and more in the direction of using indigenous authorities and structures for the exercise of control over African rural areas. The 1936 Representation of Natives Act removed the qualified franchise for Africans in the Cape and established a segregated institution, the Natives Representative Council, which would supposedly serve as a forum for African opinion.

Territorial segregation came to be embodied in two key measures: the 1913 Natives Land Act, and the 1936 Native Trust and Land Act. The former was perhaps the lynch-pin of segregationism and one of the foundation stones on which apartheid was to be built. It set aside about 8 per cent of the land area of South Africa (later to be increased) as reserves exclusively for African occupation. Blacks were for the most part prohibited from buying or leasing land outside the reserves; and restrictions were imposed on African cash tenancy and sharecropping on white-owned land, especially in the Free State. Recent research has

Olive Schreiner, who gained fame as the author of *The Story of an African Farm*
(Transvaal Archives TAB 15108)

Above:
Women from Illinge camp carry firewood to the settlement which lies 5km from the nearest road and the nearest proper habitation. The Land Act, which facilitated the removal of Africans to reserves, was the lynch-pin of segregationism
(Mayibuye Centre: photo by John Seymour)

Above right:
The 'Whites Only' signs in many public places enforced segregation on social and cultural levels
(Mayibuye Centre)

shown that these latter restrictions were not always enforced, so that sharecropping persisted in some parts of the country until the 1950s. The 1936 Act imposed further restrictions on tenancy arrangements, especially labour tenancy; and it created the South African Native Trust, which was empowered to expand the area of the reserves through the purchase of land. This land legislation became a source of enormous bitterness and anger for Africans. The measures have resulted in the eviction of millions of people from land that they once occupied, and given rise to widespread landlessness and massive hardship.

Urban segregation was constructed upon the 1923 Natives (Urban Areas) Act. This measure created the framework within which a more rigid system of urban apartheid eventually evolved. The Act provided for various forms of urban segregation: it encouraged, but did not compel, residential segregation by recommending that municipalities establish separate townships for Africans; access to urban areas became discriminatory as a rudimentary system of influx control was set up; the Act enforced fiscal segregation by requiring municipalities to establish separate 'native revenue accounts'; and the municipal disfranchisement of Africans was confirmed with the optional establishment of advisory boards, bodies that were in effect powerless and were designed to offer a facade of black representation at the local level.

Over the next few decades subsequent amendments to the 1923 Act served to tighten these various forms of urban segregation. While the real tightening occurred after 1950, some amendments in the 1930s and 1940s strengthened in particular the influx control provisions of the Act.

Segregation in the industrial work-place was another form of racial separation to become entrenched in legislation in the years after Union. This segregation was more horizontal than vertical. Black and white worked alongside each other, but from the early days of mining in the industrial era, skilled jobs tended to be reserved for whites, and Africans were largely restricted to unskilled work. This pattern was steadily reinforced after Union. The 1911 Mines and Works Act, for instance, restricted certain categories of skilled work to whites. The 1924 Industrial Conciliation Act and the 1925 Wage Act aimed to incorporate white workers into a system of official bargaining, including the right to unionisation, but excluded Africans from this system. The 1926 Job Reservation Act protected white workers in certain job categories from being displaced by black workers.

The ideology of segregation. Segregation did not simply comprise a body of laws and policies. It also came to be underpinned by a set of ideas that were designed to legitimate racial separation. These ideas gained currency and widespread acceptance among whites, most of whom came to see segregation not only as desirable but also as normal and natural.

Although the South African Native Affairs Commission set down a segregationist programme as early as 1905, the ideology of segregation was not well developed before the First World War. As the work of Saul Dubow and Paul Rich has shown, those primarily responsible for the development of segregationist thought in South Africa in the early part of the twentieth century were a group of English-speaking liberal intellectuals. Foremost among these were Howard Pim, Maurice Evans, Edgar Brookes and Charles Loram.

Their thinking was informed by certain fundamental assumptions and ideas. Some of these were based on Social Darwinist theory, which was influential at the time. Social Darwinists assumed a correlation between racial identity and mental capacity; and they posited a racial hierarchy, according to which the general capacity of Europeans was significantly superior to that of dark-skinned races. This assumption lay beneath the thinking of policy-makers and officials in the British imperial world in the early twentieth century. And it served to justify both the differential treatment of people of colour, and the maintenance of white supremacy. Although, as Dubow has observed, virulent scientific racism was not explicitly articulated on a significant scale in South Africa at the time, racist thinking was implicit in the discourse of the day — it was part of a 'commonsense' view of the world.

Social Darwinist assumptions thus forced their way into the thinking of the early liberal segregationists in South Africa. Howard Pim, for instance, assumed that racial differences were outward signs of mental and moral differences. Maurice Evans warned against miscegenation, as hybridisation and racial impurity only brought degeneration. However, these liberal segregationists of the early twentieth century were not just crude proponents of white supremacy. Indeed they tended to see segregation as a compromise between straight white domination, on the one hand, and assimilation on the other — or as a happy medium between what Loram called 'repressionism' and 'equalism'.

This brand of segregationism thus contained a strong element of benevolent paternalism, epitomised in the notion of trusteeship, according to which it was the duty of whites to act as guardians or trustees over races which were deemed to be inferior and would thus need careful guidance along the path to civilisation. Trusteeship, in the view of these segregationist thinkers, also required the maintenance of social order and stability. In the case of African society this meant the preservation of rural life. Africans were deemed to be 'naturally' rural people whose social structure could only function properly in the countryside. Thus African urbanisation was viewed as a negative process, causing social degeneration and moral deterioration.

This kind of thinking was reinforced in the 1920s with the development in South Africa of the discipline of social anthropology. Anthropological thought at the time tended to stress the distinctive character of the African social order and culture. And this seemed to justify the differential treatment of blacks according to the tenets of segregationist policy. Moreover anthropology seemed to give segregation a certain authority and authenticity insofar as academic 'experts' were producing empirical research and a theoretical approach which supported segregation. Indeed this anthropological work was seized upon by policy-makers and administrators determined to promote segregation as the solution to the 'native question'.

Of the white political leaders of the time it is General Hertzog whom one most readily associates with the policy of segregation. It was his Pact Government, elected in 1924, that proceeded to introduce a series of segregation bills in Parliament. Hertzog's conception of segregation was more rigid and more racist than that of the liberal segregationists. Indeed, in the eyes of such liberals, Hertzog's views tainted the policy of segregation, so much so that in the late 1920s liberals like Brookes and Pim recanted and abandoned segregationist ideology.

Smuts also espoused segregation, supporting the more paternalist, protective conception of the policy. While believing in political and territorial segregation he left open the possibility of the African élite being assimilated. He remained, though, an ardent white supremacist, quite able to support Hertzog in the passing of the Native Representation of Voters Act and the Native Trust and Land Act of 1936.

The historiography of segregation. Scholars who have analysed segregation, as practised in South Africa during the first half of the twentieth century, have in various ways tried to address some fundamental questions. How, for instance, does one best explain segregation? Where and when did it originate? Was it something new, or did it represent a continuation of older policies? What was its fundamental purpose — to keep races apart, or to sustain a system of labour exploitation? These are questions that have given rise to considerable debate and a variety of interpretations.

For those on the right of the ideological spectrum these questions have generally

Cartoon of Edgar Brookes by D C Boonzaier. Although Brookes was one of the group of English-speaking liberal intellectuals primarily responsible for the development of segregationist thought in South Africa, he later recanted and abandoned this ideology
(South African Library)

The Bantu Education Act of 1953 was designed to separate the races at a fundamental level. Cramped classrooms and an inferior syllabus were the inevitable consequences
(Mayibuye Centre)

not posed an analytical problem. For such thinkers segregation was simply a reflection of assumed realities — the existence of different race groups in South Africa, the supposed natural tendency of each race group to live apart from the others, and the friction that allegedly results from racial integration. Thus, according to this view, segregation has always been a natural, normal policy or practice. Nor was it an artificial contrivance, but something that evolved over the years, almost of its own accord.

On the other hand, from the 1930s liberal scholars, after the earlier phase of liberal segregationism had passed, tended to see segregation as something abnormal and unnatural. The 1930s was a decade of growing black urbanisation, and it was this phenomenon in particular that seemed to show up the artificiality of segregation. Industrialisation and urbanisation, in the eyes of liberals, were leading inevitably to a greater integration of the races. Attempts to perpetuate or tighten segregationist policies were therefore considered to be unrealistic. Indeed segregation increasingly came to be viewed by liberals as a relic from the past, representing a carry-over of an old white frontier mentality into the modern industrial era. Segregation was a survival of the nineteenth century Boer republican tradition which would allow for no equality between black and white. Both archaic and artificial, segregation, according to this liberal view, could only hamper the process of modernisation and industrialisation in twentieth-century South Africa.

In the past two or three decades this liberal view of segregation has come under attack. Radical scholars, working in a Marxist tradition, have not seen segregation as dysfunctional to modernisation and industrialisation. Rather has the opposite been the case, with segregation serving the cause of capitalist development. Thus, in this view, the 1913 Land Act was not so much designed to introduce territorial segregation, but rather to underpin a system of cheap labour. The main function of the reserves was to support migrant labour which was so essential to the profitability of the mining industry. Political segregation and repression were necessary to limit the capacity of the black working-class to organise and act against its own exploitation.

Recently this line of argument has been refined. Dubow, for instance, has argued that it is an oversimplified view to explain segregation simply in terms of capital's needs. He rather suggests a weaker link between segregation and capitalism, seeing the former as a policy designed to limit the dislocation of the social order during a time of rapid industrialisation. Segregation was, in Dubow's words, 'primarily a defensive strategy aimed at consolidating white supremacy in the face of the challenge posed by the emergence of an African proletariat'.

Conclusion. While segregation should be viewed in its political, ideological and legislative dimensions, it can only be understood properly when set in the social and economic context of the time — especially in the context of industrialisation and urbanisation. It should also be seen as marking a distinctive phase in South African history, covering the first half of the twentieth century. This is not to say that elements of segregationist thinking and practice cannot be found long before the twentieth century; and there was considerable continuity between the segregation era and the later apartheid era. What was distinctive about the former era was the attempt by white political leaders and intellectuals to give segregation legislative substance and ideological coherence.

(P Maylam)

Sekhukhune

MOGOKGOMENG, TRANSVAAL, *c.*1810 — MANOGE, TRANSVAAL, 1882

Paramount chief of the Pedi of the eastern Transvaal from 1861. On the death of his father Sekwati, Sekhukhune seized the leadership of the Pedi from

Mampuru, his half-brother and the rightful heir. Boer encroachment on their lands forced the Pedi to wage a prolonged struggle to try to retain their independence, first against the Boers themselves and then, after the annexation of the Transvaal in 1877, against the British. In 1879 Sekhukhune's warriors were defeated by a superior force of Swazi and British under Sir Garnet Wolseley, and Sekhukhune's power was finally broken.

Seme, Pixley ka Isaka

INANDA, NATAL, 1881 — JOHANNESBURG, 1951

Founder of the ANC. A lawyer, with degrees from Columbia University (USA) and Jesus College (Oxford), Seme was the main founder of the South African Native National Congress (SANNC). He had for some time favoured a 'native union' in which Africans would forget their tribal conflicts and unite against racist laws. On 8 January 1912 he addressed the first meeting of the new Congress in Bloemfontein and called for Africans to insist on their representation in the Union Parliament. He became the first treasurer of SANNC (which by 1923 was known as the ANC), but did not play a major role in the organisation in the 1920s. A conservative figure who did not believe in confrontation with the government, Seme became the new president of the ANC in 1930, replacing Josiah Gumede. During his presidency the ANC went into sorry decline. In 1935, Seme and DDT Jabavu of the Cape Native Voters Convention agreed to create an All African Convention to unite resistance against the removal of the Cape African vote, but Seme did not play a leading role in the new organisation.

Separate Development

As the term 'apartheid' had attracted so much odium, the term 'separate development' was substituted for it in government parlance in the 1950s. It is associated particularly with Dr H F Verwoerd. As Minister of Native Affairs (1950–1958) and then Prime Minister (1958–1966), he expounded the ideology of separate development or what he called 'good neighbourliness'. According to him, it meant that different peoples should develop on their own lines; in practice, it meant white domination and black inferiority. A barrage of legislation passed in the 1950s sought to implement this ideology. One aspect was the creation of Bantustans, which Verwoerd said could be given independence.

Shaka

NEAR MELMOTH, NATAL, *c.* 1787 — DUKUZA, ZULULAND, 1828

Zulu ruler (1816–1828). Illegitimate son of Senzangakona, a Zulu chieftain, Shaka served as a commander in Dingiswayo's Mthethwa empire (1810–1816). He used his exceptional military talents to build up the Zulu into a formidable fighting force, conquering all the groups in the area, and initiating a chain of violence. By the mid-1820s the Zulu kingdom was the greatest power in south-east Africa. In 1828 Shaka was murdered by his half-brother Dingane who then became king.

Sharpeville

Township near Vereeniging in the southern Transvaal where on 21 March 1960 police panicked and opened fire on a crowd of Pan Africanist Congress (PAC) anti-pass law demonstrators. Sixty-nine blacks were killed and 180 were injured. The shooting was universally condemned. A week later, the PAC and African National Congress were banned and a state of emergency was declared. The crisis led to an outflow of both capital and skills, and to further international pressure on South Africa to change its apartheid policy, but after a moment of indecision the government continued on the same road. Sharpeville remained a symbol of the brute force which lay behind apartheid.

Sekhukhune
(Transvaal Archives TAB 24475)

Above:
By the mid-1820s, Shaka's kingdom was the greatest power in south-east Africa
(Africana Museum)

Below:
Sharpeville, March 1960. Demonstrators flee as police open fire
(Mayibuye Centre)

Above:
Sir Theophilus Shepstone
(Local History Museum, Durban)

Far right:
Walter Sisulu addressing a rally after his release
(Mayibuye Centre)

Shepstone, Sir Theophilus

WESTBURY-ON-TRYM, ENGLAND, 1817 — PIETERMARITZBURG, 1893

Administrator. The son of a Wesleyan missionary, Shepstone was appointed diplomatic agent to the tribes of Natal in 1845 and Secretary for Native Affairs of Natal in 1856. In that post, he masterminded the establishment of segregated locations for Africans in Natal and devoted much of his energy to preventing contact between his black wards and white labour seekers. Shepstone's annexation and administration of the Transvaal (1877–1879) were followed by his retirement from public life in 1880.

Simonstown

Located on the eastern side of the Cape Peninsula, forty kilometres south of Cape Town, it is named after Simon van der Stel, Dutch East India Company Commander at the Cape in the late seventeenth century. From 1741 it was used as a winter anchorage by the Dutch navy when strong north-westerly winds made Table Bay unsuitable. In 1814 it became the headquarters of the British South Atlantic Naval Squadron. Since then it has become South Africa's principal naval base.

Sisulu, Walter Max Ulyate

ENCOBO, TRANSKEI, 1912 —

A trade unionist who joined the African National Congress (ANC) in 1940, Sisulu opposed African involvement in the Second World War and supported Anton Lembede and the Youth League. In 1949 he became a member of the Transvaal

Executive of the ANC and in the 1950s was arrested and banned under the Suppression of Communism Act. After a tour of Eastern bloc countries, Israel, China and Great Britain, his views were modified and he supported the multiracial Congress Alliance. One of the Rivonia trialists, he was sent to Robben Island in 1964. He was, with Mandela, the leading elder statesman on the Island, and was much revered by young members of the ANC. He was eventually released in 1989. He continued to be active as an ANC leader in the early 1990s.

Simonstown. In 1814 it became the headquarters of the British South Atlantic Naval Squadron
(Africana Museum)

Slagter's Nek Rebellion (1815)

Rebellion which followed from the refusal of a frontier farmer, Frederik Bezuidenhout, to obey an order to appear in court to answer charges of maltreating a Khoi servant. Bezuidenhout was shot dead while resisting arrest by a detachment of Khoi soldiers. His brother, vowing revenge for his death, invited Ngqika to join in resistance to the colonial government. The uprising was suppressed at Slagter's Nek and the leaders were publicly executed. The event — the rope broke the first time the execution was attempted — long remained in the memory of the frontier farmers, and was later in the century revived as an example of British cruelty and oppression by those who wished to mobilise Afrikaners into a nationalist movement.

Slavery

The Dutch East India Company (VOC) traded in slaves in South Asia and the

East Indies and extended its use of slave labour to its colony at the Cape. The first slaves arrived with Van Riebeeck. Subsequently slaving expeditions were sent from Cape Town to Mozambique and Madagascar, but the majority of slaves came from Asia aboard vessels carrying other trading goods between Batavia and Europe.

By 1838, when slavery was ended, there were 36 000 slaves in the colony. Slaves were used by the VOC on its cattle and defence posts as well as on public works in Cape Town. They were sold to colonists to be employed on the grain and wine farms of the southwestern Cape. Some were owned by pastoralists, although the indigenous Khoi and San were more often used as workers on frontier farms. Most Capetonians had slaves as domestic servants and artisans.

Slave labour formed the mainstay of the work-force of the Cape. Profits obtained from their work could be as high as those made by the owners of slave plantations in the eighteenth century Caribbean and North America. Contrary to the opinion often expressed by contemporaries and by some more recent apologists, slaves at the Cape could be treated just as brutally as in other colonial slave societies. Although the VOC offered nominal protection to slaves from the worst abuse of their owners, it was not until the late 1820s that effective control was obtained by the British government over physical punishment. Slaves were restricted from travelling without passes, could be sold at public auctions and until the 1820s were unable to marry. Some acquired small amounts of money or livestock from earnings permitted by their owners, but the majority lacked any resources of their own.

Enforced deference to owners led to a high degree of paternalism and dependency which shaped the character of labour relations and racial attitudes in the Cape. Most settlers associated slaves and indigenous people with manual labour and as a result class and wealth differences became closely associated with race. The level of slave manumission (that is, the acquisition of freedom) was very low. Only in Cape Town did a significant 'free black' (ex-slave) community emerge. Some free blacks even owned slaves themselves, but in general they lacked the resources to challenge the settler monopoly of wealth and status.

Slaves came from a wide variety of places, speaking many languages and holding a range of belief systems. So there did not develop a strongly distinctive slave culture of the kind found in the colonial Americas. Rather slaves contributed to a broader popular culture, infused with both settler and indigenous elements. Slave languages played an important part in the emergence of the creole that became Afrikaans. Together with the political exiles

Above:
African captives being driven off into slavery, *c.* 1800
(Africana Museum)

Left:
Slaves could be sold at public auctions
(Cape Archives M 259)

'Malay fruit hawker'. Slaves brought by the Dutch from Asia formed the basis of a thriving Muslim community in Cape Town. Many spoke Malay and retained some Malay customs
(Africana Museum)

brought by the Dutch from Asia, slaves formed the basis of a thriving Muslim community in Cape Town. The earliest Afrikaans texts were written by Cape Muslims in Arabic script.

Until the nineteenth century, the Cape depended on imported slaves to maintain its work-force. The majority of these were male, and there was thus a sexual imbalance. Even where family ties were forged, couples could be broken up and children sold. But after the abolition of the slave trade in 1808 a higher proportion of slaves were Cape-born (children of slave women were born into slavery) and kinship networks emerged. Families, however, were still often separated from each other amongst different owners.

Slaves resisted their condition in a number of ways. Rebellion was difficult because the owners held the power, and slaves were physically separated in relatively small units on remote farms. But many slaves ran away, some escaping from the colony altogether and becoming part of the mixed Oorlam and Griqua communities. A community of runaway slaves also existed for almost a century at Cape Hangklip, on False Bay near Cape Town, frustrating attempts by the authorities to capture them. Other less dramatic forms of resistance included working slowly or inefficiently, breaking tools and poisoning food. Not all slaves acted in such ways. Paternalism and deference, particularly of household domestic slaves, led many to identify with their owners.

In the early nineteenth century important changes took place in Cape slave society. The abolition of the slave trade cut off external supplies, and high infant mortality levels made it difficult to maintain slave numbers from local births. The wine farms on which many slaves worked suffered a slump in the late 1820s, while wool production, the boom sector of the colony's economy, was in any case less dependent on slaves. As colonial settlement expanded in the eastern Cape, a more mobile labour force was needed. Hence merchants and new commercial pastoral farmers began to oppose slavery and opt for cheap wage labour. The slaves themselves became more assertive and laid complaints against their owners to the authorities. There were even two rebellions (1808 and 1825) in a bid for freedom. Neither was very widespread and both were swiftly crushed, but the colonists were alarmed. Thus when the British Parliament abolished slavery in 1834 (with a four-year period of apprenticeship until final emancipation in 1838) there was only muted opposition from the slave owners.

Slave emancipation did not alter the social structure of the colony. No land or capital was provided for the freed slaves, and although some moved to the towns and villages, and particularly to the mission stations after 1838, many other remained on the farms as permanent or seasonal workers. Families were united and many women withdrew from farm work. But most freed slaves lacked the resources to obtain a truly equal position in Cape society.

Slavery thus had a major impact on the economy and society of the Cape. In addition the coercive nature of slavery influenced other types of labour use. Khoi and San children captured in raids were indentured as forced workers. In the eastern Cape during the early nineteenth century

'Slave trade', by George Morland. Family members were often separated from one another amongst different slave owners
(Africana Museum)

some indigenous Africans were also captured and enslaved by settler farmers. These labour methods were extended to the interior after the 1830s. Slave raiding took place in the Delagoa Bay region and indentured labour was widely used in the trekker Republics.

(NA Worden)

Smith, Sir Henry (Harry) George Wakelyn

WHITTLESEY, NORTH CAMBRIDGE, 1787 — LONDON, 1860

Governor of the Cape Colony and High Commissioner for South Africa from 1847 to 1852, Smith was a distinguished veteran of the Napoleonic wars who had served as deputy to Sir Benjamin D'Urban in the mid-1830s. A bombastic High Commissioner, he implemented a new frontier policy of annexation and direct rule by magistrates, and extended British rule northwards to the Vaal River, with the creation of the Orange River Sovereignty in 1848. His policies helped lead to war in 1850, and he was recalled in 1852.

Smuts, Jan Christian

BOVENPLAATS, NEAR RIEBEECK WEST, CAPE, 1870 — IRENE, PRETORIA, 1950

Statesman, soldier, Prime Minister (1919–1924 and 1939–1948). A brilliant scholar, Smuts gained academic distinction at Cambridge University, where he read law. He became Attorney-General of the Transvaal in 1897 and led a Boer commando during the South African War (1899–1902). With his friend and colleague Louis Botha he advocated a policy of conciliation after the war. He was one of the chief architects of the Union of South Africa, and then became a dynamic member of Botha's cabinet. During the First World War he commanded the South African forces in East Africa, and gained international acclaim as a member of the British war cabinet and a draughtsman of the plans to establish the League of Nations. His turbulent and controversial first premiership ended in defeat at the polls in 1924. His South African Party joined with Hertzog's National Party and he became Deputy Prime Minister. He became Prime Minister again in September 1939, when he insisted that the country enter the Second World War. He played a prominent role internationally during the war, and was one of the founders of the United Nations. Domestically, the political tide turned against him after the war and he was defeated in the 1948 election. One of the most remarkable of South Africa's leaders, Smuts was a humanist who failed to recognise that the white electorate needed to be shifted towards more enlightened race policies.

Above:
Meeting held on Devil's Peak (1904–1905) in commemoration of the emancipation of slaves
(Cape Archives E 7892)

Above:
Sir Harry Smith, Governor of the Cape from 1847 to 1852
(Cape Archives M 506a)

Left:
Jan Christian Smuts
(South African National Museum of Military History)

Sobhuza I, (Somhlolo, Raputsa)

d. SWAZILAND, 1839

Founder of the Swazi nation. Having inherited the chieftainship of the Dlamini section of the Ngwane in about

1815, Sobhuza ruled on the upper Phongolo River, but after a battle with Zwide of the Ndwandwe, he fled with his followers northwards to what is now Bremersdorp, where he built Elangeni as his headquarters. From that site Sobhuza subjugated the neighbouring smaller Sotho and Nguni clans and consolidated his power base to form the Swazi nation. Sobhuza, who preferred peace to conflict, was conciliatory to Shaka and Soshangane, and he hid with his followers from Dingane's army in 1828 and 1836. His son Mswati II was able to succeed to a significant chiefdom.

Right:
Robert Sobukwe, first President of the PAC
(Mayibuye Centre)

Sobukwe, Robert Mangaliso
GRAAFF-REINET, 1924 — KIMBERLEY, 1978

Pan Africanist Congress (PAC) leader. Sobukwe joined the African National Congress (ANC) Youth League while attending Fort Hare University. A schoolteacher, then university lecturer, Sobukwe came increasingly to question ANC strategy and in 1958 he advocated a breakaway from the ANC. In 1959 the PAC was founded with Sobukwe as President. After the PAC's anti-pass law campaign (1960) Sobukwe was imprisoned on Robben Island for nine years. On his release, he was restricted, though allowed to practise law in Kimberley.

Lord Charles Somerset, Governor of the Cape from 1814 to 1826
(Transvaal Archives TAB 34487)

Somerset, Lord Charles Henry
GLOUCESTERSHIRE, 1767 — BRIGHTON, 1831

Cape Governor. A direct relation of the British royal family, Somerset's career began in the army but changed direction when he entered Parliament in 1796. He was offered the governorship of the Cape Colony in 1813. To deal with the problem of the defence of the Eastern Frontier, he advocated the introduction of British settlers, 5 000 of whom arrived in 1820. He had earlier tried to negotiate with the Xhosa, recognising Ngqika as paramount chief, but after the war of 1819 he forced Ngqika to give up the land between the Keiskamma and the Fish rivers, which became 'neutral territory'. A man who could not tolerate dissent, Somerset was angered by the critical comments made about his authoritarianism in the first non-government publications which were issued at the Cape in the 1820s, and tried to suppress them.

Sotho

The Sotho are conventionally divided into the southern Sotho, the northern Sotho and the western Sotho or Tswana, who are treated separately (*see* Tswana).

The Southern Sotho. Sotho-speakers settled the area south of the Vaal from about 1500.

Far right:
Sotho warrior by Charles Bell. The distinctive shield, breastplate and plumed head-dress were favoured by the Sotho-speakers
(Africana Museum)

Fokeng, who were early settlers in the region south-east of the fertile Caledon River, and Kwena chiefdoms who crossed over the Vaal River between 1550 and 1650, settled along the upper reaches of the Caledon. The two lineages intermarried but the Kwena seem to have become the more dominant. In about 1600 the two communities crossed the Vaal to settle in the Heidelberg district but remigrated after nearly a century. Other Sotho clans consisted of the Taung, an affiliate of the Hoja, a very early lineage that had been absorbed by later immigrants or forced into the Kalahari Desert, and the Tlokwa and Phuting, both of whom were related to the Kgatla and lived along the Wilge and Elands rivers.

The Southern Sotho lived in small villages of between 50 and 100 people and new chiefdoms proliferated as chiefs tended to ignore the authority of the parent group. The uniting of chiefdoms into larger 'confederations' did not occur as it did amongst the Tswana. The Sotho constructed distinct settlements that indicated the growth of a distinct Sotho identity separate from that of the Tswana. Trade was also more localised.

Following the onset of the Difaqane, the Sotho were attacked by Nguni-speaking refugees, principally the Hlubi and Matiwane's Ngwane, from across the Drakensberg in 1821. Some Sotho chiefdoms, such as Moletsane's Taung and Sebetwane's Kololo, fled across the Vaal adding to the instability there, whilst the Tlokwa under Mma-Ntatsi and Sekonyela, and the Mokoteli of Moshweshwe struggled for control of the region south of the Vaal. Sebetwane was the only Sotho leader to develop a conquest state among the Lozi of the upper Zambesi.

In the Sotho region Moshweshwe eventually established a paramountcy over the southern Sotho. This he did by building up his cattle herds and by a judicious policy of appeasing his enemies and attracting followers to his mountain fortresses at Buthe and Thaba Bosiu. By 1840 he had attracted about 40 000 adherents, including Moletsane who had been unable to establish himself north of the Vaal. Moshweshwe established contact with French missionaries whom he invited to settle in his kingdom in 1833. Later these missionaries acted as a source of support against the Boers.

Moshweshwe's mountain fortress at Thaba Bosiu (Africana Museum)

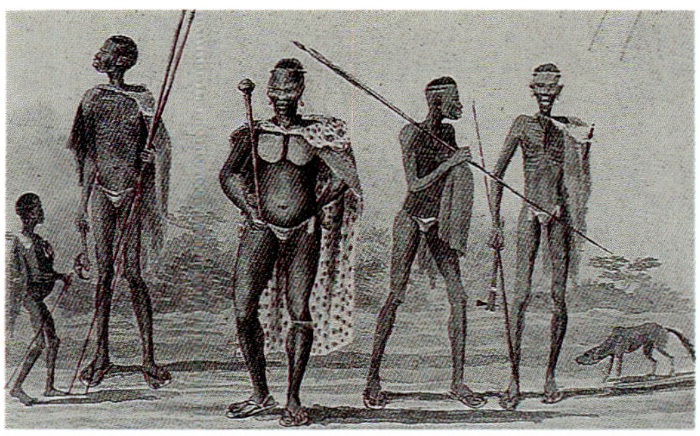

Far left:
A group of Kwena refugees, 1835, by C D Bell. Following the onset of the Difaqane Tswana chiefdoms such as the Kwena were attacked by Nguni-speakers and were driven from the territory north of the Vaal (Africana Museum)

After 1836 the area of trans-Orangia was plunged into war due to conflicting land claims between the African and Kora chiefdoms and the Boers of the Orange Free State. The British attempted to demarcate borders in the region but they were not respected and the British authorities were forced to implement alternative policies that added to the confusion. This led to wars between Moshweshwe and the British on the one hand, and the Orange Free State and the Sotho on the other. Once again Moshweshwe followed a policy based on diplomatic trade-offs and force to ensure that the Sotho remained in possession of their land.

Though Moshweshwe's relationship with the British was contradictory, in 1868 the value of maintaining close contact with them paid off when they intervened in the Second Sotho-Free State war to prevent a certain catastrophe among the Basotho. Though at the Treaty of Aliwal North which followed, the Basotho were forced to give up choice land to the Orange Free State, Moshweshwe negotiated with the British who declared his territory of Basutoland to be a British colony. For three years the territory was administered through the British High Commission but in 1871 the Cape government took over responsibility for Basutoland. The relations between the colonial administration and the Basotho were strained in 1880 when the former attempted to disarm the Basotho leading to the so-called Gun War. Peace returned in 1884 when the British again assumed full control.

Most of the Basotho not living in Basutoland were scattered on farms in the Orange Free State, facing, throughout the twentieth century, the problems of land shortage and poor wages. Many families resorted to sharecropping with white farmers in order to survive. In terms of the homeland policy the nearly two million southern Sotho in 1976 were designated citizens of QwaQwa, a small, mountainous territory on the north-east of modern Lesotho. Voluntary or forced removals of Sotho families off white farms in the 1960s and 1970s increased the population of QwaQwa, making it one of the worst rural slums in South Africa.

Top:
An illustration depicting village life from *Les Basoutos* by E Casalis, published in 1859
(Africana Museum)

Bottom:
African chiefdoms in the late eighteenth century

The Northern Sotho. The northern Sotho were once under the power of the Pedi kingdom though they were not ethnically homogeneous prior to the advent of Pedi paramountcy. The Pedi were a Kgatla offshoot who migrated north from the Pretoria district to the Leolu mountains in about the mid-seventeenth century, an area occupied by many small chiefdoms. The nucleus of the Pedi under Thobele settled in the Steelpoort valley. Here Thobele built up a confederacy of chiefdoms based around his own Maroteng chiefdom which assumed royal status. This was achieved by attracting some chiefdoms through the loan of cattle and by conquering others. The identity of subject people was retained however and the Pedi and immigrant Kgatla existed side by side on the north-eastern highveld. By the beginning of the nineteenth century the Pedi were acting as middlemen trading ivory, cattle and furs with the Thonga at Maputo Bay, and redirecting European or Asian goods such as cloth and beads to the chiefdoms of the central and western highveld. Pedi influence was being directly exerted as far as the Rustenburg area in 1820 where the paramount Thulare was intervening in Fokeng affairs.

Pedi power was challenged in 1822 when the Khumalo (later the Ndebele) under Mzilikazi settled with the Ndzundza close to the Steelpoort River. At this time the Pedi were in crisis following a civil war and the recent passage of the Ndwandwe under Zwide who had moved through the area causing havoc. This allowed the still small Khumalo chiefdom the chance to grow in strength and eventually exert some control in the Pedi heartland.

After the Difaqane, Sekwati, one of the surviving sons of Thulare, restored the Pedi kingdom, settling at a new mountain capital called Phiring. The rise of new forces in the region, such as the Swazi and Zulu kingdoms, meant that the Pedi had to compete for control of subjects who might shift their allegiance to other people. The Pedi formed close links with the Zulu during Sekwati's rule, but remained constant enemies of the Swazi. The situation was made more complex by the arrival of the Boers at Lydenburg and the later establishment of the South African Republic (SAR). The Boers generally treated the Pedi

Top:
'Capturing Sekhukhune's stronghold', from *The Graphic*, 24 January 1880
(Transvaal Archives TAB 15483)

Above:
After 1922 the Communist Party began to pay more attention to Africans and set about working for a 'Native Republic'
(Photograph supplied by Tom Lodge)

with caution after the Soutpansberg Boers under Potgieter had been defeated by the Pedi in 1852. However certain Boer factions considered the Pedi to be tributaries of the Swazi and advanced claims to Pedi land through their Swazi allies. Further tension developed over issues of access to land (especially as gold had been discovered at Lydenburg), labour and taxation, making war almost inevitable.

In 1876 burghers attacked the Pedi, but their protective stronghold coupled with the fact that the Pedi had acquired guns, mainly through wages earned as migrant workers, meant that the combined Boer-Swazi army was held at bay. After a war of attrition however, Sekhukhune sued for peace. Following the British annexation of the Transvaal in 1877 Sekhukhune disclaimed any allegiance to the SAR and by extension to the Transvaal colony. The British interpreted his defiant attitude as a threat to their new administration in the Transvaal and eventually sent forces against him, one in 1878 and another, much larger, in 1879. The Pedi were defeated, their chief imprisoned, and they were forced into a location much smaller than their original homeland. The era of their independence was over. A later act of Pedi resistance took place in the twentieth century when during the so-called Sekhukhuneland revolt they opposed the imposition of a government-appointed chief in 1958.

(A Manson)

South African Communist Party (SACP)

The Communist Party of South Africa was formed in 1921 by an amalgamation of numerous small socialist groups, including the International Socialist League. Initially the Communist Party was dominated by white members and its actions focused mainly on white working class interests. This was evident in the 1922 strike on the Witwatersrand in which the party played a leading role and urged 'workers of the world' to 'unite and fight for a white South Africa'. After 1922, however, the party began to pay more attention to Africans and by 1928 most of its members were black. By then the party had accepted the idea of working for a 'Native Republic', which would be followed by a classless society. African nationalism was seen as the first stage of the social revolution. Prominent communists, such as S P Bunting, Solly Sachs and W H Andrews did not support this policy and were suspended from the party. Communist Party membership dwindled from 1 750 in 1928 to 150 in 1935, and the party found itself isolated from the masses.

Towards the end of the 1930s the party managed to resuscitate itself by organising an anti-Fascist campaign, and by working with black trade unions. In 1950 the Nationalist government passed the Suppression of Communism Act, outlawing the Communist Party, which disbanded. Three years later, the party, renaming itself the South African Communist Party, reformed as an underground organisation and concentrated on working within the Congress Alliance. In 1961 SACP and African National Congress (ANC) leaders formed Umkhonto we Sizwe, marking the start of a new formal alliance between the two organisations. Many leading communists were amongst those arrested at Rivonia in 1963, and the underground SACP was effectively smashed. Thereafter nearly all SACP activities were conducted from outside the country. In February 1990 the SACP was unbanned, and it slowly emerged from the underground, launching itself as an official political party, espousing the idea of a negotiated settlement, and becoming increasingly pragmatic on economic policy. Many of its leading

Solly Sachs, prominent member of the Communist Party
(Mayibuye Centre)

Right:
Yusuf Dadoo and Joe Slovo at a London demonstration during the Rivonia Trial. Many leading communists were amongst those arrested in 1963, and the underground SACP was effectively smashed
(Mayibuye Centre/IDAF)

Above:
J D Rheinallt Jones, one of the founders of the South African Institute of Race Relations
(South African Library)

members continued to hold key offices in the ranks of the ANC, and the alliance of the two organisations remained intact despite calls by opponents for its dissolution.

South African Defence Force

The Union Defence Force was created in 1912, two years after the formation of Union. It was called out by the Botha government to suppress white strikers on the Rand (1913), but it was not yet sufficiently organised to provide protection against increasing militancy, and Smuts had to ask the Governor-General for imperial troops to assist in keeping order. In January 1914 government troops were used to crush the general strike, and in September the outbreak of the First World War precipitated the Afrikaner Rebellion, which was put down by Afrikaner commandos. In the same month Defence Force troops invaded German South West Africa. Government troops were also used to suppress the Bondelswarts uprising and the Rand Rebellion (1922). Abroad, Union Defence Force troops participated in both the First and Second World Wars, fighting in Africa, Europe and the Middle East.

The South African Defence Force (SADF), as it was known from 1957, consisted of a Permanent Force, Citizen Force and Commando Force, subdivided into the army, the navy (established in 1922) and the air-force (established in 1920). In the mid-1970s two further branches were added, the medical service and the special forces. The ballot system introduced in 1957 was scrapped in 1968 when national military service was introduced, and all white male citizens were obliged to perform military service from the age of 18.

From the 1960s the SADF expanded rapidly, evolving into the most formidable military machine in Africa. In the 1970s and 1980s SADF units launched attacks against government opponents in neighbouring countries, and covertly supported Renamo in Mozambique. On the domestic front, SADF troops were deployed extensively in black townships from 1984, acting together with the South African Police in quelling disturbances. The reputation of the SADF suffered severely as information emerged about secret units, such as the Civil Cooperation Bureau, involved in dirty tricks, including assassinations.

Below:
SADF troops were deployed extensively in black townships from 1984
(Mayibuye Centre)

South African Institute of Race Relations

A research body, primarily concerned with improving black/white relations, founded in 1929 by a small group of intellectuals led by J D Rheinallt Jones. The Institute acted as a pressure group on the government until 1948, but with the advent of National Party government it was sidelined as a 'liberal', even dangerous body. It continued to collect and publish material on the effects of segregation and discrimination, its most significant publication being its annual *Survey of Race Relations*. It also organised seminars, discussion groups and meetings. In the early 1990s it was no longer the target of government attack and instead came under criticism from the left for its links with Inkatha and for the extent to which it blamed the African National Congress for the continuing violence.

South African Party

Political party formed in 1911 after Union from a coalition which included the Afrikaner Bond of the Cape and Het Volk of the Transvaal. Under the leadership first of Botha and then Smuts, it strove to conciliate English and Afrikaans-speaking South Africans within the framework of the British Commonwealth. The South African Party was defeated in the 1924 elections by the Pact Government, and remained in opposition until 1933, when it formed a coalition with, and then in 1934 merged with the National Party to form the United Party.

President Paul Kruger with the SAR coat of arms and Marthinus Steyn with the OFS coat of arms. Kruger struggled throughout his 12-year presidency to regain complete independence for the SAR
(National Cultural History Museum)

South African Republic
(1852–1902)

Afrikaner state — also known as the Transvaal Republic — lying between the Vaal and Limpopo Rivers, which was granted its independence by Britain in the Sand River Convention of 1852. At this time small, farming trekker communities were widely dispersed across the vaguely defined territory. Factionalism hampered Transvaal politics, and only in 1860 did the various groups unite under a constitution, which reserved franchise rights and citizenship exclusively for whites, and precluded Africans from owning land. Also living between the Vaal and Limpopo were a considerable number of independent African chiefdoms who opposed Boer expansion. This frequently led to conflict, resulting in the weaker African communities being broken up, and the remnants becoming squatters and servants on white-owned farms.

Transvaal government was weak, corrupt, unstable and debt-ridden. In 1877, to promote its federation scheme, Britain annexed the South African Republic (SAR), but the Afrikaners resorted to arms to recover their independence, which they regained, subject to certain provisos, in 1881 after the British forces had been overwhelmed at the Battle of Majuba.

Paul Kruger, first elected President in 1883, struggled throughout his eighteen-year presidency to regain complete independence for the SAR, and to preserve Afrikaner control of it. His expansion plans west, north and east were thwarted, and the SAR remained encircled by Britain. The discovery of the Witwatersrand gold reef in 1886 transformed the SAR from an impoverished, rural backwater into the fast-growing economic hub of southern Africa. It also resulted in a tremendous influx of foreign fortune-seekers. Tension with Britain increased after the disastrous Jameson Raid of 1895, in which Cecil Rhodes attempted to topple Kruger's government. The raid itself helped lead to the outbreak of the South African War four years later in 1899. In 1900 the SAR was occupied by British troops and when the war ended in 1902 the former SAR became the Crown Colony of the Transvaal, which in 1907 regained self-government and in 1910 became a province of the Union of South Africa.

South African War (1899–1902)

The causes of the South African War of 1899–1902, known popularly as the Anglo-Boer War, lay in Britain's nineteenth century empire-building in the subcontinent. Having controlled the Cape Colony comfortably since 1815, British leaders took a generally complacent view of their overall power in the region. They allowed migrant Boer populations to establish their own settler Republics (the Transvaal and the Orange Free State) in the interior. Thereafter, except for a brief period in the 1870s, these new agriculturally-based states experienced little British interference in their affairs.

But the discovery of gold in the South African Republic (Transvaal) in 1886 transformed this situation. Within little more than a decade, the Witwatersrand mines had become the world's largest single source of gold, and the economic centre of South Africa had shifted from the British Cape Colony to an independent Boer Republic. Meanwhile, Britain was growing

Above:
The English lion and the Boer bull – how the South African War was depicted by *Le Petit Journal* on 19 November 1899. This French illustrated newspaper adopted a pro-Boer stance throughout the war
(Private Collection)

increasingly uneasy about Germany extending its political and commercial influence there. With established imperial interests exposed to threatening new pressures, British leaders now also feared the possible eventual loss of strategic Cape naval facilities to a European great power rival and its upstart Boer ally.

These imperial system concerns were accompanied by a much greater worry. With London the financial capital of world trade, an efficient and profitable gold-mining industry was vital to British ends. Yet the

Right:
Boer sentries pose in front of their ox-hide tent, 1900
(National Cultural History Museum)

Transvaal government was rather slow to assist mining development in the 1890s, giving priority to the needs of landowning Boer society. Disgruntled mineowners claimed that successful long-term mining as a British interest could only be attained by the removal of the Transvaal regime of President Paul Kruger. The future of gold, and of heavy British investment in the industry, now seemed to depend on a loose common purpose between the imperial government and capitalists, and the willingness of that government to move against the South African Republic.

The 1895 Jameson Raid, a botched plot to unseat the Kruger regime, and a subsequent menacing imperial demand that the Transvaal make political reforms to favour British interests, pushed the Republic to the end of its tether. Standing up to intensifying imperial aggression, the Transvaal, supported by the Orange Free State, declared war in October 1899. They did so to preserve their independence against British imperialists who saw their removal as the only way of guaranteeing vital British material and strategic interests in southern Africa.

In the ensuing conflict, Britain anticipated a quick and easy victory. Instead, imperial power experienced a devastating shock. For before Britain's badly-organised and indifferently-led forces could be reinforced, Boer armies penetrated deep into British territory, inflicting several major defeats on British troops in December 1899. Early in 1900, the tide began to turn. Reorganised and strengthened under more competent command, the British push began. By June, the enemy had been driven back and its field armies were disintegrating. With the Republics seemingly conquered, British generals considered the war at an end.

But then followed nearly two years of highly effective guerrilla warfare by Boer commando units which, living off the countryside, kept the imperial army of occupation at bay with continuous attacks, sabotage, and other forms of military harassment. To isolate commandos from their lifeline of rural support and food supply, the British Commander-in-Chief, Horatio Kitchener, adopted a scorched earth policy, destroying crops and burning thousands of farms in the Boer states. In addition he instituted notorious concentration camps to house Boer women and children removed from the land. African communities were also adversely affected

The Battle of Spion Kop, 24 January 1900. Over 300 British soldiers died and 1 653 were wounded. The Boers, however, suffered 50 dead and 120 wounded (Africana Museum)

by scorched earth tactics, with many refugees being driven into separate black concentration camps where over 14 000 blacks died, mainly from epidemics.

Britain's determination to defeat the Boers, and deepening misery as the war dragged on, eventually eroded the will and capacity of Boer leaders to continue fighting. While they could not develop an anti-imperial alliance with local African societies, blacks themselves were collaborating in increasing numbers with British forces, and resisting republican authority. To make matters worse, numerous poorer Boers had lost faith in the republican cause, and were serving the British Army as National Scouts, against their former commando compatriots.

Faced with this bleak situation, and a willingness by Britain to strike a negotiated peace settlement, Boer military leaders accepted what became known as the Peace of Vereeniging at a conference in May 1902. Although its terms required the Republics to surrender their independence, Britain promised massive economic assistance for post-war reconstruction.

By the end, Britain had put almost 450 000 soldiers into the field, the Boers about 88 000 combatants. In the greatest and most costly war fought by the British between 1815 and 1914, it had taken the self-styled greatest empire in the world nearly three years to defeat two of the colonial world's smallest states. Fighting claimed the lives of 22 000 imperial troops and over 7 000 Boer soldiers, in addition to numerous casualties among blacks who became involved in hostilities. For despite imperial and Republican propaganda that the war was strictly a 'white man's' affair, both camps made considerable use of black labour for both unskilled and skilled war duties. In fact, so great was the contribution of African and coloured people to the British war effort, that approximately 100 000 black men were engaged by the military, as many as 30 000 of whom were armed on active service. Ultimately, in a region where four-fifths of the population was black, a major war could not be fought

In early 1900 the tide began to turn in favour of the British. This painting depicts General Buller's relief of Ladysmith and his reception by General White on 28 February 1900 (National Cultural History Museum)

Above:
May 1900, Boer prisoners of war march through the streets of St Helena to Deadwood Camp. Each week saw the tiresome march of about 200 Boer prisoners from the harbour to the camp while the rest of the prisoners remained on board the ship. By the end of the war there were 2 000 prisoners in the camp
(National Cultural History Museum)

Top right:
Treating the wounded, March 1900. The war claimed the lives of 22 000 imperial troops and over 7 000 Boer soldiers, as well as numerous casualties among blacks who became involved in hostilities
(Transvaal Archives TAB 32202)

Right:
Hindu soldiers, Pretoria, 1901. The war was never simply an 'Anglo-Boer' affair and as many as 30 000 African and coloured people were armed on active service
(Africana Museum)

without them exercising an influence.

With Boer society divided between republican die-hards and those who threw in their lot with the British in the latter stages of the war, and with blacks entangled in the conflict, the South African War was never a simple 'Anglo-Boer', imperial war. It also took on the character of a civil war between parts of South African society. Peace in 1902 also ended this civil war impasse.

With peace concluded, three factors were now expected to secure the substance of Britain's vital interests in South Africa. Imperial supremacy was no longer contested. The brisk capitalist development of the Transvaal into a territory better able to meet the labour and other demands of the mining industry, could proceed apace. Finally, as Britain needed the collaboration of local settlers, imperial strategy rested on conciliating white inhabitants of the former Republics by granting them the latitude to decide on whether to extend the franchise to blacks after their achievement of self-government. As most blacks in the Republics had expected a British victory to lead to some improvement in their position, there was bitter disenchantment as white settlers were appeased at their expense in the aftermath of the war.

(W R Nasson)

South West Africa, *see* Namibia

Soweto

The largest black urban community in South Africa, southwest of Johannesburg. It grew out of the shantytowns and slums that arose with the arrival of black labourers from the rural areas between the First and Second World Wars. In 1976 Soweto was the site of a massive uprising, which began as a political protest against the government's insistence that Afrikaans be used as the medium of instruction in Soweto's high schools, and spread from Soweto across the country.

Soweto Revolt, *see* Township Revolt

Sport

From 1948 onwards it was official government policy to prevent interracial contacts in sport. This meant no multiracial teams, no competitions between teams of different races in South Africa, and no multiracial teams representing South Africa abroad. As South Africa was excluded from sporting events and organisations, and her sporting ties with the rest of the world diminished, the government began to allow integrated sport, first at international level (1971) and then at national level (1973). It was hoped that this would allow South Africa to participate in international sporting events while maintaining strict apartheid at local provincial levels. In the 1980s rebel tours were undertaken by overseas sports teams, willing to break the sports boycott against the country for the cash benefits. The repeal of some apartheid laws in 1991 led to South Africa's acceptance into the international sporting community, and her participation in the 1992 Barcelona Olympics.

Squatting

In rural areas those called squatters were black cultivators who farmed land belonging to white farmers in return for rent or the provision of ninety to 180 days of labour each year. Such squatters were often the original occupiers of the land, who had been forced off it when whites took it over. In the urban areas squatters were those who, unable to afford or find a home, erected shelters on unoccupied land within or just outside the town. On the Witwatersrand in the 1940s a huge squatter population grew as a result of urbanisation during the Second World War, and with the abolition of influx control in the 1980s the squatter population of the towns again increased dramatically.

State of Emergency

Legislation of 1953 provided for the declaration of a state of emergency. The first was proclaimed a week after Sharpeville and continued from 30 March to 30 August 1960. Emergency regulations gave the government sweeping powers of arrest, detention, search and seizure. In 1985 a second state of emergency was declared. Except for the period March to June 1986, there was a state of emergency in force from 1985 to 1990. The government used its emergency powers to severely restrict extra-parliamentary activities, and to suppress the insurrection which had begun in 1984.

Above:
Soweto, the largest black urban community in South Africa, grew out of the shanty towns and slums of the inter-war period
(Mayibuye Centre/IDAF)

Steyn, Marthinus Theunis

RIETFONTEIN, 1857 — BLOEMFONTEIN, 1916

Advocate, judge and President of the Orange Free State. He was called to the Bar in 1882 and appointed Attorney General of the Orange Free State six years later. He believed that the Boer states should cooperate with the colonies, but was strongly opposed to Lord Milner and British imperialism. He tried to negotiate Uitlander voting rights, but Chamberlain was not in favour of his proposal. After war broke out in 1899, and the British stated that they had no intention of recognising the independence of the Boer states, Steyn joined Kruger and Joubert in approving the use of guerrilla tactics against the British. The war destroyed his health, but he continued to support Afrikaner nationalism until his death in 1916.

Above:
Marthinus Theunis Steyn, President of the Orange Free State
(Transvaal Archives TAB 279)

Left:
Township youths flee from police fire during the State of Emergency, 1986
(Mayibuye Centre)

Sir Andries Stockenström
(Cape Archives E 416)

Stockenström, Sir Andries

CAPE TOWN, 1792 — LONDON, 1864

Cape politician and frontier administrator of relatively enlightened views. As an ensign in the Cape Corps, Stockenström fought in the war of 1811–1812. Appointed first Deputy Landdrost of Graaff-Reinet, and then in 1815 Landdrost, he was responsible for governing an enormous frontier region. Able to sympathise to some extent with the Xhosa, he opposed the armed expeditions of burghers across the frontier to retake stolen stock. In 1820 he was appointed a member of the Council of Advice and then Commissioner General for the Eastern Province. He supported Ordinance 50 of 1828, which placed people of colour equal before the law with whites, but felt that it should be accompanied by a law against vagrancy. After resigning as Commissioner General in 1833, he gave evidence to a select committee of the House of Commons in England in which he criticised the reprisals system. He was then appointed Lieutenant-Governor of the Eastern Districts by the Secretary of State for the colonies, Lord Glenelg. A malicious campaign was mounted against him on his return and he was dismissed by Glenelg's successor. He continued to oppose British policy on the frontier, and he supported the introduction of representative government in the colony. After the eventual introduction of representative government in 1853, he became a member of the Legislative Council and was instrumental in having legislation passed which placed burghers on an equal footing with the military. He resigned in 1856 and went to Europe.

Stone Age

Stone Age is the term used by archaeologists to refer to the period between the first appearance of stone artefacts some 2 to 2,5 million years ago and the appearance of tools of bronze or iron in the last 5 000 years. Stone tools did not however appear everywhere that early nor were they replaced by bronze or iron tools in all parts of the world. The pre-colonial past in southern Africa is essentially Stone Age, with the exception that in the last 2 000 years iron-using agricultural peoples spread into the eastern parts of the subcontinent. Hunter-gatherers and pastoralists who shared the landscape with farmers did not, as far as we know, smelt metals and were thus technologically Stone Age people.

Because we know that chimpanzees in the wild make and use tools of wood and reed as well as stone, we must assume that early hominids of 7 to 3 million years ago may have too. Stone, however, is the best preserved artefactual material and stone flaking is more recognisable than the shaping of wood or reed and thus stone tools have been taken as key indicators of artefact-making abilities. It may obviously prove extremely difficult to recognise the casual and informal use of stones or other materials prior to the deliberate shaping of tools or the repeated use of preferred locations to do this.

The first recognisable stone artefacts are found in sites in Ethiopia and Kenya in deposits dating between 2,2 and 2,5 million years ago. The fact that such stones are flaked in patterned ways, were brought in to the sites from quarries or sources elsewhere and are associated in concentra-

Below:
Early Stone Age artefacts in position on an ancient campsite
(UCT Archaeology)

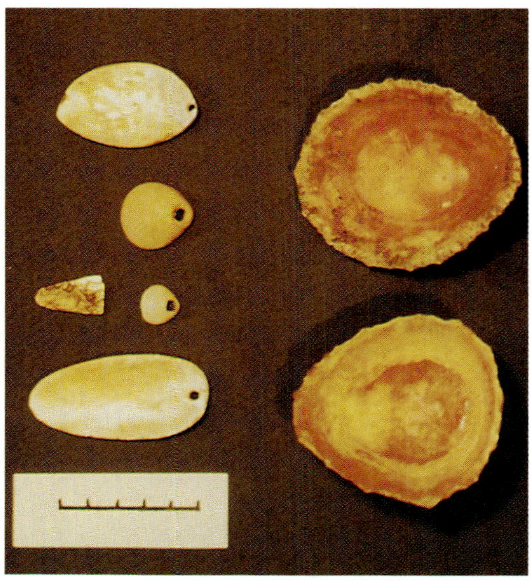

Below right:
Shell pendants and shells used as paint pots from Elands Bay Cave
(UCT Archaeology)

tions with animal bones, helps define them as tools. Such tools are, however, fairly simple consisting mostly of cobbles of rock and flakes struck from them, and used to obtain and process plant and animal foods.

In sub-Saharan Africa the Stone Age is for convenience subdivided into Earlier, Middle and Later Stone Ages as a reflection of increasing sophistication in stone tool making. Although dating is not resolved and archaeologists differ on the details of classification, the boundary between Earlier and Middle Stone Ages is usually taken as about 150 000 years ago and that between Middle and Later Stone Ages as about 30 000 to 40 000 years ago.

The most notable changes through time in stone tools have been a decrease in size and an increase in standardisation and variety of types as the tools became more uniquely designed for specific tasks and more obviously intended to be mounted on shafts or on handles as parts of composite equipment. Thus towards the end of the Stone Age artefacts were made of more than just stone alone, with the use of wood for handles, resin and sinews for glue and binding, and stone for the working edges. Indigenous hunter-gatherers of southern Africa, those known variously as Bushmen or San, were the surviving Later Stone Age people encountered by colonial society.

The Later Stone Age (LSA), by virtue of its more recent dating, is the best known part of the southern African Stone Age sequence. Excavations have revealed much of the hunting and gathering lifestyle of LSA people and have produced bones and plant remains that reflect dietary residues, whilst other archaeological studies have illustrated the symbolic and religious nature of LSA rock paintings. Some 3 000 years ago all the inhabitable parts of the subcontinent were occupied by stone tool-making hunter-gatherers. After 2 000 years ago, partly through the movement of people and partly through local innovation, borrowing and integration, hunter-gatherer groups were increasingly replaced by iron-working agriculturalists or stone-using stock keepers. Eventually these processes were interrupted by colonial settlement some 300 years ago. The Stone Age thus survived late in southern Africa but was quickly swept aside by colonists armed with more deadly weapons and aided by introduced diseases.

(J Parkington)

Far left:
A section through the Later Stone Age deposits at Elands Bay Cave. The scale rods lie on a surface that is 11 000 years old
(UCT Archaeology)

Strijdom, Johannes Gerhardus

KLIPFONTEIN, 1893 — CAPE TOWN, 1958

Politician and Prime Minister. Strijdom began practising law after the Great War, during which he lived in South West Africa. A believer in an Afrikaner Republic, he nevertheless supported Smuts and Hertzog until Malan broke away to form the Purified National Party in 1934. For a time he was the only member of that party from the Transvaal in Parliament; for his strongly held views, he was known as 'the lion of the North'. He succeeded Malan as Prime Minister and under his leadership the policy of apartheid was intensified. He openly conceded that it meant *baasskap*, that is white domination.

Above:
J G Strijdom. He succeeded Malan as Prime Minister
(Cape Archives AG 15906)

Strikes

Between 1907 and 1922 South Africa experienced serious, and often violent, industrial unrest focused mainly on the Witwatersrand. A series of strikes by white mine workers about conditions of work and black competition in 1907, 1913 and 1914 culminated in a general strike in 1922. The strike developed into an armed revolt, which was put down by the army using aircraft and artillery against the mainly Afrikaans-speaking strikers. In these and other strikes, black and white workers failed to act jointly.

Below:
The mine workers' strike in Johannesburg, 1922. The strike developed into an armed revolt which was put down by the army using aircraft and artillery
(Die Burger)

Far right:
Helen Suzman during the 1974 elections
(Rapport Library)

Unrest among African mine workers manifested itself in strikes in 1913 and 1914, and climaxed in 1920 with a strike involving some 71 000 African workers on twenty-one mines. Much of black worker discontent was rooted in low wages and economic exploitation. During and after the Second World War, black workers became increasingly militant. In reaction to a massive wave of strikes beginning in late 1942 the government made strikes by Africans illegal. A series of strikes and riots on the Witwatersrand gold mines culminated in a serious strike in 1946, in which 73 000 black miners led by the African Mine Workers' Union went on strike over low wages, dangerous living and working conditions and poor rations.

In 1973 the widespread, spontaneous outbreak of unofficial black strike activity in Durban was the signal for change, and reached a climax with the massive Soweto stay-at-home in 1976. In 1979 the government recognised black trade unions for the first time, and new labour legislation removed most of the restrictions on black unionisation and created new conditions favourable for collective bargaining. But the 1980s saw a massive upsurge in strike activity by unions: in 1981 there were 342 strikes involving 92 842 workers, in 1990 855 strikes involving 341 097 workers.

Mswati II, the king of Swaziland in the early nineteenth century
(South African Library)

Suzman, Helen

GERMISTON, TRANSVAAL, 1917 —

Politician, member of Parliament from 1953 to 1989, and one of South Africa's most prominent liberal parliamentarians. Suzman was a lecturer in Economic History at the University of the Witwatersrand before she entered Parliament as a United Party (UP) representative in 1953. She was one of the group of liberal dissidents who broke away from the UP in 1959 to form the Progressive Party (PP). Re-elected to Parliament in 1961, she remained the sole PP member of Parliament for the next thirteen years, doggedly voicing her opposition to the government's apartheid policies.

Swaziland

A major Swazi state was created under Sobhuza I and his son Mswati II in the early nineteenth century. In the face of Zulu threats, the Swazi turned to the whites in the Transvaal as potential allies. Eventually concessions extracted from Swazi rulers undermined the kingdom, which was disposed of by treaties between the Transvaal and British governments. By the time Swaziland had become a High Commission territory (1907) nearly two-thirds of the land was legally owned by whites. South African governments long wanted to incorporate Swaziland and the other High Commission territories, but Britain led it to independence in 1968. In February 1982 Swaziland signed a secret non-aggression pact with South Africa.

T

Tambo, Oliver Reginald

BIZANA, CAPE, 1917 — JOHANNESBURG, 1993

Politician. A founding member of the African National Congress (ANC) Youth League (1944), Secretary-General of the ANC (1954–1958), acting President-General (1967–1977), and President-General from 1977 to 1990. The son of a Pondoland peasant farmer, Tambo went to Fort Hare University, taught briefly and then became a lawyer in a practice with Nelson Mandela in Johannesburg. Active in the ANC all his adult life, he went into exile shortly before the ANC was banned in 1960. He then headed the ANC's external mission, setting up offices in a number of countries and its headquarters in Lusaka, Zambia. He suffered a severe stroke in 1989. Two years later he resettled in South Africa.

Oliver Tambo, President-General of the ANC from 1977 to 1990
(Mayibuye Centre)

Taung Child

Fossilised skull of early hominid. Discovered in the lime deposits of Taung in November 1924, this skull was to provide valuable clues to the origins of man. Its significance was perceived by Professor Raymond Dart who recognised that it showed features midway between man and the apes. The Taung child, so named because the state of development of its teeth revealed that it had died at the age of three or four years, had walked upright and its brain, although small, displayed human-like features. In his report to the British scientific journal *Nature*, Dart suggested that the skull belonged to a member of an extinct ape family with characteristics similar to those of man. He named it *Australopithicus africanus* — the southern ape of Africa.

Theal, George McCall

NEW BRUNSWICK, CANADA, 1837 — WYNBERG, CAPE TOWN, 1919

South Africa's first great historian. Theal, who wrote prolifically, is known particularly for his eleven volume *History of South Africa*, the bulk of which was written in the 1880s. While teaching at Lovedale in the 1870s, he conducted oral research into the history of the Xhosa people, and began publishing general works on South Africa's past. He transcribed documents on the history of Basutoland (Lesotho) and produced a number of volumes on the genealogy of old Cape families. He collected numerous documents from Britain and the Netherlands, and his research resulted in the thirty-six volume *Records of the Cape Colony*. He gave very few references to his sources in his histories, however, making it difficult for other scholars to verify the accuracy of his work.

Thonga (Tsonga, Tonga, Shangaan)

Name for the people who occupied the coastal belt of south-east Africa stretching from Kosi Bay to the Save River. Thonga traded first with the Arabs and then with the Portuguese for hundreds of years in iron, copper, ivory and slaves. Under pressure of Nguni raids in the early 1800s, Thonga settlers were driven westwards into the Transvaal. In 1895 Britain annexed the Thonga territory south of Delagoa Bay in order to prevent the Transvaal from gaining access to the sea.

Tlhaping

The most southerly group of western Sotho (Tswana), they lived north of

G M Theal, South Africa's first great historian
(South African Library)

the Orange River by the late eighteenth century. The first whites to meet Sotho-speakers arrived in their capital, Dithakong, in 1801. In 1823 they were attacked by marauders, and only the firepower of the Griqua saved the Tlhaping from defeat in the battle of Dithakong. In the early nineteenth century they cultivated extensively, but their land and independence gradually eroded as the nineteenth century developed. A range of grievances led the Tlhaping into rebellion against the Cape Colony in 1878 and again in 1896.

Tobruk

Strategically situated harbour on the Libyan coast. Ten thousand South Africans were among the Allied troops sent to defend it during the Second World War. When the Germans captured it in 1942 they were all taken prisoner. In South Africa even leaders of the Communist Party fanned the patriotism of the people by calling for Tobruk to be avenged.

Life in the Tobruk garrison, 11 July 1942. A devotional service is held around one of the anti-aircraft guns which were used for the defence of Tobruk
(South African National Museum of Military History)

Total Strategy

Doctrine elaborated by the military from 1977 and formally announced by Prime Minister Botha in 1979. It was designed to counter what was termed the 'total onslaught', the idea that the main threat to South Africa came from Marxism rather than from the continuation of apartheid policies. As part of the 'total strategy', the government set about trying to create a constellation of southern African states, by offering neighbouring and Bantustan governments mainly economic incentives to maintain a moderate stance towards South Africa, and to keep the African National Congress out of their territory. The climax of this part of total strategy was the signing of the Nkomati Accord between South Africa and Mozambique in March 1984. Another element of 'total strategy' was massive destabilisation of Angola and other states in the region. At home Botha introduced limited reforms. The government eliminated some segregation laws, repealed the bans on multiracial political parties and interracial sex and marriage, and ended job reservation and influx control. In 1984 a tricameral parliament was convened, designed to give coloureds and Indians a political voice. However, after 1986 the reform programme ground to a halt and by the time Botha resigned in 1989, total strategy had come to be viewed as irrelevant by most senior Nationalist politicians, especially in the light of the *glasnost* of President Gorbachev of the Soviet Union.

Township Revolt

Most of the resistance movements which occurred in the townships and towns of South Africa before the 1970s were localised, sporadic, short-lived and piecemeal. They included squatter movements and bus boycotts, pass demonstrations and beer protests. They did not pose a serious challenge to State power. That was true even of the Sharpeville crisis. But the Soweto revolt, and the massive, almost countrywide township uprisings which followed in the 1980s were of a different order.

The economic recession in the early 1970s, the growth in the Black Consciousness movement which encouraged political assertiveness amongst the black petty bourgeoisie, the collapse of the Portuguese regimes in Angola and Mozambique in 1974, the explosion of industrial strikes from 1973 which spread from Durban to East London and the Rand, and the increasing transparency of State indecisiveness, had combined to create a crisis situation in the townships by 1976. The establishment of Regional Administration

Boards to run the townships had meant that municipal subsidies were withdrawn. As a result rents in the townships increased, housing expenditure decreased, and services and welfare services deteriorated. The catalyst came with the new law enforcing Afrikaans as a medium of instruction in African secondary schools. On 16 June 1976, 15 000 school pupils marched towards Orlando West Junior Secondary School. In attempting to disperse them, the police shot into the crowd leaving at least two dead and many injured. That day Soweto rose in revolt, beer halls and administration offices were burned and barricades were set up. The risings spread to at least 80 other communities including Kagiso, Thembisa and other townships on the Rand, but also to Natal and the western and eastern Cape.

Further township protests continued sporadically from 1977 over schooling, which continued to be disrupted, and rent increases. Community action also became linked to union strategies, as in the consumer boycott in 1979 of Fatti's and Moni's products. In February 1982, 100 000 workers stopped work to protest Neil Aggett's death in detention. But from September 1984 violence began on a scale equal to that of the Soweto revolt, and soon became as widespread. After mass stayaways in townships in the Vaal Triangle, including Sebokeng, Sharpeville and Boipatong, violence spread to townships in the eastern Cape and Natal. At Uitenhage more than 20 people were killed by the police in their attempts to stop a march of 4 000 people from Langa township. A state of emergency was imposed on 36 magisterial districts in July 1985 in an attempt by the government to put a lid on the unrest in the townships. It was only a nation-wide state of emergency and the deployment of large numbers of troops in the townships that brought the revolt to an end in 1987.

Teenager Hector Petersen was the first to die in the confrontation with police on 16 June 1976
(Mayibuye Centre/IDAF)

The first Trades Union Congress, Johannesburg 25–26 March 1925
(Africana Museum)

Trade Unions

The first trade unions were craft unions formed in Cape Town by white printers and carpenters in 1881. Skilled white mine workers on the Witwatersrand formed trade unions after 1890, such as the powerful all-white Mine Workers' Union formed in 1902, which launched a number of strikes over conditions of work and the job colour bar. Black workers were prohibited from striking, and were excluded from participating in the collective bargaining process. Despite this, black unions were formed, the largest the Industrial and Commercial Workers' Union, established in 1919.

In 1946, over 70 000 black miners led by the African Mine Workers' Union, went on strike for four days. Black trade unions were legalised in 1979, and within five years they had a membership of over one million workers, and had assumed a significant political role at a time when the leading black political parties were banned.

Transkei

The 'land across the Kei River', lying between the Great Kei River and the

Transkei's Prime Minister Kaiser Matanzima addressing his first press conference after independence. Next to him is Digby Koyana, the new Minister of Foreign Affairs
(Rapport Library)

southern border of Natal, and between the Drakensberg mountains and the Indian Ocean. Sometime in the first millenium the Transkei was occupied by Nguni-speakers practising mixed farming. Shipwrecked travellers in the sixteenth century found Xhosa-speaking peoples as far south as the Mthatha River. Trekboer expansion eastwards had, by the 1770s, brought white frontier farmers in contact with the settled Xhosa population, first in what became the Ciskei, but gradually involving also the people east of the Kei. The last of the frontier wars in 1877–1878 saw a final desperate bid by the Gcaleka Xhosa for continued independence. After this colonial troops occupied their country and a Cape administration was imposed. A further major rebellion broke out two years later, which was put down by Cape forces in 1881. Between 1879 and 1894 the Transkeian regions, Griqualand East, Pondoland and Tembuland were incorporated within the Cape Colony, bringing the whole of the Transkei under white domination. From 1894 territorial councils began to be established, eventually grouped under a single General Council for the Transkeian Territories.

The largest of the African reserves, the Transkei was the first to become a Bantustan or homeland. In 1963 a Legislative Assembly was introduced, all of whose actions had to be approved by South Africa. Kaiser Matanzima, the first leader of the Transkei, imprisoned political opponents without trial and imposed emergency regulations which he renewed annually. In 1976 the Transkei was given nominal 'independence'. Since Major-General Bantu Holomisa took power in a military coup in 1987, the territory has remained under military rule.

'Hottentot kraal on the banks of the Gariep', by W J Burchell, 1811. The area known as the TransGariep was originally inhabited by Khoisan hunters and herders
(Africana Museum)

Transorangia

The 'land beyond the Orange River', also known as the TransGariep from the Korana word for Orange River, *Garieb*. The area was originally inhabited by Khoisan hunters and herders, and black farmers were present in the north-eastern Orange Free State by AD 1 000. By the 1840s Griqua under Adam Kok were living in the southernmost part, Rolong under Moroka were in the east, and two major Sotho states had emerged, that under Moshweshwe east of the Caledon River, and the Tlokwa state under Sekonyela west of the Caledon. Voortrekkers had also settled in Transorangia, some of whom occupied the Winburg region. Constant unrest led Cape Governor Napier to attempt to exercise indirect control over the territory in the early 1840s. The aim was to protect the Cape's northern frontier by means of subsidised buffer states without incurring heavy military expenditure. However, this proved ineffective, and in 1848 Britain annexed the entire territory between the Orange and Vaal Rivers as the Orange River Sovereignty.

Transport

In South Africa, transport remained primitive until the mid-nineteenth century. The ox-wagon was the only means of inland transport, as there were no navigable rivers and the sparsely populated interior presented physical obstacles to development. But with the discovery after 1860 of diamonds and gold, railways and roads developed rapidly, and within 100 years South Africa became the most highly industrialised country in Africa.

'Transvaal steam train', by G H Thompson. With the mineral discoveries of the 1860s, South Africa's railway network developed rapidly (Africana Museum)

With roads and railways extremely costly to build and maintain, the development of the transport infrastructure was from the first almost exclusively a state undertaking. As a result, it was subject to political interests that were often at variance with social and economic considerations. For instance, under conditions imposed by the Group Areas Act (1966), the great majority of the work-force lived often at considerable distances from their places of employment, which necessitated heavy subsidisation of commuter transport. By the early 1980s the transport system was described as 'a confusion of state and local authority monopolies, privileged franchises, restrictive licences and ... government and local authority interference'. From this period, legislation attempted to rationalise and privatise the sector. Some partly privatised toll roads were introduced in an attempt to broaden the base for development and maintenance. Provision was made for the privatisation of South African Transport Services as Transnet in 1990 — a move aggressively resisted by the unions aligned with the Congress of South African Trade Unions within the industry. The dramatic rise of the black kombi-taxi industry in this period heightened the inadequacies of subsidised commuter traffic, and focused attention on deregulation of the industry. The late 1980s and early 1990s saw violent 'taxi wars' in the Cape and Transvaal as both legal and illegal operators contested their interests in a limited market.

Transvaal

The 'land across the Vaal River', which became the northernmost province of South Africa, lying between the Vaal and Limpopo Rivers. The area has been inhabited by Bantu-speaking farmers for at least the last thousand years. In the 1820s and 1830s most of the region was disrupted by the Difaqane. Populations were uprooted and dislocated, and in some of the land, apparently 'empty', Voortrekkers began settling in 1836. They defeated Mzilikazi's Ndebele, who withdrew north across the Limpopo, and claimed the central highveld by right of conquest. The trekkers lived in isolated communities, widely dispersed amongst African populations and encircled by relatively powerful Zulu, Swazi, Pedi, Venda and Ndebele states on the periphery of the highveld.

In 1852 Britain recognised the independence of whites living north of the Vaal, but it was only in 1857 that these scattered groups were brought together under the central authority of the South African Republic, as the Transvaal state was called. For most of the nineteenth century the nascent state was weak and poorly governed, and lacked a sound economic base.

White encroachment on black lands was resisted, but one after another the African states were defeated with the aid of British arms, so that by the end of the 1800s white control over almost the entire area between the Vaal and Limpopo Rivers had been established. The final pockets of independent African rule in the far north were taken over at the end of the century.

The discovery of gold on the Witwatersrand in 1886 helped to precipitate the South African War (1899–1902), in which the South African Republic lost its independence. The Transvaal became a Crown Colony and in 1910 a province of the Union, with Pretoria, the provincial capital, as the national capital. Johannesburg, on the Witwatersrand, lies at the centre of the vast mineral wealth of the Transvaal, and is South Africa's largest city, and the mining, industrial, commercial and financial heart of South Africa.

Transvaal Republic, *see* South African Republic

Transvaal War of Independence, *see* Anglo-Transvaal War

Trekboers

Dutch-speaking semi-nomadic frontier farmers who moved into the interior with their livestock. From the beginning of the 1700s the increase in herds and the exhaustion of pastures led the cattle farmers further and further away from the settled areas of Cape Town. The lands in the interior were plentiful and cheap, and teemed with game. In addition, there were no geographical barriers impeding movement. Once the first range of mountains behind Cape Town itself had been crossed, the trekboer ascended the flat inland plateau where, in return for a small annual rent, he could lay claim to a 6 000 acre loan farm which he could sell or bequeath. The government made little effort to follow the trekboers, and their attempts to define boundaries proved ineffective in curbing expansion.

The trekboers lived isolated existences, thinly scattered over a vast hinterland. Their economy was as primitive as their living conditions, and contact with markets was rare. The Khoisan peoples with whom they came in contact as they trekked north and east, were dispossessed of their lands, killed, ejected or turned into squatters or labourers on trekboer farms. By the 1770s trekboers in the eastern Cape had encountered the Xhosa living in the Zuurveld. Xhosa-trekboer relations speedily deteriorated over competition for grazing land, and in 1779 the first of many frontier wars broke out. Unlike the Voortrekkers, the trekboers were keen to have the Cape government extend its authority over

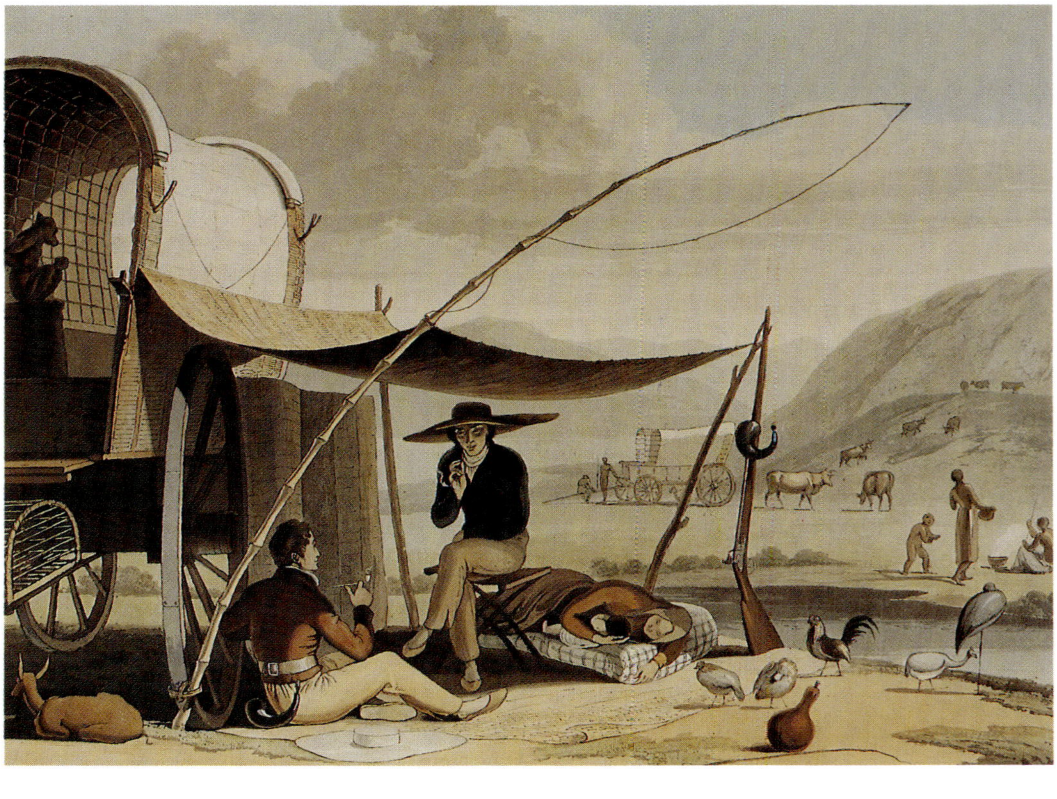

A trekboer encampment as depicted by Samuel Daniell. These semi-nomadic cattle farmers moved into the northern and eastern Cape interior during the eighteenth century. They lived simply, thinly scattered over a vast hinterland
(Africana Museum)

them, and considered themselves colonial subjects, even those living in Transorangia in the 1830s who had no intention of returning to the Cape. Accustomed to loading their possessions onto an oxwagon and going off in search of a better loan farm in the interior, the trekboers paved the way for the Great Trek.

Trichardt (Tregardt), Louis

SWELLENDAM DISTRICT, 1783 — LOURENÇO MARQUES, 1838

Voortrekker leader. Trichardt's route took him from the Kei River area, where he lived among the Xhosa having leased land from their leader Hintsa (1833), to Standerton and Middelburg, and via the Soutpansberg to De Doorns. His group encountered that of J J Janse van Rensburg and later Potgieter's reconnaissance patrol. Trichardt's aim was to reach Delagoa Bay, which he did after an epic trek lasting eight months. However, the costs were high and in crossing the Drakensberg he suffered numerous setbacks, among them malaria and cattle sickness, and many of his party died.

Trichardt was the only Voortrekker leader to keep a diary, which provides invaluable information on the black communities he encountered, and also on the fauna, flora and climatic conditions of the Transvaal. He died in Lourenço Marques in 1838, possibly from malaria.

Tswana

From evidence of their material culture it can be inferred that the people who gave rise to the Tswana congregated in the central, western and possibly eastern regions of the Transvaal about AD 1 000. They did not arrive in 'waves' of migration as earlier thought. From here there was a gradual process of population growth over the following two or three centuries during which time a common language probably began to emerge. Most Tswana chiefdoms recognise as their 'founding fathers' three leaders, Morolong, Mokgatla and Masilo. From the mid-fifteenth century a process of fairly rapid division occurred so that by the beginning of the eighteenth century the Tswana occupied most of the choice land on the central and western highveld. In the south-west of this plateau they co-existed relatively peacefully with the San and Khoi people though competition for resources probably intensified with population growth in an area of limited summer rainfall.

The precise dispersal pattern of the main Tswana lineages is difficult to reconstruct. The followers of Morolong moved west towards the Kalahari in about 1500. The Hurutshe then followed them to the headwaters of the Marico (Madikwe) River soon after the beginning of the sixteenth century. However two other lineages began to disperse at about the same time. Some

This painting entitled 'Bechuana huts' by Charles Davison Bell, depicts the typical rondavel dwelling of the Tswana
(Africana Museum)

Kwena lineages crossed the Vaal River, intermarrying and eventually dominating the Fokeng, who had settled there earlier. Another Kwena group settled north of the Hurutshe along the Crocodile River. Further divisions among the Kwena gave rise to the Ngwaketse and Ngwato of modern Botswana. The Kgatla lineage also emerged as a dominant group, settling, eventually, in the Pretoria and Rustenburg districts, and in a region east of Pretoria in the Leolu mountains where the Pedi settled. A sub-group of the Kgatla, the Tlokwa, emerged as a separate community in the Pilanesberg district, in the northern Transvaal and in northern Botswana. Lastly there was a migration of Nguni-speakers from across the Drakensberg who settled widely in the region of the Sotho-Tswana. These people are known as the 'Transvaal Ndebele' or Ndzundza, but they are not to be confused with the Ndebele under Mzilikazi who came later onto the highveld.

The pattern of Tswana history up to the end of the eighteenth century was characterised by the twin process of fission and amalgamation. Communities divided because of environmental factors such as drought, water or land shortage or because of disputes over succession. Amalgamation occurred where strong chiefs could attract followers by offering economic security or military protection.

This constantly shifting pattern makes it difficult to provide a precise account of the history of the various Tswana chiefdoms.

Right:
'Bechuana ivory carrier and young girl carrying milk' by Thomas Baines. Whereas cattle were a means of subsistence, ivory had significance only as a trade item
(Africana Museum)

Of significance was the move from the Madikwe River by the Rolong and their subsequent settlement and dominance south of the Molopo River, and the pre-eminence of the Hurutshe in the western Transvaal. These chiefdoms established what can be likened to confederacies, by incorporating client communities and controlling trade in cattle, furs, metals (several Tswana chiefdoms were renowned metalsmiths) and, from the mid-eighteenth century, ivory. The Rolong essentially controlled the north-south axis of trade, from across the Orange River to present-day Namibia, and the Hurutshe the west-east axis from the southern Kalahari to the central Transvaal. The Hurutshe knew every community living to their east as far as the Mozambique coast. The power of the Rolong and Hurutshe did not remain unchallenged, however. By the mid-eighteenth century the Tlhaping, with the assistance of the Kora, had shaken off Rolong hegemony. The Rolong divided into four separate groups following the death of their chief Tau in a battle in about 1760. The Hurutshe too came under pressure from the Ngwaketse to their west who wished to break their monopoly over trade. A notable feature of these Tswana confederacies was the size and organisation of their settlements. The Rolong, Hurutshe and Tlhaping capitals for example were built in stone and contained from fifteen to twenty thousand inhabitants. They were divided into districts with areas set aside for habitation, cultivation and herding of stock.

From the last quarter of the eighteenth century nearly all the Tswana chiefdoms found themselves embroiled in conflict similar to that which affected the Nguni-speakers. This conflict took the form of raids for cattle and women but the underlying causes seem to have been related to

Far right:
'A group of Barolong Men, 1834', by Charles Bell. The Rolong controlled the north-south axis of trade, from across the Orange River to present-day Namibia
(Africana Museum)

competition over arable and grazing land and control of trade. The most militarised Tswana chiefdom was the Ngwaketse who, had circumstances permitted, would have brought the Tswana to the south and east into an enlarged state under their control. Before this could happen, however, new intruders erupted on to the highveld.

This precipitated a 'Time of Troubles', commonly known as the Difaqane. Though its origins are still debated, its effects among the Tswana were recorded by European missionaries and travellers who had arrived among the Tswana at the beginning of the nineteenth century. Several groups of refugees entered the western highveld from 1821, disrupting the pattern of communal life and driving Tswana chiefdoms from regions they had long occupied. Some Tswana were protected by missionaries during this time, the most celebrated instance being in 1823 when Robert Moffat of the London Missionary Society (LMS), together with a combined Griqua and Tlhaping force, drove a destitute horde away from the Tlhaping capital at Dithakong. The Ndebele under Mzilikazi established themselves in the Marico district in 1832. From this base they established a powerful state, incorporating some Tswana and driving others south of the Molopo River. Only in the 1830s were some Tswana chiefdoms able to reconstruct themselves, in some instances with missionary help. For example, Moroka's Rolong settled at Thaba 'Nchu in 1833 with the Wesleyan missionaries.

Post-Difaqane reconstruction proved difficult for most Tswana communities, because the 1830s saw the arrival of other intruders on the highveld. These included the Griqua and the trekkers from the Cape. The latter regarded many Tswana as their subjects on the grounds that they had displaced the all-powerful Ndebele. Tswana living in the South African Republic were subject to tribute and labour demands, and competed with the Boers for land. Those on the fringes of the SAR, such as the Rolong, faced continual pressures on their land by groups of 'freebooters' who tried to establish independent 'Republics' on their land.

After the discovery of diamonds in the region of modern Kimberley, the Tlhaping and Thlaro had to contest for land rights against other claimants. Though these communities resisted by taking up arms against the colonisers in 1878 and 1896, they eventually fell under British control.

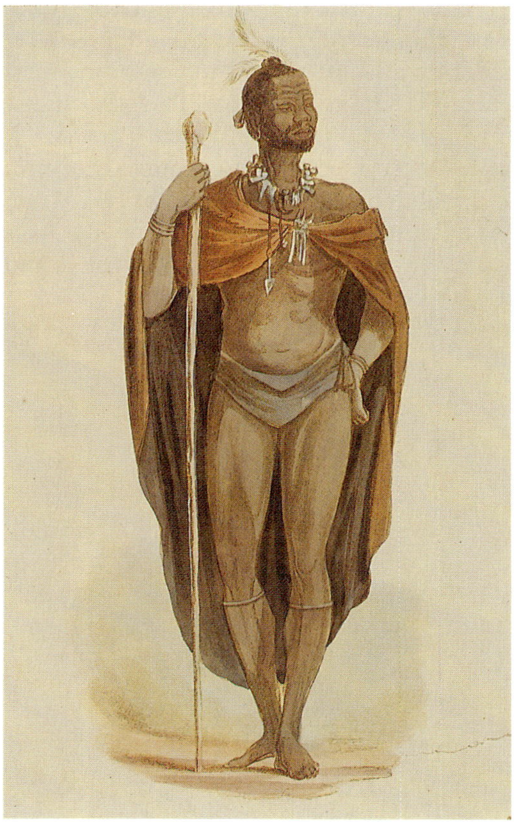

Top:
Tswana women preparing their harvest for storage
(Africana Museum)

Above:
Ndebele warriors attacking, by C D Bell. From their base in the Marico district they established a powerful state, incorporating some Tswana and driving others out of the area
(Africana Museum)

Left:
A tribesman of the Bechuana from N Pritchard's *Natural History of Man*, 1855
(Africana Museum)

In 1871 the Tlhaping were placed under the authority of the Crown Colony of Griqualand West which in 1880 was transferred to the Cape. Those Tswana living nearer to the SAR were also placed under Crown Colony rule in 1885, due largely to the efforts of the LMS missionary, Revd John Mackenzie, who convinced the British of the need to establish a protectorate over the Tswana. In 1895 this territory too was transferred to the authority of the Cape Colony. Moroka's Rolong at Thaba 'Nchu similarly struggled to maintain a measure of independence from their powerful neighbours — Moshweshwe's Sotho kingdom and the Orange Free State. The Free Staters attempted to alienate land from the Rolong and eventually intervened in a succession dispute in 1884 to seize Rolong farms.

The pressures of being caught between the competing forces of British imperialism and Boer rapacity caused severe rifts between the Tswana chiefdoms living between the Orange and Molopo Rivers. These rivalries were taken into the South African War in 1899 when the Tswana found themselves active participants on both sides. Those who hoped for political and economic rewards for assisting the British had their hopes dashed after the war.

From 1910 the Tswana formed part of the Union of South Africa and shared the experiences of Africans in a similar position. The main features of this period were a restriction on land occupation, migrancy and curtailed political rights that led to an erosion of economic and social life. A relative and generally unrecognised form of independence was reinstated in 1977 when the Republic of Bophuthatswana was formed in line with the policy of grand apartheid.

(A Manson)

Tutu, Desmond Mpilo

KLERKSDORP, 1931 —

Archbishop and Nobel Peace Prize winner. After attending Saint Peter's Theological College, Tutu was ordained in 1961; he received an MA in Theology in Britain in 1966. During the following decade he was employed by the World Council of Churches, appointed Anglican Dean of Johannesburg, and then Bishop of Lesotho, before becoming General Secretary of the South African Council of Churches. In the 1980s he emerged as perhaps the most eloquent and powerful of the critics of the apartheid regime and supporter of sanctions against it. He participated in numerous demonstrations and consequently lost his passport. In 1984 he was awarded the Nobel Peace Prize and two years later he became the first African Anglican Archbishop of Cape Town. He continued to participate actively in political matters, though after February 1990 his role became more that of adviser than leader.

Far right:
In the 1980s Archbishop Tutu emerged as a powerful critic of the apartheid regime and supported sanctions against it
(Mayibuye Centre)

U

Uitlanders

Foreigners, mainly British immigrants, thousands of whom came to the Transvaal after the discovery of gold on the Witwatersrand in 1886. The Uitlander influx threatened to engulf the impoverished, rural Afrikaner society of the Transvaal Republic, and Kruger saw in Uitlander demands for the franchise a threat to the political independence of his country. The Uitlander franchise issue was the ostensible reason for the Jameson Raid (1895) and contributed to the outbreak of the South African War (1899).

Ulundi, Battle of (1879)

One of the battles which followed the British invasion of Zululand which began in January 1879. At Isandlwana the British suffered a humiliating defeat; at Rorke's Drift they managed to resist the Zulu attack. The morale of the Zulu force was broken at the battles of Khambula and Gingindlovu. Cetshwayo made overtures for peace, but Chelmsford wished to restore his reputation and sought further confrontation on the Mahlabatini plain near Ondini. The Zulu launched a rather reluctant attack, and the British set fire to the royal homestead; the Zulu army 'melted away'. Cetshwayo was captured the following month, ending the war.

Umkhonto we Sizwe (Spear of the Nation)

Military wing of the African National Congress (ANC), established by Nelson Mandela and other ANC and South African Communist Party leaders in 1961. Unable to obtain political concessions by peaceful means, the ANC embarked on a campaign of sabotage. The main targets were economic installations and symbols of political significance. In 1962 Mandela was arrested and a year later most of the Umkhonto leadership was arrested at its headquarters in Rivonia near Johannesburg, tried and sentenced to life imprisonment. In exile, Umkhonto leaders tried to prepare for guerrilla war by obtaining support for training, arming and funding its cadres; help was given by African and Soviet bloc countries. After the Soweto uprising in 1976, Umkhonto resumed sabotage activities in South Africa. Following negotiations with the government, the ANC in 1991 agreed to suspend the armed struggle, but Umkhonto was not disbanded and its weapons not handed over.

Top:
Lord Chelmsford's last victory at Ulundi, 4 July 1879
(The Brenthurst Library)

Above:
Umkhonto cadres in an Angolan training camp during the late 1970s
(Mayibuye Centre)

Union

After the South African War (1899–1902) attempts were made to eliminate economic competition between the four colonies and encourage closer political ties between them. Sir Alfred Milner, by creating a South African Customs Union and a single Central South African Railways hoped to promote the federal cause. His successor, Lord Selborne, in a memorandum of 1907 urged political federation as a means of staving off economic collapse. A National Convention (1908–1909) agreed on political unification of all four colonies and the Union of South Africa came into being on 31 May 1910.

United Democratic Front (UDF)

A multiracial umbrella organisation comprising over 600 affiliated civic, church, sports, trade union and other organisations. It was formed in 1983 to coordinate resistance to the proposed racially structured tricameral constitution. The largest anti-apartheid movement since the banning of the African National Congress (ANC) in 1960, it subscribed to non-violence and the Freedom Charter, and was highly active in the campaign for human and political rights. The man most closely identified with the organisation was Dr Allan Boesak, president of the World Alliance of Reformed Churches. Between 1985 and 1987 almost the entire leadership corps, some 8 000 people, were restricted, and several key members were murdered, including Matthew Goniwe. In February 1988 UDF activities were restricted by the state, and thereafter it continued under the mantle of the Mass Democratic Movement. A year after the unbanning of the ANC in 1990, the UDF disbanded.

United Nations (UN)

Smuts had drafted the original declaration of aims in the preamble to the UN Charter and South Africa was a founder member of the organisation. However apartheid came under increasing attack over the years, and in 1974 South Africa's credentials were rejected by the General Assembly, which prevented the country from speaking in that forum. The Security Council imposed a mandatory

South Africa, a respected founder member of the United Nations, was pilloried and reviled because of her apartheid policies. In 1974 South Africa's credentials were rejected by the General Assembly and she was thus prevented from speaking at that forum (Cartoon by Abe Berry)

arms embargo in 1977. On the Namibian issue, however, South Africa increasingly worked with the world body, and in 1991 the General Assembly began to urge the restoration of ties with South Africa, because of progress in ending apartheid, though South Africa did not regain its seat in that body.

United Party (United South African Nationalist Party)

Born in 1934 by the amalgamation of Hertzog's National Party and Smuts's South African Party, the United Party (UP) was a white supremacist party, which in the course of time became a mainly English-speaking party. In 1939 Hertzog and his followers left the UP over South Africa's entry into the war. The UP's surprise defeat in the 1948 general election, followed by the deaths of Jan Hofmeyr and Smuts, left the party in disarray. It refused to reject racism and even at times sought to outbid the National Party in proposing racial solutions, thinking that in that way it might return to power. Sir de Villiers Graaff provided weak leadership. In 1959 eleven liberal members of Parliament broke away in disgust and formed the Progressive Party. During 1975–1977 the UP split twice and then disintegrated.

Universities

These developed from university colleges which taught but did not examine or award degrees, such as the University of the Cape of Good Hope (later the University of South Africa), founded in 1873 by royal charter. In 1916 the South African Native College was established at Fort Hare in the Ciskei, and in the same year the universities of Cape Town and Stellenbosch became fully-fledged independent teaching-examining universities. Other universities followed: the Witwatersrand (1923), Pretoria (1930), Natal (1950), Orange Free State (1950), Rhodes (1951), Potchefstroom (1951), Port Elizabeth (1965), and Rand Afrikaans University (1966). In 1959 the government passed legislation which prohibited the historically white universities from accepting black students. Four ethnic universities were established, and Fort Hare was taken over by the government as a university for Xhosa-speakers. New universities were established for coloureds (Western Cape) and Indians (Durban

Westville). By 1990 the country had twenty-one universities. In 1991 the universities were granted freedom to admit whom they wished.

Urban Development

Pre-colonial urban development was confined to the Sotho. Dithakong, on the Kuruman River, had a population of over 10 000 in 1802 and other settlements were even larger. Often on hilltops, each centred on an independent chief and his followers. They were destroyed by Tlokwa invasion in the 1820s and did not contribute to later urban processes.

Towns built by whites were typically colonial. There were four main reasons for their existence — security, administration, religion and trade. This was reflected in their uniform spatial structure, with streets organised on a grid pattern. The Dutch Reformed Church was usually the dominant institution in inland towns while the market-place, often large enough to accommodate teams of oxen, formed the centre of commercial life.

Rudimentary local government was based on the 1836 Cape Municipal Ordinance (No 9), adapted by Natal in 1847, the Orange Free State (OFS) in 1856 and the South African Republic in 1883. In the Cape the Municipal Act of 1882 provided for more sophisticated municipalities, under

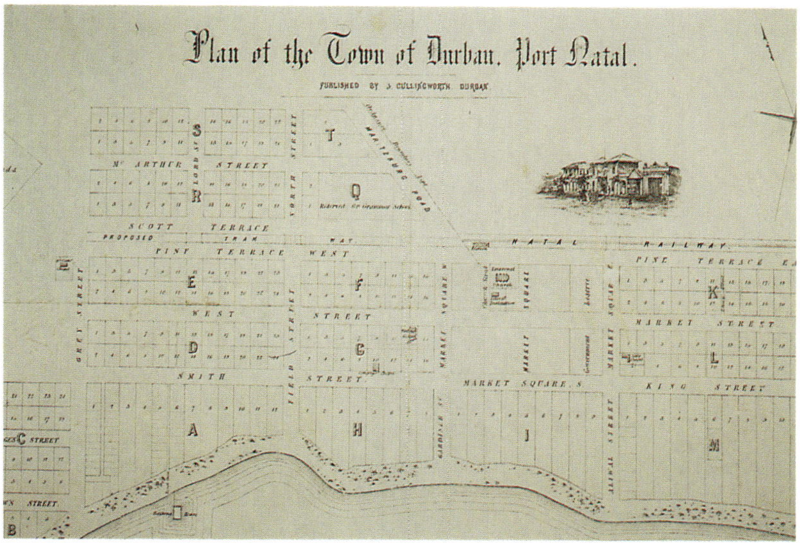

Top:
Students working in the library at Fort Hare, 1950. In 1959 control of the college passed to the Department of Bantu Education and it became an ethnic university for Xhosa-speakers
(Mayibuye Centre)

Above:
Plan of the town of Durban, Port Natal. Like other colonial towns, its streets were organised on a grid pattern
(Local History Museum Collection, Durban)

Left:
Hottentot's Holland and Somerset West, 1847, by G F Angas. This village lay at the foot of the mountains over which the high road led to the interior of the Colony by way of Sir Lowry's Pass, which was opened in 1830
(Africana Museum)

the supervision of the Cape Colonial Office Health Department from 1881. South Africa's first municipal medical officer of health was appointed in Cape Town in 1883. Transvaal local government remained primitive both because of central government weakness and, after 1886, Boer reluctance to cede authority to Uitlanders. Johannesburg's only local institution was a Sanitary Board, until British annexation introduced modern forms of municipal control after 1903. In 1904 similar reforms were introduced into the OFS.

Lacking indigenous urbanisation, early Dutch settlements were not segregated but, by 1910, a number of factors had promoted residential separation. In the eastern Cape the Fingo location provided land for Mfengu purchase from 1856. The desire to restrict Indian commercial competition in Durban and Johannesburg led to separate Indian areas, while Kimberley introduced a compound system to control the African workers on the diamond-fields. In Cape Town the first African location was erected under the Public Health Act in 1901, ostensibly to halt a plague epidemic.

Until the twentieth century urbanisation was associated with British commercial enterprise. Afrikaner migration to the towns increased from the 1920s. African migration was slower, but was precipitated by both World Wars and rural impoverishment. By 1991, 89 per cent of whites and 50 per cent of blacks were urbanised while urban growth rates were over 3 per cent per year.

Housing was a major consideration, and mixed inner city slums a focus of attention. The 1920 Housing Act and the 1934 Slums Act empowered municipalities to demolish slums and provided loans for sub-economic housing. This legislation removed poor whites to new, segregated suburbs and partially alleviated black housing with such developments as the Eastern Native Township in Johannesburg.

Residential segregation remained rudimentary but Colonel Stallard's doctrine that blacks were unsuited to urban life except as temporary labour became entrenched in interwar legislation such as the 1923 Natives (Urban Areas) Act. This enabled municipalities to establish African locations, to be funded on the 'Durban system' whereby the revenues from municipal beer halls were paid into a Native Revenue Account, and the Act made possible the implementation of influx control through passes. African resentment of municipal control of beer brewing, which was integral to urban culture and the economic survival of women, led to riots in Durban in 1929 and 1930. Municipalities were slow to utilise the 1923 Act. By 1937 only eleven towns had implemented influx control, although more had established locations.

The emergence of town planning as a discipline also encouraged segregation. South African town planners, often engineers, were influenced by the idea of the 'efficient city' rather than social concerns.

'Cape Town from Camps Bay Road, 1846', by G F Angas. At this date the two churches were still the most prominent buildings in Cape Town and the town had not yet encroached along the Salt River shore or far up the slopes of the mountain (Africana Museum)

View of Cape Town station and Foreshore, 1962. The Foreshore scheme, designed to reshape the city, envisaged the disappearance of much of District Six
(Cape Archives CA 68)

The Transvaal Provincial Ordinance No 11 of 1931 became the model for all the provinces, leading to more ambitious compulsory reshaping of cities, such as the Cape Town foreshore scheme which envisaged the disappearance of much of District Six.

Municipal autonomy was weakened increasingly by other legislation before 1948. The 1937 Native Laws Amendment Act gave central government power to enforce influx control, while the 1944 Housing Amendment Act empowered the National Housing and Planning Commission to intervene in local housing policy.

The National Party victory in 1948 reinforced this process. Under the 1950 Group Areas Act individuals lost the last rights to live where they chose and towns were gradually restructured to conform with this rezoning. The removal of coloureds from District Six in Cape Town after 1967 led to prolonged resistance and international opprobrium. In 1972 coloureds lost their Cape municipal franchise. The establishment of Administration Boards in 1972 removed African urban administration from the municipalities, regulating influx control, housing and labour and funded by beer monopolies and rents. Occasionally conflict arose when municipalities resisted this process. In the 1950s, for example, the Johannesburg City Council objected to the razing of Sophiatown, Martindale and Newclare.

Initially Nationalist government policy improved the housing situation, exacerbated by the Second World War, and huge townships, like Soweto, were built on city fringes. The National Housing Commission established the principles of location layout while the National Building Research Institute developed low cost housing, both contributing to a distinctive pattern of township structure.

In the 1960s the policy of border industries and tighter influx control halted building, leading to overcrowding in existing townships from the 1970s. The breakdown of Bantustan economies increased the pace of urbanisation, resulting in huge illegal squatter settlements. Most formal areas lacked basic amenities such as electricity, contributing to urban pollution, while sewerage and water supply were grossly inadequate in squatter camps. High infant mortality rates and tuberculosis were major health problems.

Growing militancy over pass laws, education, rents and transport led to government loss of control in the townships. By the 1980s their fiscal base weakened as beer monopoly profits declined and rent boycotts were instituted. The creation of Urban Bantu Councils in 1968 and Community Councils in 1977 failed to gain legitimacy as black local authorities. Private organisations like the Urban Foundation, funded by business, attempted to alleviate urban ills.

The beginnings of a squatter settlement, Johannesburg 1948
(Transvaal Archives TAB 31989)

Influx control was lifted in 1986, after which squatter settlements gained official recognition, but local government remained a problem and violence often became endemic, as conflict over scarce resources intensified. After political parties were unbanned in 1990, this violence was politicised, as Inkatha and the African National Congress vied for power in Natal, while migrant worker hostels were a focus of similar unrest in the Transvaal. Since 1990 moves have been afoot to establish joint municipal councils, but inadequate housing and services and huge budget deficits remain unsolved problems.

(E B van Heyningen)

Urban Foundation

Following the Soweto uprising in 1976, big business interests in South Africa decided to become actively involved in improving the quality of life for the country's urban black population. The Urban Foundation was established, with its first director ex-judge Jan Steyn, and was chiefly occupied with improving black housing. It invested nearly half a billion rands in development and housing loans between 1978 and 1988, and launched over 800 housing projects in black townships. Another major area of activity was the upgrading of educational and recreational facilities in black areas. In the early 1990s more money became available for such projects through the Independent Development Trust, set up with government money allocated to social development purposes.

V

Van der Kemp, Johannes Theodorus

ROTTERDAM, NETHERLANDS, 1747 — CAPE TOWN, 1811

Missionary. Van der Kemp first served in the Dutch army and then trained as a medical doctor before joining the London Missionary Society. He was one of their first missionaries to be sent to the Cape, arriving there in 1799. The first in a long line of radical priests, he worked among the Xhosa on the eastern frontier and then among the Khoikhoi, first at Graaff-Reinet and later at a new settlement near Algoa Bay, the famous Bethelsdorp mission which was established in 1803. He brought the Khoikhoi's living and working conditions to public attention in a series of harsh and detailed complaints and, as a result, antagonised the local colonists. He was subsequently prohibited by the Governor of the Cape from residing at Bethelsdorp. After his death, the newly created circuit court looked into his accusations of colonist maltreatment of the Khoikhoi.

Revd Johannes van der Kemp of the London Missionary Society (Africana Museum)

Van der Stel, Simon

MAURITIUS, 1639 – CAPE TOWN, 1712

Dutch East India Company Governor and Commander of the Cape from 1679 to 1699. In order to promote the well-being of the settlement, Van der Stel effected a marked improvement in the quality of the Cape wines, transformed the Company's garden, reorganised the Cape defences and greatly reduced the Cape's annual deficits. Farms were granted to settlers in Stellenbosch (1679) and in Drakenstein (1686). When Van der Stel retired to farm his Constantia estate, he was succeeded by his son, Willem Adriaan.

Van der Stel, Willem Adriaan

HAARLEM, NETHERLANDS, 1664 – LISSE, NETHERLANDS, 1733

Dutch East India Company Governor of the Cape from 1699 to 1707. Son of Simon van der Stel, Willem Adriaan, like his father before him, used his position to enrich himself, and soon owned large tracts of the best arable land and numerous cattle farms and slaves. Sixty-three free burghers drew up a petition of complaint and this led eventually to his dismissal. Historians have differed in their judgements of Willem Adriaan, some seeing him as unjustly treated, pointing out that his accusers were economic competitors, but the

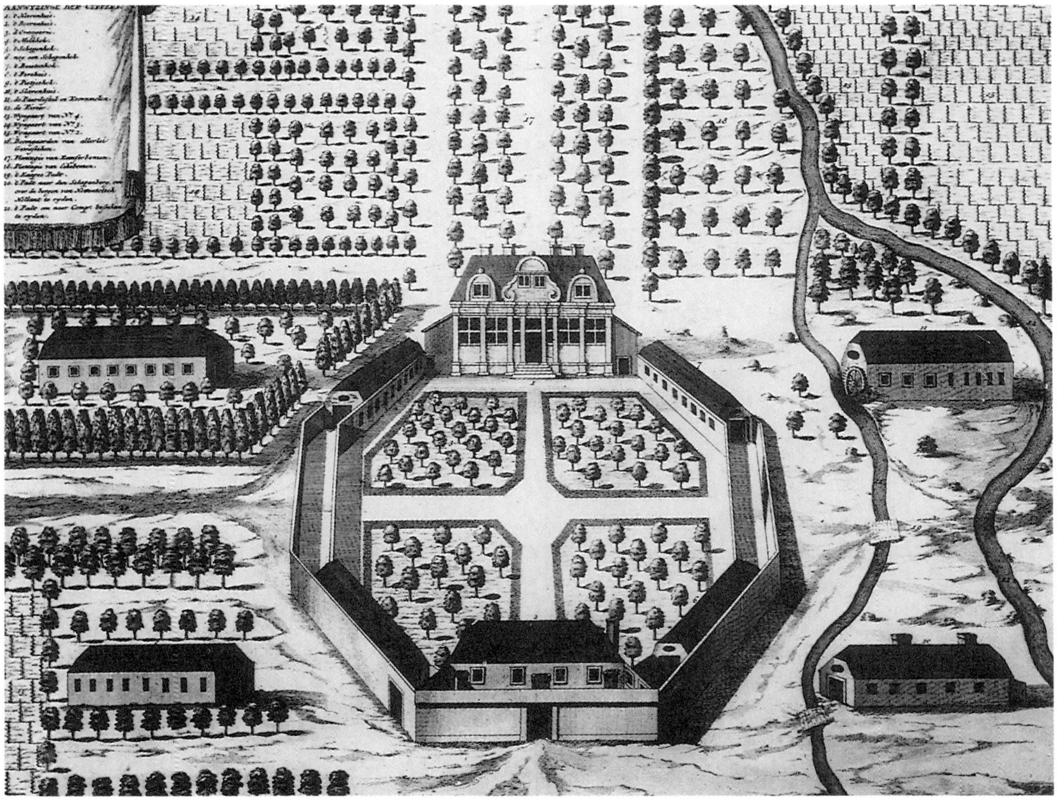

Vergelegen, the estate of Willem Adriaan van der Stel, as pictured by the complaining burghers in 1712. The illustration depicts the free burghers' claims concerning the extensive nature of the estate with its numerous vineyards, plantations and slave quarters (Cape Archives M 140)

more common view is that he met his just deserts.

Van Riebeeck, Jan Anthonisz

CULEMBORG, NETHERLANDS, 1619 — BATAVIA, DUTCH EAST INDIES, 1677

Founder of white settlement at the Cape and first Commander of the Cape (1652–1662). Van Riebeeck had joined the Dutch East India Company (VOC) as assistant-surgeon in 1639, and in 1652 the VOC sent him out to the Cape to build a fort and supply the Company fleets with fruit, vegetables and meat. The VOC was the greatest trading corporation of that time, and the Cape was to be the link between the Netherlands and its eastern empire centred in Java. Van Riebeeck arrived on 6 April 1652, as commander of an expedition of five ships with eighty Company employees. Besides the fruit and vegetables grown, wheat was sown and viticulture introduced, and in 1657 nine Company servants were allowed to establish private farms at Rondebosch. Under Van Riebeeck's rule slaves were imported and the first war was fought (1659–1660) against Khoi pastoralists on whose land the settlement had begun to encroach.

Portrait of Jan Van Riebeeck by H J Slijper, 1972, after the original by Craeij
(William Fehr Collection)

Vegkop, Battle of (1836)

The first significant battle between Africans and the Voortrekkers. A trekker commando led by Hendrik Potgieter attacked the Ndebele, who blocked their route northwards. A counter attack was launched by the Ndebele against the trekkers, sheltered in a laager at the base of Doringkop (later Vegkop) in the Heilbron district. Their wagons were tied together and thorn trees were used as a barricade. The trekkers were able to resist the Ndebele attack, though they lost most of their cattle, sheep and trek oxen. Four hundred and thirty Ndebele were killed, and only two trekkers lost their lives. After the battle the trekkers continued their march north.

Venda

Bantu-speakers who live in the extreme north of South Africa. Their language is distinct, though is closely connected with both Shona, which is spoken in most of Zimbabwe, and Sotho. From at least the seventeenth century Venda have inhabited the fertile Soutpansberg mountains south of the Limpopo River. The Venda state Thovela, which existed in the early eighteenth century, absorbed a number of Shona groups. The Venda built in stone, mined gold, copper and tin, hunted for ivory and traded with the Shona. Their rugged and inaccessible habitat helped enable them to withstand the impact of the Difaqane ('Time of Troubles') and the Great Trek in the 1820s and 1830s. For a long time the Venda resisted encroachment on their territory by the Transvaal Boers, but in 1898 a Boer expedition succeeded in driving them from their mountain strongholds, and the Venda chief, Mphephu, and about 10 000 followers fled across the Limpopo River. Their conquest marked the end of the process of colonial subjugation in South Africa.

Vereeniging, Treaty of (1902)

Treaty that ended the South African War, which, despite its name, was signed in Pretoria on 31 May 1902. Initial Boer approval to it was given at Vereeniging, close to the Vaal, when representatives of the British and ex-republican Boer governments met to discuss peace terms. In terms of the Treaty, the independence of the South African Republic and the Orange Free State was ended, a general amnesty was declared, Britain agreed to pay three million pounds to alleviate the ravages of war, and political autonomy was promised to the ex-republics. The question of a black franchise was to be settled after the defeated Boers had been granted self-government. Altogether, the terms were considered very moderate, and this persuaded such Boer generals as Smuts and Botha to work with the British after the war.

Top:
Battle of Vegkop by H Egersdörfer. Under attack from the Ndebele, the Voortrekkers tied their wagons together and used thorn trees as a barricade
(South African Library)

Above:
Delegates and their families at the Peace Conference at Vereeniging, May 1902. The treaty which came out of this conference was signed in Pretoria
(National Cultural History Museum)

Verwoerd, Hendrik Frensch

AMSTERDAM, HOLLAND, 1901 — CAPE TOWN, 1966

Politician, Prime Minister of South Africa from 1958 to 1966. Verwoerd's family came out to South Africa from the Netherlands when he was two years old. After a brilliant academic career he was appointed professor of applied psychology at the University of Stellenbosch (1927), where he taught until his appointment as editor of *Die Transvaler*, a Nationalist daily newspaper in Johannesburg, in 1937. As Minister of Native Affairs in Malan's cabinet from 1950 he was responsible for much key apartheid legislation.

Following Strijdom's death (1958) Verwoerd became Prime Minister and he proceeded to implement his apartheid programme ruthlessly. He survived an assassination attempt in 1960 and saw that as evidence that God was on his side. Under his leadership South Africa became a Republic (1961). In 1966 Verwoerd was stabbed to death in the House of Assembly by a deranged messenger, Tsafendas, who was committed to a mental hospital and never sentenced for his deed.

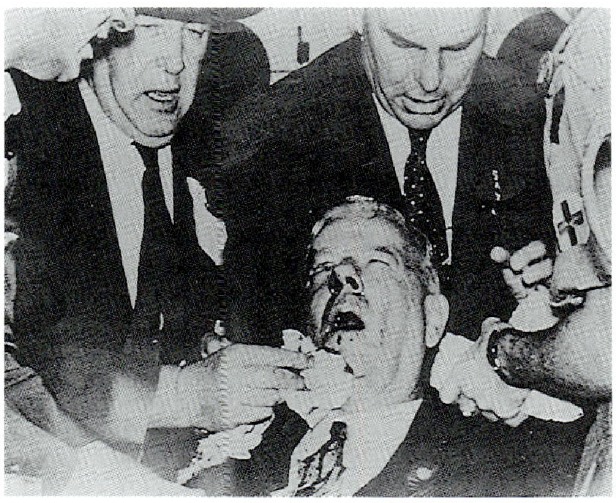

Far left:
Verwoerd after the attempt on his life at the Rand Easter Show, April 1960
(Rapport Library)

Voortrekkers

Name given to those Afrikaner frontier farmers who set out on what became known as the Great Trek. Some 15 000 left the eastern Cape Colony between 1834 and 1840 to establish their own states in the interior. They wished to escape from a British government whose policies they had come to detest. Meaning merely 'pioneers' the term has also been applied to the Griqua and other frontier groups.

Vorster, Balthazar Johannes (John)

JAMESTOWN, CAPE, 1915 — CAPE TOWN, 1983

Politician and Prime Minister of South Africa from 1966 to 1978. A general in the Ossewabrandwag who had Nazi sympathies, Vorster was interned during the Second World War for his anti-war activities. As Minister of Justice in Verwoerd's cabinet from 1961, he pushed through a succession of tough laws de-

B J Vorster, Prime Minister of South Africa from 1966 to 1978
(Rapport Library)

signed to deter subversion, and his strong-arm tactics made him the natural successor to Verwoerd on the latter's death in 1966. As Prime Minister, Vorster was relatively pragmatic, introducing some reformist changes in domestic policy, and in foreign affairs pursuing a policy of detente. His fall from office resulted from the Muldergate 'Information' scandal. Citing 'health reasons' he first resigned as Prime Minister, but accepted the office of State President. When his involvement in the scandal became public he was forced to resign that office in 1979.

W

Walvis Bay

Harbour on the coast of Namibia, so named because of the whales encountered there. From the 1830s Walvis Bay was increasingly used by traders, missionaries and collectors of guano, and was annexed by Britain in 1878. It was incorporated into the Cape Colony in 1884 and retained by Britain despite German annexation of the rest of South West Africa. Walvis Bay was included in South Africa by the Act of Union in 1910, but from 1922 it was administered as part of South West Africa. From 1977 it was again brought under South African administration, and in 1978 it was accepted by the Western Contact Group, then engaged in negotiations on the future of Namibia, that the issue of the incorporation of Walvis Bay would be left over for bilateral discussions between South Africa and Namibia after the latter's independence. Such discussions were held, and in August 1992 it was announced that an agreement had been reached on joint administration of the enclave, through which most of Namibia's trade passes. A year later the negotiating forum at the World Trade Centre agreed that Walvis Bay should become part of Namibia.

War of the Axe (Seventh Frontier War, 1846–1847)

A war sparked off by an incident involving a patrol sent to arrest a Xhosa suspected of stealing an axe from a shop in Fort Beaufort. The breakdown of the treaty system devised after the previous war, the Sixth Frontier War (1834–1835), was a more fundamental cause, as was the desire of the white settlers for more land. This war dragged on longer than any previous frontier war and ended with the Xhosa in effect surrendering for lack of food. In its closing phases, Governor Smith proclaimed the annexation of the land eastwards to the Kei as British Kaffraria.

Water Resources

In South Africa water is a scarce resource, limited by unfavourable climatic conditions, an uneven geographic distribution relative to demand, and by the need to share it with other countries. The predominant source of water in the country is surface run-off from rainfall — water that is carried off an area by streams and rivers. Some 40 per cent of this water is lost by spillage, evaporation from storage, and the fact that not all of it can be diverted for use before reaching the sea. A second source of water is underground water, often the only

Walvis Bay in 1861 by Thomas Baines
(William Fehr Collection)

Kowie River, Cape of Good Hope, 1840 by W Purser
(Africana Museum)

source available to isolated communities. Underground water was increasingly tapped, and by 1980 an estimated 13 per cent of all water used came from underground sources. In the early part of the century, water resources were developed and used chiefly for agricultural purposes, irrigation being the largest single water consumer. From the 1940s there has been a rapid rise in water consumption for urban and industrial purposes. The two largest water projects to date have been the Orange River scheme, completed in the 1960s, and the Highlands Water scheme in Lesotho, construction of which began in the early 1990s.

Wheat Industry

Wheat was one of the first crops planted by the Dutch at the Cape, and wheat farming was one of the main economic activities under Dutch East India Company rule. During the eighteenth century wheat production increased considerably in response to increased demand by the official establishment, visiting foreign ships, and the Dutch Eastern Empire. The mineral discoveries brought about a sudden increase in the consuming population, and led to the opening up of rail communications between the Cape wheat producing districts and the inland consuming centres. The resulting demand for wheat was met by greater production, supplemented by importation of large quantities of wheat. After the First World War, South Africa was still unable to satisfy her own wheat requirements. As a result of restrictions on wheat imports and the encouragement of domestic production, imports gradually ceased and in the 1980s South Africa was able to export considerable quantities of her crop.

Wheat threshing machine. Wheat was one of the first crops planted by the Dutch at the Cape
(South African Library)

White Politics

Despite important class, occupational, regional and language differences which caused serious divisions among them, white people succeeded in conquering the African inhabitants of southern Africa during the last three decades of the nineteenth century. The South African War (1899–1902) further exacerbated tensions between whites, but there were powerful pressures which drew whites together in the years immediately after the war. Two factors in particular urged whites towards political unity. Firstly, economic disputes and conflicts of interest threatened further open strife with grave potential consequences for the economy of the entire region. Meanwhile, the Zulu rebellion in Natal in 1906 alerted whites in southern Africa to the necessity of a more coherent and consistent policy towards Africans and other people of colour, which would better serve white interests.

Thus, only eight years after the end of the South African War, the four South African colonies merged to form the Union of South Africa on 31 May 1910. The constitution — negotiated with relative ease by Afrikaner and English-speaking white leaders from all four colonies at the National Convention in 1908 and 1909 — gave whites almost total control of political representation. They opted for the creation of a unitary state with a sovereign central Parliament, which exercised control over all provincial and local institutions. The executive was responsible to the majority party in the House of Assembly (the lower house of Parliament), which was elected by voters at least once every five years; the Senate (the upper house) was indirectly elected and had limited powers; and there was no bill of rights. English and Dutch were made the official languages of the country, ensuring their equal status in the constitution. Another significant feature of the constitution was the method of division of the country into constituencies: delimitation commissions were empowered to give sparsely populated rural constituencies 15 per cent fewer voters than the average, and more densely populated urban constituencies 15 per cent more. The advantage gained by the country areas was to provide a vital advantage to parties with a rural support base.

A compromise was reached with regard to the franchise. Cape delegates at the Convention wanted the non-racial franchise of the Cape, where over 15 per cent of the electorate was coloured or African, to be extended to the whole country. Transvaal and Orange River Colony representatives, strongly supported by those from Natal, were insistent that no black should be permitted to vote for members of the central Parliament. It was agreed that the franchise laws then existing in each colony be maintained, and that no black be able to stand for election to Parliament. In effect, this meant that the political rights of coloureds and Africans in the Cape were greatly reduced, and that whites had a virtual monopoly of the political process in the Union.

Opening of Parliament, Cape Town, 15 March 1905
(South African Library)

Between 1910 and 1948, whites consolidated their political power and their control over the state. The relationship between Afrikaners and English-speakers — which involved both ethnic and class factors — was the dominant issue of white politics during these years, but differences between whites never jeopardised their powerful political position. Successive governments pursued segregationist policies, which strengthened the control of whites over blacks. Afrikaner politicians also strove to loosen the legal right of the British government to intervene in South Africa and to develop an independent foreign policy.

The South African Party (SAP) led by Louis Botha, a former Boer general and a wealthy farmer who became the first Prime Minister, won the 1910 election with mainly Afrikaner support on its policy of reconciliation between English-speakers and Afrikaners. Its main opposition was the Unionist Party, which drew much of the capitalist and urban English vote, but which had similar policies to the SAP. Tension between Botha and his Minister of Justice, J B M Hertzog, over the policy of reconciliation caused the SAP to split, and in 1914 Hertzog formed the National Party, which was committed to weakening South Africa's imperial links and to advancing the economic and cultural interests of Afrikaners. Thereafter, the SAP and the Unionists worked increasingly closely together against the National Party, until the Unionists were absorbed by the SAP in 1921.

The SAP lost much Afrikaner support in

Right:
General Louis Botha and General Jan Smuts during the First World War. Botha was Prime Minister and Smuts his Minister of Defence
(National Cultural History Museum)

Far right:
General Hertzog arrives in Cape Town for a session of Parliament, July 1939
(Rapport Library)

the rural areas of the Transvaal, Orange Free State and the Cape after South Africa's entry into the First World War in support of Britain. A short rebellion against the government in 1914 by extreme Afrikaner nationalists was quickly suppressed, but provided an ideological focus against Botha and Jan Smuts, Botha's successor as Prime Minister in 1919, who were perceived as lackeys of Britain. The SAP also alienated white workers, who participated in a number of strikes in 1913 and 1914 over their working conditions and competition from blacks, whose labour was attractive to mineowners because it was much cheaper than the employment of whites. In 1922, semi-skilled whites were replaced by blacks, provoking a bitter strike which was brutally suppressed by Smuts's government. This resulted in an electoral pact between the Nationalists and the smaller Labour Party, which had represented white workers in Parliament since 1910, and the SAP was defeated in 1924.

The National Party followed a programme of increased employment opportunity for whites by promoting industrial development, supporting state-owned industry and offering tariff protection to private industries which employed a high proportion of whites. White farming was also sustained by cheap state loans and guaranteed prices. Afrikaans replaced Dutch as an official language in 1925, and large numbers of Afrikaners began to be employed in the civil service. After 1926, English-speakers and Afrikaners became deeply divided over the design of a new national flag, but Hertzog's moves to achieve full autonomy and equality of status with Britain for South Africa and other dominions, which achieved final fruition in the Statute of Westminster in 1931, were less controversial.

The severe depression of 1929–1933 greatly weakened South Africa's economy, and led to a coalition government between Hertzog and Smuts in March 1933 and a merger between them to form the United Party in 1934. The United Party enjoyed the support of the majority of the electorate during the rest of the 1930s, as the economy improved and white poverty declined. Neither the Dominion Party, a small pro-British party with a Natal support base, nor the Purified National Party, which broke away from Hertzog under D F Malan, a newspaper editor and Dutch Reformed church minister, over his cooperation with Smuts, offered a significant threat to the United Party. The Purified Nationalists did, however, build considerable strength during the 1930s on the basis of an ardent Afrikaner nationalism, using the 1938 Great Trek celebrations effectively to promote the party. The United Party split in 1939 on the issue of South African participation in the Second World War. Hertzog, who argued for a policy of strict neutrality, lost the premiership after a parliamentary vote went against him. Smuts became Prime Minister and led South

In 1939 Smuts became Prime Minister and led South Africa into the war against Germany (Transvaal Archives TAB 5285)

Africa into the war against Germany.

Despite these divisions between whites in the decades after Union, they found common ground with one another over policy towards blacks. The policy of segregation, which developed mainly as a complex form of labour control, began to be implemented almost immediately after Union. The two main pieces of legislation were the Natives Land Act of 1913, which established the principle of territorial separation and prohibited Africans from buying or leasing land outside of demarcated reserves, and the Natives (Urban Areas) Act of 1923, which extended segregation to urban areas by giving the authorities power to create locations to house Africans and regulate access to them. Other legislation provided for job reservation, the creation of separate administrative structures for Africans and the control of movement of Africans between the reserves and urban areas. In 1936, the African franchise in the Cape was removed, and replaced with a system which entitled African Cape voters to elect three white members of Parliament to represent them.

Smuts's power during the Second World War, which boosted South Africa's manufacturing capability and accelerated urbanisation, was never seriously challenged. Afrikaners remained divided: many supported Smuts, attempts at reconciliation between Hertzog and Malan failed, while the Ossewabrandwag, a Nazi-style paramilitary organisation, engaged in acts of sabotage and competed with Malan for leadership among Afrikaners. The National Party worked hard, however, to overcome differences among Afrikaners, and by 1948 succeeded in building bridges between the main classes of urban and rural Afrikaners by appealing to their common ethnic affiliation and by concentrating on the state of race relations and their doctrine of racial separation, labelled apartheid. They portrayed Smuts as a distant figure out of touch with domestic issues and working-class Afrikaners, and exploited discussions within the United Party over the viability of segregation as evidence of vacillation. In the 1948 election, the National Party won a slim majority of seats, although substantially fewer votes than the United Party, and was able to form a government.

The new government was deeply committed to the maintenance of white supremacy, but it was initially even more concerned to ensure that its parliamentary majority was not lost. It incorporated six South West African seats into the South African Parliament and redrew electoral boundaries in order to guarantee victory in the election of 1953. In 1955, after constitutional methods had failed, the government eliminated coloureds from the common voters' roll by enlarging the Senate and the Appeal Court with people sympathetic to their cause. By 1958, the National Party had secured the support of the overwhelming number of Afrikaners: it increased state and public investment in the economy, which greatly assisted the economic advancement of Afrikaner workers. State institutions, the civil service, the police and army were Afrikanerised, while Afrikaner business in the private sector was favoured by the state, enabling Afrikaner entrepreneurs to challenge the domination of En-

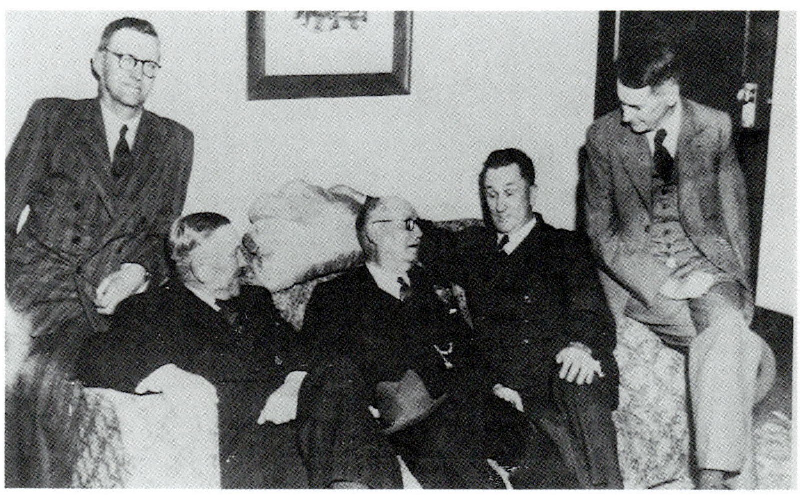

National Party leaders assemble in Pretoria before Dr Malan appoints his cabinet in 1948. From left, C R Swart, N C Havenga, Dr Malan, J G Strijdom and Dr E J Jansen (Rapport Library)

glish-speakers in commerce, mining, finance and manufacture by the late 1960s. The government also succeeded in achieving another long-cherished goal in 1961, when South Africa became a Republic, completing the process of withdrawal from Britain.

It was the implementation of its apartheid policies which proved most instrumental in securing white domination. Although it is conventionally accepted that the National Party was elected in 1948 with a clearly formulated plan of action, there was no blueprint which was systematically implemented. Policies were formulated and shaped according to ideology, but were also influenced by pragmatism and more immediate circumstances. The National Party needed to reconcile different class interests — farmers, businessmen and workers — within Afrikanerdom, as well as accommodate English-speaking capital and United Party-dominated urban local authorities during the 1950s. It was thus unable to impose an unfettered 'master plan' on South African society.

Nevertheless, by 1960, a large number of different laws were on the statute books which combined to have far-reaching consequences on society. The National Party believed that racial purity was of fundamental importance, and the Mixed Marriages Act (1949) and the Immorality Act (1950) were designed to prevent interracial sexual and marital relationships. The Population Registration Act (1950) was passed to categorise all South Africans according to race. The Group Areas Act (1950) enforced residential separation, while the Separate Amenities Act (1953) segregated public amenities and aimed to eliminate non-racial contact. The Natives Act (1952) compelled blacks to carry passes, thereby giving the authorities further power to regulate the movement of blacks. The Bantu Education Act (1953) introduced state-controlled education for Africans, which was designed to bolster white domination by ensuring that Africans were trained for menial tasks. The Bantu Authorities Act (1951) and the Promotion of Bantu Self-Government Act (1959) eliminated the representation of Africans in Parliament by whites, and set up structures whereby people in the reserves — later called Bantustans or homelands — would eventually be granted limited self-government.

The government of H F Verwoerd achieved a long-cherished goal in 1961 when South Africa became a Republic (Rapport Library)

White opposition to the government's programmes within Parliament was ineffectual. The United Party never developed a coherent and attractive plan to counter the National Party during the 1950s, and was hampered by weak leadership. The party enjoyed temporary vitality during the campaign to oppose the removal of the franchise from coloureds, but the main thrust came from an extra-parliamentary grouping called the Torch Commando, which was founded by ex-servicemen to oppose the violation of the constitution. A small number of whites vigorously opposed the growing battery of apartheid laws by forming the non-racial Liberal Party in 1953, but it never enjoyed voter support. In 1959, the liberal wing of the United Party split to form the Progressive Party, but only secured a single seat in Parliament in the election of 1961. Support for the United Party continued to ebb during the 1960s as the National Party began to attract English-speaking voters in significant numbers.

From the mid-1950s, the state began to augment the coercive legislation already on the statute books in order to enforce white domination yet further. Various laws enabled detention without trial and gave government ministers sweeping powers to ban organisations, prohibit public meetings and control the activities of individuals. The police force was enlarged, while conscription for whites was introduced in 1967. During the 1960s, as the economic disparities between whites became less pronounced during a period of high economic growth, the majority of whites drew together politically under the National Party administration. Social engineering programmes of the state, particularly the forced removals of Africans into the homelands, became more confident during this period, and were opposed by few whites.

From the mid-1970s, however, white politics began to alter in significant ways, as the National Party was forced to respond to growing international constraints, the end of the economic boom of the 1960s and early 1970s, and increasing internal discontent. Pressures to reform apartheid, which reached its peak during the premiership of one of its leading ideologues, H F Verwoerd (1958–1966), mounted from the 1970s, leading to tensions within Afrikanerdom in particular. A small group had broken away from the National Party under the leadership of Albert Hertzog in 1969 to form the Herstigte Nasionale Party to fight any modification of 'pure' apartheid. As reformists began to experiment with different strategies after P W Botha became Prime Minister in 1978, significant hardline opposition began to make its voice heard, until a group of Nationalists left to form the Conservative Party under the leadership of A P Treurnicht in 1982. Meanwhile, in 1977, the Progressive Federal Party — a fusion of the Progressive Party and the liberal remnants of the United Party, which disbanded in that year — became the official opposition in Parliament, though remained numerically small (with 17 seats to the 134 of the National Party).

P W Botha introduced constitutional changes in 1984 which, though claiming to end white domination of politics by bringing coloureds and Indians into Parliament, perpetuated white power in all significant areas of public life. The constitution made provision for three racially separate houses of Parliament, for whites, coloureds and Indians respectively, in which each was to look after their 'own affairs'. The numerical dominance of the white house, coupled with unprecedented powers centred on an executive State President (which office P W Botha assumed), meant that white control of politics continued. A state of emergency between 1986 and 1990 was evidence of the necessity of using force to maintain white supremacy.

After 1989, when F W de Klerk became State President, white politics were further transformed when the need for negotiations with all South Africans about a future political dispensation was recognised by the National Party. De Klerk won a referendum in March 1992 from the white electorate with a two-thirds majority to pursue a negotiated settlement and end the white monopoly on political power.

(N D Southey)

Above:
April 1989, the new Democratic Party leaders, (from left) Wynand Malan, Dennis Worrall and (far right) Zach de Beer
(Rapport Library)

Left:
The President's Council, the supreme decision-making body, consisted of nominated members with a Nationalist majority, and a minority of Coloured, Indian and Opposition MPs. Africans were excluded
(Cartoon by Abe Berry)

'Wind of Change' Speech

Famous speech delivered by visiting British Prime Minister Harold Macmillan to the South African Parliament on 3 February 1960 at the conclusion of a tour through the African continent. Impressed

Below:
British Prime Minister Harold Macmillan arrived at D F Malan airport on 1 February 1960. He was received by Dr Verwoerd
(South African Library)

by the strength of African nationalism, Macmillan was convinced that an irresistible 'wind of change' was blowing throughout the continent, that South Africa could not remain isolated from it, and that therefore apartheid should be abandoned and political power extended to all on the basis of individual merit. Prime Minister Verwoerd rejected this analysis, telling Macmillan that South Africa was different, that the whites would remain in charge and that ethnic nationalism among Africans could find outlets in the new Bantustans.

Wine Industry

The first vines were imported to the Cape by Jan van Riebeeck in 1655 and planted in the Dutch East India Company garden. The free burghers were encouraged to plant vineyards, and the wine industry of the southwestern Cape expanded rapidly. Wine and brandy were not much exported, for apart from Constantia wine, the quality remained poor. In 1813 the duty on Cape wines entering Britain was reduced to one-third of what it had previously been, and the wine industry boomed. By 1822, wine exports exceeded all other Cape exports together, and saved the colony from insolvency. However, when Britain began to withdraw the preferential tariffs in 1825 and 1831, the Cape wine industry started to collapse. To stabilise the industry, a central wine growers' organisation was established in 1918, the Ko-operatiewe Wijnbouwers-Vereniging (KWV) which today exercises almost complete control over all aspects of the production of wines and spirits in South Africa.

Wodehouse, Sir Philip Edmond
NORFOLK, 1811 — LONDON, 1887

Colonial Governor, expansionist. Wodehouse succeeded Sir George Grey as Cape Governor and High Commissioner in South Africa (1862–1870). He tried to increase the strength of the executive in a time of recession, and to introduce a more efficient colonial administration. He was opposed to responsible government for the Cape on the grounds that the colony's re-

Far right:
Sir P E Wodehouse, Governor of the Cape from 1862 to 1870
(Cory Library)

Right:
The vineyards of Paarl. Painting by G F Angas
(Africana Museum)

sources were inadequate for full self-government. Perhaps his most important step was to support the British annexation of Basutoland in 1868. In 1869 he and Brand of the Orange Free State signed the second convention of Aliwal North, which established the new boundaries of Basutoland and confirmed the loss of the Sotho land west of the Caledon River.

Women

Women have never constituted a homogeneous group in South African history. This makes a brief history of the position of women a problematic task. Nevertheless, given the pervasiveness of various forms of male dominance historically (one manifestation of which is the invisibility of women in many influential texts), the durability of patriarchal gender relations does provide a certain thematic unity to the diverse experiences of women in different epochs and societies.

In the past ten years a gathering momentum in research has increased our knowledge about women's roles and gender relations historically, although many gaps remain. Little is known about women in the history of hunter-gatherer societies, but the broad outlines of the position of women in Bantu-speaking agricultural societies in the more recent pre-colonial era have begun to be charted.

Jeff Guy argues that the oppression of women, in the form of the control of women's reproductive and productive labour by men, was the axis on which these pre-capitalist farming societies turned. Given the low level of technological development, wealth and power depended (in contrast to capitalist societies) on the accumulation of people rather than things. This was realised through the control of women's fertility — their capacity to bear children, the future productive members of society. Why and how this control came to vest in men, within the patriarchal homestead, rather than in women themselves, remains obscure. The high social value placed on fertility however, did give women an important, if prescribed, status within the homestead, as did their substantial role in the production of food.

The colonial period initiated a far-reaching disruption and reorganisation of indigenous gender relations and the introduction of new groupings of women, from Europe and also the Indian sub-continent, to the region. Henceforth race and class were as significant in shaping the life chances of South African women as their gender, while different conceptions and expectations of womanhood challenged older formulations.

Settler society, both Boer and British, was sternly patriarchal — in 1883 the South African writer, Olive Schreiner, lamented that 'to be born a woman was to be born branded'. Under capitalism women were not recognised for the economic contribution they made as unwaged housewives and farmworkers. In the nineteenth century, colonial legislators reinterpreted indigenous legal systems through the prism of their own ethnocentric views on

Far left:
A sketch by Thomas Baines of a Xhosa woman at work. Xhosa society was male-dominated and the work of women – agriculture, pottery, basket-making and child-rearing – carried with it a far lower status than that of men
(© The Brenthurst Press)

Left:
Distinguished author and feminist Olive Schreiner
(South African Library)

women's position; in the process they both exaggerated and fossilised the subordinate status of black women under customary law. At the same time, Christianity introduced new conceptions of marriage and women's roles that challenged the polygamous collectivity of the pre-colonial homestead and promoted a double domesticity for African women, as domestic workers in white households or institutions and as Christian wives and mothers within their own homes.

The disorganisation of gender relations was accelerated by the discovery of gold and the launching of South Africa's industrial revolution, predicated as it was on a parasitic system of male migrant labour that depended on women to sustain the productivity and social integrity of the rural homestead. In the first half of the twentieth century successive white governments relied largely on the informal sanctions of rural chiefs and male elders, boosted by local municipal restrictions, to contain African women within the reserves. As a result, the proletarianisation and urbanisation of black women proceeded much more slowly than for other groups; as late as 1951 only a little over 20 per cent of African women were living in the urban areas. Much of the social cost of maintaining the rural homestead under deteriorating economic conditions was borne by African women. African marriages became less stable and gender relations more strained as women took on more responsibilities within their households in the absence of their men. The reverberations of these interlocked processes spread unevenly, however, so that the timing and extent of women's exposure to these stresses differed from region to region.

Colonial society also offered women limited opportunities for improving, or attempting to improve, their lot. For thousands of working-class women who immigrated from Britain in the course of the nineteenth century, colonial society offered upward social mobility into a racialised élite; most white women were also able to assign the most burdensome aspects of their domestic responsibilities to black servants, male and female. Although far more circumscribed, some black women also perceived avenues of opportunity in the new order. Christianity, for instance, preached the subservience of women to their husbands, but its stress on individual responsibility and the companionship of men and women in marriage attracted numbers of black women faced with unwanted arranged marriages and onerous family obligations.

In the twentieth century racial and gender hierarchies have been restructured. As secondary industry expanded, women were drawn into waged work outside the home, encouraging the emergence of a less restrictive ideology of female domesticity. However, employed women constituted a highly segmented and vulnerable labour force, divided both horizontally along racialised lines and vertically in terms of a sexual division of labour. This clustered women in certain areas of the labour force, stereotyped as 'women's work', which tended to be very poorly paid and carry low status — teaching, nursing, service and clerical work and, within manufacturing, the garment and food industries.

White women, many of them newly proletarianised Afrikaners, were the first to enter the industrial labour force in any numbers, finding their way into the bottom rungs of especially the garment industry in the 1920s and 1930s. During the 1940s white women began to advance into an expanding service sector, as clerks, secretaries and salespeople, while growing numbers of black women replaced them on the factory floor. This had major implications for the organisation of women workers. The Garment Workers' Union of the 1930s and 1940s fought hard, initially with some success, to organise women across colour lines but this became increasingly difficult to sustain in the face of a hostile, segregationist state and the stratified interests of women themselves.

Changes in the life experiences of women were reflected in their political or-

The Union Brand Jellies factory c. 1930. Women were clustered in certain areas of the labour force, stereotyped as 'women's work' which tended to be poorly paid and carried low status
(South African Library)

Above left:
The first woman registers for the Parliamentary voters roll, 13 January 1931. Although this signalled a liberalisation of attitudes about women's involvement in public affairs, enfranchisement was restricted to white women exclusively
(South African Library)

ganisation. An all-white women's suffrage movement succeeded in obtaining the vote for white women in 1930 after many years of campaigning. This signalled a liberalisation of attitudes about women's involvement in public affairs, but the exclusive enfranchisement of white women was used by the Hertzog government to dilute the limited black franchise in the Cape. It thus exacerbated the gulf separating white women from black. Given their marginal economic and social status, black women's organisational energies tended to focus on material issues at a community level such as housing and the right to brew and sell beer. From the 1940s, however, women became more active in the national liberation movement. In the 1950s African women were galvanised into militant, nationwide protest against legislation designed to bring them within the national pass laws net. The legislation indicated how far the economy of the reserves had declined — only through coercion could black, and especially black female, urbanisation be countered. Under the overall leadership of the multiracial Federation of South African Women (FSAW) and its major affiliate, the ANC Women's League, tens of thousands of women participated in a series of demonstrations around the country. In the aftermath of the Sharpeville massacre, however, the ANC Women's League was forced to regroup in exile, the FSAW collapsed, and passes became compulsory for African women in 1963. Between then and the abolition of influx control in 1986, African women were regarded by the state as 'surplus appendages' with no assured rights to be in the urban areas. This intensified their economic vulnerability. Their protests played a major role in the collapse of the pass system. In the new era begun in 1990, the question of women's rights was placed on the agenda, but moves towards equality

Above right:
International Women's Day protest outside the Chamber of Mines in Johannesburg, March 1988
(Mayibuye Centre)

with men were, for the most part, slow and incomplete.

(C Walker)

Wool Industry

The wool industry originated with the introduction of merino sheep into the Cape Colony in 1789. When Cape farmers switched from the indigenous fat-tailed sheep which had played so important a part in the economy of the eighteenth century to the breeding of Spanish merinos, wool production expanded rapidly. By 1841 the Cape was exporting over one million pounds, in weight, of

Left:
The indigenous fat-tailed sheep played an important part in the economy of the eighteenth century. Sketch by Samuel Daniell
(Africana Museum)

Left:
Selective breeding resulted in the improved Cape sheep and by 1841 the Cape was exporting over one million pounds, in weight, of wool annually
(Africana Museum)

wool annually, three-fifths of it coming from the eastern Cape, and wool had become the most important colonial export. Filling the gap after the collapse of the wine industry, wool remained the leading colonial export until after the discovery of diamonds. The value of wool exports rose steadily, peaking at over three million pounds in 1872, after which it fluctuated. Even since the development of mining and secondary industry, wool has remained a major earner of foreign exchange (some R845 million in 1991), and one of South Africa's main agricultural exports.

Below:
The South African Native Labour Corps, France 1916
(Africana Museum)

Above:
A rousing welcome awaited Field-Marshall J C Smuts when he visited his men in the Western Desert
(South African National Museum of Military History)

World War, First (1914–1918)

With the outbreak of the First World War on 4 August 1914, the Union of South Africa, as part of the British Empire, was automatically at war with Germany. The Union government's decision to invade German South West Africa (in accordance with Britain's request) precipitated an armed rebellion by dissident Afrikaners opposed to South Africa's involvement in the war. After the rebellion had been suppressed, South African forces captured German South West Africa. In 1916 Smuts took command of the East African campaign against the German forces there. More than 60 000 South Africans fought, and over 1 500 died, in East Africa. A South African Brigade fought in the Somme offensive in 1916, and took savage losses especially in the battle of Delville Wood. A South African Native Labour Contingent, comprising 21 000 blacks, was not allowed to bear arms, but dug trenches and did other work for the British army in France. In February 1917 some 700 of these men were drowned at sea when the troopship *Mendi* sank. Altogether, over 12 000 South Africans died during the war. General Smuts played a vital role in decisions concerning the war as a member of the Imperial war cabinet, helping, for example, to organise the Royal Air Force.

World War, Second (1939–1945)

The announcement on 3 September 1939 that Britain was at war with Germany, brought to an end the Fusion Government, with Smuts and Hertzog differing on the issue of South Africa's entry into the war. The issue was debated in Parliament, and Hertzog's motion asserting the country's neutrality was defeated. Hertzog resigned and Smuts formed the new government, which promptly severed relations with Germany (6 September). The decision to enter the war precipitated a series of massive ideological conflicts in the country. Union forces took part in the reconquest of Ethiopia from the Italians (1940–1941), and seized Madagascar (1942). They participated in the North African campaigns against German and Italian forces, 10 000 men being trapped by Rommel at Tobruk, and fought in Italy. Altogether some 397 655 South Africans served in the armed forces, including 123 000 blacks who were confined to noncombatant roles. Close on 9 000 South Africans died in the war.

X

Xhosa

Xhosa is the name generally given to the indigenous peoples of the eastern Cape and Transkei. The so-called Xhosa are not, however, historically or linguistically homogeneous.

The *amaXhosa* (Xhosa nation) proper occupied the lands west of the Mbashe River at the time of their first encounter with white colonists in 1736. The name Xhosa originates from a Khoikhoi term meaning 'angry men'. Oral tradition relates that the first king of the Xhosa was Cirha, who was dethroned by his younger brother Tshawe on account of his stinginess. This incident occurred some time before 1600, and ever since the amaTshawe have been the royal clan of the amaXhosa.

The Xhosa kingdom was not very centralised, and each Tshawe chief was relatively autonomous within his own chiefdom. As the generations passed, the chiefs dispersed over a wide area, expanding the Xhosa kingdom by means of subjecting the Khoikhoi and other independent clans to Tshawe authority. During the reign of Phalo (1715–1775), the Tshawe dynasty became effectively sub-divided between the Great House of Gcaleka and the Right-Hand House of Rharhabe. The amaRharhabe bore the brunt of the frontier wars, and divided yet again between the followers of Ngqika (d. 1829), who collaborated with the colonial forces, and Ndlambe (d. 1828), who resisted them.

During the nine frontier wars (1779–1878), the amaXhosa received very little help from their neighbours. They were shattered by the Nongqause catastrophe (1856–1857), and dispersed among the white farmers of the Karoo and the eastern Cape. They were the first black people to become widely known to whites, and it is perhaps in part on that account that the name 'Xhosa' has been adopted as the generic term used by outsiders to describe eastern Cape Africans as a whole.

The *Thembu* people occupy the inland region west of Xhosaland, the stretch of country running approximately from

Above:
Charge of the Gwanga. In June 1846, during the Seventh Frontier War, the Xhosa suffered heavy losses when they made the tactical error of crossing open territory in the daylight
(National Cultural History Museum)

Left:
'Xhosa settlement on the Eastern Cape Frontier', by François le Vaillant
(The Brenthurst Library)

Above:
Hamilton Hope, the magistrate of Qumbu, who was murdered in the Mpondomise Rebellion of 1880. The incident came to be known as Hope's War
(South African Library)

Above:
The Mfengu proved to be responsive to the Christian message preached by Revd John Ayliff of Butterworth
(South African Library)

Far right:
'Xhosa men, one with traditional long-stemmed pipe'. Pencil sketch by Thomas Baines
(© The Brenthust Press)

Umtata to Queenstown. They were constantly at war with the Xhosa, and consequently tended to ally with the colonial power. When Ngangelizwe of the Thembu was defeated in battle by Sarili of the Gcaleka Xhosa in 1875, he appealed to the British government for protection, thus precipitating the colonial annexation of Thembuland. In recent years the Thembu have produced some outstanding political leaders, including African National Congress President Nelson Mandela and Transkei politician Kaiser Matanzima.

The *Mpondomise* were based around the sources of the Umzimvubu River and it seems that the Mpondomise kingdom was once fully equal in status and power to its Xhosa, Thembu and Mpondo neighbours. The Mpondomise were fatally weakened by dynastic rivalry in the eighteenth century, and further broken up by the Mfecane invasions of the early nineteenth. On the eve of the colonial occupation of Transkei, they were again divided between the senior chief Mhlontlo and his cousin Mditshwa. Mhlontlo asked for British protection, a move which he almost immediately regretted. The Mpondomise rebelled in 1880, an incident known as 'Hope's War' because of the murder of Hamilton Hope, the magistrate of Qumbu. Most of the Mpondomise lands were confiscated, and their chieftainship was abolished. Today, the Mpondomise occupy only a fraction of their old territory in the districts of Tsolo and Qumbu.

The *Mpondo* occupy the coastal region between the Umtata River and the Natal border. Thanks to the inspired leadership of their great king Faku (d. 1867), they survived two Zulu invasions and emerged from the Mfecane period as the dominant power in the eastern Transkei. Faku persuaded most of the minor chiefdoms in this area to accept Mpondo overlordship; recalcitrants were coerced by his warrior son, Ndamase. Mpondoland remained independent long after the remainder of Transkei was annexed to the Cape Colony. Finally, in 1894, having failed to find a pretext for annexation, the government of Cecil Rhodes bluntly required the Mpondo king Sigcawu to submit to colonial rule.

Although there is no conclusive historical evidence, it may be assumed that the Xhosa, Thembu, Mpondo and Mpondomise had drifted westwards from the direction of present-day Natal before the seventeenth century. Other, smaller nations followed, most notably the *Xesibe* about the beginning of the eighteenth century and the *Bomvana* towards its end. The beginning of the nineteenth century saw, however, much greater and more aggressive invasions directly attributable to the Mfecane upheavals.

The *Bhaca* originated among the Debe Nguni of Natal. The Debe Nguni had never constituted a single political entity, but they shared certain common cultural characteristics, such as the custom of cutting slits on their faces. They were fused into a political unit by their great hero Chief Madzikane (d. 1824), who had magical powers. He is credited by the Bhaca with destroying an entire Zulu army by summoning a snowstorm which froze them to death. Madzikane's Bhaca lived off plunder and ate their meat raw. After Madzikane died in battle against the Thembu, the fortunes of the Bhaca declined, but they preserved their distinct identity through an uneasy alliance with Faku.

A more numerous wave of immigrants from Natal were the so-called *Mfengu* (meaning 'those who wander about, seeking service'). The Mfengu were not in fact a single group, but fragments of various nations (such as amaBhele, amaHlubi and amaZizi) which had been scattered by the Mfecane. Many of them had found their way into Transkei under the leadership of Matiwane, chief of the amaNgwane. After Matiwane's defeat at the battle of Mbholompho (1828), his followers scattered as servants among the Thembu and Gcaleka Xhosa. They proved very responsive to the Christian message preached by Reverend John Ayliff of Butterworth. When the British army invaded Transkei during the 1834–1835 Frontier War, Ayliff advised the Mfengu to join it. They did so, and the colonial authorities rewarded them for their loyalty by giving them large tracts of confiscated land in districts such as Peddie and Victoria East.

The Mfengu were genuine converts to European civilisation. In May 1835, they

swore a great oath that they would obey the government, educate their children and accept Christianity. They embraced the market economy and became prosperous peasants during the heyday of Cape liberalism. Others became teachers, churchmen and government clerks. After the passage of the Glen Grey Act (1894) and the erosion of the Cape non-racial franchise, many Mfengu began to feel betrayed. They soon became the most articulate critics of colonial segregationism, and they played an important part in the establishment of 'independent churches' free from white control.

It should be clear, then, that the various groups now labelled Xhosa come from varied historical, ethnic and cultural backgrounds. In the early nineteenth century, there was a world of difference between the amaXhosa, who cut off the first joint of their little fingers, the Bhaca, who slit their faces, and the Mfengu, who pierced their ears. The Xhosa and the Thembu circumcised, but the Mpondo did not. The Rharhabe spoke something like today's standard Xhosa, but the Mpondo dialect was closer to Zulu, and the Bhaca spoke a dialect all of their own. These cultural and ethnic distinctions have, however, tended to evaporate over time, and such as still remain are regarded as local curiosities rather than socially significant markers.

Xhosa people do not share a single history, nor do they possess a single spectacular hero figure such as Shaka or Moshweshwe to epitomise a common past. But perhaps it is the very diversity of the Xhosa past that defines their social and political ethos. Political authority among the Xhosa was never centralised and absolute — it was always divided and diffuse. The right of popular rebellion against unjust rulers has been a factor in Xhosa politics ever since the overthrow of Cirha before 1600. Culturally, the Xhosa have always been a very open society, which not only absorbed ongoing waves of migrants from Natal but also integrated sizable communities of Sotho and Khoisan origin. The early exposure of the Xhosa people to the ideas and techniques of missionaries and liberals, together with their later subordination as migrant labourers in the South African economy, has further orientated Xhosa political consciousness away from a narrow ethnic awareness and towards a broader South Africanism.

(J B Peires)

Above:
Xhosa village *c.* 1800 by Ludwig Alberti. Xhosa began migrating west of the Kei River during the early seventeenth century. By the 1780s, they were well established in the Zuurveld
(Africana Museum)

Xuma, Alfred Bitini

ENGCOBO, TRANSKEI, *c.* 1893 — DUBE, SOWETO, 1962

Physician and President General of the African National Congress (ANC). Xuma qualified as a primary school teacher in South Africa before obtaining a medical degree in America. He was the first black person to obtain a PhD from the London School of Tropical Medicine and Hygiene. Returning to South Africa, he opposed the removal of the Cape African franchise and advocated its extension to the rest of the country. His obvious abilities as a politician led to his election first as Vice-President of the All African Convention (1935), and then as President General of the ANC in 1939. In his ten years in that office he did much to revive the organisation. He introduced a new constitution, and in 1943 a document entitled *African Claims* set out new demands for equality for Africans. At the party congress in 1949 he was ousted in favour of someone whom the more radical Youth Leaguers thought they could influence.

Above:
Sarili, chief of the Gcaleka Xhosa
(Cory Library)

Left:
Dr A B Xuma, President-General of the ANC in 1939
(Africana Museum)

Y

Yussuf, Joseph (Sheik)
INDONESIA, 1626 — NEAR CAPE TOWN, 1699

Muslim leader. An influential religious figure who taught at the palace of the Sultan of Bantam (western Java) and then resisted the Dutch, fighting from the forests of Java. After he had surrendered on the promise of a pardon, the Dutch East India Company, fearing his power and influence, banished him to the Cape (1694). There he soon acquired a reputation as a man of great spiritual power, and as the Muslim community grew in South Africa he was remembered as a pioneer and saint. A *kramat* (holy place) near Faure was built in his memory.

Sheik Joseph's memorial at Faure
(Africana Museum)

Z

ZAR, *see* South African Republic

ZAR, *see* South African Republic

Zulu Kingdom

The kingdom of the Zulu came into being in the late 1810s and early 1820s, and existed until the early 1880s. It is difficult to get a clear picture of its history because of the power of the heavily romanticised images of the Zulu past which have been created since the late nineteenth-century by popular writers, politicians and film-makers. Academic research has tended to focus mainly on the emergence of the kingdom under Shaka, son of Senzangakhona, and its destruction in the time of Cetshwayo kaMpande: relatively little work has been done on the period in between.

The establishment of Zulu domination north and south of the Thukela River was a product of half a century of increasing political conflict in a region that extended from southern Mozambique and the eastern Transvaal through Swaziland and Natal to the northern Transkei. Historians are still vigorously debating the causes of this conflict. In part, at least, it seems to have been a consequence of the expansion of an international trade at Delagoa Bay (present-day Maputo) after about 1760, first in ivory and later in cattle. Some historians have recently argued that the rise of a trade in slaves after 1810 also needs to be taken into account.

In the struggle to control trade routes and sources of trade goods, a number of chiefdoms in the Delagoa Bay hinterland were able to expand the areas under their control. By the late 1810s a confrontation was developing between the Ndwandwe on the Mkhuze River and the Mthethwa between the White Mfolozi and Mhlathuze Rivers. The defeat of the Mthethwa provided the opportunity for the Zulu chiefdom, which had previously been subordinate to them, to become the dominant polity south of the White Mfolozi. Soon afterwards, the break-up of the Ndwandwe chiefdom enabled the Zulu to extend an initially shaky domination northwards as far as the Mkhuze.

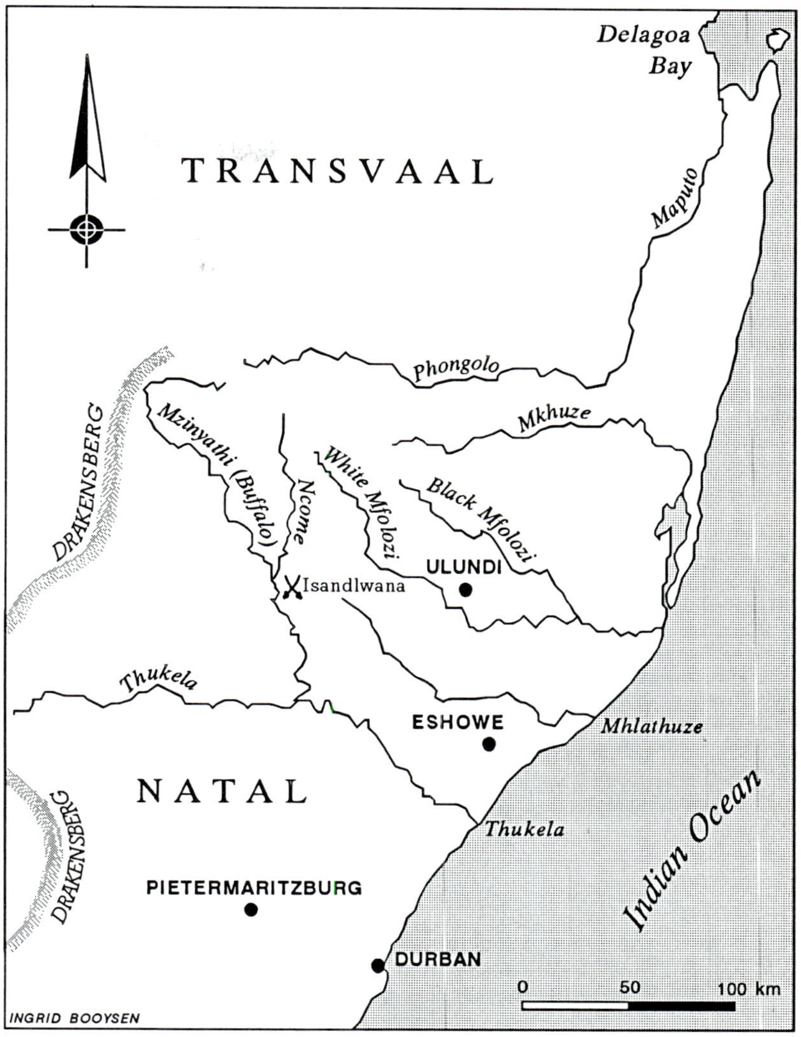

Above:
Map of the Zulu kingdom and neighbouring regions

Left:
There were no European eyewitnesses to the assassination of King Shaka by two of his brothers in 1828. This has not stopped numerous European artists from using their imaginations to try to depict this incident. This nineteenth century illustration shows one such depiction (Africana Museum)

Popular accounts by white and black writers alike have generally exaggerated the role played by Shaka in the history of the early Zulu kingdom. But there can be little doubt that he was an able military leader and an astute and ruthless politician. The kingdom which consolidated under his rule in the 1820s was one of the most powerful polities in southern Africa, but its size and strength should not be

A view of King Dingane's capital, Mgungundlovu. The drawing was made in 1835 by Allen Gardiner, the first missionary to visit the Zulu kingdom (Local History Museum Collection, Durban)

exaggerated. Its core territory lay between the Thukela and the Black Mfolozi: beyond this, Zulu authority shaded off into regions whose chiefs gave allegiance to Shaka but acted with varying degrees of autonomy. Inside the kingdom, Shaka faced persistent if muted opposition from a number of senior chiefs, and from within the Zulu royal house itself. Resistance to his rule culminated in his assassination in a 'palace coup' in 1828.

In the reign of Dingane (1828–1840), Shaka's brother and one of his assassins, stresses and conflicts within the kingdom grew markedly. In part these were caused by the failure of several cattle-raiding expeditions launched by the Zulu leadership against neighbouring states. Without large herds of cattle at its disposal, the Zulu royal house found it difficult to maintain the allegiance of politically important chiefs and army officers. Internal strains were exacerbated by an increase in external political pressures. In the last years of Shaka's reign, British traders from the Cape had begun to play an important role in the affairs of the Zulu state. From the early 1830s, the number of traders operating in the kingdom was growing, and from the mid-1830s British and American missionaries were beginning to establish themselves in it.

In the late 1830s a combination of external and internal pressures led to violent conflict in the kingdom. The incursions of parties of Boer trekkers from the Cape into the region south of the Thukela was followed by war with the Zulu and the defeat of Dingane's army at the Ncome (Blood) River. Soon afterwards, Mpande, one of the king's brothers, broke away with a large following. In 1840, with the assistance of the Boers, Mpande drove Dingane out and established himself as ruler of the territories north of the Thukela. The Boers held on to the region to the south, but in 1842 were in turn defeated by the British. The following year the area south of the Thukela was annexed as the colony of Natal.

Through the 1840s Mpande managed to keep his hold on power, but by the early 1850s his authority was being undermined by some of his subordinate chiefs. A dispute between two of the king's sons

Right:
This well-known painting, 'Umpanda reviewing his troops at Nonduengu', was made by an English artist, George Angas, who visited the Zulu kingdom in 1847. (KwaNodwengu, near modern-day Ulundi, was one of King Mpande's capitals.) Recent research by art critics indicates that Angas's idealised portrayals of Zulu life cannot be taken as wholly accurate (Africana Museum)

Far left:
Another painting by Angas, entitled 'Zulu soldiers of King Panda's army'. Angas's paintings are now seen more as reflections of artistic conventions in mid-nineteenth century England than as reliable documentation of Zulu culture
(Africana Museum)

Above:
Detail from a romanticised painting of the Battle of Isandlwana, January 1879. It was made in the late nineteenth or early twentieth century by M E Newman on an engraving originally published in *The Graphic* of 15 March 1879. As far as is known, both the engraving and the painting were imaginary depictions. The artist's main concern was to show the heroism of British troops in the face of death at the hands of a 'savage' enemy
(Local History Museum Collection, Durban)

over the succession to the kingship brought the developing crisis to a head. Mpande backed one son, Mbuyazi, while a number of powerful chiefs backed the other, Cetshwayo. In 1856, in a fierce battle near the mouth of the Thukela, Cetshwayo emerged victorious. After this he was the dominant political figure in the kingdom, though Mpande retained important ritual powers until his death in 1872.

In the 1860s and 1870s the Zulu kingdom faced increasing pressures from outside its borders. In Natal, British officials were seeking to play off some of Cetshwayo's brothers against him. To the north-west, Boer farmers from the Transvaal were encroaching on lands which the Zulu regarded as theirs. In the face of these pressures, the senior chiefs in the kingdom began for the first time to unite under Zulu leadership. At the same time, Cetshwayo was trying to rebuild the power of the royal house, which had seriously declined since the conflicts of the 1850s.

In the mid-1870s, imperial Britain began manoeuvring to establish firmer domination in southern Africa. By 1877 the British High Commissioner in South Africa, Sir Bartle Frere, was planning a war against the Zulu kingdom, which he saw as a major obstacle to the expansion of British influence. At the end of 1878, Frere found a pretext for sending Cetshwayo an ultimatum which he knew the Zulu king could not accept, and in January 1879 British troops invaded the kingdom.

Early in the war the united Zulu kingdom succeeded in destroying a strong British force at Isandlwana. But once the British had resumed their march on Ulundi, Cetshwayo's capital, and had defeated the Zulu armies in a series of pitched battles, individual chiefs began to break their allegiance to the Zulu king, and to make separate peace terms with the invaders. In July the British burnt Ulundi, and the following month Cetshwayo was captured and sent into exile in the Cape. In a hastily-made settlement, the British divided up his kingdom among thirteen appointed chiefs, and then proceeded to withdraw.

In the early 1880s violent conflict broke out between supporters of the Zulu royal house and its enemies, who were actively supported by British colonial officials. In 1883 the British government attempted to restore order by allowing Cetshwayo to return as ruler of part of his former kingdom. But within a few months his forces had been heavily defeated, and Cetshwayo himself had sought protection from the British. His death at Eshowe in 1884 signalled the end of the old Zulu order. By the end of the 1880s the former kingdom had been partitioned between Boers and British, and the men who had fought in the Zulu armies were being forced in increasing numbers to leave their homes to find wage-work in Natal and the Transvaal. Any sense of a common Zulu identity had been largely destroyed: not until well into the twentieth century did it begin to revive.

(J B Wright)

Zuurveld (Suurveld)

Land between the Bushman's and Fish Rivers in the eastern Cape, whose oc-

Pass of the Great Fish River, 1841, by W Purser. The Xhosa occupied the Zuurveld region between the Great Fish and Bushman's rivers before the arrival of the trekboers (Africana Museum)

cupants, the Xhosa, first encountered trekboers from the Cape in the 1770s. Competition for pastureland between Xhosa and trekboers led to war in 1779, the first of what came to be known as the frontier wars. In 1812 twenty thousand Xhosa were driven out of the Zuurveld. Military outposts were constructed and in 1820 five thousand British immigrants were settled there as a barrier against Xhosa penetration into the colony.

Zwide

c. 1790 — *c.* 1830

Ndwandwe ruler. He built up the Ndwandwe, a loose confederation of people who lived north of the Mthethwa in what became known as Zululand. In one of a number of conflicts with his neighbours, he defeated the Ngwane-Dlamini under Sobhuza at the Phongola River. In 1818 he defeated Dingiswayo, chief of the Mthethewa, opening the way for Shaka's rise to power. When the Ndwandwe attacked Shaka's Zulu, they were defeated at the Battle of Gqokoli Hill, and Zwide was forced to move inland to the upper reaches of the Nkomati River.

FURTHER READING

General Works

Cameron, T and Spies, S B (eds). *A New Illustrated History of South Africa* (2nd edition). Johannesburg: Southern Book Publishers, 1991

Davenport, T R H. *South Africa. A Modern History* (4th edition). London: Macmillan, 1991

Oakes, D (ed). *Reader's Digest Illustrated History of South Africa* (2nd edition). Cape Town: Reader's Digest, 1992

Omer-Cooper, J D. *History of Southern Africa.* London: James Currey, 1987

Pampallis, J. *Foundations of the New South Africa.* Cape Town: Maskew Miller Longman, 1991

Thompson, L. *A History of South Africa.* Sandton: Radix, 1990

Van Aswegen, H J. *History of South Africa to 1854.* Pretoria: Academia, 1990

African National Congress

Barrell, H. *MK: The ANC's Armed Struggle.* Johannesburg: Penguin, 1990

Ellis, S and Sechabe, T. *Comrades and Cadres: The African National Congress and the South African Communist Party in Exile.* London: James Currey, 1992

Gerhart, G. *Black Power in South Africa.* Berkeley: University of California Press, 1987

Holland, H. *The Struggle: A History of the African National Congress.* London: Grafton, 1989

Afrikaners

Fisher, J. *The Afrikaners.* London: Cassell, 1969

Giliomee, H and Schlemmer, L. *From Apartheid to Nation-building.* Cape Town: Oxford University Press, 1989

Kapp, P H. 'Afrikaanse kultuurverenigings as kultuurverskynsels' in *Suid-Afrikaanse Tydskrif vir Kultuurgeskiedenis* 1992, 6 (2)

Moodie T D. *The Rise of Afrikanerdom: Power, Apartheid and the Afrikaner Civil Religion.* Berkeley: University of California Press, 1975

Apartheid (*see* **White Politics**)

Ormond, R. *The Apartheid Handbook: A Guide to South Africa's Everyday Racial Policies* (2nd edition). New York: Penguin Books, 1986

Stadler, A. *The Political Economy of Modern South Africa.* Cape Town: David Philip, 1987

Black Politics

Lodge, T. *Black Politics in South Africa since 1945.* London: Longman, 1983

Lodge, T and Nasson, B. *All Here and Now: Black Politics in South Africa during the 1980s.* Cape Town and New York: David Philip and the Ford Foundation, 1991

Marx, A W. *Lessons of Struggle: South African Internal Opposition, 1960–1990.* Cape Town: Oxford University Press, 1992

Mufson, S. *Fighting Years: Black Resistance and the Struggle for a New South Africa.* Boston: Beacon Press, 1990

Odendaal, A. *Vukani Bantu: The Beginnings of Black Protest Politics in South Africa to 1912.* Cape Town: David Philip, 1984

Simons, H J and R E. *Class and Colour in South Africa, 1850–1950.* Harmondsworth: Penguin, 1969

Walshe, P. *The Rise of African Nationalism in South Africa.* Cape Town: Ad Donker, 1987

Britain in South Africa

Boucher, M and Penn, N (eds). *Britain at the Cape, 1795–1803.* Johannesburg: The Brenthurst Press, 1992

Cape

Elphick, R and Giliomee, H (eds). *The Shaping of South African Society, 1652–1840.* Cape Town: Maskew Miller Longman, 1989

Cape Town

Studies in the History of Cape Town, vols 1–6

Chinese

Human, L. *The Chinese People of South Africa: Freewheeling on the Fringes.* Pretoria: Unisa, 1984

Richardson, P G L. *Chinese Mine Labour in the Transvaal.* London: Macmillan, 1982

Christianity

Chidester, D. *Religions of South Africa.* London and New York: Routledge, 1992

Prozesky, M (ed). *Christianity in South Africa.* Bergvlei, Southern Book Publishers, 1990

Villa-Vicencio, C. *Trapped in Apartheid: A Socio-Theological History of the English-speaking Churches.* Cape Town: David Philip, 1988

Ciskei

Anonymous. 'Ethnicity and Pseudo-Ethnicity in the Ciskei', in *The Creation of Tribalism in Southern Africa*, Vail, L (ed). London: James Currey, 1989

Coloureds

Adhikari, M. *Let us Live for Our Children: The Teachers' League of South Africa, 1913–1940.* Cape Town: UCT Press/ Buchu Books, 1993

Lewis, G. *Between the Wire and the Wall: A History of South African 'Coloured' Politics.* Cape Town: David Philip, 1987

Van der Ross, R. *The Rise and Decline of Apartheid: A Study of Political Movements among the Coloured People of South Africa, 1880–1985.* Cape Town: Tafelberg, 1986

Economic Development

Houghton, D H. *The South African Economy.* Cape Town, Oxford University Press, 1964

Jones, S and Muller, A. *The South African Economy 1910–1990.* London: Macmillan, 1992

Education

Behr, A L. *Education in South Africa. Origins, Issues and Trends, 1652–1988.* Pretoria: Academia, 1988

Kallaway, P (ed). *Apartheid and Education.* Johannesburg: Ravan, 1984

Malherbe, E G. *Education in South Africa, 1652–1922.* Cape Town: Juta, 1925

Malherbe, E G. *Education in South Africa, 1923–1975.* Cape Town: Juta, 1977

Foreign Relations

Barber, J and Barratt, J. *South Africa's Foreign Policy – The Search for Status and Security 1945–1988.* Johannesburg: Southern Book Publishers, 1990

Geldenhuys, D. *The Diplomacy of Isolation: South Africa's Foreign Policy Making.* Johannesburg: Macmillan, 1984

Frontiers

Lamar, H and Thompson, L M (eds). *The Frontier in History.* New Haven: Yale University Press, 1981

Legassick, M. 'The frontier tradition in South African historiography', in Marks, S and Atmore, A (eds). *Economy and Society in Pre-Industrial South Africa.* London, 1980

Indians

Bhana, S and Brian, J B. *Setting Down Roots: Indian Migrants in South Africa 1860–1911.* Johannesburg: Witwatersrand University Press, 1990

Pachai, B. *The International Aspects of the South African Indian Question 1860–1971.* Cape Town: C Struik Pty Ltd, 1971

Iron Age

Hall, M. *The Changing Past. Farmers, Kings and Traders in Southern Africa, 200–1860.* Cape Town: David Philip, 1897

Phillipson, D. *African Archaeology.* Cambridge: Cambridge University Press, 1985.

Khoikhoi

Elphick, R. *Khoikhoi and the Founding of White South Africa.* Johannesburg: Ravan, 1985

Smith, A B and Pheiffer, R H. *The Khoikhoi in the Eighteenth Century: Drawings in the South African Library.* Cape Town: S A Library, 1993

Literature

Chapman, M. *South African English Poetry: A Modern Perspective.* Johannesburg: Ad Donker, 1984

Chapman, M. *Soweto Poetry.* Johannesburg: McGraw-Hill, 1982

Christie, S, Hutchings, G and Maclennen, D. *Perspectives on South African Fiction.* Johannesburg: Ad Donker, 1980

Gordimer, N. *Black Interpreters.* Johannesburg: Ravan Press, 1973

Gray, S. *Southern African Literature: And Introduction.* Cape Town: David Philip, 1979

Mphahlele, E. *The African Image.* London: Faber, 1962

Van Wyk Smith, M. *Grounds of Contest: A Survey of South African Literature.* Cape Town: Juta & Co Ltd, 1990

Mining

Webb, A C M. 'Mining in South Africa', in Coleman, F L (ed). *Economic History of South Africa.* Pretoria: Haum, 1983

Namibia

Herbstein, D and Evenson, J. *The Devils are Among Us. The War for Namibia.* London: Zed Press, 1989

Du Pisani, A. *SWA/Namibia: The Politics of Continuity and Change.* Johannesburg: Jonathan Ball Publishers, 1985

Rock Art

Dowson, T A. *Rock Engravings of Southern Africa.* Johannesburg: Witwatersrand University Press, 1992

Lewis-Williams, J D and Dowson, T A. *Images of Power: Understanding Bushman Rock Art.* Johannesburg: Southern Book Publishers, 1989

Yates, R, Parkington, J and Manhire, T. *Pictures of the Past: A History of the Interpretation of Rock Paintings and Engravings of Southern Africa.* Pietermaritzburg: Centaur Publications, 1990

Rural Change

Beinart, W. Delius, P and Trapido, S (eds). *Putting a Plough to the Ground: Accumulation and Dispossession in Rural South Africa*. Johannesburg: Ravan Press, 1986

Crush, J, Jeeves, A and Yudelman, D. *South Africa's Labour Empire: A History of Black Migrancy to the Gold Mines*. Cape Town: David Philip, 1991

Keegan, T. *Rural Transformations in Industrialising South Africa*. Johannesburg and London: Ravan Press and Macmillan, 1987

Segregation

Cell, J W. *The Highest Stage of White Supremacy*. Cambridge: Cambridge University Press, 1982.

Dubow, S. *Racial Segregation and the Origins of Apartheid in South Africa, 1919–1936*. London: Macmillan, 1989

Slavery

Elphick, R and Giliomee, H (eds). *The Shaping of South African Society, 1652–1840* (2nd edition). Cape Town, 1989

Ross, R. *Cape of Torments: Slavery and Resistance in South Africa*. London, 1983

Worden, N. *Slavery in Dutch South Africa*. Cambridge, 1985

Worden, N and Crais, C (eds). *Breaking the Chains: Slavery and Emancipation in the Nineteenth Century Cape Colony*. Johannesburg, 1993

South African War

Nasson, B. *Abraham Esau's War: A Black South African War in the Cape, 1899–1902*. Cambridge and Cape Town: Cambridge University Press and David Philip, 1991

Pakenham, T. *The Boer War*. London: Weidenfeld & Nicholson, 1979

Warwick, P (ed). *The South African War: The Anglo-Boer War, 1899–1902*. London: Longman, 1980

Urban Development

Maylam, P. 'The rise and decline of urban apartheid in South Africa', in *African Affairs*, 83(354), January 1990

White Politics

Johnson, S. *South Africa: No Turning Back*. Bloomingdale: Indiana University Press, 1989

Marks, S and Trapido, S (eds). *The Politics of Race, Class and Nationalism in Twentieth Century South Africa*. London and New York: Longman, 1987

Posel, D. *The Making of Apartheid, 1948–1961: Conflict and Compromise*. Oxford: Clarendon Press, 1991

Thompson, L. *The Political Mythology of Apartheid*. New Haven: Yale University Press, 1985

Thompson, L and Prior, A. *South African Politics*. Cape Town: David Philip, 1982

Women

Berger, I. *Threads of Solidarity. Women in South African Industry 1900–1980*. London: James Currey, 1992

Bozzoli, B and Nkotsoe, M. *Women of Phokeng. Consciousness, Life Strategy and Migrancy in South Africa 1900–1983*. Johannesburg: Ravan Press, 1991

Walker, C (ed). *Women and Gender in Southern Africa to 1945*. Cape Town: David Philip and London: James Currey, 1990

Xhosa

Peires, J B. *The House of Phalo: A History of the Xhosa People in the Days of their Independence*. Johannesburg: Ravan Press, 1981

Zulu Kingdom

Duminy, A and Guest, B (eds). *Natal and Zululand from Earliest Times to 1910: A New History*. Pietermaritzburg, 1989.

Guy, J. *The Destruction of the Zulu Kingdom: The Civil War in Zululand, 1879–1884*. London, 1979

Laband, J. *Kingdom in Crisis: the Zulu Response to the British Invasion of 1879*. Pietermaritzburg, 1992.

INDEX

Figures in **bold** represent illustrations